SAS® Programming 2: Data Manipulation Techniques

Course Notes

SAS® Programming 2: Data Manipulation Techniques Course Notes was developed by Rob McAfee and Kathy Passarella. Additional contributions were made by Michele Ensor, Brian Gayle, Richard Hallquist, Mark Jordan, Linda Mitterling, Georg Morsing, and Kent Reeve. Editing and production support was provided by the Curriculum Development and Support Department.

SAS® Programming 2: Data Manipulation Techniques Course Notes

---

Book code E1510, course code LWPRG2/PRG2, prepared date 29Jun2009. LWPRG2_003

ISBN 978-1-60764-238-1

Table of Contents

Course Description viii

Prerequisites ix

Chapter 1 Introduction 1-1

1.1 Course Logistics 1-3

Demonstration: Using the Help Facility 1-6

1.2 Course Overview 1-15

1.3 SAS Syntax Review 1-23

1.4 Navigating the SAS Windowing Environment (Self-Study) 1-31

1.5 Solutions 1-38

Solutions to Student Activities (Polls/Quizzes) 1-38

Chapter 2 Controlling Input and Output 2-1

2.1 Outputting Multiple Observations 2-3

Exercises 2-16

2.2 Writing to Multiple SAS Data Sets 2-20

Demonstration: Creating Multiple Data Sets 2-25

Exercises 2-31

2.3 Selecting Variables and Observations 2-35

Exercises 2-51

2.4 Chapter Review 2-54

2.5 Solutions 2-55

Solutions to Exercises 2-55

Solutions to Student Activities (Polls/Quizzes) 2-60

Solutions to Chapter Review 2-64

Chapter 3 Summarizing Data 3-1

3.1 Creating an Accumulating Total Variable 3-3

Exercises 3-17

3.2 Accumulating Totals for a Group of Data 3-21

Exercises 3-42

3.3 Chapter Review 3-47

3.4 Solutions 3-48

Solutions to Exercises 3-48

Solutions to Student Activities (Polls/Quizzes) 3-54

Solutions to Chapter Review 3-57

Chapter 4 Reading Raw Data Files 4-1

4.1 Reading Raw Data Files with Formatted Input 4-3

Exercises 4-20

4.2 Controlling When a Record Loads 4-24

Exercises 4-49

4.3 Additional Techniques for List Input (Self-Study) 4-52

4.4 Chapter Review 4-74

4.5 Solutions 4-75

Solutions to Exercises 4-75

Solutions to Student Activities 4-78

Solutions to Chapter Review 4-82

Chapter 5 Data Transformations 5-1

5.1 Introduction 5-3

5.2 Manipulating Character Values (Part 1) 5-10

Exercises 5-25

5.3 Manipulating Character Values (Part 2) 5-29

Exercises 5-53

5.4 Manipulating Numeric Values 5-58

Exercises 5-70

5.5 Converting Variable Type 5-73

Exercises 5-97

5.6 Chapter Review 5-100

5.7 Solutions 5-101

Solutions to Exercises 5-101

Solutions to Student Activities (Polls/Quizzes) 5-108

Chapter Review Answers 5-115

Chapter 6 Debugging Techniques 6-1

6.1 Using the PUTLOG Statement 6-3

Demonstration: Determining Logic Errors 6-12

6.2 Using the DEBUG Option 6-17

Demonstration: Identifying Logic Errors with the DATA Step Debugger 6-21

Demonstration: Setting Breakpoints 6-35

Exercises 6-42

6.3 Chapter Review 6-44

6.4 Solutions 6-45

Solutions to Exercises 6-45

Solutions to Student Activities (Polls/Quizzes) 6-48

Solutions to Chapter Review 6-50

Chapter 7 Processing Data Iteratively 7-1

7.1 DO Loop Processing 7-3

Exercises 7-31

7.2 SAS Array Processing 7-34

Exercises 7-47

7.3 Using SAS Arrays 7-52

Exercises 7-69

7.4 Chapter Review 7-72

7.5 Solutions 7-73

Solutions to Exercises 7-73

Solutions to Student Activities (Polls/Quizzes) 7-79

Solutions to Chapter Review 7-83

Chapter 8 Restructuring a Data Set 8-1

8.1 Rotating with the DATA Step 8-3

Exercises 8-24

8.2 Using the TRANSPOSE Procedure 8-28

Exercises 8-49

8.3 Chapter Review 8-52

8.4 Solutions 8-53

Solutions to Exercises 8-53

Solutions to Student Activities (Polls/Quizzes) 8-56

Solutions to Chapter Review 8-58

Chapter 9 Combining SAS Data Sets 9-1

9.1 Using Data Manipulation Techniques with Match-Merging 9-3

Demonstration: Match-Merging Data Sets That Lack a Common Variable 9-14

Exercises 9-22

9.2 Chapter Review 9-27

9.3 Solutions 9-28

Solutions to Exercises 9-28

Solutions to Student Activities (Polls/Quizzes)......9-30

Solutions to Chapter Review......9-33

Chapter 10 Other SAS Languages......10-1

10.1 An Overview of Other Languages......10-3

10.2 Using the SQL Procedure......10-5

Exercises......10-21

10.3 The SAS Macro Language......10-25

Exercises......10-37

10.4 Chapter Review......10-40

10.5 Solutions......10-41

Solutions to Exercises......10-41

Solutions to Student Activities (Polls/Quizzes)......10-44

Solutions to Chapter Review......10-47

Chapter 11 Learning More......11-1

11.1 SAS Resources......11-3

11.2 Beyond This Course......11-6

Appendix A Index......A-1

Course Description

This course is for those who need to learn data manipulation techniques using SAS DATA and PROCEDURE steps to access, transform, and summarize SAS data sets. The course builds on the concepts that are presented in the SAS® Programming 1: Essentials course and is not recommended for beginning SAS software users.

To learn more…

For information on other courses in the curriculum, contact the SAS Education Division at 1-800-333-7660, or send e-mail to training@sas.com. You can also find this information on the Web at support.sas.com/training/ as well as in the Training Course Catalog.

For a list of other SAS books that relate to the topics covered in this Course Notes, USA customers can contact our SAS Publishing Department at 1-800-727-3228 or send e-mail to sasbook@sas.com. Customers outside the USA, please contact your local SAS office.

Also, see the Publications Catalog on the Web at support.sas.com/pubs for a complete list of books and a convenient order form.

Prerequisites

Before attending this course, you should have at least six months of experience writing SAS programs or have completed the SAS® Programming 1: Essentials course and used SAS for at least one month. Specifically, you should be able to

- submit a SAS program
- diagnose and correct syntax errors
- examine descriptor and data portions of a SAS data set
- access SAS data libraries
- read and create SAS data sets
- read Excel spreadsheets
- read delimited raw data files
- examine data errors when reading raw data files.
- use SAS procedures to validate data
- clean invalid data
- create variables
- combine SAS data sets
- use global statements
- use labels and formats, including user-defined formats
- subset observations
- direct output to external files
- produce summary reports using the FREQ and MEANS procedures

Chapter 1 Introduction

1.1 Course Logistics **1-3**

Demonstration: Using the Help Facility 1-6

1.2 Course Overview **1-15**

1.3 SAS Syntax Review **1-23**

1.4 Navigating the SAS Windowing Environment (Self-Study) **1-31**

1.5 Solutions **1-38**

Solutions to Student Activities (Polls/Quizzes) 1-38

1.1 Course Logistics

Objectives

- Explain the naming convention that is used for the course files.
- Compare the three levels of exercises that are used in the course.
- Describe at a high level how data is used and stored at Orion Star Sports & Outdoors.
- Use the Help facility.

3

Filename Conventions

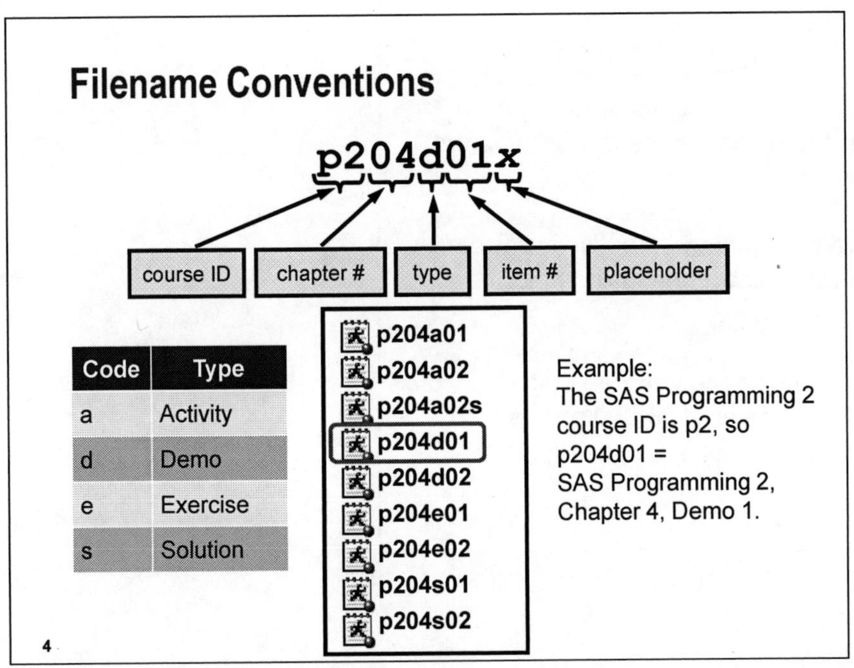

Code	Type
a	Activity
d	Demo
e	Exercise
s	Solution

4

Three Levels of Exercises

Level 1	The exercise mimics an example presented in the section.
Level 2	Less information and guidance are provided in the exercise instructions.
Level 3	Only the task you are to perform or the results to be obtained are provided. Typically, you will need to use the Help facility.

You are not expected to complete all of the exercises in the time allotted. Choose the exercise or exercises that are at the level you are most comfortable with.

5

Orion Star Sports & Outdoors

Orion Star Sports & Outdoors is a fictitious global sports and outdoors retailer with traditional stores, an online store, and a large catalog business.

The corporate headquarters is located in the United States with offices and stores in many countries throughout the world.

Orion Star has about 1,000 employees and 90,000 customers, processes approximately 150,000 orders annually, and purchases products from 64 suppliers.

6

Orion Star Data

As is the case with most organizations, Orion Star has a large amount of data about its customers, suppliers, products, and employees. Much of this information is stored in transactional systems in various formats.

Using applications and processes such as SAS Data Integration Studio, this transactional information was extracted, transformed, and loaded into a data warehouse.

Data marts were created to meet the needs of specific departments such as Marketing.

7

Business Scenarios

Throughout the course, business scenarios introduce and provide context for using the techniques to manipulate the data.

The business scenarios cover a variety of situations and will always include

- a sample of the input data
- the transformations needed
- the desired output.

8

Using the Help Facility

This demonstration shows how to find documentation for a topic and how to store frequently used Help pages in Favorites.

Using SAS 9.2 Help and Documentation

Open SAS Help by selecting **Help** ⇨ **SAS Help and Documentation** or by clicking the **Help** button on the toolbar.

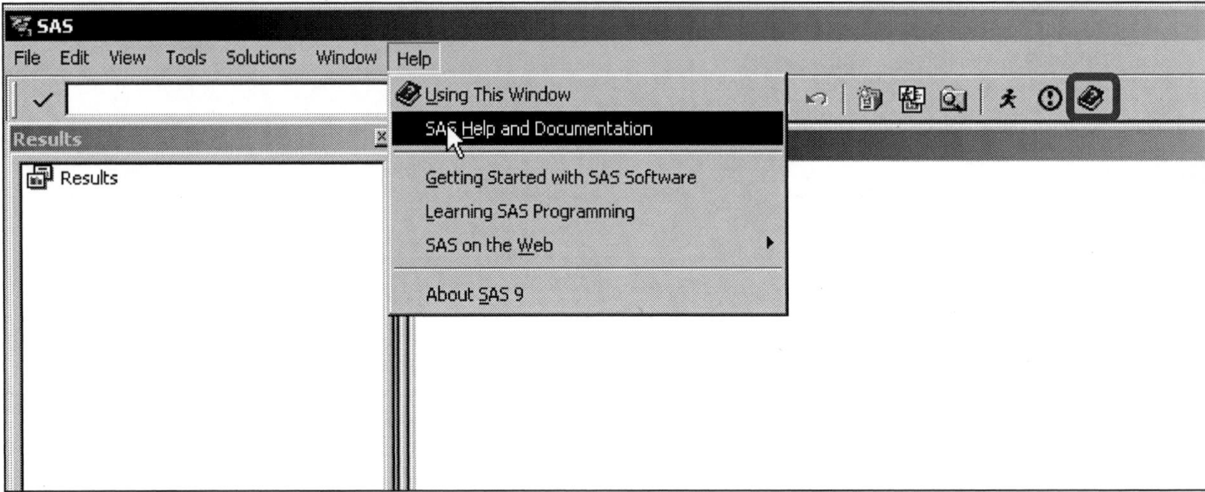

The SAS Help and Documentation window opens.

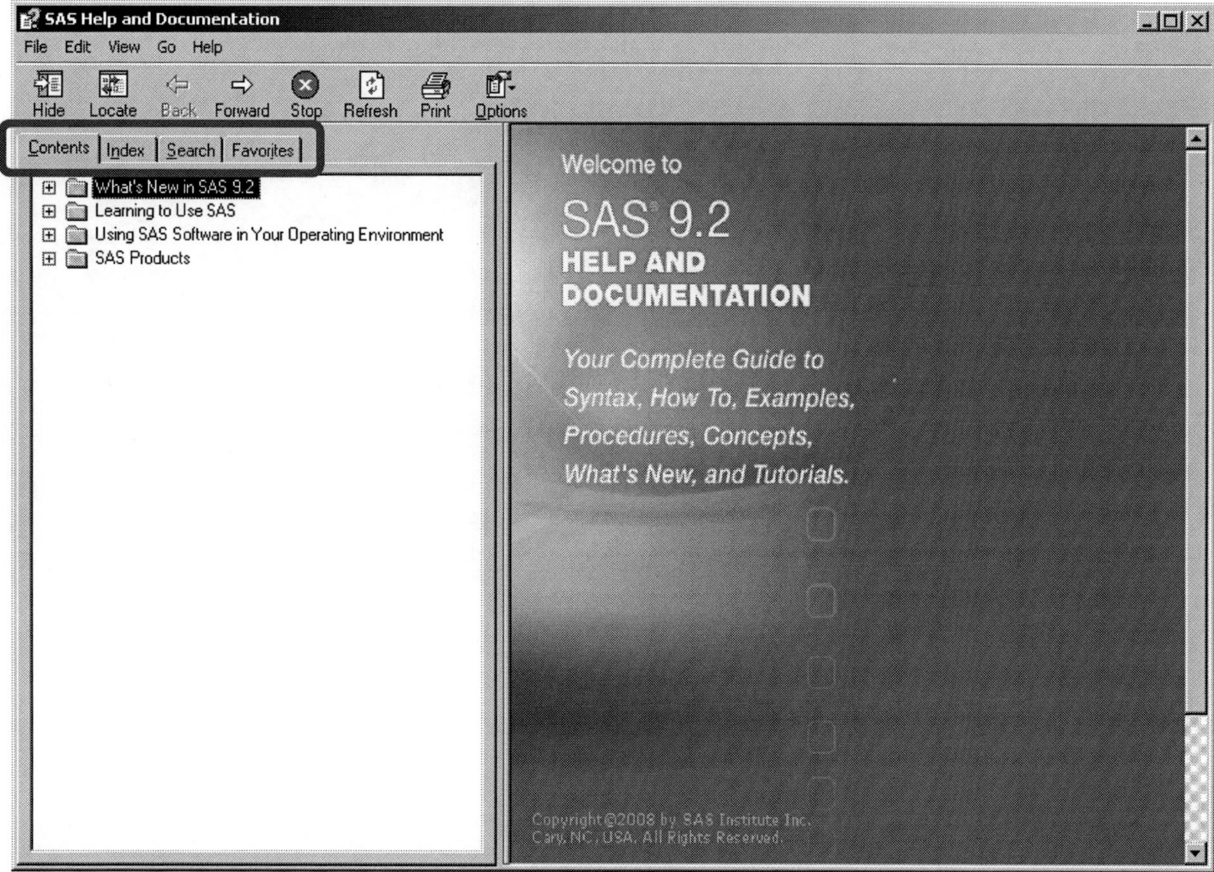

The window contains a menu bar, toolbar, and four tabs.

Contents	Use this tab to view an expandable/contractible table of contents.
Index	Use this tab to search the index.
Search	Use this tab to search the document contents for words, phrases, and so on.
Favorites	Use this tab to store or bookmark your favorite or frequently used pages.

Using the Contents Tab

Select the Contents tab to view a table of contents, similar to that of a printed book. Clicking on a plus sign (+) expands a list, and clicking on a minus sign (-) collapses a list.

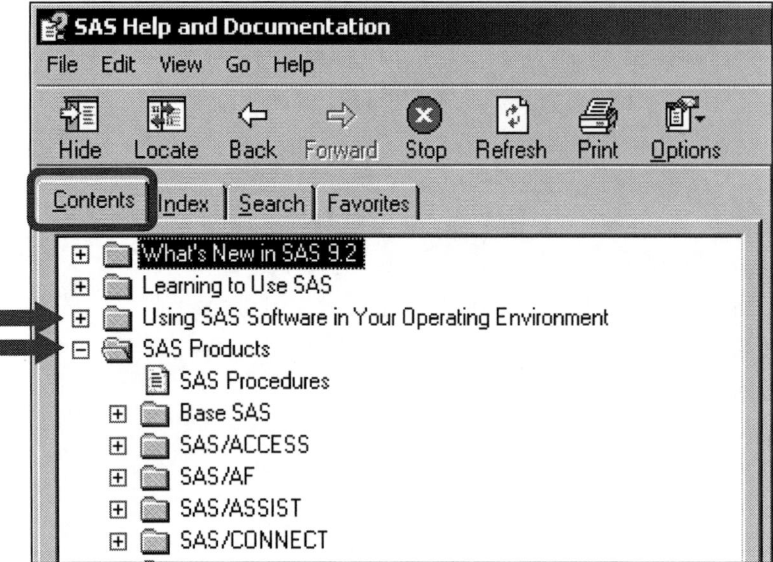

The SAS 9.2 Language Reference: Dictionary

A useful section is the Dictionary of Language Elements. To access this section, select **SAS Products** ⇨ **Base SAS** ⇨ **SAS 9.2 Language Reference: Dictionary** ⇨ **Dictionary of Language Elements**.

The sections available at this location include Formats, Functions, Informats, Statements, and SAS System Options.

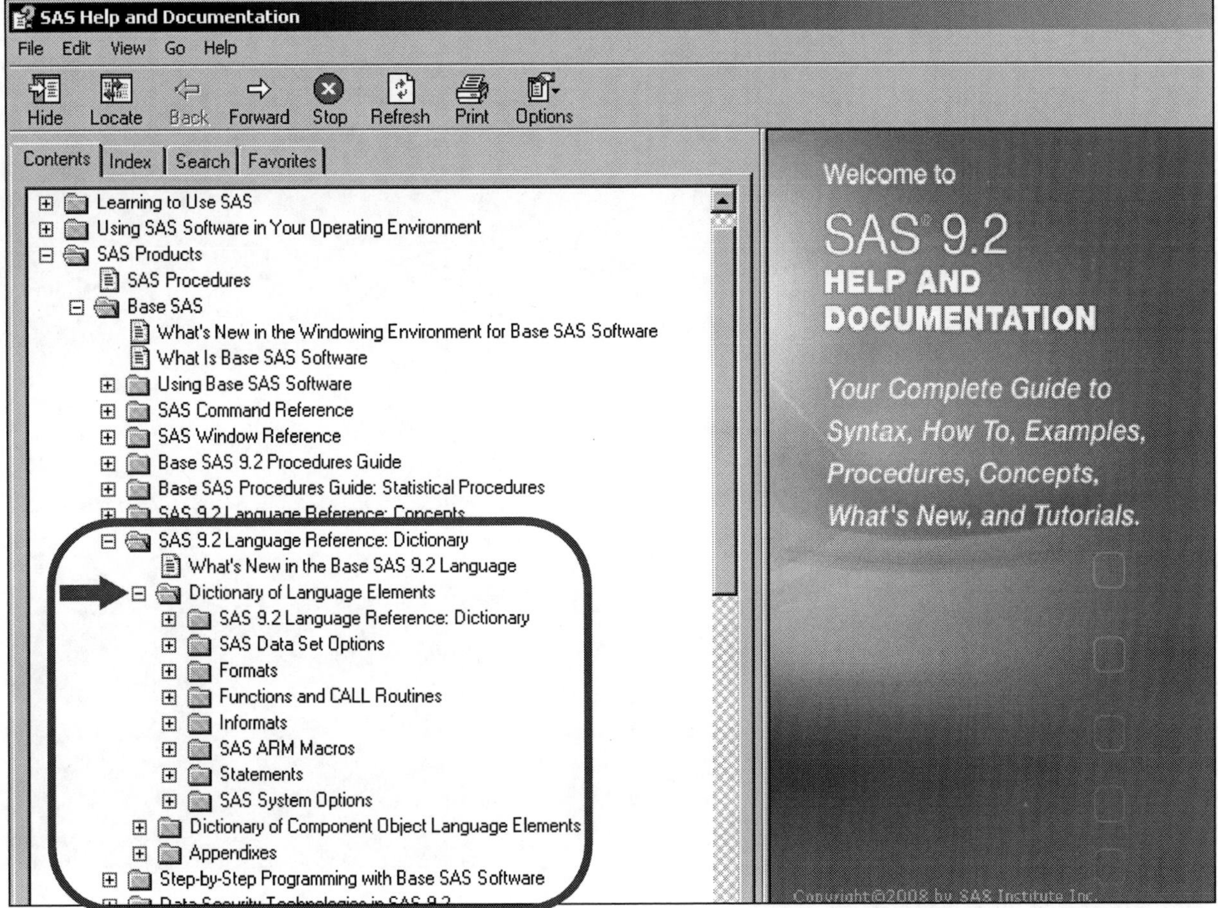

Step-by-Step Programming with Base SAS Software

Another useful section is Step-by-Step Programming with Base SAS Software. To access this section, select **SAS Products** ⇨ **Base SAS** ⇨ **Step-by-Step Programming with Base SAS Software**.

The subsections offer an easy to use overview of SAS concepts and programming.

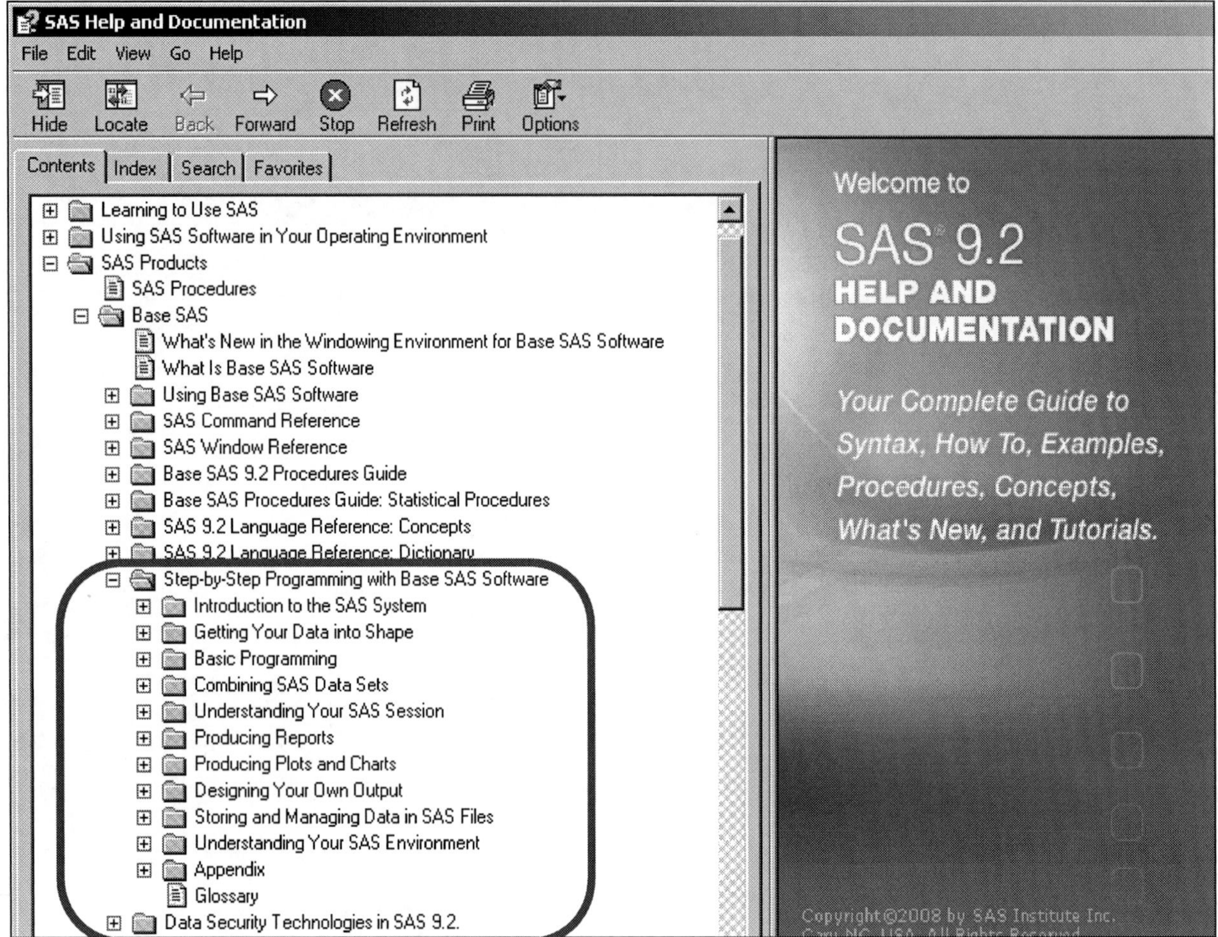

Using the Index Tab

Select the **Index** tab and type the keyword that you want to find. As you are typing the keyword, the area below the text box displays matching topics, if any are found.

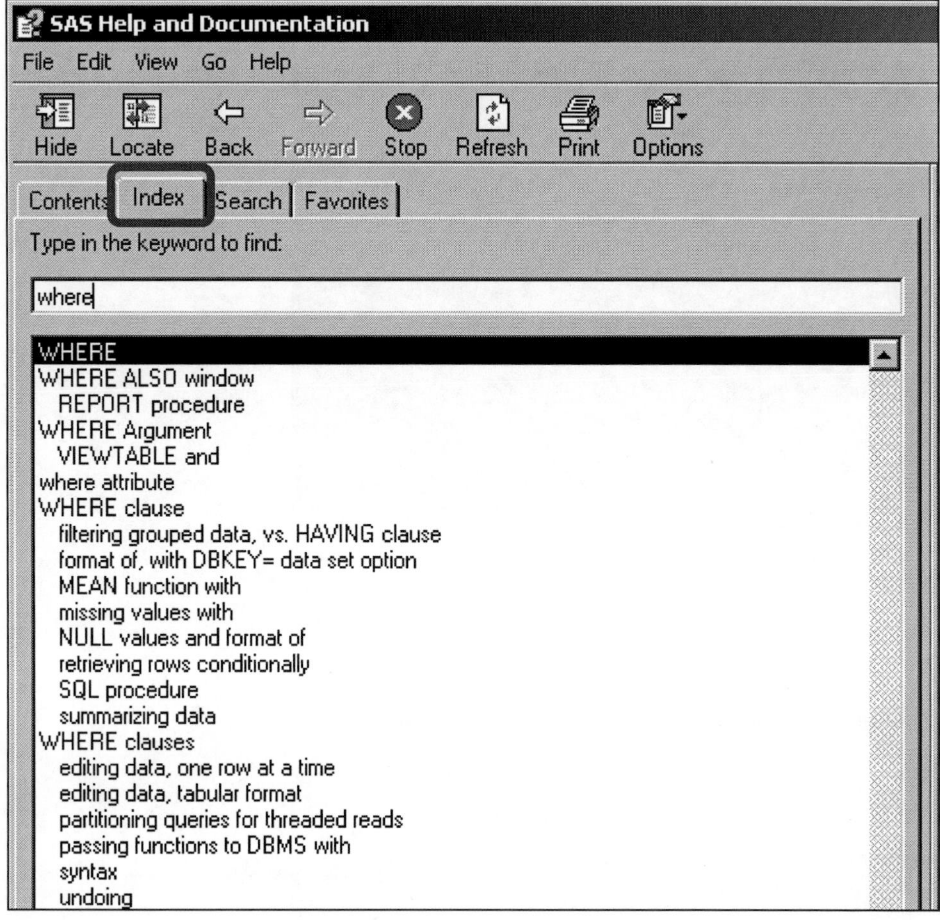

Using the Search Tab

Select the **Search** tab, type the keyword to find, and click the **List Topics** button or press ENTER. The search results are displayed below the text box. Select the desired topic and click the **Display** button.

This searches the entire document and might generate more results than expected.

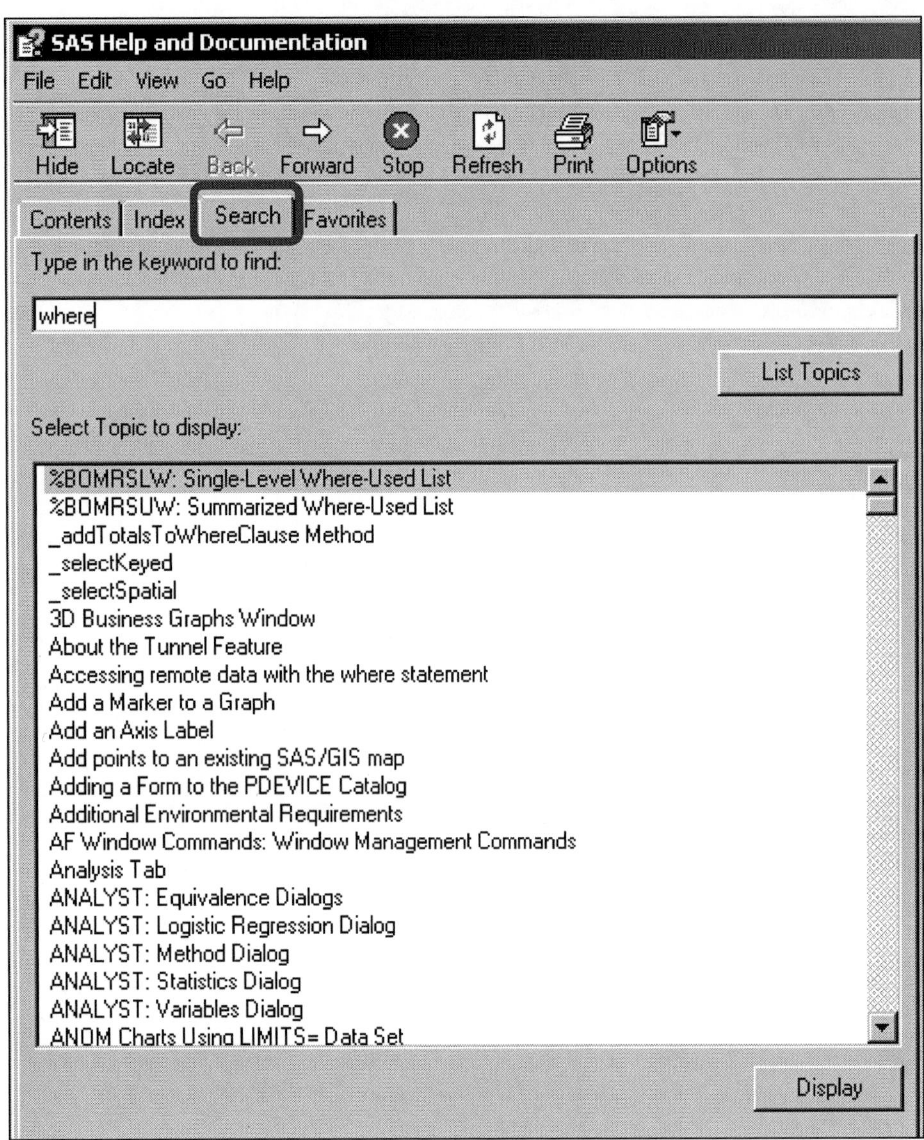

Using the Favorites Tab

Navigate to the desired page and select the **Favorites** tab. The topic is displayed in the Current topic text box at the bottom of the window.

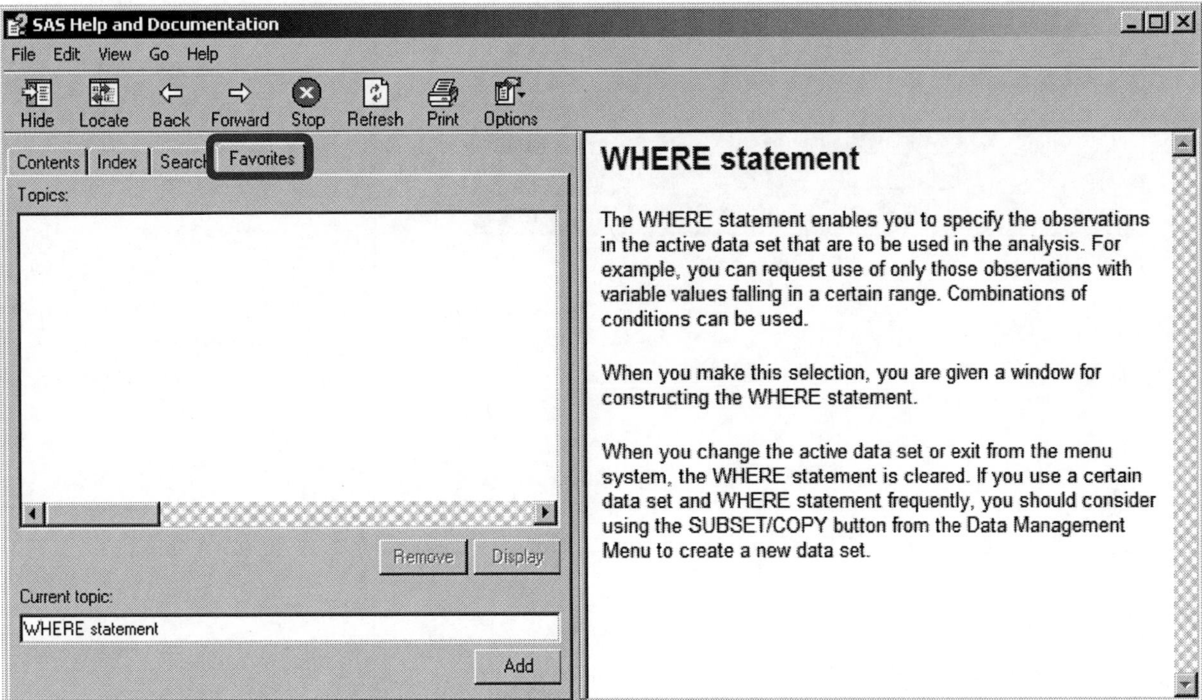

Click the **Add** button to add this topic to your list of Favorites.

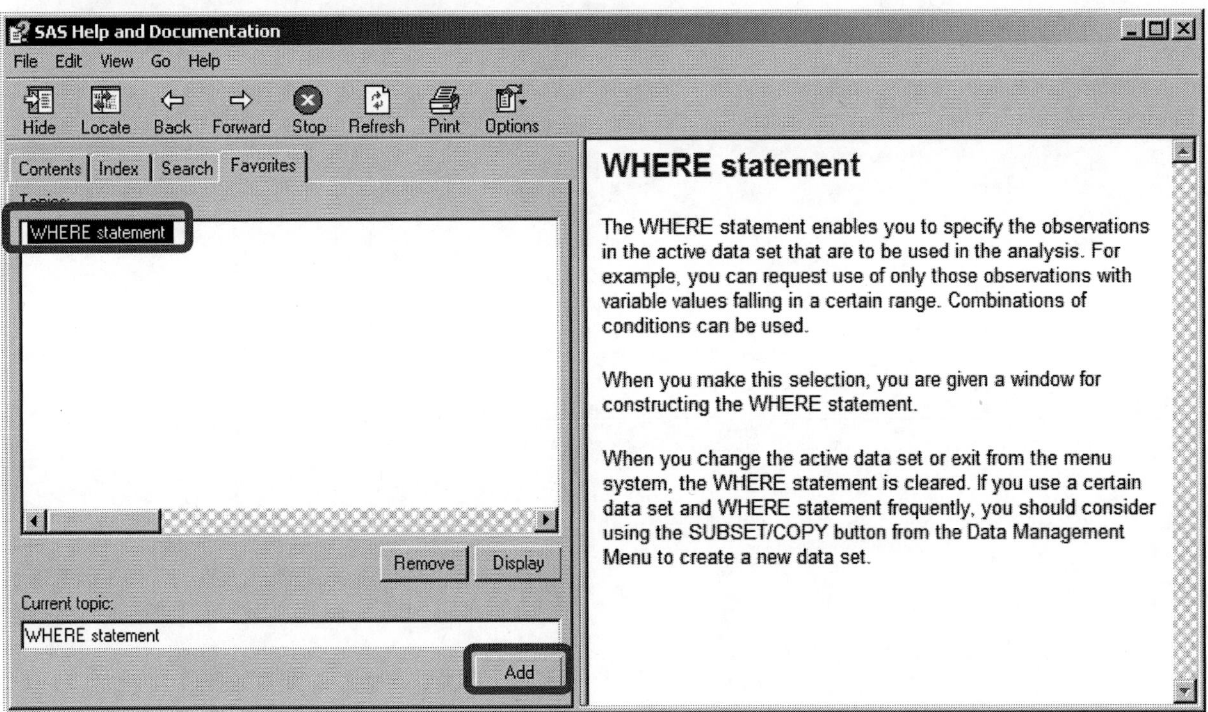

Setup for the Poll

Use SAS Help to navigate to DATA Step Processing.

Click the **Contents** tab and select:
- ⇨ **SAS Products**
  - ⇨ **Base SAS**
    - ⇨ **SAS 9.2 Language Reference: Concepts**
      - ⇨ **DATA Step Concepts**
        - ⇨ **DATA Step Processing**

Add this location to your Favorites.

11

1.01 Poll

Were you able to open the Help facility and add DATA Step Processing to your Favorites?

❍ Yes

❍ No

12

1.2 Course Overview

Objectives

- List data manipulation tools and techniques.
- Identify examples of data manipulation that are discussed in the course.

14

Manipulating Data in the DATA Step

Data is rarely in the form needed for analysis and reporting. Data manipulation is often required to transform the data.

- The DATA step is often the best choice for data manipulation.
- It offers
  - flexible programming capabilities
  - a vast library of data manipulation functions.

15

Other Data Manipulation Techniques

Other tools and techniques:

- The SORT, SQL, and TRANSPOSE procedures are useful for data manipulation and transformation.
- The SAS macro facility can make your code more flexible.
- Debugging techniques can help to identify logic errors.

What type of data manipulation is examined?

16

Creating Multiple Data Sets

A DATA step can be used to create multiple SAS data sets.

DATA Step

17

Creating Accumulating Totals

A DATA step can be used to create accumulating totals.

SAS Data Set

SaleDate	SaleAmt	Mth2Dte
01APR2007	498.49	498.49
02APR2007	946.50	1444.99
03APR2007	994.97	2439.96
04APR2007	564.59	3004.55

18

Summarizing Data Sets

A DATA step can be used to summarize data sets.

SAS Data Set

Salary	Dept
42000	SALES
34000	ADMIN
87000	ENGINR
60000	SALES
39000	ADMIN
79000	ENGINR

→ DATA Step →

SAS Data Set

Dept	DeptSal
ADMIN	73000
ENGINR	166000
SALES	102000

19

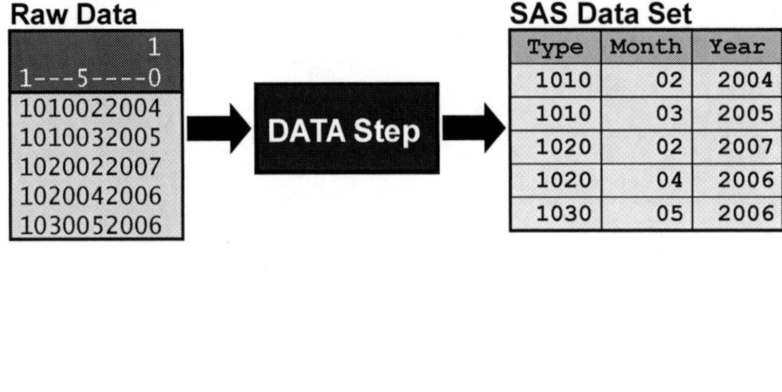
Reading a Raw Data File
A DATA step can be used to read from a raw data file to create a SAS data set.
Raw Data
1
1---5----0
1010022004
1010032005
1020022007
1020042006
1030052006
DATA Step
SAS Data Set
Type Month Year
1010 02 2004
1010 03 2005
1020 02 2007
1020 04 2006
1030 05 2006
20

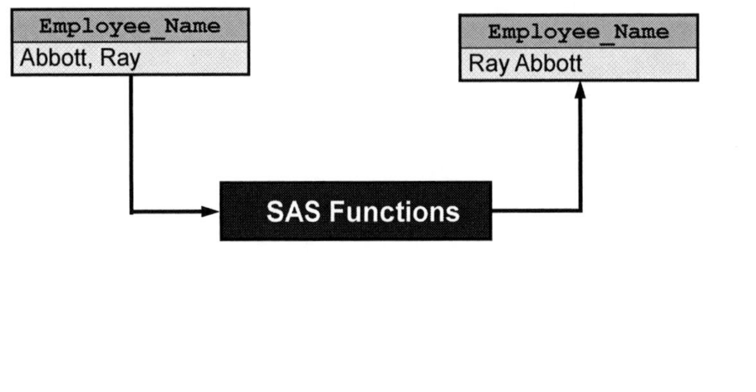
Manipulating Character Values
The DATA step offers many functions and operators to manipulate character values.
Employee_Name
Abbott, Ray
Employee_Name
Ray Abbott
SAS Functions
21

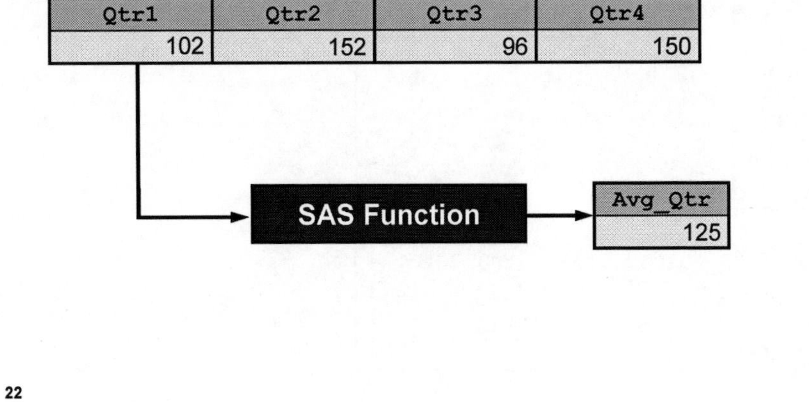
Manipulating Numeric Values
The DATA step also offers functions and operators to manipulate numeric values.
Qtr1
Qtr2
Qtr3
Qtr4
102
152
96
150
SAS Function
Avg_Qtr
125
22

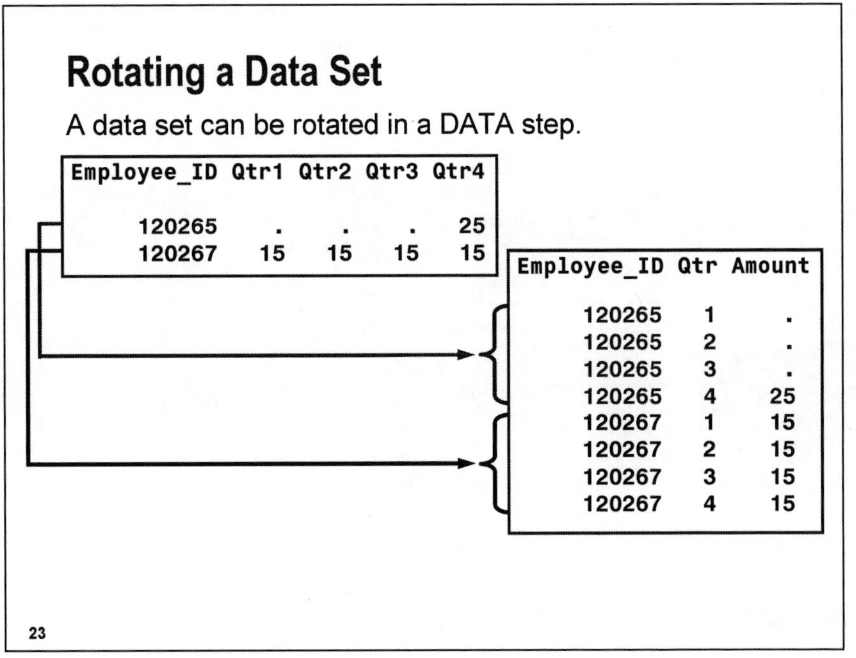
Rotating a Data Set
A data set can be rotated in a DATA step.
Employee_ID Qtr1 Qtr2 Qtr3 Qtr4
120265 . . . 25
120267 15 15 15 15
Employee_ID Qtr Amount
120265 1 .
120265 2 .
120265 3 .
120265 4 25
120267 1 15
120267 2 15
120267 3 15
120267 4 15
23

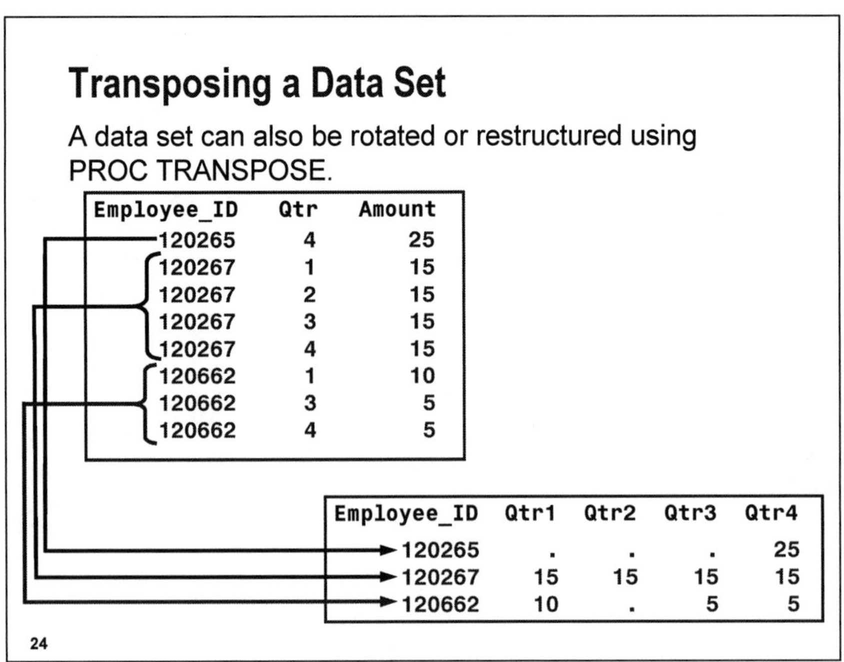

Transposing a Data Set
A data set can also be rotated or restructured using PROC TRANSPOSE.
Employee_ID Qtr Amount
120265 4 25
120267 1 15
120267 2 15
120267 3 15
120267 4 15
120662 1 10
120662 3 5
120662 4 5
Employee_ID Qtr1 Qtr2 Qtr3 Qtr4
120265 . . . 25
120267 15 15 15 15
120662 10 . 5 5
24

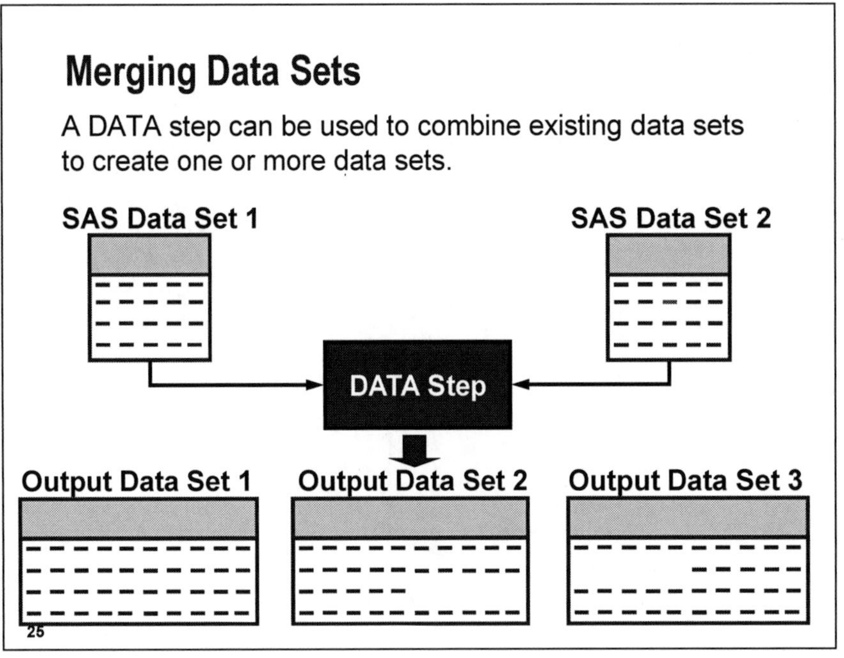

Merging Data Sets
A DATA step can be used to combine existing data sets to create one or more data sets.
SAS Data Set 1
SAS Data Set 2
DATA Step
Output Data Set 1
Output Data Set 2
Output Data Set 3
25

Joining Data Sets

The SQL procedure can also be used to combine existing data sets using various types of joins.

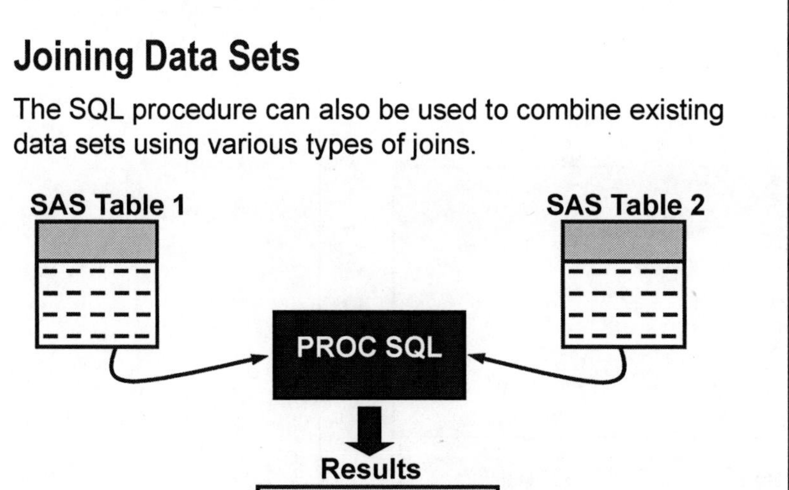

26

Using the Macro Language

The SAS macro language can be used to make your code more flexible.

```
proc print data=orion.order_fact;
   where year(order_date)=2006;
   title "Orders for 2006";
run;
```

```
proc print data=orion.order_fact;
   where year(order_date)=2007;
   title "Orders for 2007";
run;
```

```
proc print data=orion.order_fact;
   where year(order_date)=2008;
   title "Orders for 2008";
run;
```

27

Using Debugging Techniques

DATA step debugging techniques can help you locate errors in your code.

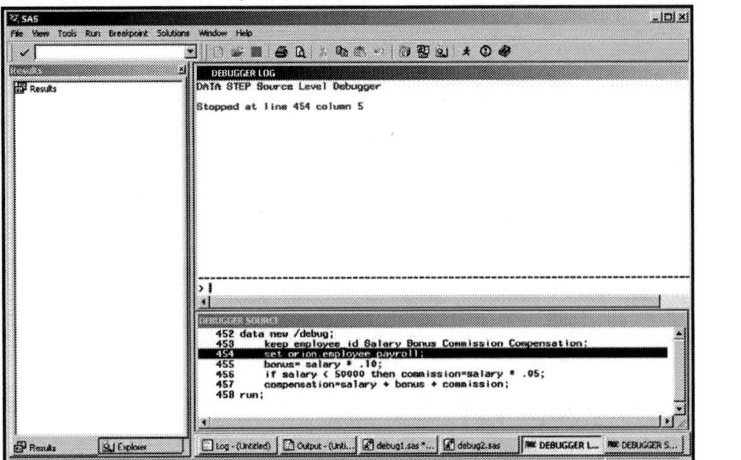

28

1.3 SAS Syntax Review

Objectives

- Explain the steps and statements in a sample SAS program.

31

SAS Program (Review)

A SAS program consists of one or more DATA steps, PROC steps, and global statements.

p201d01.sas

```
libname orion 's:\workshop';
data work.qtr1salesrep;
proc sort data=work.qtr1salesrep;
proc format;

options nodate pageno=1;
ods html file='salesrep.html' style=sasweb;
proc print data=work.qtr1salesrep label noobs;
ods html close;
```

32

p201d01

The LIBNAME Statement (Review)

The LIBNAME statement is a global statement that is used to define a **libref** and associate it with a SAS library.

PROG2Review.sas *

```
libname orion 's:\workshop';
data work.qtr1salesrep;
   set orion.sales;
```

The LIBNAME statement varies by operating system as shown in the following table.

Platform	LIBNAME Statement
Windows	`libname orion 's:\workshop';`
UNIX	`libname orion '.';`
z/OS (OS/390)	`libname orion '.workshop.sasdata';`

33

The DATA Step (Review)

This DATA step creates **`work.qtr1salesrep`** using **`orion.sales`** as input.

PROG2Review.sas *

```
libname orion 's:\workshop';
data work.qtr1salesrep;
   set orion.sales;
   where Job_Title contains 'Rep';
   BonusMonth=month(Hire_Date);
   if BonusMonth in (1,2,3);
   if Country='US' then Bonus=500;
   else if Country='AU' then Bonus=300;
   Compensation=sum(Salary,Bonus);
   keep First_Name Last_Name Country Gender Salary
        Hire_Date BonusMonth Bonus Compensation;
   label First_Name='First Name'
         Last_Name='Last Name'
         Hire_Date='Date of Hire'
         BonusMonth='Month of Bonus';
   format Hire_Date ddmmyy10.;
run;
```

34

The SORT Procedure (Review)

The SORT procedure rearranges the observations in **work.qtr1salesrep** and places them in order by descending **Last_Name** within **Country**.

```
PROG2Review.sas *
libname orion 's:\workshop';
data work.qtr1salesrep;

proc sort data=work.qtr1salesrep;
   by Country descending Last_Name;
run;
```

The OUT= option in the SORT procedure can be used to create an output data set, instead of overwriting the input data set.

35

The FORMAT Procedure (Review)

The FORMAT procedure creates user-defined formats and informats, and stores them in the SAS catalog **work.formats** by default.

```
PROG2Review.sas *
libname orion 's:\workshop';
data work.qtr1salesrep;
proc sort data=work.qtr1salesrep;

proc format;
   value $ctryfmt 'AU'='Australia'
                  'US'='United States';
run;
```

The formats and informats can be used for the remainder of the SAS session.

36

The OPTIONS Statement (Review)

The OPTIONS statement is a global statement that is used to set SAS system options.


```
libname orion 's:\workshop';
⊞data work.qtr1salesrep;
⊞proc sort data=work.qtr1salesrep;
⊞proc format;

options nodate pageno=1;
```

The options remain in effect until they are modified or the session ends.

37

ODS – The Output Delivery System (Review)

The Output Delivery System (ODS) enables you to produce output in a variety of formats, including HTML, RTF, PDF, and the default SAS listing.

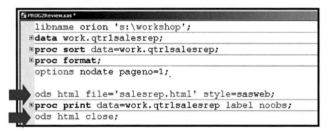

```
libname orion 's:\workshop';
⊞data work.qtr1salesrep;
⊞proc sort data=work.qtr1salesrep;
⊞proc format;
options nodate pageno=1;

ods html file='salesrep.html' style=sasweb;
⊞proc print data=work.qtr1salesrep label noobs;
ods html close;
```

The ODS statements above create an HTML file, salesrep.html, using the output produced by the PROC PRINT step.

38

The PRINT Procedure (Review)

The PRINT procedure prints the observations in a SAS data set and uses all or some of the variables.

PROG2Review.sas *

```
ods html file='salesrep.html' style=sasweb;
proc print data=work.qtr1salesrep label noobs;
   var Last_Name First_Name BonusMonth Bonus;
   title1 'Quarter 1 Orion Sales Reps';
   title2 'Males Only';
   footnote 'Confidential';
   format Bonus  dollar8.;
   where Gender='M';
   by Country;
run;
ods html close;
```

The PRINT procedure above includes TITLE and FOOTNOTE statements, which are global statements and do not need to be enclosed in a DATA or PROC step.

39

Program Output

Partial PROC PRINT Output (SAS Output window)

```
                  Quarter 1 Orion Sales Reps
                          Males Only

---------------------- Country=AU ----------------------

                   First       Month of
     Last Name     Name          Bonus          Bonus

     Wills         Matsuoka        1             $300
     Surawski      Marinus         1             $300
     Shannan       Sian            1             $300
     Scordia       Randal          2             $300
     Pretorius     Tadashi         3             $300
     Nowd          Fadi            1             $300
     Magrath       Brett           1             $300
```

40

Program Output

Partial PROC PRINT Output (HTML format)

Quarter 1 Orion Sales Reps
Males Only

Country=AU

Last Name	First Name	Month of Bonus	Bonus
Wills	Matsuoka	1	$300
Surawski	Marinus	1	$300
Shannan	Sian	1	$300
Scordia	Randal	2	$300
Pretorius	Tadashi	3	$300
Nowd	Fadi	1	$300
Magrath	Brett	1	$300

41

1.02 Quiz

Open and submit **p201a01**. Modify the program so that the $ctryfmt format is applied to `Country`, and the titles and footnotes are cleared at the end of the program.

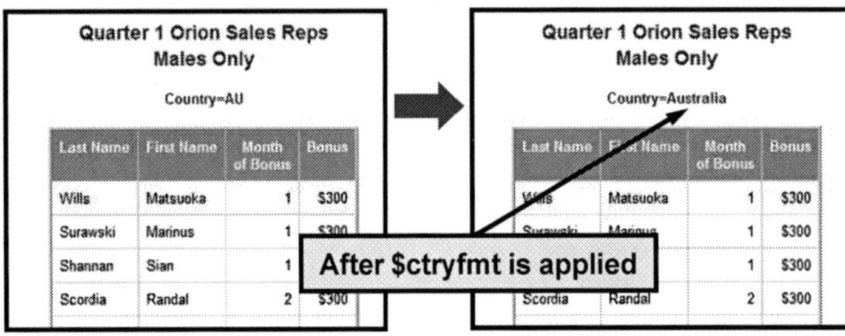

43

The following is a syntax guide to statements and procedures you should know before you start this class.

SAS System Options

```
OPTIONS DATE|NODATE;
OPTIONS NUMBER|NONUMBER;
OPTIONS LINESIZE|LS=n;
OPTIONS PAGESIZE| PS=n;
OPTIONS PAGENO=n;
OPTIONS CENTER|NOCENTER;
OPTIONS DTRESET|NODTRESET;
```

LIBNAME Statement

```
LIBNAME libref 'SAS-data-library' <options>;
```

Reading Excel Worksheets

```
LIBNAME libref 'physical-file-name' <options>;
```

Examining SAS Data Set Descriptor Portion

```
PROC CONTENTS DATA=SAS-data-set;
RUN;
```

```
PROC CONTENTS DATA=libref._ALL_ NODS;
RUN;
```

Reading Delimited Raw Data Files

```
DATA SAS-data-set(s);
      INFILE 'filename' <DLM='delimiter'> <DSD>;
      INPUT variable <$> variable <:informat> ... ;
      <additional SAS statements>
RUN;
```

Reading and Concatenating SAS Data Sets

```
DATA SAS-data-set(s);
      SET SAS-data-set(s);
      <additional SAS statements>
RUN;
```

Appending SAS Data Sets

```
PROC APPEND BASE = SAS-data-set
                    DATA = SAS-data-set <FORCE>;
RUN;
```

Subsetting Observations

```
WHERE expression;
```

```
IF expression THEN DELETE;
```

```
IF expression;
```

Subsetting Variables

```
DROP variable-list;
```

```
KEEP variable-list;
```

Merging SAS Data Sets

```
DATA SAS-data-sets;
      MERGE SAS-data-sets;
      BY BY-column(s);
      <additional SAS statements>
RUN;
```

Functions

```
YEAR(SAS-date)
QTR(SAS-date)
MONTH(SAS-date)
DAY(SAS-date)
WEEKDAY(SAS-date)
TODAY()
MDY(month, day, year)
```

```
UPCASE(argument)
```

```
SUM(argument1,argument2, . . .)
```

Titles and Footnotes

```
TITLEn 'text';
```

```
FOOTNOTEn 'text';
```

Examining SAS Data Set Data Portion

```
PROC PRINT DATA=SAS-data-set
           <NOOBS LABEL SPLIT='split-character'>;
    VAR variable-list;
RUN;
```

SAS Data Set Options

```
SAS-data-set(DROP=variable-list)
```

```
SAS-data-set(KEEP=variable-list)
```

```
SAS-data-set(IN=variable)
```

```
SAS-data-set(RENAME=(old-variable=new-variable
                     old-variable=new-variable ...))
```

Conditional Processing

```
IF expression THEN statement;
ELSE IF expression THEN statement;
ELSE statement;
```

```
IF expression THEN DO;
    statements
END;
ELSE IF expression THEN DO;
    statements
END;
```

Sorting Data

```
PROC SORT DATA=input-SAS-data-set
          <OUT=output-SAS-data-set>;
    BY <DESCENDING> by-variables;
RUN;
```

Grouping Observations

```
BY <DESCENDING> by-variables;
```

Directing Output to External Files

```
ODS destination FILE='filename.ext'
                <STYLE = style-definition>;
SAS code generating output
ODS destination CLOSE;
```

Formats and Labels

```
LABEL variable='label'
      variable='label' . . . ;
```

```
FORMAT variable(s) format;
```

```
PROC FORMAT;
    VALUE format-name range1='label'
                      range2='label'
                      . . . ;
RUN;
```

Creating New Variables

```
new-variable = expression;
```

```
LENGTH variable(s) <$> length;
```

Data Summarization and Validation Procedures

```
PROC MEANS DATA=SAS-data-set
           <options statistics>;
    CLASS variable(s);
    VAR variable(s);
RUN;
```

```
PROC FREQ DATA=SAS-data-set <options>;
    TABLES variable(s) </ option(s)>;
RUN;
```

```
PROC UNIVARIATE DATA=SAS-data-set;
    VAR variable(s);
RUN;
```

1.4 Navigating the SAS Windowing Environment (Self-Study)

These instructions are intended for students navigating the SAS windowing environment on SAS classroom machines. They might not be appropriate for all sites.

Navigating the SAS Windowing Environment on Windows

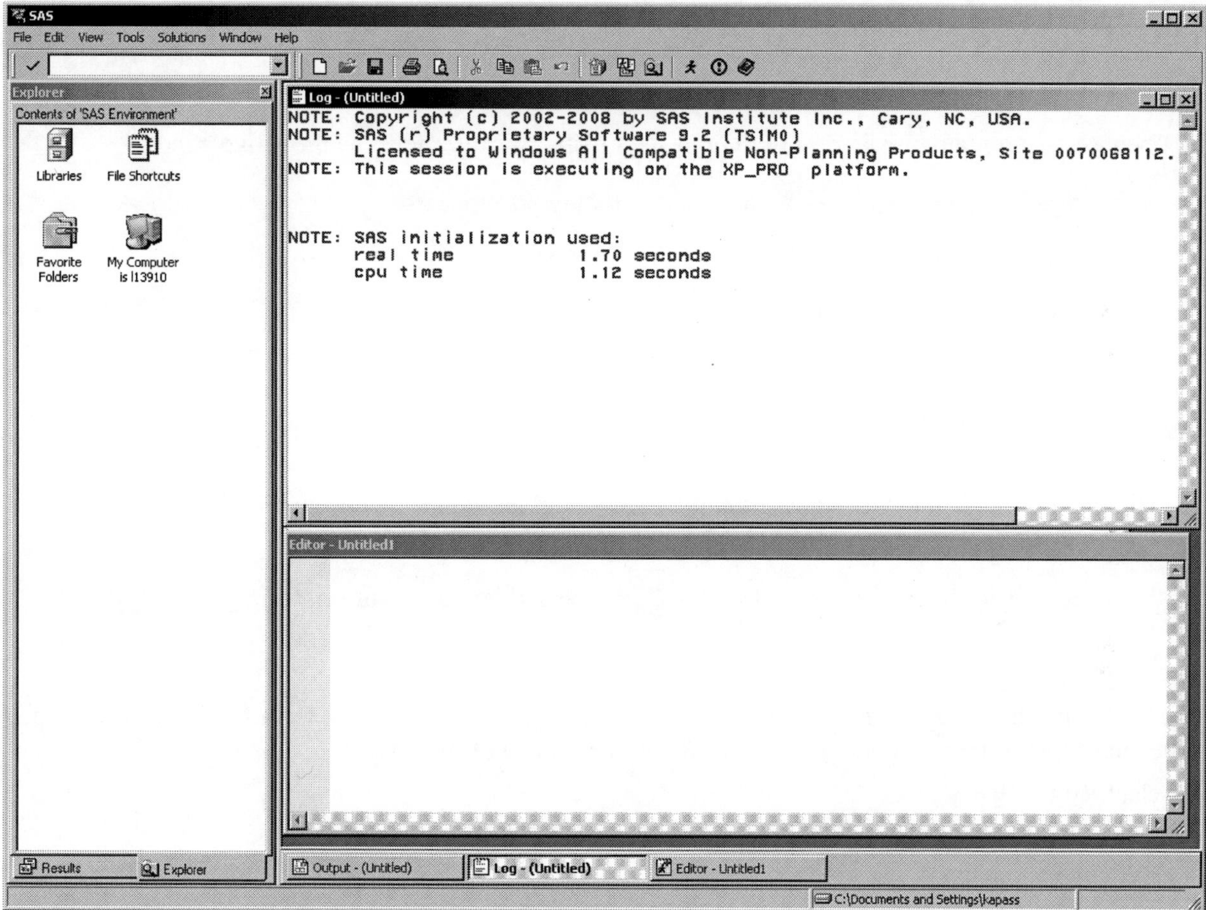

The Enhanced Editor (the default editor on Windows) is only available on the Windows operating system. Unlike the Program Editor, it does not automatically clear when code is submitted, and you can have multiple Enhanced Editor windows open simultaneously. You can use the Program Editor (the default editor in SAS 6 and earlier) by selecting **View** ⇨ **Program Editor**.

Navigating the Windows

To navigate to any window, do one of the following:

- Select the window button at the bottom of the screen (if the window is open).
- Select the window name from the View drop-down menu.
- Type the name of the window in the command bar and press the ENTER key.

To close any window, do one of the following:

- Select [X] in the upper-right corner of the window.
- Type `end` in the command bar, and press the ENTER key.

Opening a SAS Program

To open a SAS program, the Program Editor or the Enhanced Editor must be the active window.

1. Select **File** ⇨ **Open** or select [Open icon]. A Windows dialog box appears.
2. Navigate through the folders and highlight the program.
3. Select **OK**.

Submitting a SAS Program

To submit a program, the Program Editor or the Enhanced Editor must be the active window, and the code to be submitted must be in the window.

1. Highlight the code that you want to submit. (This is not necessary if you submit the entire contents of the window.)
2. Issue the SUBMIT command by selecting [Submit icon], pressing the F3 key, or selecting **Run** ⇨ **Submit**.

Recalling Submitted Code

The Program Editor is cleared automatically every time that code is submitted from it. To recall submitted code, make the Program Editor the active window, and do one of the following:

- Select **Run** ⇨ **Recall**.
- Type `recall` in the command bar, and press the ENTER key.
- Use the F4 shortcut key.

The RECALL command can also be used from the Enhanced Editor to retrieve lost code that was submitted.

Saving a SAS Program

To save a SAS program, the Program Editor or the Enhanced Editor must be the active window, and the code you want to save must be in the window.

1. Select **File** ⇨ **Save** or select **File** ⇨ **Save As...**. A Windows dialog box appears.
2. Navigate to the folder in which you want to save the program.
3. Type a name for the program in the appropriate box.
4. Select **OK**.

Clearing Windows

To clear a window, do one of the following:

- Activate the window, type `clear` in the command bar, and press the ENTER key.
- Activate the window and select **Edit** ⇨ **Clear All**.
- Type `clear` and the name of the window on the command bar and press the ENTER key.

Issuing Multiple Commands at Once

To issue more than one command at the same time, type the commands in the command bar separated by semicolons.

For example, to clear both the Log and Output windows, type the following on the command bar:

```
clear log; clear output
```

Navigating the SAS Windowing Environment on UNIX

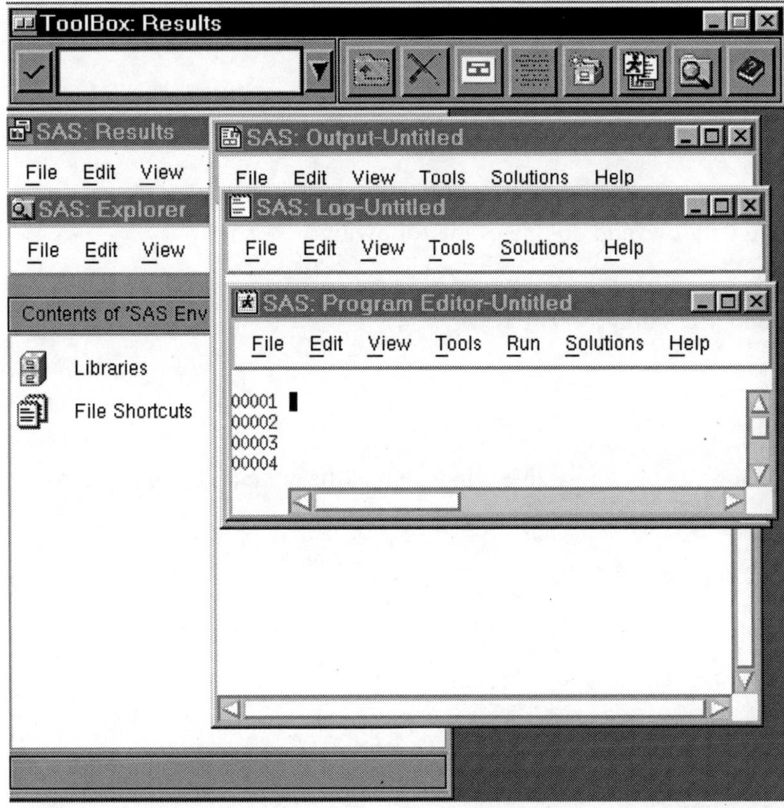

In the UNIX environment, SAS windows are floating, not docked. There is a floating toolbar with a command bar and shortcut icons. Drop-down menus are at the top of each window.

Navigating the Windows

To activate any window, do one of the following:

- Select the window icon at the bottom of the screen.
- Select the window name from the View drop-down menu.
- Type the window name on the command bar, and press the ENTER key.

Submitting a Program

To submit a SAS program, the Program Editor must be the active window and contain the code that you want to submit. Do any of the following to submit the contents of the Program Editor:

- Type `submit` on the command bar, and press the ENTER key.
- Use the F3 key.
- Select [icon] from the toolbar.
- Select **Run** ⇨ **Submit**.

To submit a portion of the code, do the following:

- Highlight the code to be submitted.
- Select **Run** ⇨ **Submit Clipboard**.

Recalling Submitted Code

The Program Editor is cleared automatically every time that code is submitted from it. To recall submitted code, make the Program Editor the active window, and do one of the following:

- Select **Run** ⇨ **Recall**.
- Type `recall` on the command bar, and press the ENTER key.
- Use the F4 shortcut key.

Saving a SAS Program

To save a SAS program, the Program Editor must be the active window, and the code that you want to save must be in the window.

1. Select **File** ⇨ **Save** or select **File** ⇨ **Save As...**. A dialog box appears.
2. Navigate to the directory in which you want to save the program.
3. Type a name for the program in the appropriate box.
4. Select **OK**.

Clearing Windows

To clear a window, do one of the following:

- Activate the window, type `clear` on the command bar, and press the ENTER key.
- Activate the window and select **Edit** ⇨ **Clear All**.
- Type `clear` and the name of the window on the command bar, and press the ENTER key.

Issuing Multiple Commands at Once

To submit more than one command at the same time, type the commands, separated by semicolons, on the command bar and press the ENTER key.

For example, to clear both the Log and Output windows, type the following on the command bar:

```
clear log; clear output
```

Navigating the SAS Windowing Environment on z/OS

Each time that you log on. do the following:

1. open the Output window by typing `output` on any command line and pressing the ENTER key.
2. issue the following command from the command line of the Output window. (This prevents suspended output.)

```
autoscroll 0
```

Navigating the Windows

- Each window contains a command line.
- You can open any window by typing its name on any command line and pressing the ENTER key.
- The PageUp and PageDown keys on your keyboard move from one open window to another.
- F7 and F8 enable you to scroll up and down within a window.
- To close any window and return to the Program Editor, issue the END command or use the F3 key. If the Program Editor is active, the F3 key submits the code in the window.
- To maximize a window, type **Z** on the command line and press the ENTER key. To restore the window to normal size, type **Z** on the command line of the maximized window and press the ENTER key.

Including a SAS Program

To include a SAS program in your session, the Program Editor must be the active window.

1. Type **include '*name-of-SAS-program*'** on the command line of the Program Editor window.
2. Press the ENTER key.

Submitting a Program

To submit a SAS program, the Program Editor must be the active window and contain the code that you want to submit. To submit code, do one of the following:

- Type `submit` on the command line of the Program Editor, and press the ENTER key.
- Use the F3 key.

Recalling Submitted Code

The Program Editor is cleared automatically every time that code is submitted from it. To recall submitted code, make the Program Editor the active window and do one of the following:

- Type `recall` on the command line of the Program Editor, and press the ENTER key.
- Use the F4 key.

Saving a SAS Program

To save a SAS program, the Program Editor must be the active window and contain the code that you want
to save.

1. Type **`file 'name-of-SAS-program'`** on the command line of the Program Editor window.
2. Press the ENTER key. A note appears at the top of the window.

Clearing Windows

To clear a window, do one of the following:

- Type **`clear`** on the command line of that window and press the ENTER key.
- Type **`clear`** and the name of the window to be cleared on any command line and press the ENTER key.

Editing SAS Program Code in the UNIX and z/OS Environments

Program Editor Line Number Commands

Most Windows users utilize copy and paste commands. However, the Program Editor in all three environments allows the use of line number commands. Use these commands to copy, paste, or delete program code.

I	inserts one line (after) the current line.
I*n*	inserts *n* lines (after) the current line.
IB	inserts one line (before) the current line.
IB*n*	inserts *n* lines (before) the current line.

D	deletes the current line.
D*n*	deletes *n* lines.
DD	deletes a block of lines. Type **`dd`** on the first and last lines of the block.

R	repeats the current line once.
R*n*	repeats the current line *n* times.
RR	repeats a block of lines once. Type **`rr`** on the first and last lines of the block.

Moving and Copying Code

To copy or move one line of code, do the following:

1. Type **`c`** (to copy) or **`m`** (to move) the line that you want to copy or move.
2. Type **`a`** (for after) or **`b`** (for before) on the appropriate line to indicate where you want to copy or move the specified line.

To copy or move a block of lines of code, do the following:

1. Type `cc` or `mm` on the first line that you want to copy or move.
2. Type `cc` or `mm` on the last line that you want to copy or move.
3. Type `a` (for after) or `b` (for before) on the appropriate line to indicate where you want to copy or move the block of lines.

Line number commands are not available in the Windows Enhanced Editor.

1.5 Solutions

Solutions to Student Activities (Polls/Quizzes)

1.02 Quiz – Correct Answer

Open and submit **p201a01**. Modify the program so that the $ctryfmt format is applied to **Country**, and the titles and footnotes are cleared at the end of the program.

```
ods html file='salesrep.html' style=sasweb;
proc print data=work.qtr1salesrep label noobs;
   var Last_Name First_Name BonusMonth Bonus;
   title1 'Quarter 1 Orion Sales Reps';
   title2 'Males Only';
   footnote 'Confidential';
   format Bonus  dollar8. country $ctryfmt.;
   where Gender='M';
   by Country;
run;
ods html close;
title;
footnote;
```

Modify the existing FORMAT statement or add another.

Add null TITLE and FOOTNOTE statements.

44

p201a01s

Chapter 2 Controlling Input and Output

2.1 Outputting Multiple Observations 2-3

Exercises 2-16

2.2 Writing to Multiple SAS Data Sets 2-20

Demonstration: Creating Multiple Data Sets 2-25

Exercises 2-31

2.3 Selecting Variables and Observations 2-35

Exercises 2-51

2.4 Chapter Review 2-54

2.5 Solutions 2-55

Solutions to Exercises 2-55

Solutions to Student Activities (Polls/Quizzes) 2-60

Solutions to Chapter Review 2-64

2.1 Outputting Multiple Observations

Objectives

- Explicitly control the output of multiple observations to a SAS data set.

3

Business Scenario – A Forecasting Application

The growth rate of six departments at Orion Star is stored in the **`Increase`** variable in the data set **`orion.growth`**. If each department grows at its predicted rate for the next two years, how many employees will be in each department at the end of each year?

Listing of **`orion.growth`**

Department	Total_ Employees	Increase
Administration	34	0.25
Engineering	9	0.30
IS	25	0.10
Marketing	20	0.20
Sales	201	0.30
Sales Management	11	0.10

4

A Forecasting Application

The output SAS data set, **forecast**, should contain 12 observations. Two observations are written for each observation read.

Partial Listing of **forecast**

Department	Total_ Employees	Increase	Year
Administration	42.500	0.25	1
Administration	53.125	0.25	2
Engineering	11.700	0.30	1
Engineering	15.210	0.30	2
IS	27.500	0.10	1
IS	30.250	0.10	2

5

2.01 Quiz

Which of the following occur at the end of a DATA step iteration?

```
data forecast;
   set orion.growth;
   total_employees=
      total_employees * (1+increase);
run;
```

?

a. Reinitialize the PDV.

b. Implicit OUTPUT; implicit RETURN.

c. Read the next observation.

7

Explicit Output

The explicit OUTPUT statement writes the contents of the program data vector (PDV) to the data set or data sets being created. The presence of an explicit OUTPUT statement overrides implicit output.

```
data forecast;
   set orion.growth;
   Year=1;
   Total_Employees=Total_Employees*(1+Increase);
   output;
   Year=2;
   Total_Employees=Total_Employees*(1+Increase);
   output;
run;
```

No Implicit OUTPUT;

9 p202d01

Using an explicit OUTPUT statement without arguments causes the current observation to be written to all data sets that are named in the DATA statement.

The explicit OUTPUT statement causes immediate output but not an immediate return to the top of the DATA step. The implicit RETURN statement still occurs at the bottom of the step.

Compilation

```
data forecast;
   set orion.growth;
   Year=1;
   Total_Employees=Total_Employees*(1+Increase);
   output;
   Year=2;
   Total_Employees=Total_Employees*(1+Increase);
   output;
run;
```

PDV – Program Data Vector

Department $ 20	Total_ Employees N 8	Increase N 8

10 ...

Compilation

```
data forecast;
   set orion.growth;
   Year=1;
   Total_Employees=Total_Employees*(1+Increase);
   output;
   Year=2;
   Total_Employees=Total_Employees*(1+Increase);
   output;
run;
```

PDV

Department $ 20	Total_ Employees N 8	Increase N 8	Year N 8

11 ...

Compilation

```
data forecast;
   set orion.growth;
   Year=1;
   Total_Employees=Total_Employees*(1+Increase);
   output;
   Year=2;
   Total_Employees=Total_Employees*(1+Increase);
   output;
run;
```

Write descriptor portion of output data set

PDV

Department $ 20	Total_ Employees N 8	Increase N 8	Year N 8

work.forecast

Department $ 20	Total_ Employees N 8	Increase N 8	Year N 8

12

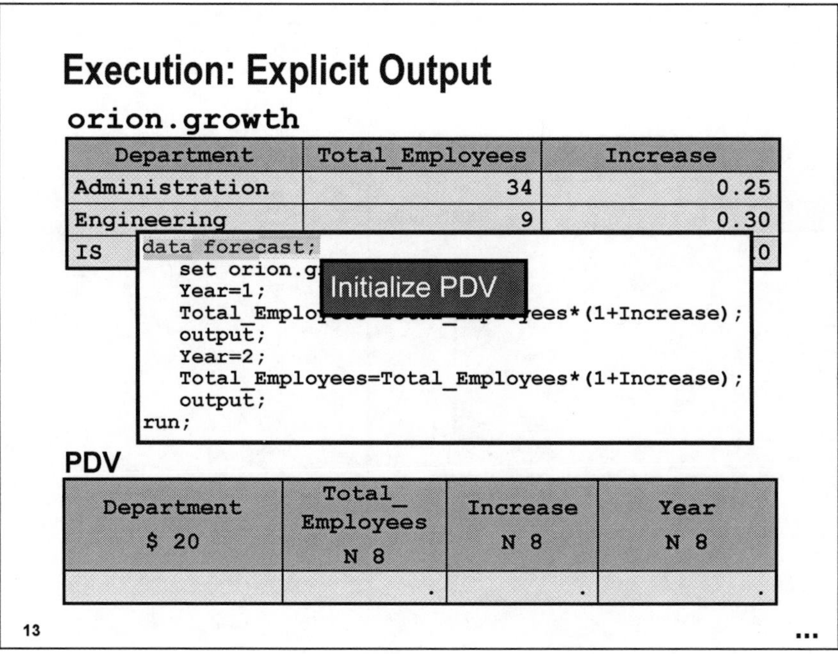
Execution: Explicit Output
orion.growth
Department | Total_Employees | Increase
Administration | 34 | 0.25
Engineering | 9 | 0.30
IS
data forecast;
set orion.g
Year=1;
Total_Emplo
ees*(1+Increase);
output;
Year=2;
Total_Employees=Total_Employees*(1+Increase);
output;
run;
Initialize PDV
PDV
Department $ 20
Total_ Employees N 8
Increase N 8
Year N 8
.
.
.
13
...

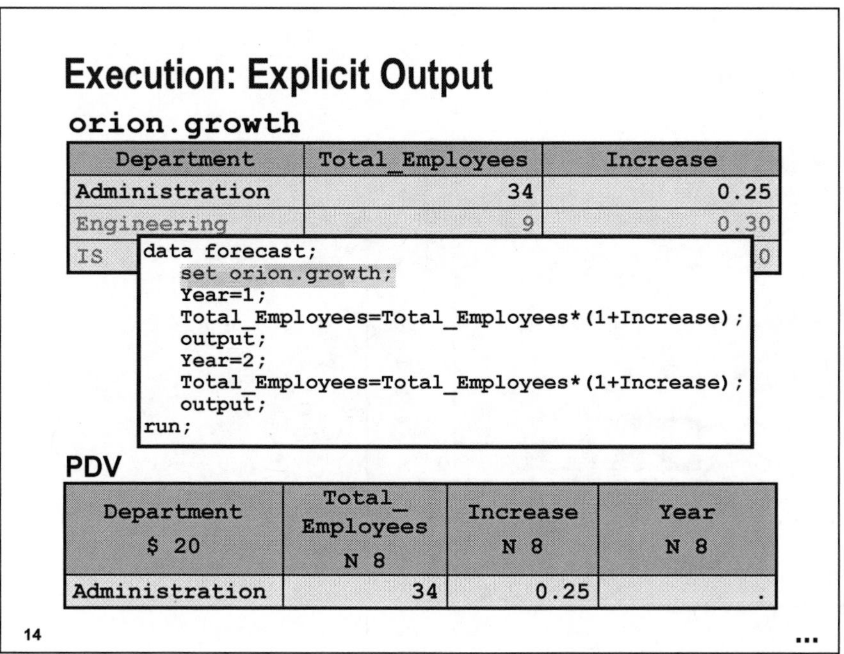
Execution: Explicit Output
orion.growth
Department | Total_Employees | Increase
Administration | 34 | 0.25
Engineering | 9 | 0.30
IS
data forecast;
set orion.growth;
Year=1;
Total_Employees=Total_Employees*(1+Increase);
output;
Year=2;
Total_Employees=Total_Employees*(1+Increase);
output;
run;
PDV
Department $ 20
Total_ Employees N 8
Increase N 8
Year N 8
Administration
34
0.25
.
14
...

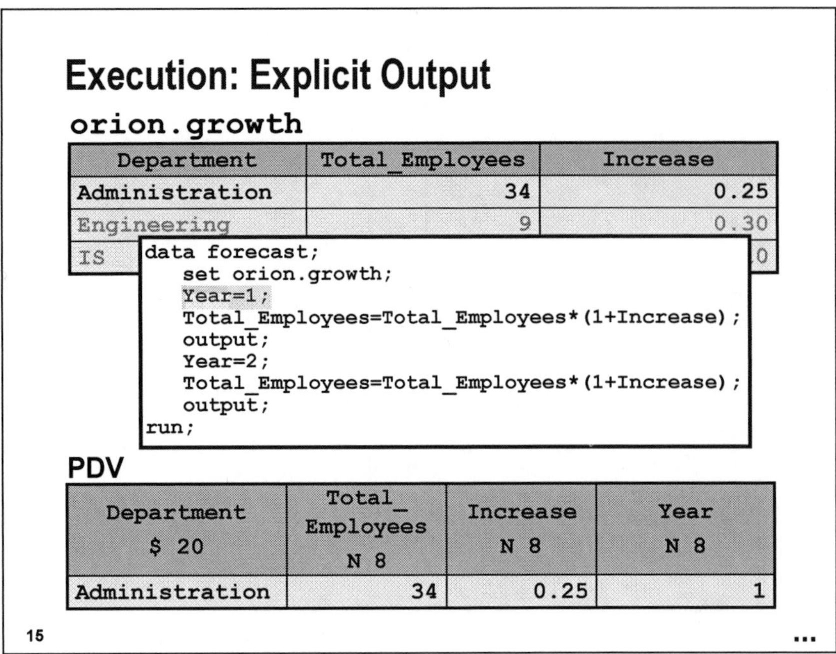
Execution: Explicit Output
orion.growth
Department
Total_Employees
Increase
Administration
34
0.25
Engineering
9
0.30
IS
data forecast;
set orion.growth;
Year=1;
Total_Employees=Total_Employees*(1+Increase);
output;
Year=2;
Total_Employees=Total_Employees*(1+Increase);
output;
run;
PDV
Department $ 20
Total_ Employees N 8
Increase N 8
Year N 8
Administration
34
0.25
1
15
...

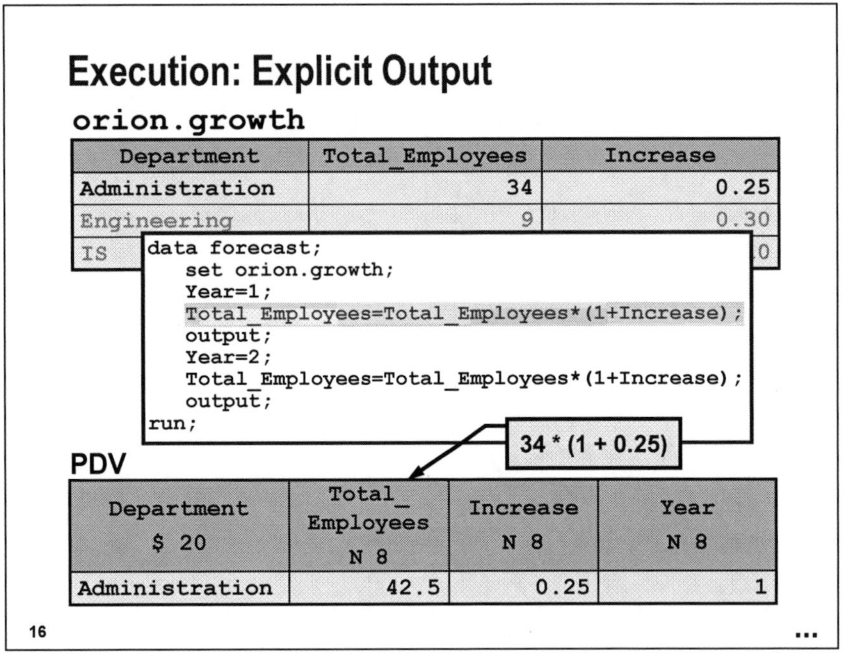
Execution: Explicit Output
orion.growth
Department
Total_Employees
Increase
Administration
34
0.25
Engineering
9
0.30
IS
data forecast;
set orion.growth;
Year=1;
Total_Employees=Total_Employees*(1+Increase);
output;
Year=2;
Total_Employees=Total_Employees*(1+Increase);
output;
run;
34 * (1 + 0.25)
PDV
Department $ 20
Total_ Employees N 8
Increase N 8
Year N 8
Administration
42.5
0.25
1
16
...

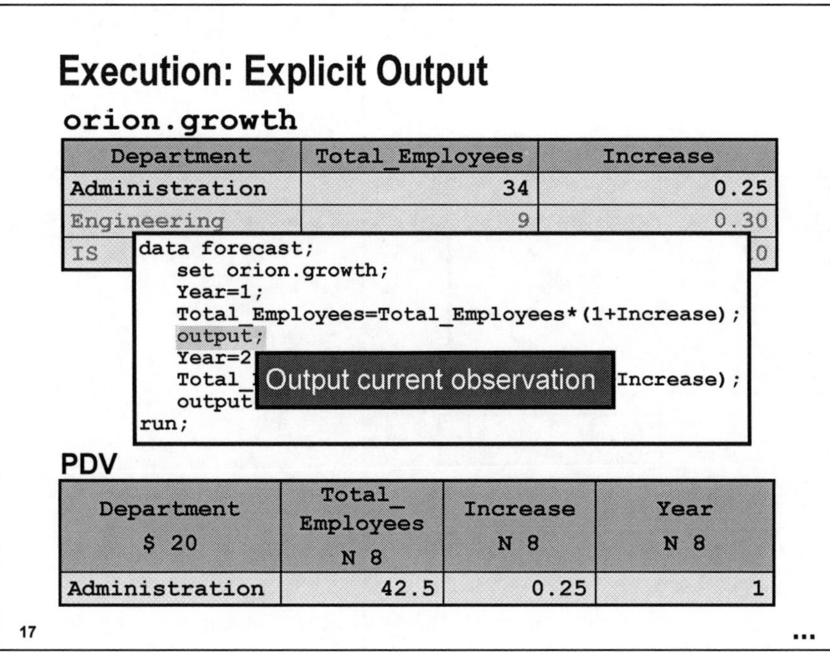
Execution: Explicit Output
orion.growth
Department
Total_Employees
Increase
Administration
34
0.25
Engineering
9
0.30
IS
data forecast;
set orion.growth;
Year=1;
Total_Employees=Total_Employees*(1+Increase);
output;
Year=2
Total_
Increase);
output
run;
Output current observation
PDV
Department
$ 20
Total_
Employees
N 8
Increase
N 8
Year
N 8
Administration
42.5
0.25
1
17

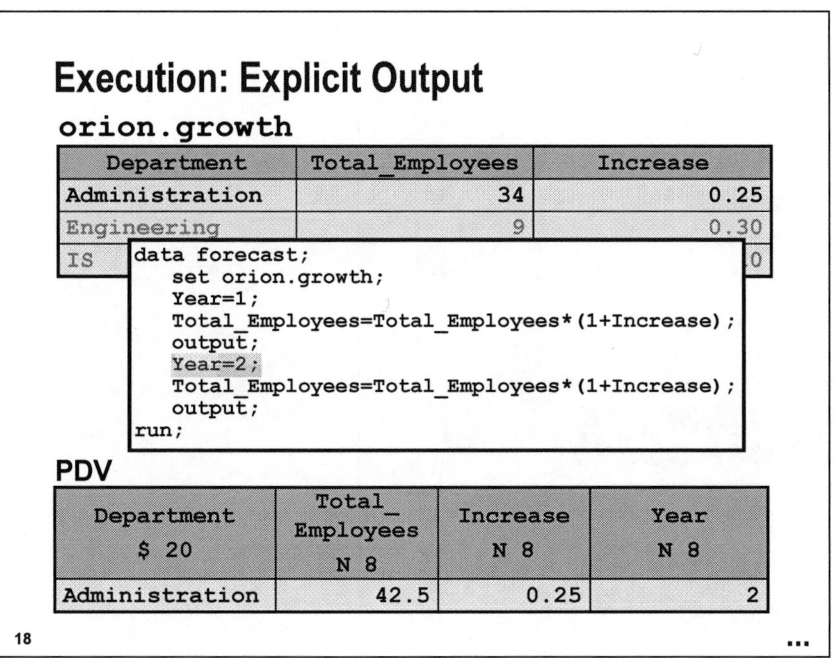
Execution: Explicit Output
orion.growth
Department
Total_Employees
Increase
Administration
34
0.25
Engineering
9
0.30
IS
data forecast;
set orion.growth;
Year=1;
Total_Employees=Total_Employees*(1+Increase);
output;
Year=2;
Total_Employees=Total_Employees*(1+Increase);
output;
run;
PDV
Department
$ 20
Total_
Employees
N 8
Increase
N 8
Year
N 8
Administration
42.5
0.25
2
18

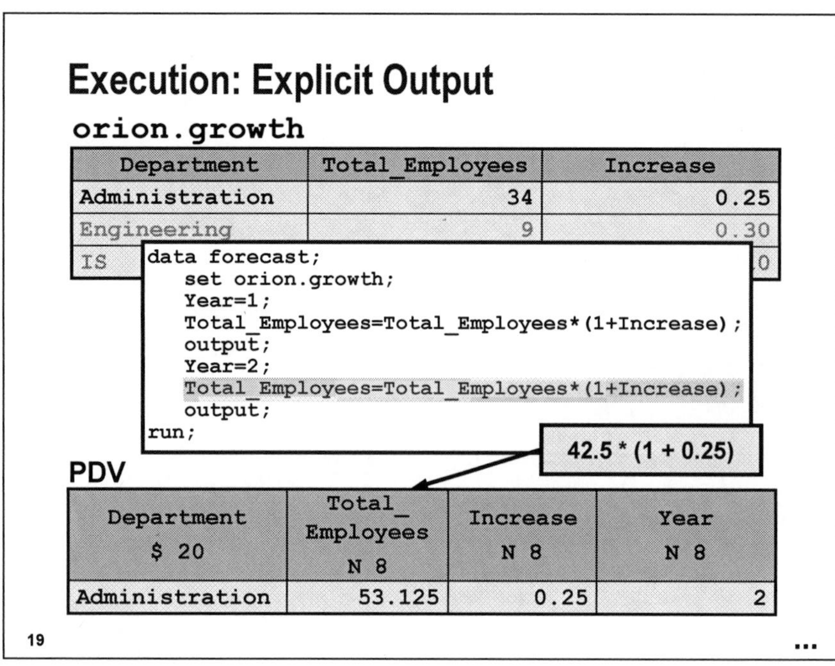
Execution: Explicit Output
orion.growth
Department
Total_Employees
Increase
Administration
34
0.25
Engineering
9
0.30
IS
data forecast;
set orion.growth;
Year=1;
Total_Employees=Total_Employees*(1+Increase);
output;
Year=2;
Total_Employees=Total_Employees*(1+Increase);
output;
run;
42.5 * (1 + 0.25)
PDV
Department
$ 20
Total_
Employees
N 8
Increase
N 8
Year
N 8
Administration
53.125
0.25
2
19

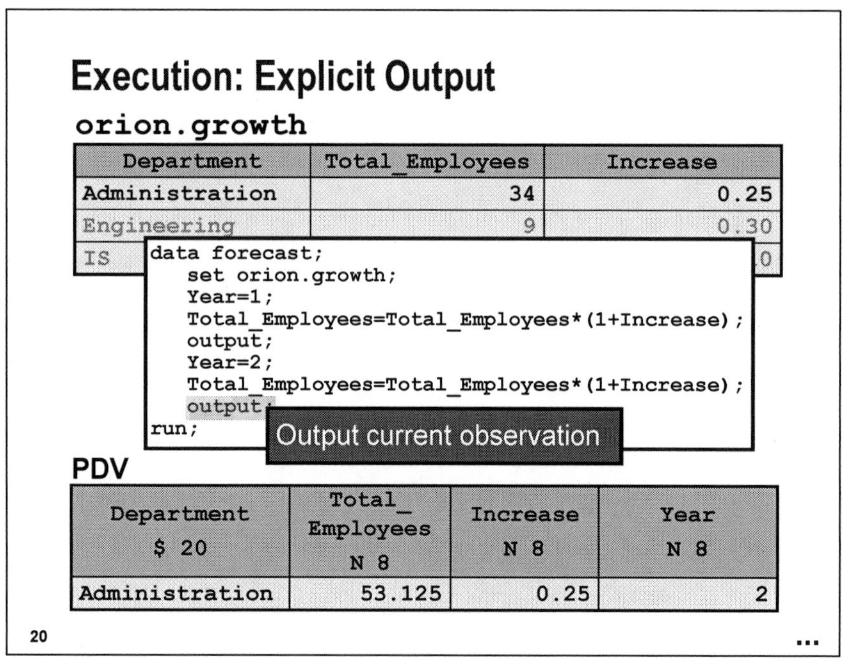
Execution: Explicit Output
orion.growth
Department
Total_Employees
Increase
Administration
34
0.25
Engineering
9
0.30
IS
data forecast;
set orion.growth;
Year=1;
Total_Employees=Total_Employees*(1+Increase);
output;
Year=2;
Total_Employees=Total_Employees*(1+Increase);
output;
run;
Output current observation
PDV
Department
$ 20
Total_
Employees
N 8
Increase
N 8
Year
N 8
Administration
53.125
0.25
2
20

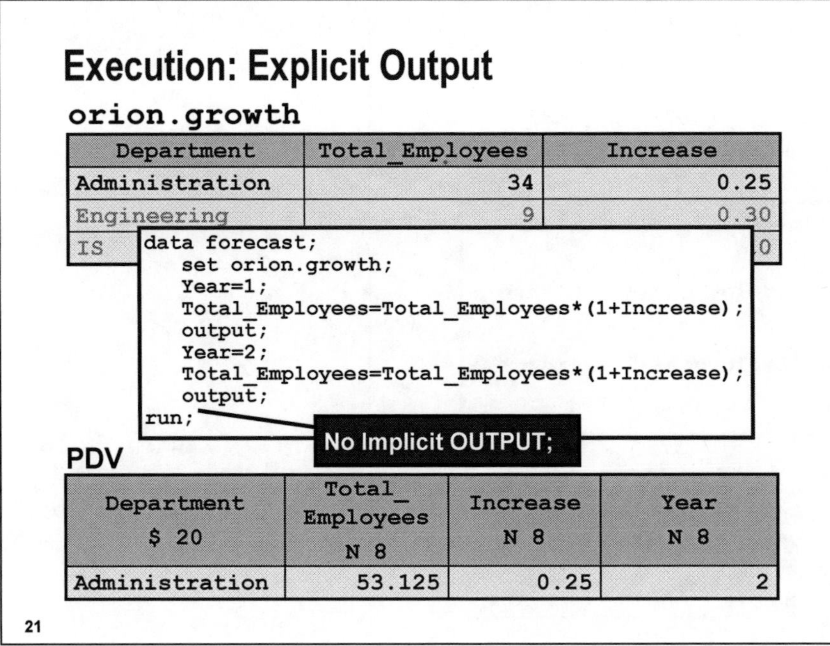

Output: A Forecasting Application

The **forecast** data set contains two observations after the first iteration of the DATA step.

work.forecast

Department	Total_ Employees	Increase	Year
Administration	42.500	0.25	1
Administration	53.125	0.25	2

22

Setup for the Poll

Prior to the second iteration of the DATA step, some variables in the program data vector will be reinitialized. .

```
data forecast;
   set orion.growth;
   Year=1;
   Total_Employees=Total_Employees*(1+Increase);
   output;
   Year=2;
   Total_Employees=Total_Employees*(1+Increase);
   output;
run;
```

PDV

Department $ 20	Total_ Employees N 8	Increase N 8	Year N 8
Administration	53.125	0.25	2

24

2.02 Multiple Answer Poll

Which variable(s) will be reinitialized?

a. `Department`

b. `Total_Employees`

c. `Increase`

d. `Year`

25

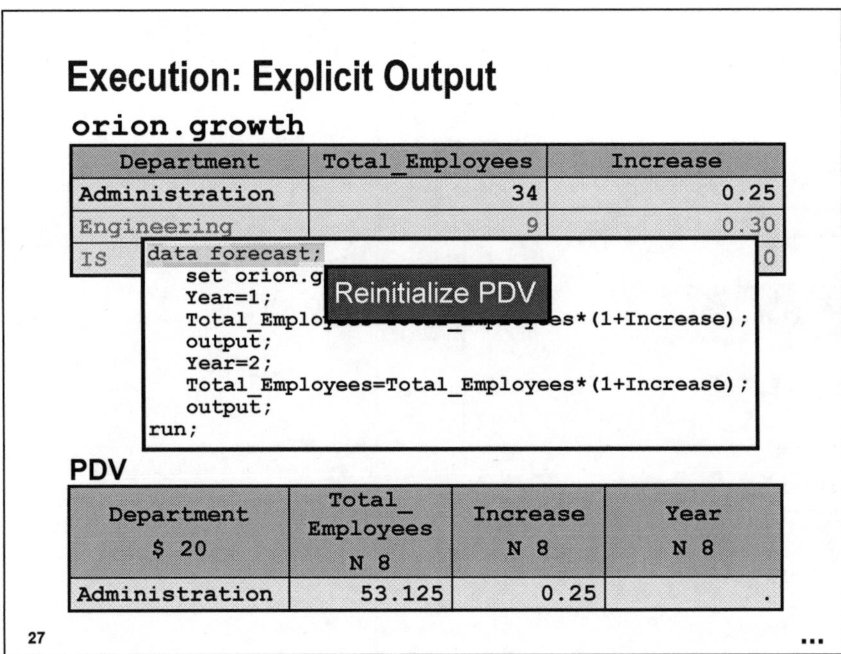

Execution: Explicit Output
orion.growth
Department
Total_Employees
Increase
Administration
34
0.25
Engineering
9
0.30
IS
data forecast;
set orion.g
Year=1;
Reinitialize PDV
Total_Emplo
es*(1+Increase);
output;
Year=2;
Total_Employees=Total_Employees*(1+Increase);
output;
run;
PDV
Department
$ 20
Total_
Employees
N 8
Increase
N 8
Year
N 8
Administration
53.125
0.25
.
27
...

When the program data vector is reinitialized, the values of variables created by INPUT and assignment statements are set to missing. Variables that you read with a SET statement are not set to missing, because they will be overwritten when the next observation is read.

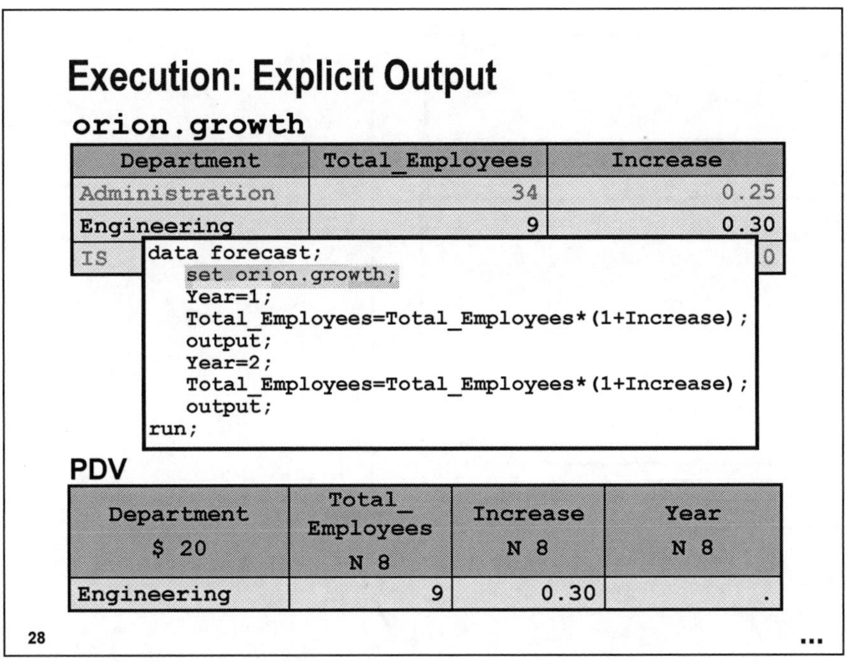

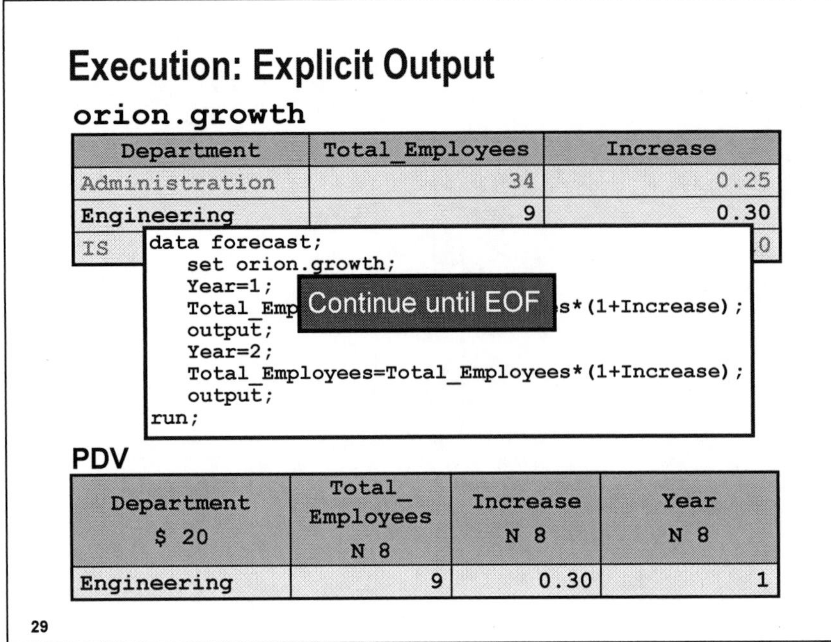

Check the Results

Partial SAS Log

```
NOTE: There were 6 observations read from the data set
      ORION.GROWTH.
NOTE: The data set WORK.FORECAST has 12 observations
      and 4 variables.
```

Partial PROC PRINT Output

```
                          Total_
Department               Employees     Year

Administration             42.500        1
Administration             53.125        2
Engineering                11.700        1
Engineering                15.210        2
IS                         27.500        1
IS                         30.250        2
Marketing                  24.000        1
Marketing                  28.800        2
```

30

2.03 Quiz

Open and submit **p202a01**. Modify the DATA step to write only one observation per department. Show the number of employees after two years.

Desired Results

```
                        Total_
Department           Employees    Year

Administration          53.125       2
Engineering             15.210       2
IS                      30.250       2
Marketing               28.800       2
Sales                  339.690       2
Sales Management        13.310       2
```

32

p202a01

Exercises

These exercises use SAS data sets stored in a permanent SAS data library.

- Submit the appropriate LIBNAME statement to define an **ORION** libref.

Windows	`libname orion 's:\workshop';`
UNIX	`libname orion '.';`
z/OS (OS/390)	`libname orion '.workshop.sasdata';`

If you are using SAS on your own computer, you might need to change the location specified for the SAS data library.

Example: `libname orion 'C:\SAS_Education\LWPRG2';`

- Check the log to confirm that the SAS data library was assigned.

```
NOTE: Libref ORION was successfully assigned as follows:
```

- Use the EXPLORER window to view the contents of the **orion** library.

Level 1

1. Outputting Multiple Observations

The **orion.prices** data set contains price information for Orion Star products.

Partial Listing of **orion.prices** (50 Total Observations)

```
  Product_ID       Unit_Price   Factor

210200100009         $34.70      1.01
210200100017         $40.00      1.01
210200200023         $19.80      1.01
210200600067         $67.00      1.01
210200600085         $39.40      1.01
210200600112         $21.80      1.01
210200900033         $14.20      1.01
210200900038         $20.30      1.01
210201000050         $19.60      1.01
210201000126          $6.50      1.01
```

a. Write a DATA step to create a new data set that forecasts unit prices for the next three years. This data set will contain three observations for each input observation read from **orion.prices**.

- Open file **p202e01**. It reads **orion.prices** and creates a new data set named **work.price_increase**.
- Use explicit OUTPUT statements to forecast unit prices for the next three years, using **Factor** as the annual rate of increase.

b. Print the new data set.

- Include only **Product_ID**, **Unit_Price** and **Year** in the report.
- Verify your results.

Partial PROC PRINT Output (150 Total Observations)

Obs	Product_ID	Unit_Price	Year
1	210200100009	$35.05	1
2	210200100009	$35.40	2
3	210200100009	$35.75	3
4	210200100017	$40.40	1
5	210200100017	$40.80	2
6	210200100017	$41.21	3
7	210200200023	$20.00	1
8	210200200023	$20.20	2
9	210200200023	$20.40	3
10	210200600067	$67.67	1

Level 2

2. Outputting Multiple Observations

The data set **orion.discount** contains information about various discounts that Orion Star runs on its products.

Partial Listing of **orion.discount**

Product_ID	Start_ Date	End_Date	Unit_Sales_ Price	Discount
210100100027	01MAY2007	31MAY2007	$17.99	70%
210100100030	01AUG2007	31AUG2007	$32.99	70%
210100100033	01AUG2007	31AUG2007	$161.99	70%
210100100034	01AUG2007	31AUG2007	$187.99	70%
210100100035	01MAY2007	31MAY2007	$172.99	70%
210100100038	01JUL2007	31JUL2007	$59.99	60%
210100100039	01JUN2007	31AUG2007	$21.99	70%
210100100048	01AUG2007	31AUG2007	$13.99	70%

a. Due to excellent sales, all discounts from December 2007 will be repeated in July 2008. Both the December 2007 and the July 2008 discounts will be called the Happy Holidays promotion.

- Create a new data set named **work.extended** that contains all discounts for the Happy Holidays promotion.
- Use a WHERE statement to read only observations with a start date of 01Dec2007.
- Create a new variable, **Promotion**, which has the value `Happy Holidays` for each observation.
- Create another new variable, **Season**, that has a value of `Winter` for the December observations and `Summer` for the July observations.
- July 2008 discounts should have a start date of 01Jul2008 and an end date of 31Jul2008.
- Drop the **Unit_Sales_Price** variable.
- Use explicit OUTPUT to write two observations for each observation read.

b. Print the new data set.

- Add an appropriate title
- Verify the results.

Partial PROC PRINT (332 Total Observations)

All discount ranges with the Happy Holidays promotion

Obs	Product_ID	Start_ Date	End_Date	Discount	Promotion	Season
1	210200100007	01DEC2007	31DEC2007	50%	Happy Holidays	Winter
2	210200100007	01JUL2008	31JUL2008	50%	Happy Holidays	Summer
3	210200300013	01DEC2007	31DEC2007	50%	Happy Holidays	Winter
4	210200300013	01JUL2008	31JUL2008	50%	Happy Holidays	Summer
5	210200300025	01DEC2007	31DEC2007	50%	Happy Holidays	Winter

Level 3

3. Using Conditional Logic to Output Multiple Observations

The data set **orion.country** contains information on country names as well as various lookup codes.

Listing of **orion.country**

Country	Country_Name	Population	Country_ ID	Continent_ ID	Country_Former Name
AU	Australia	20,000,000	160	96	
CA	Canada	.	260	91	
DE	Germany	80,000,000	394	93	East/West Germany
IL	Israel	5,000,000	475	95	
TR	Turkey	70,000,000	905	95	
US	United States	280,000,000	926	91	
ZA	South Africa	43,000,000	801	94	

a. Create a new data set that contains one observation for each current country name as well as one observation for each former country name.

- Use conditional logic and explicit OUTPUT statements to create a data set named **work.lookup**.
- If a country has a former country name, write two observations: one with the current name in the **Country_Name** variable and another with the former country name in the **Country_Name** variable.
- Drop the variables **Country_FormerName** and **Population**.
- Create a new variable named **Outdated** with values of either Y or N to indicate whether the observation represents the current country name.

b. Print the new data set with an appropriate title.

PROC PRINT Output

Current and Outdated Country Name Data

Obs	Country	Country_Name	Country_ ID	Continent_ ID	Outdated
1	AU	Australia	160	96	N
2	CA	Canada	260	91	N
3	DE	Germany	394	93	N
4	DE	East/West Germany	394	93	Y
5	IL	Israel	475	95	N
6	TR	Turkey	905	95	N
7	US	United States	926	91	N
8	ZA	South Africa	801	94	N

2.2 Writing to Multiple SAS Data Sets

Objectives

- Create multiple SAS data sets in a single DATA step.
- Use conditional processing to control the data set(s) to which an observation is written.

37

Business Scenario

Use the **orion.employee_addresses** data set as input to create three new data sets: **usa**, **australia**, and **other**.

- The **usa** data set will contain observations with a **Country** value of `US`.
- The **australia** data set will contain observations with a **Country** value of `AU`.
- Observations with any other **Country** value will be written to the **other** data set.

38

Browse the Input Data Set

```
proc print data=orion.employee_addresses;
   var Employee_Name City Country;
run;
```

Partial PROC PRINT Output

Obs	Employee_Name	City	Country
1	Abbott, Ray	Miami-Dade	US
2	Aisbitt, Sandy	Melbourne	AU
3	Akinfolarin, Tameaka	Philadelphia	US
4	Amos, Salley	San Diego	US
5	Anger, Rose	Philadelphia	US
6	Anstey, David	Miami-Dade	US
7	Antonini, Doris	Miami-Dade	US
8	Apr, Nishan	San Diego	US
9	Ardskin, Elizabeth	Miami-Dade	US
10	Areu, Jeryl	Miami-Dade	US
11	Arizmendi, Gilbert	San Diego	US
12	Armant, Debra	San Diego	US

39

p202d02

Creating Multiple DATA Sets

Multiple data sets can be created in a DATA step by listing the names of the output data sets in the DATA statement.

DATA <*SAS-data-set-1* ... *SAS-data-set-n*>;

You can direct output to a specific data set or data sets by listing the data set names in the OUTPUT statement.

OUTPUT <*SAS-data-set-1* ... *SAS-data-set-n*>;

An OUTPUT statement without arguments writes to every SAS data set listed in the DATA statement.

40

If you do not specify a SAS data set name or the reserved name _NULL_ in a DATA statement, then SAS automatically creates data sets with the names **data1**, **data2**, and so on in the Work library by default.

Data sets named in the OUTPUT statement **must** appear in the DATA statement.

 To specify multiple data sets in a single OUTPUT statement, separate the data set names with a space:

```
output data1 data2;
```

Creating Multiple SAS Data Sets

Create three new data sets: **usa**, **australia**, and **other**.

```
data usa australia other;
   set orion.employee_addresses;
   if Country='AU' then output australia;
   else if Country='US' then output usa;
   else output other;
run;
```

41

p202d03

Check the SAS Log

Three data sets were created. The log shows that US was the most frequently occurring value.

Partial SAS Log

```
NOTE: There were 424 observations read from the data set
      ORION.EMPLOYEE_ADDRESSES.
NOTE: The data set WORK.USA has 311 observations and 9
      variables.
NOTE: The data set WORK.AUSTRALIA has 105 observations and
      9  variables.
NOTE: The data set WORK.OTHER has 8 observations and 9
      variables.
```

42

Efficient Conditional Processing

It is more efficient to check values in order of decreasing frequency.

```
data usa australia other;
   set orion.employee_addresses;
   if Country='US' then output usa;
   else if Country='AU' then output australia;
   else output other;
run;
```

```
NOTE: There were 424 observations read from the data set
      ORION.EMPLOYEE_ADDRESSES.
NOTE: The data set WORK.USA has 311 observations and 9
      variables.
NOTE: The data set WORK.AUSTRALIA has 105 observations and
      9 variables.
NOTE: The data set WORK.OTHER has 8 observations and 9
      variables.
```

43

2.04 Quiz

Consider the results of the previous DATA step.

Can all three data sets be printed with a single PRINT procedure?

Partial SAS Log

```
NOTE: There were 424 observations read from the data set
      ORION.EMPLOYEE_ADDRESSES.
NOTE: The data set WORK.USA has 311 observations and 9
      variables.
NOTE: The data set WORK.AUSTRALIA has 105 observations and
      9 variables.
NOTE: The data set WORK.OTHER has 8 observations and 9
      variables.
```

45

Displaying Multiple SAS Data Sets

The PRINT procedure can only print one data set. A separate PROC PRINT step is required for each data set.

```
title 'Employees in the United States';
proc print data=usa;
run;

title 'Employees in Australia';
proc print data=australia;
run;

title 'Non US and AU Employees';
proc print data=other;
run;

title;
```

47

p202a02s

Creating Multiple Data Sets

p202d03a

This demonstration illustrates the creation of multiple data sets.

Creating Multiple Data Sets

Open **p202d03a** and submit the DATA step to create three data sets: **usa**, **australia**, and **other**. Examine the log. Most observations were written to **usa** and **australia**, while only eight observations were written to **other**.

Partial SAS Log

```
NOTE: There were 424 observations read from the data set ORION.EMPLOYEE_ADDRESSES.
NOTE: The data set WORK.USA has 311 observations and 9 variables.
NOTE: The data set WORK.AUSTRALIA has 105 observations and 9 variables.
NOTE: The data set WORK.OTHER has 8 observations and 9 variables.
```

Submit the three PROC PRINT steps to display the data sets. Examine the values of the **Country** variable in the output. The observations in **other** have lower case **Country** values: `au` and `us`. The upcase function can be used to cause case to be ignored.

Case-insensitive Comparisons

Submit the modified DATA step to use the upcase function as shown below.

```
data usa australia other;
   set orion.employee_addresses;
   if upcase(Country)='AU' then output australia;
   else if upcase(Country)='US' then output usa;
   else output other;
run;
```

The following is an alternate approach that permanently converts the **Country** values to upper case.

```
data usa australia other;
   set orion.employee_addresses;
   Country=upcase(Country);
   if Country='AU' then output australia;
   else if Country='US' then output usa;
   else output other;
run;
```

Examine the log. No observations were written to **other**.

```
NOTE: There were 424 observations read from the data set ORION.EMPLOYEE_ADDRESSES.
NOTE: The data set WORK.USA has 316 observations and 9 variables.
NOTE: The data set WORK.AUSTRALIA has 108 observations and 9 variables.
NOTE: The data set WORK.OTHER has 0 observations and 9 variables.
```

Using a SELECT Group

An alternate form of conditional execution uses a SELECT group.

```
SELECT <(select-expression)>;
     WHEN-1 (value-1 <...,value-n>)
          statement;
    <...WHEN-n (value-1 <...,value-n>)
          statement;>
    <OTHERWISE statement;>
END;
```

The *select-expression* specifies any SAS expression that evaluates to a single value.

✎ Often a variable name is used as the *select-expression*.

50

Using a SELECT Group

The previous task can be rewritten using a SELECT group:

```
data usa australia other;
   set orion.employee_addresses;
   select (Country);
      when ('US') output usa;
      when ('AU') output australia;
      otherwise output other;
   end;
run;
```

The SELECT statement processes the WHEN statements from top to bottom, so it is more efficient to check the values in order of decreasing frequency.

51 p202d04

Check the SAS Log

Results using SELECT are the same as IF-THEN/ELSE results.

Partial SAS Log

```
NOTE: There were 424 observations read from the data set
      ORION.EMPLOYEE_ADDRESSES.
NOTE: The data set WORK.USA has 311 observations and 9
      variables.
NOTE: The data set WORK.AUSTRALIA has 105 observations and 9
      variables.
NOTE: The data set WORK.OTHER has 8 observations and 9
      variables.
```

52

The OTHERWISE Statement

The OTHERWISE statement is optional, but omitting it results in an error when all WHEN conditions are false.

```
SELECT <(select-expression)>;
    WHEN-1 (value-1 <…,value-n>)
        statement;
    <…WHEN-n (value-1 <…,value-n>)
        statement;>
    <OTHERWISE statement;>
END;
```

Use the OTHERWISE statement followed by a null statement to prevent SAS from issuing an error message.

```
otherwise;
```

53

2.05 Quiz

Open the file **p202a03** and submit it. View the log, identify and correct the problem, and resubmit the program.

```
data usa australia;
   set orion.employee_addresses;
   select (Country);
      when ('US') output usa;
      when ('AU') output australia;
   end;
run;
```

55

p202a03

Test for Multiple Values in a WHEN Statement

Multiple values can be listed in the WHEN expression.

```
data usa australia other;
   set orion.employee_addresses;
   select (Country);
      when ('US','us') output usa;
      when ('AU','au') output australia;
      otherwise output other;
   end;
run;
```

Partial SAS Log

```
NOTE: There were 424 observations read from the data set
      ORION.EMPLOYEE_ADDRESSES.
NOTE: The data set WORK.USA has 316 observations and 9 variables.
NOTE: The data set WORK.AUSTRALIA has 108 observations and 9
      variables.
NOTE: The data set WORK.OTHER has 0 observations and 9 variables.
```

57

p202d04

Using Functions in a Select Expression

An alternate solution uses the UPCASE function.

```
data usa australia other;
   set orion.employee_addresses;
   select (upcase(Country));
      when ('US') output usa;
      when ('AU') output australia;
      otherwise output other;
   end;
run;
```

Partial SAS Log

```
NOTE: There were 424 observations read from the data set
      ORION.EMPLOYEE_ADDRESSES.
NOTE: The data set WORK.USA has 316 observations and 9 variables.
NOTE: The data set WORK.AUSTRALIA has 108 observations and 9
      variables.
NOTE: The data set WORK.OTHER has 0 observations and 9 variables.
```

58 p202d04

Using DO-END in a SELECT Group

Use DO and END statements to execute multiple statements when an expression is true.

```
data usa australia other;
   set orion.employee_addresses;
   select (upcase(country));
      when ('US') do;
         Benefits=1;
         output usa;
      end;
      when ('AU') do;
         Benefits=2;
         output australia;
      end;
      otherwise do;
         Benefits=0;
         output other;
      end;
   end;
run;
```

59 p202d04

Omitting the Select Expression

The *select-expression* can be omitted in a SELECT group:

SELECT;
    WHEN (*expression-1*)
        statement;
  <...**WHEN** (*expression-n*)
        statement;>
  <**OTHERWISE** *statement*;>
END;

Each WHEN expression evaluates to true or false.

- If true, the associated statement(s) is executed.
- If false, SAS proceeds to the next WHEN statement.
- If all WHEN expressions are false, then the statement(s) following the OTHERWISE statement executes.

60

Omitting the Select Expression

This version of the current example omits the SELECT expression:

```
data usa australia other;
   set orion.employee_addresses;
   select;
      when (country='US') output usa;
      when (country='AU') output australia;
      otherwise output other;
   end;
run;
```

Partial SAS Log

```
NOTE: There were 424 observations read from the data set
      ORION.EMPLOYEE_ADDRESSES.
NOTE: The data set WORK.USA has 311 observations and 9 variables.
NOTE: The data set WORK.AUSTRALIA has 105 observations and 9
      variables.
NOTE: The data set WORK.OTHER has 8 observations and 9 variables.
```

61 p202d04

 See SAS documentation for more information about using SELECT groups.

Exercises

Level 1

4. Creating Multiple SAS Data Sets

The data set **orion.employee_organization** contains information about employee job titles, departments, and managers.

Partial Listing of **orion.employee_organization** (424 Total Observations)

```
Employee_                                                  Manager_
   ID        Job_Title                  Department            ID

  120101     Director                   Sales Management     120261
  120102     Sales Manager              Sales Management     120101
  120103     Sales Manager              Sales Management     120101
  120104     Administration Manager     Administration       120101
  120105     Secretary I                Administration       120101
  120106     Office Assistant II        Administration       120104
  120107     Office Assistant III       Administration       120104
```

a. Create a separate data set for each department.

   Name the data sets **work.admin**, **work.stock**, and **work.purchasing**.

   Use conditional logic and explicit OUTPUT statements to write to these data sets depending on whether the value of **Department** is `Administration`, `Stock & Shipping`, or `Purchasing`, respectively. Ignore all other **Department** values.

   Hint: Be careful with capitalization and the spelling of the **Department** values.

b. Print **work.admin** and verify your results.

   Add an appropriate title.

Partial Listing of **work.admin** (34 Total Observations)

```
                        Administration Employees

            Employee_                                                 Manager_
    Obs        ID       Job_Title                      Department         ID

     1       120104     Administration Manager      Administration     120101
     2       120105     Secretary I                 Administration     120101
     3       120106     Office Assistant II         Administration     120104
     4       120107     Office Assistant III        Administration     120104
     5       120108     Warehouse Assistant II      Administration     120104
     6       120109     Warehouse Assistant I       Administration     120104
     7       120110     Warehouse Assistant III     Administration     120104
     8       120111     Security Guard II           Administration     120104
```

c. Print **`work.stock`** and verify your results.

Add an appropriate title.

Partial Listing of **`work.stock`** (26 Total Observations)

Stock and Shipping Employees

Obs	Employee_ ID	Job_Title	Department	Manager_ ID
1	120670	Shipping Manager	Stock & Shipping	120659
2	120671	Shipping Agent III	Stock & Shipping	120670
3	120672	Shipping Manager	Stock & Shipping	120659
4	120673	Shipping Agent II	Stock & Shipping	120672
5	120677	Shipping Manager	Stock & Shipping	120659
6	120678	Shipping Agent III	Stock & Shipping	120677
7	120679	Shipping Manager	Stock & Shipping	120659
8	120680	Shipping Agent I	Stock & Shipping	120679
9	120681	Shipping Agent II	Stock & Shipping	120679
10	120682	Shipping Agent I	Stock & Shipping	120679

d. Print **`work.purchasing`** and verify your results.

Add an appropriate title.

Partial Listing of **`work.purchasing`** (18 Total Observations)

Purchasing Employees

Obs	Employee_ ID	Job_Title	Department	Manager_ ID
1	120728	Purchasing Agent II	Purchasing	120735
2	120729	Purchasing Agent I	Purchasing	120735
3	120730	Purchasing Agent I	Purchasing	120735
4	120731	Purchasing Agent II	Purchasing	120735
5	120732	Purchasing Agent III	Purchasing	120736
6	120733	Purchasing Agent I	Purchasing	120736
7	120734	Purchasing Agent III	Purchasing	120736
8	120735	Purchasing Manager	Purchasing	120261
9	120736	Purchasing Manager	Purchasing	120261
10	120737	Purchasing Manager	Purchasing	120261

Level 2

5. Creating Multiple SAS Data Sets with Derived Values

The data set **orion.orders** contains information on in-store, catalog, and Internet orders as well as delivery dates.

Partial Listing of **orion.orders** (490 Total Observations)

Order_ID	Order_ Type	Employee_ID	Customer_ID	Order_ Date	Delivery_ Date
1230058123	1	121039	63	11JAN2003	11JAN2003
1230080101	2	99999999	5	15JAN2003	19JAN2003
1230106883	2	99999999	45	20JAN2003	22JAN2003
1230147441	1	120174	41	28JAN2003	28JAN2003
1230315085	1	120134	183	27FEB2003	27FEB2003

a. Orion Star wants to study catalog and Internet orders that were delivered quickly, as well as those that went slowly.

- Create three data sets named **work.fast**, **work.slow**, and **work.veryslow**.
- Write a WHERE statement to read only the observations with **Order_Type** equal to 2 (catalog) or 3 (Internet).
- Create a variable named **ShipDays** that is the number of days between when the order was placed and when the order was delivered.
- Handle the output as follows:
  - Output to **work.fast** when the value of **ShipDays** is less than 3.
  - Output to **work.slow** when the value of **ShipDays** is 5 to 7.
  - Output to **work.veryslow** when the value of **ShipDays** is greater than 7.
  - Do not output an observation when the value of **ShipDays** is 3 or 4.
- Drop the variable **Employee_ID**.
- There should be 80 observations in **work.fast**, 69 observations in **work.slow**, and 5 observations in **work.veryslow**.

Of the 490 observations in **orion.orders**, only 230 are read due to the WHERE statement.

b. Print your results from **work.veryslow** with an appropriate title.

Listing of **work.veryslow** (5 Total Observations)

Orders taking more than 7 days to deliver

Obs	Order_ID	Order_ Type	Customer_ID	Order_ Date	Delivery_ Date	Ship Days
1	1231305521	2	16	27AUG2003	04SEP2003	8
2	1236483576	2	70108	22JUL2005	02AUG2005	11
3	1236965430	3	70165	08SEP2005	18SEP2005	10
4	1237165927	3	79	27SEP2005	08OCT2005	11
5	1241298131	2	2806	29JAN2007	08FEB2007	10

Level 3

6. Using a SELECT Group

Write a solution to the previous exercise. Using SELECT logic instead of IF-THEN/ELSE logic. Refer to SAS documentation to explore the use of a compound expression in a SELECT statement. Print the data set **`work.veryslow`**.

2.3 Selecting Variables and Observations

Objectives

- Control which variables are written to an output data set during a DATA step.
- Control which variables are read from an input data set during a DATA step.
- Control how many observations are processed from an input data set during a DATA or PROC step.

65

Business Scenario

Create three data sets that are subsets of **orion.employee_addresses** based on the value of the **Country** variable.

Name the data sets **usa**, **australia**, and **other**, and write different variables to each output data set.

66

Controlling Variable Output (Review)

By default, SAS writes all variables from the input data set to every output data set.

In the DATA step, the DROP and KEEP statements can be used to control which variables are written to output data sets.

67

Controlling Variable Output (Review)

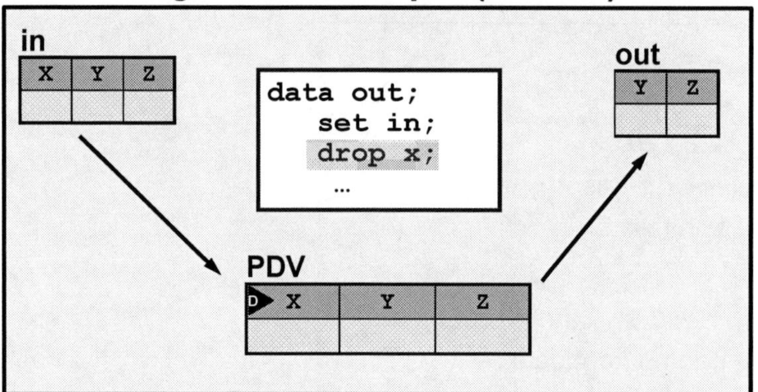

The DROP and KEEP statements affect output data sets. The statements can be used when reading from a SAS data set or from a raw data file.

68

Display Information About the Variables

The **orion.employee_addresses** data set contains nine variables.

```
proc contents data=orion.employee_addresses;
run;
```

Partial PROC CONTENTS Output

```
        ---Alphabetic List of Variables and Attributes---

             #    Variable          Type    Len

             6    City              Char     30
             9    Country           Char      2
             1    Employee_ID       Num       8
             2    Employee_Name     Char     40
             8    Postal_Code       Char     10
             7    State             Char      2
             3    Street_ID         Num       8
             5    Street_Name       Char     40
             4    Street_Number     Num       8
```

69 p202d05

The DROP Statement

The DROP statement drops variables from every output data set.

```
data usa australia other;
   drop Street_ID;
   set orion.employee_addresses;
   if Country='US' then output usa;
   else if Country='AU' then output australia;
   else output other;
run;
```

Partial SAS Log

```
NOTE: There were 424 observations read from the data set
      ORION.EMPLOYEE_ADDRESSES.
NOTE: The data set WORK.USA has 311 observations and 8 variables.
NOTE: The data set WORK.AUSTRALIA has 105 observations and 8
      variables.
NOTE: The data set WORK.OTHER has 8 observations and 8 variables.
```

70 p202d05

Controlling Variable Output

The task is to drop **`Street_ID`** and **`Country`** from **`usa`**, drop **`Street_ID`**, **`Country`**, and **`State`** from **`australia`**, and keep all variables in **`other`**.

USA

Employee_ ID	Employee_Name	Street_ Number	Street_Name	City	State	Postal_ Code
121044	Abbott, Ray	2267	Edwards Mill Rd	Miami-Dade	FL	33135
120761	Akinfolarin, Tameaka	5	Donnybrook Rd	Philadelphia	PA	19145
120656	Amos, Salley	3524	Calico Ct	San Diego	CA	92116

Australia

Employee_ ID	Employee_Name	Street_ Number	Street_Name	City	Postal_ Code
120145	Aisbitt, Sandy	30	Bingera Street	Melbourne	2001
120185	Bahlman, Sharon	24	LaTrobe Street	Sydney	2165
120109	Baker, Gabriele	166	Toorak Road	Sydney	2119

Other

Employee_ ID	Employee_Name	Street_ID	Street_ Number	Street_Name	City	State	Postal_ Code	Country
121019	Desanctis, Scott	9260121087	765	Greenhaven Ln	Philadelphia	PA	19102	us
120997	Donathan, Mary	9260121069	4923	Gateridge Dr	Philadelphia	PA	19152	us
120747	Farthing, Zashia	9260123756	763	Chatterson Dr	San Diego	CA	92116	us

71

The DROP= Data Set Option

The DROP= data set option can be used to exclude variables from a specific output data set.

General form of the DROP= data set option:

SAS-data-set(DROP=*variable-1* <*variable-2 ...variable-n*>)

72

The DROP= Option on an Output Data Set

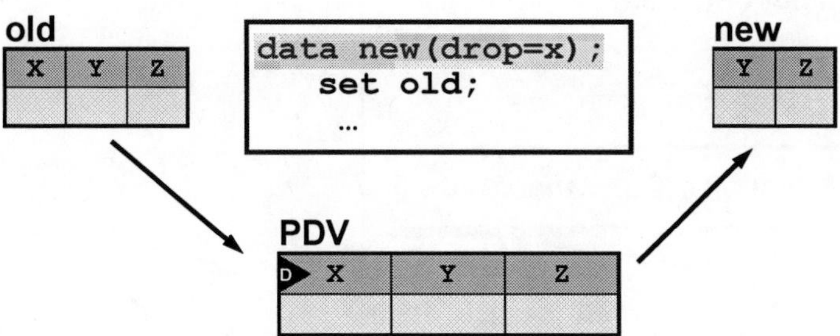

The specified variables are **not** written to the output data set; however, all variables are available for processing.

73

Using the DROP= Data Set Option

```
data usa(drop=Street_ID Country)
     australia(drop=Street_ID State Country)
     other;
   set orion.employee_addresses;
   if Country='US' then output usa;
   else if Country='AU' then
        output australia;
   else output other;
run;
```

```
NOTE: There were 424 observations read from the data set
      ORION.EMPLOYEE_ADDRESSES.
NOTE: The data set WORK.USA has 311 observations
      and 7 variables.
NOTE: The data set WORK.AUSTRALIA has 105 observations
      and 6 variables.
NOTE: The data set WORK.OTHER has 8 observations
      and 9 variables.
```

74 p202d06

The KEEP= Data Set Option

The KEEP= data set option can be used to specify which variables to write to a specific output data set.

General form of the KEEP= data set option:

SAS-data-set(KEEP=*variable-1* <*variable-2* ... *variable-n*>)

75

The KEEP= Option on an Output Data Set

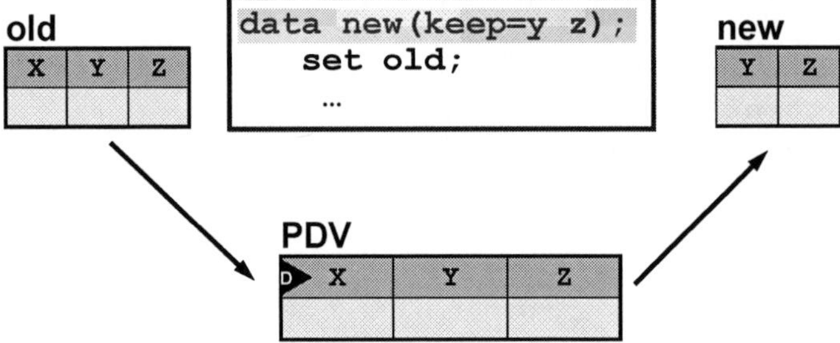

Only the specified variables are written to the output data set; however, all variables are available for processing.

76

Using the DROP= and KEEP= Options

The DROP= and KEEP= options can both be used in a SAS program.

```
data usa(keep=Employee_Name City State)
     australia(drop=Street_ID State)
     other;
   set orion.employee_addresses;
   if Country='US' then output usa;
   else if Country='AU' then output australia;
   else output other;
run;
```

 Attempting to drop and keep the same variable in a data set results in a warning.

77 p202d07

In many cases, you have a choice between using a DROP= or KEEP= data set option (or DROP or KEEP statements). Often the data set option or statement that minimizes the amount of typing is selected.

2.06 Quiz

The data set **orion.employee_addresses** contains nine variables. How many variables will be in the **usa**, **australia**, and **other** data sets?

```
data usa(keep=Employee_Name City State Country)
     australia(drop=Street_ID State Country)
     other;
   set orion.employee_addresses;
   if Country='US' then output usa;
   else if Country='AU' then output australia;
   else output other;
run;
```

79 p202a04

Using DROP= on an Input Data Set

When a **DROP=** data set option is used on an input data set, the specified variables are not read into the PDV, and therefore are **not** available for processing.

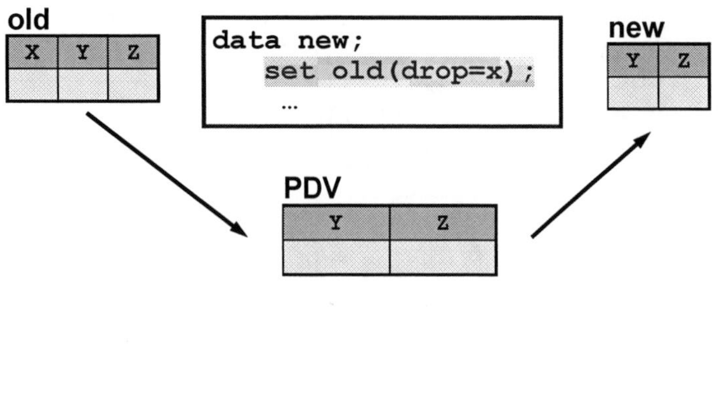

81

Using KEEP= on an Input Data Set

When a **KEEP=** data set option is used on an input data set, only the specified variables are read into the PDV, and therefore **are** available for processing.

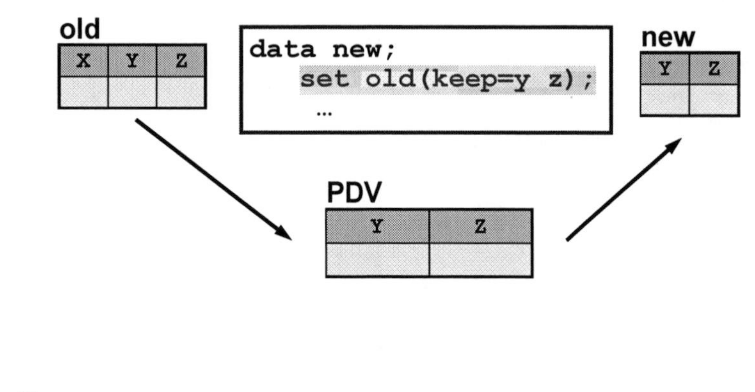

82

2.07 Quiz

Open file **p202a05** and submit it. The intent is to drop **`Country`**, **`Street_ID`**, and **`Employee_ID`** from every data set, and to drop **`State`** from **`australia`**. What is wrong with the program?

```
data usa australia(drop=State) other;
   set orion.employee_addresses
       (drop=Country Street_ID Employee_ID);
   if Country='US' then output usa;
   else if Country='AU' then output australia;
   else output other;
run;
```

84 p202a05

An Improved Solution

Use a combination of the DROP= option and the DROP statement to achieve the desired results.

```
data usa australia(drop=State) other;
  set orion.employee_addresses
      (drop=Street_ID Employee_ID);
  drop Country;
  if Country='US' then output usa;
  else if Country='AU' then output australia;
  else output other;
run;
```

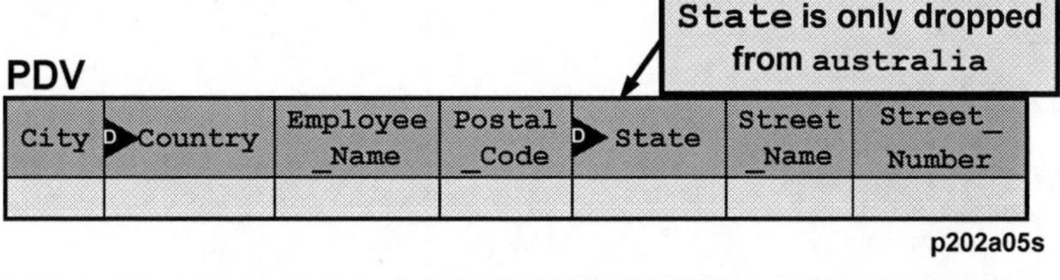

86 p202a05s

✎ If a DROP or KEEP statement is used in the same step as a data set option, the statement is applied first.

Check the SAS Log

Partial SAS Log

```
NOTE: There were 424 observations read from the data set
      ORION.EMPLOYEE_ADDRESSES.
NOTE: The data set WORK.USA has 311 observations
      and 6 variables.
NOTE: The data set WORK.AUSTRALIA has 105 observations
      and 5 variables.
NOTE: The data set WORK.OTHER has 8 observations
      and 6 variables.
```

87

Controlling Variable Input

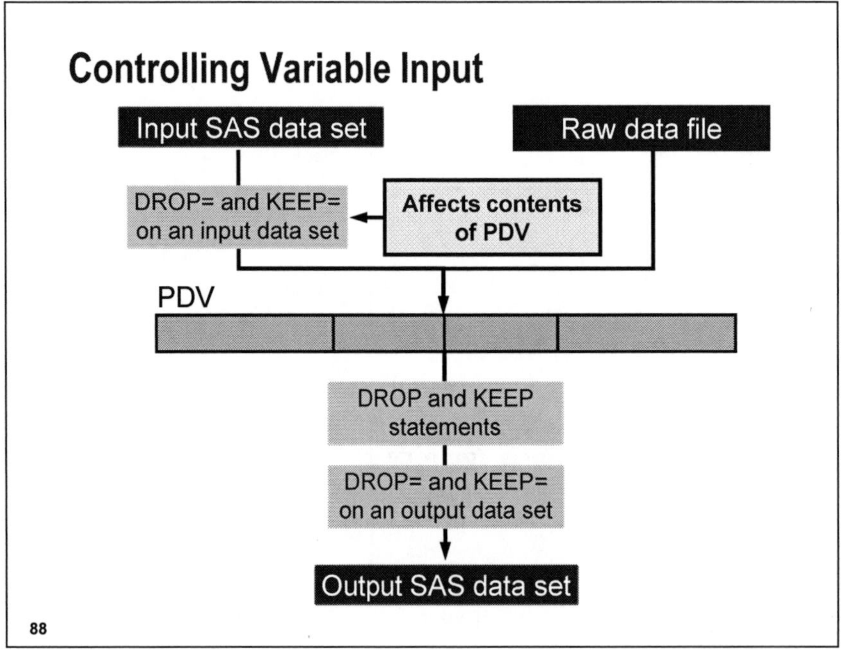

88

The DROP= and KEEP= data set options can be used to exclude variables from processing during a PROC step:

```
proc print data=orion.employee_addresses
              (keep=Employee_Name City State Country);
run;
```

However, the DROP= and KEEP= data set options do **not** affect the order in which the variables are processed.

Controlling Which Observations Are Read

By default, SAS processes every observation in a SAS data set, from the first observation to the last. The FIRSTOBS= and OBS= data set options can be used to control which observations are processed.

The FIRSTOBS= and OBS= options are used with input data sets. You cannot use either option with output data sets.

90

The OBS= Data Set Option

The OBS= data set option specifies an ending point for processing an input data set.

General form of OBS= data set option:

SAS-data-set(OBS=*n*)

This option specifies the number of the last observation to process, not how many observations should be processed.

91

n specifies a positive integer that is less than or equal to the number of observations in the data set, or zero.

✎ The OBS= data set option overrides the OBS= system option for the individual data set.

To guarantee that SAS processes all observations from a data set, you can use the following syntax:

SAS-data-set(OBS=MAX)

Using the OBS= Data Set Option

This OBS= data set option causes the DATA step to stop processing after observation 100.

```
data australia;
   set orion.employee_addresses (obs=100);
   if Country='AU' then output;
run;
```

Partial SAS Log

```
NOTE: There were 100 observations read from the data set
      ORION.EMPLOYEE_ADDRESSES.
NOTE: The data set WORK.AUSTRALIA has 24 observations and
      9 variables.
```

92 p202d08

The FIRSTOBS= Data Set Option

The FIRSTOBS= data set option specifies a starting point for processing an input data set. This option specifies the number of the first observation to process.

General form of the FIRSTOBS= data set option:

SAS-data-set (FIRSTOBS=*n*)

FIRSTOBS= and OBS= are often used together to define a range of observations to be processed.

93

n specifies a positive integer that is less than or equal to the number of observations in the data set.

The FIRSTOBS= data set option overrides the FIRSTOBS= system option for the individual data set.

To guarantee that SAS processes all observations from the start of a data set, you can use the following syntax:

SAS-data-set(FIRSTOBS=1)

Using OBS= and FIRSTOBS= Data Set Options

The FIRSTOBS= and OBS= data set options cause the SET statement below to read 51 observations from `orion.employee_addresses`. Processing begins with observation 50 and ends after observation 100.

```
data australia;
   set orion.employee_addresses
      (firstobs=50 obs=100);
   if Country='AU' then output;
run;
```

94

p202d09

Check the SAS Log

Partial SAS Log

```
data australia;
     set orion.employee_addresses(firstobs=50 obs=100);
     if Country='AU' then output;
run;

NOTE: There were 51 observations read from the data set
      ORION.EMPLOYEE_ADDRESSES.
NOTE: The data set WORK.AUSTRALIA has 13 observations and
      9 variables.
```

95

Controlling Which Records Are Read

The FIRSTOBS= and OBS= options can be used in an INFILE statement when SAS reads from raw data files.

```
data employees;
  infile 'emps.dat' firstobs=11 obs=15;
  input @1 EmpID 8. @9 EmpName $40.
        @153 Country $2.;
run;
proc print data=employees;
run;
```

✎ The syntax is different. In an INFILE statement, the options are not enclosed in parentheses.

96 p202d10

Check the Output

Partial SAS Log

```
45   data employees;
46     infile 'emps.dat' firstobs=11 obs=15;
47     input @1 EmpID 8. @9 EmpName $40. @153 Country $2.;
48   run;

NOTE: 5 records were read from the infile 'emps.dat'.
NOTE: The data set WORK.EMPLOYEES has 5 observations and
      3 variables.
```

PROC PRINT Output

Obs	EmpID	EmpName	Country
1	121017	Arizmendi, Gilbert	US
2	121062	Armant, Debra	US
3	121119	Armogida, Bruce	US
4	120812	Arruza, Fauver	US
5	120756	Asta, Wendy	US

97

Using OBS= and FIRSTOBS= in a PROC Step

The FIRSTOBS= and OBS= data set options can also be used in SAS procedures. The PROC PRINT step below begins processing at observation 10 and ends after observation 15.

```
proc print data=orion.employee_addresses
           (firstobs=10 obs=15);
   var Employee_Name City State Country;
run;
```

98 p202d11

Check the Output

Partial SAS Log

```
proc print data=orion.employee_addresses
           (firstobs=10 obs=15);
   var Employee_Name City State Country;
run;

NOTE: There were 6 observations read from the data set
      ORION.EMPLOYEE_ADDRESSES.
```

PROC PRINT output shows the original observation numbers.

PROC PRINT Output

Obs	Employee_Name	City	State	Country
10	Areu, Jeryl	Miami-Dade	Fl	US
11	Arizmendi, Gilbert	San Diego	CA	US
12	Armant, Debra	San Diego	CA	US
13	Armogida, Bruce	Philadelphia	PA	US
14	Arruza, Fauver	Miami-Dade	FL	US
15	Asta, Wendy	Philadelphia	PA	US

99

Adding a WHERE Statement

When the FIRSTOBS= or OBS= option and the WHERE statement are used together, the following occurs:

- the subsetting WHERE is applied first
- the FIRSTOBS= and OBS= options are applied to the resulting observations.

The following step includes a WHERE statement and an OBS= option.

```
proc print data=orion.employee_addresses
           (obs=10);
   where Country='AU';
   var Employee_Name City Country;
run;
```

100 p202d12

Check the Output

Partial SAS Log

```
proc print data=orion.employee_addresses
           (obs=10);
   where Country='AU';
   var Employee_Name City Country;
run;

NOTE: There were 10 observations read from the data set
      ORION.EMPLOYEE_ADDRESSES.
      WHERE Country='AU';
```

PROC PRINT Output

```
Obs   Employee_Name

  2   Aisbitt, Sandy             Melbourne    AU
 17   Bahlman, Sharon            Sydney       AU
 18   Baker, Gabriele            Sydney       AU
 22   Baran, Shanmuganathan      Sydney       AU
 23   Barbis, Viney              Sydney       AU
 24   Barcoe, Selina             Melbourne    AU
 25   Barreto, Geok-Seng         Sydney       AU
 31   Billington, Kareen         Sydney       AU
 34   Blanton, Brig              Melbourne    AU
 37   Body, Meera                Sydney       AU
```

The WHERE statement is applied first, and then 10 observations are processed.

101

The procedure processed observations 1 through 10 after the subsetting WHERE was applied. The value in the OBS column reflects the observation number from the original data set.

Exercises

Level 1

7. Specifying Variables and Observations

The data set **orion.employee_organization** contains information on employee job titles, departments, and managers.

Partial Listing of **orion.employee_organization** (424 Total Observations)

```
         Employee_                                                     Manager_
           ID          Job_Title                      Department          ID

         120101     Director                     Sales Management      120261
         120102     Sales Manager                Sales Management      120101
         120103     Sales Manager                Sales Management      120101
         120104     Administration Manager       Administration        120101
         120105     Secretary I                  Administration        120101
         120106     Office Assistant II          Administration        120104
         120107     Office Assistant III         Administration        120104
```

a. Create two data sets: one for the Sales department and another for the Executive department.

- Name the data sets **work.sales** and **work.exec**.
- Output to these data sets depending on whether the value of **Department** is `Sales` or `Executives`, respectively. Ignore all other **Department** values.
- The **work.sales** data set should contain three variables (**Employee_ID**, **Job_Title**, and **Manager_ID**) and have 201 observations.
- The **work.exec** data set should contain two variables (**Employee_ID** and **Job_Title**) and have four observations.

b. Print only the first six observations from **work.sales**.

- Use a data set option to display only the first six observations.
- Add an appropriate title.

Listing of First Six Observations from **work.sales**

```
                Sales Employees

        Employee_                        Manager_
 Obs       ID          Job_Title            ID

  1      120121     Sales Rep. II        120102
  2      120122     Sales Rep. II        120102
  3      120123     Sales Rep. I         120102
  4      120124     Sales Rep. I         120102
  5      120125     Sales Rep. IV        120102
  6      120126     Sales Rep. II        120102
```

c. Print selected observations from **work.exec**.

- Use data set options to process only observations 2 and 3.
- Add an appropriate title.

Listing of Observations 2 and 3 from **work.exec**

```
                              Executives

                       Employee_
                 Obs      ID                Job_Title

                  2     120260     Chief Marketing Officer
                  3     120261     Chief Sales Officer
```

Level 2

8. Specifying Variables and Observations

The data set **orion.orders** contains information on in-store, catalog, and Internet orders as well as delivery dates.

Partial Listing of **orion.orders** (490 Total Observations)

Order_ID	Order_ Type	Employee_ID	Customer_ID	Order_ Date	Delivery_ Date
1230058123	1	121039	63	11JAN2006	11JAN2006
1230080101	2	99999999	5	15JAN2006	19JAN2006
1230088186	1	120455	11	17JAN2006	17JAN2006
1230106883	2	99999999	45	20JAN2006	22JAN2006
1230147441	1	120174	41	28JAN2006	28JAN2006

a. Create two data sets, **work.instore** and **work.delivery**, to analyze in-store sales.

- Use a WHERE statement to read only observations with **Order_Type** equal to 1.
- Create a variable **ShipDays** that is the number of days between when the order was placed and when the order was delivered.
- Output to **work.instore** when **ShipDays** is equal to 0.
- Output to **work.delivery** when **ShipDays** is greater than 0.
- The **work.instore** data set should contain three variables (**Order_ID**, **Customer_ID**, and **Order_Date**).

  The **work.delivery** data set should contain four variables (**Order_ID**, **Customer_ID**, **Order_Date**, and **ShipDays**).
- Test this program by reading the first 30 observations that satisfy the WHERE statement. Check the SAS log to verify that no warnings or errors were reported.

> Of the 490 observations in **orion.orders**, only 230 are read due to the WHERE statement.

b. Modify the program to read the full **orion.orders** data set.

c. Print your results from **`work.delivery`** with an appropriate title.

Partial Listing of **`work.delivery`** (10 Total Observations)

```
                        Deliveries from In-store Purchases

                                                        Order_     Ship
             Obs        Order_ID      Customer_ID         Date     Days

               1      1231468750               52    25SEP2003       5
               2      1231657078               63    29OCT2003       4
               3      1232648239               49    07APR2004       8
```

d. Use PROC FREQ to display the number of orders per year in **`work.instore`**. Add an appropriate title.

Hint: Format the variable **`Order_Date`** with a YEAR. format. Restrict the analysis to the variable **`Order_Date`** with a TABLES statement.

PROC FREQ Output

```
                      In-stock Store Purchases, By Year

                              The FREQ Procedure

                       Date Order was placed by Customer

                                                Cumulative    Cumulative
        Order_Date    Frequency     Percent      Frequency      Percent
        ----------------------------------------------------------------
              2003          43       17.20             43        17.20
              2004          50       20.00             93        37.20
              2005          27       10.80            120        48.00
              2006          67       26.80            187        74.80
              2007          63       25.20            250       100.00
```

2.4 Chapter Review

Chapter Review

1. What statement is used to request explicit output?

2. To what data set will it write?

3. How can multiple data sets be created in a DATA step?

4. If multiple data sets are being created, to which data set will the OUTPUT statement write?

104

continued...

Chapter Review

5. What data set option controls which variables are written to a data set?

6. When the KEEP= data set option is specified on an input data set, all variables are available for processing. True or False?

7. When FIRSTOBS= and OBS= options are used in the SET statement, what does the OBS= value indicate?

106

2.5 Solutions

Solutions to Exercises

1. **Outputting Multiple Observations**

   a. Write a DATA step to create a new data set that forecasts unit prices for the next three years.

```
data work.price_increase;
   set orion.prices;
   Year=1;
   Unit_Price=Unit_Price * Factor;
   output;
   Year=2;
   Unit_Price=Unit_Price * Factor;
   output;
   Year=3;
   Unit_Price=Unit_Price * Factor;
   output;
run;
```

   b. Print the new data set.

```
proc print data=work.price_increase;
   var Product_ID Unit_Price Year;
run;
```

2. **Outputting Multiple Observations**

   a. Use explicit output to create a data set containing discounts from the Happy Holidays promotion.

```
data work.extended;
   set orion.discount;
   drop unit_sales_price;
   where Start_Date='01dec2007'd;
   Promotion='Happy Holidays';
   Season='Winter';
   output;
   Start_Date='01jul2008'd;
   End_Date='31jul2008'd;
   Season='Summer';
   output;
run;
```

   b. Print the new data set.

```
title 'All discount ranges with the Happy Holidays promotion';
proc print data=work.extended;
run;
title;
```

3. Using Conditional Logic to Output Multiple Observations

a. Create a new data set that contains observations for current and former country names.

```
data work.lookup;
   set orion.country;
   Outdated='N';
   output;
   if Country_FormerName ne ' ' then do;
      Country_Name=Country_FormerName;
         Outdated='Y';
         output;
   end;
   drop Country_FormerName Population;
run;
```

b. Print the new data set.

```
title 'Current and Outdated Country Name Data';
proc print data=work.lookup;
run;
title;
```

4. Creating Multiple SAS Data Sets

a. Use conditional logic to create separate data sets for each of the different departments.

```
data work.admin work.stock work.purchasing;
   set orion.employee_organization;
   if Department='Administration' then output work.admin;
   else if Department='Stock & Shipping' then output work.stock;
   else if Department='Purchasing' then output work.purchasing;
run;
```

b. Print the `work.admin` data set.

```
title 'Administration Employees';
proc print data=work.admin;
run;
title;
```

c. Print the `work.stock` data set.

```
title 'Stock and Shipping Employees';
proc print data=work.stock;
run;
title;
```

d. Print the `work.puchasing` data set.

```
title 'Purchasing Employees';
proc print data=work.purchasing;
run;
title;
```

Alternate Solution:

```
data work.admin work.stock work.purchasing;
   set orion.employee_organization;
   select (Department);
      when ('Administration') output work.admin;
      when ('Stock & Shipping') output work.stock;
      when ('Purchasing') output work.purchasing;
      otherwise;
   end;
run;

title 'Administration Employees';
proc print data=work.admin;
run;
title;

title 'Stock and Shipping Employees';
proc print data=work.stock;
run;
title;

title 'Purchasing Employees';
proc print data=work.purchasing;
run;
title;
```

5. **Creating Multiple SAS Data Sets with Derived Values**

   a. Create three data sets: **`work.fast`**, **`work.slow`**, and **`work.veryslow`**.

```
data work.fast work.slow work.veryslow;
   set orion.orders;
   where Order_Type in (2,3);
    /* There are several correct ways to write this WHERE statement */
   ShipDays=Delivery_Date-Order_Date;
   if ShipDays<3 then output work.fast;
   else if 5<=ShipDays<=7 then output work.slow;
   else if ShipDays>7 then output work.veryslow;
   drop Employee_ID;
run;
```

   b. Print the data set **`work.veryslow`**.

```
title 'Orders taking more than 7 days to deliver';
proc print data=work.veryslow;
run;
title;
```

6. Using a SELECT Group

a. Create three data sets using SELECT logic.

```
data work.fast work.slow work.veryslow;
   set orion.orders;
   where Order_Type in (2,3);
    /* There are several correct ways to write this WHERE statement */
   ShipDays=Delivery_Date-Order_Date;
   select;
      when (ShipDays<3) output work.fast;
      when (5<=ShipDays<=7)  output work.slow;
      when (ShipDays>7) output work.veryslow;
     otherwise;
   end;
   drop Employee_ID;
run;
```

b. Print the data set **work.veryslow**.

```
title 'Orders taking more than 7 days to deliver';
proc print data=work.veryslow;
run;
```

7. Specifying Variables and Observations

a. Use conditional logic to create two data sets named **work.sales** and **work.exec**.

```
data work.sales (keep=Employee_ID Job_Title Manager_ID)
     work.exec (keep=Employee_ID Job_Title);
   set orion.employee_organization;
   if Department='Sales' then output work.sales;
   else if Department='Executives' then output work.exec;
run;
```

b. Print the first six observations from **work.sales**.

```
title 'Sales Employees';
proc print data=work.sales (obs=6);
run;
title;
```

c. Print the observations two and three from **work.exec**.

```
title 'Executives';
proc print data=work.exec (firstobs=2 obs=3);
run;
title;
```

8. Specifying Variables and Observations

a. Create two data sets, **work.instore** and **work.delivery**, to analyze in-store sales. Test yourself by reading the first 30 observations that satisfy the WHERE statement.

```
data work.instore (keep=Order_ID Customer_ID Order_Date)
     work.delivery (keep=Order_ID Customer_ID Order_Date ShipDays);
   set orion.orders (obs=30);
   where Order_Type=1;
   ShipDays=Delivery_Date-Order_Date;
   if ShipDays=0 then output work.instore;
   else if ShipDays>0 then output work.delivery;
run;
```

b. Run this program on the full **orion.orders** data set.

```
data work.instore (keep=Order_ID Customer_ID Order_Date)
     work.delivery (keep=Order_ID Customer_ID Order_Date ShipDays);
   set orion.orders;
   where Order_Type=1;
   ShipDays=Delivery_Date-Order_Date;
   if ShipDays=0 then output work.instore;
   else if ShipDays>0 then output work.delivery;
run;
```

c. Print **work.delivery**.

```
title 'Deliveries from In-store Purchases';
proc print data=work.delivery;
run;
title;
```

d. Use PROC FREQ to display the number of orders per year in **work.instore**.

```
title 'In-stock Store Purchases, By Year';
proc freq data=work.instore;
   tables Order_Date;
   format Order_Date year.;
run;
title;
```

Solutions to Student Activities (Polls/Quizzes)

2.01 Quiz – Correct Answer

Which of the following occur at the end of a DATA step iteration?

```
data forecast;
   set orion.growth;
   total_employees=
      total_employees * (1+increase);
run;
```

Implicit OUTPUT;
Implicit RETURN;

By default, every DATA step performs an implicit OUTPUT and implicit RETURN at the end of each iteration.

8

2.02 Multiple Answer Poll – Correct Answers

Which variable(s) will be reinitialized?

a. **Department**

b. **Total_Employees**

c. **Increase**

(d.) **Year**

Variables created by INPUT and assignment statements are reinitialized. Variables read with a SET statement are not.

26

2.03 Quiz – Correct Answer

There are several ways to modify the DATA step.
Here is one solution:

```
data forecast;
   set orion.growth;
   Year=1;
   Total_Employees=Total_Employees*(1+Increase);
   Year=2;
   Total_Employees=Total_Employees*(1+Increase);
   output;
run;
```

33

p202a01s

2.04 Quiz – Correct Answer

Consider the results of the previous DATA step.

Can all three data sets be printed with a single PRINT procedure?

Partial SAS Log

```
NOTE: There were 424 observations read from the data set
      ORION.EMPLOYEE_ADDRESSES.
NOTE: The data set WORK.USA has 311 observations and 9
      variables.
NOTE: The data set WORK.AUSTRALIA has 105 observations and
      9 variables.
NOTE: The data set WORK.OTHER has 8 observations and 9
      variables.
```

No, a separate PRINT procedure is needed for each data set.

46

2.05 Quiz – Correct Answer

Open the file **p202a03** and submit it. View the log, identify and correct the problem, and resubmit the program.

```
150  data usa australia;
151     set orion.employee_addresses;
152     select (Country);
153        when ('US') output usa;
154        when ('AU') output australia;
155     end;
156  run;
ERROR: Unsatisfied WHEN clause and no OTHERWISE clause at
line 155 column 4.
```

```
data usa australia;
   set orion.employee_addresses;
   select (Country);
      when ('US') output usa;
      when ('AU') output australia;
      otherwise;
   end;
run;
```

An OTHERWISE statement is needed.

56

p202a03s

2.06 Quiz – Correct Answer

The data set `orion.employee_addresses` contains nine variables. How many variables will be in the `usa`, `australia`, and `other` data sets? **4, 6, 9**

```
data usa(keep=Employee_Name City State Country)
     australia(drop=Street_ID State Country)
     other;
   set orion.employee_addresses;
   if Country='US' then output usa;
   else if Country='AU' then output australia;
   else output other;
run;
```

Four variables are kept in `usa`, three are dropped from `australia`, and there is no DROP or KEEP for `other`.

80

2.07 Quiz – Correct Answer

Open file **p202a05** and submit it. The intent is to drop **Country**, **Street_ID**, and **Employee_ID** from every data set, and to drop **State** from **australia**. What is wrong with the program?

```
data usa australia(drop=State) other;
   set orion.employee_addresses
       (drop=Country Street_ID Employee_ID);
   if Country='US' then output usa;
   else if Country='AU' then output australia;
   else output other;
run;
```

Country is dropped on input, and therefore it is not available for processing. Every observation is written to other.

85

p202a05

Solutions to Chapter Review

Chapter Review Answers

1. What statement is used to request explicit output?
   The OUTPUT statement

2. To what data set will it write?
   The data set named in the DATA statement

3. How can multiple data sets be created in a DATA step?
   List the desired data set names in the DATA statement.

4. If multiple data sets are being created, to which data set will the OUTPUT statement write?
   It will write to every data set unless you specify a data set name in the OUTPUT statement.

105

continued...

Chapter Review Answers

5. What data set option controls which variables are written to a data set?
   The DROP= and KEEP= data set options

6. When the KEEP= data set option is specified on an input data set, all variables are available for processing.
   False. Only the variables listed in KEEP= will be in the PDV and available for processing.

7. When FIRSTOBS= and OBS= options are used in the SET statement, what does the OBS= value indicate?
   The number of the last observation to read

107

Chapter 3 Summarizing Data

3.1 Creating an Accumulating Total Variable 3-3

Exercises 3-17

3.2 Accumulating Totals for a Group of Data 3-21

Exercises 3-42

3.3 Chapter Review 3-47

3.4 Solutions 3-48

Solutions to Exercises 3-48

Solutions to Student Activities (Polls/Quizzes) 3-54

Solutions to Chapter Review 3-57

3.1 Creating an Accumulating Total Variable

Objectives

- Explain how SAS initializes the value of a variable in the PDV.
- Prevent reinitialization of a variable in the PDV.
- Create an accumulating variable.

3

Business Scenario

A retail manager for Orion Star Sportswear asked to see her department's daily sales for April, as well as a month-to-date total for each day.

Create a new data set, **mnthtot**, that includes the month-to-date total (**Mth2Dte**) for each day.

Partial Listing of **mnthtot**

SaleDate	Sale Amt	Mth2Dte
01APR2007	498.49	498.49
02APR2007	946.50	1444.99
03APR2007	994.97	2439.96
04APR2007	564.59	3004.55
05APR2007	783.01	3787.56

4

Input Data

The SAS data set **orion.aprsales** contains daily sales data from the Orion Star Sportswear department.

Partial Listing of **orion.aprsales**

SaleDate	SaleAmt
01APR2007	498.49
02APR2007	946.50
03APR2007	994.97
04APR2007	564.59
05APR2007	783.01
06APR2007	228.82
07APR2007	930.57

One observation for each day in April shows the date (**SaleDate**) and the total sales for that day (**SaleAmt**).

5

3.01 Quiz

Open and submit the program in **p203a01**. Does this program create the correct values for **Mth2Dte**?

```
data mnthtot;
   set orion.aprsales;
   Mth2Dte=Mth2Dte+SaleAmt;
run;
```

7 p203a01

Creating an Accumulating Variable

By default, variables created with an assignment statement are initialized to missing at the top of each iteration of the DATA step.

```
Mth2Dte=Mth2Dte+SaleAmt;
```

`Mth2Dte` is an example of an *accumulating variable* that needs to keep its value from one observation to the next.

9

The RETAIN Statement

The RETAIN statement prevents SAS from reinitializing the values of new variables at the top of the DATA step.

General form of the RETAIN statement:

RETAIN *variable-name <initial-value>* ...;

Previous values of retained variables are available for processing across iterations of the DATA step.

10

The RETAIN Statement – Details

The RETAIN statement

- retains the value of the variable in the PDV across iterations of the DATA step
- initializes the retained variable to missing before the first iteration of the DATA step if an initial value is not specified
- is a compile-time-only statement.

The RETAIN statement has no effect on variables that are read with SET, MERGE, or UPDATE statements; variables read from SAS data sets are automatically retained.

11

A variable referenced in the RETAIN statement appears in the output SAS data set only if it is given an initial value or referenced elsewhere in the DATA step.

Create an Accumulating Variable

Retain the values of **Mth2Dte** and set an initial value.

```
data mnthtot;
   set orion.aprsales;
   retain Mth2Dte 0;
   Mth2Dte=Mth2Dte+SaleAmt;
run;
```

If you do not supply an initial value, all the values of **Mth2Dte** will be missing.

12 p203d02

The input SAS data set must be sorted by **SaleDate** for the following method to produce the correct results.

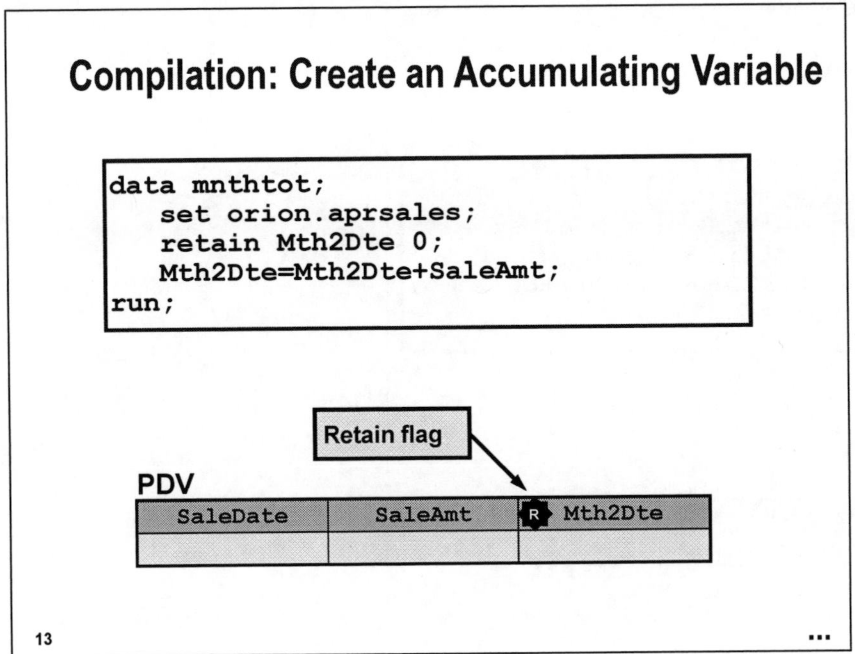
Compilation: Create an Accumulating Variable
data mnthtot;
set orion.aprsales;
retain Mth2Dte 0;
Mth2Dte=Mth2Dte+SaleAmt;
run;
Retain flag
PDV
SaleDate
SaleAmt
R
Mth2Dte
13
...

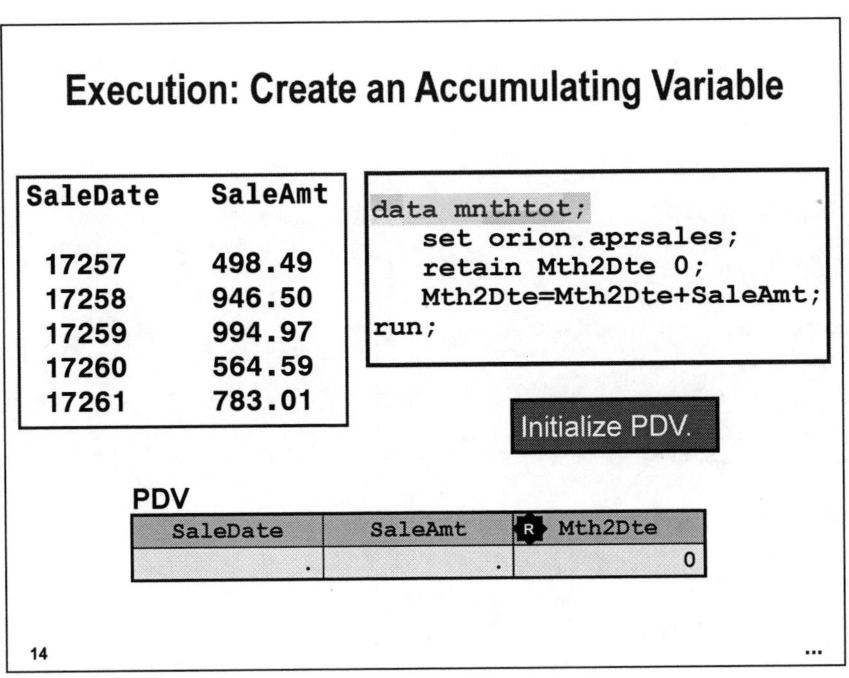
Execution: Create an Accumulating Variable
SaleDate SaleAmt
17257 498.49
17258 946.50
17259 994.97
17260 564.59
17261 783.01
data mnthtot;
set orion.aprsales;
retain Mth2Dte 0;
Mth2Dte=Mth2Dte+SaleAmt;
run;
Initialize PDV.
PDV
SaleDate
SaleAmt
R
Mth2Dte
.
.
0
14
...

Execution: Create an Accumulating Variable

SaleDate	SaleAmt
17257	498.49
17258	946.50
17259	994.97
17260	564.59
17261	783.01

```
data mnthtot;
   set orion.aprsales;
   retain Mth2Dte 0;
   Mth2Dte=Mth2Dte+SaleAmt;
run;
```

PDV

SaleDate	SaleAmt	R Mth2Dte
17257	498.49	0

15 ...

Execution: Create an Accumulating Variable

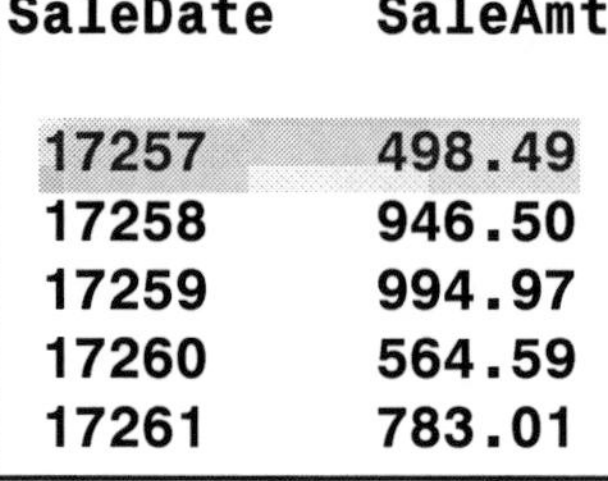

SaleDate	SaleAmt
17257	498.49
17258	946.50
17259	994.97
17260	564.59
17261	783.01

```
data mnthtot;
   set orion.aprsales;
   retain Mth2Dte 0;
   Mth2Dte=Mth2Dte+SaleAmt;
run;
```

0 + 498.49

PDV

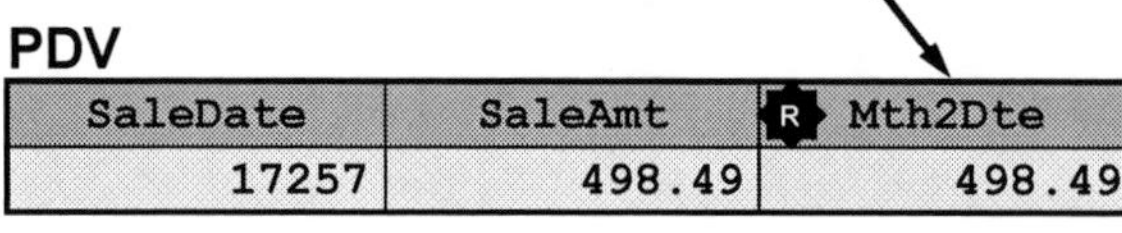

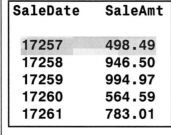

SaleDate	SaleAmt	R Mth2Dte
17257	498.49	498.49

16 ...

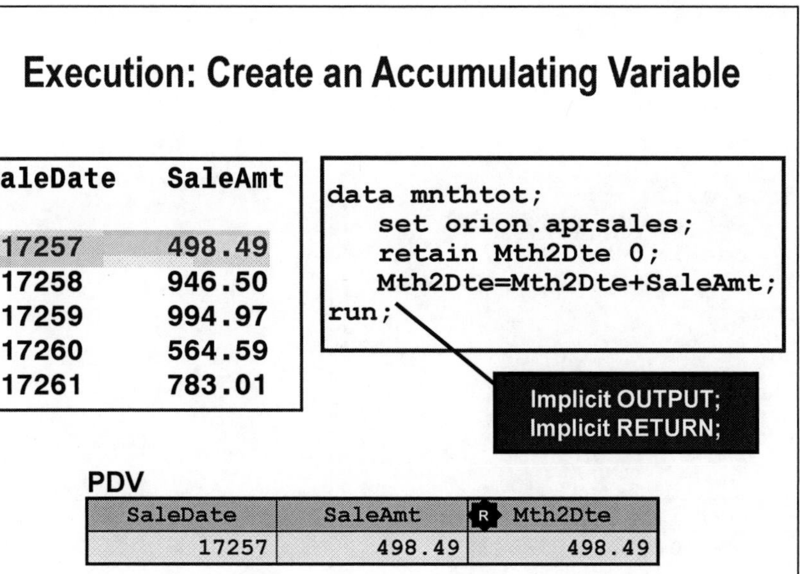
Execution: Create an Accumulating Variable
SaleDate SaleAmt
17257 498.49
17258 946.50
17259 994.97
17260 564.59
17261 783.01
data mnthtot;
set orion.aprsales;
retain Mth2Dte 0;
Mth2Dte=Mth2Dte+SaleAmt;
run;
Implicit OUTPUT;
Implicit RETURN;
PDV
SaleDate SaleAmt R Mth2Dte
17257 498.49 498.49
Write observation to mnthtot
17
...

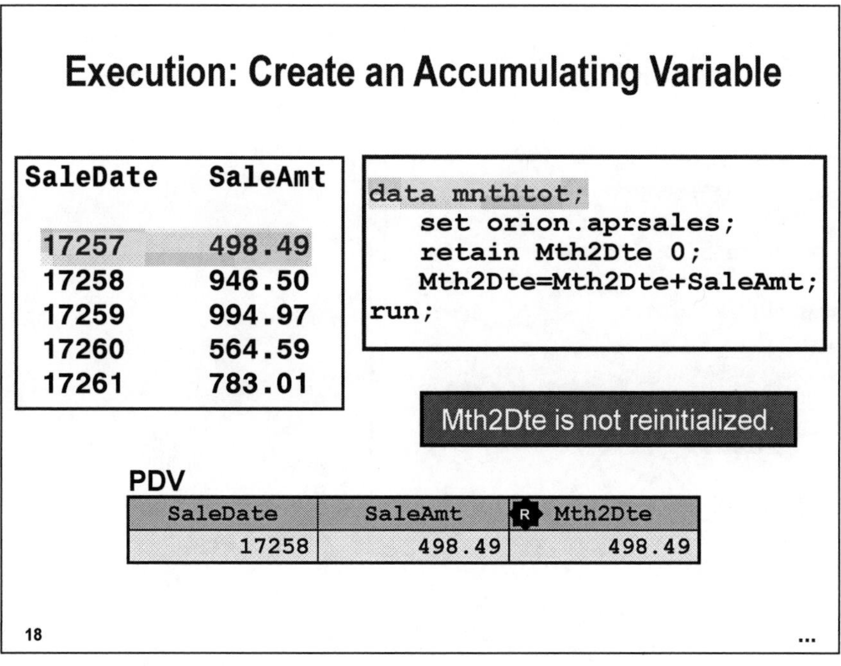
Execution: Create an Accumulating Variable
SaleDate SaleAmt
17257 498.49
17258 946.50
17259 994.97
17260 564.59
17261 783.01
data mnthtot;
set orion.aprsales;
retain Mth2Dte 0;
Mth2Dte=Mth2Dte+SaleAmt;
run;
Mth2Dte is not reinitialized.
PDV
SaleDate SaleAmt R Mth2Dte
17258 498.49 498.49
18
...

Execution: Create an Accumulating Variable

SaleDate	SaleAmt
17257	498.49
17258	946.50
17259	994.97
17260	564.59
17261	783.01

```
data mnthtot;
   set orion.aprsales;
   retain Mth2Dte 0;
   Mth2Dte=Mth2Dte+SaleAmt;
run;
```

PDV

SaleDate	SaleAmt	R Mth2Dte
17258	946.50	498.49

19 ...

Execution: Create an Accumulating Variable

SaleDate	SaleAmt
17257	498.49
17258	946.50
17259	994.97
17260	564.59
17261	783.01

```
data mnthtot;
   set orion.aprsales;
   retain Mth2Dte 0;
   Mth2Dte=Mth2Dte+SaleAmt;
run;
```

498.49 + 946.50

PDV

SaleDate	SaleAmt	R Mth2Dte
17258	946.50	1444.99

20 ...

Execution: Create an Accumulating Variable

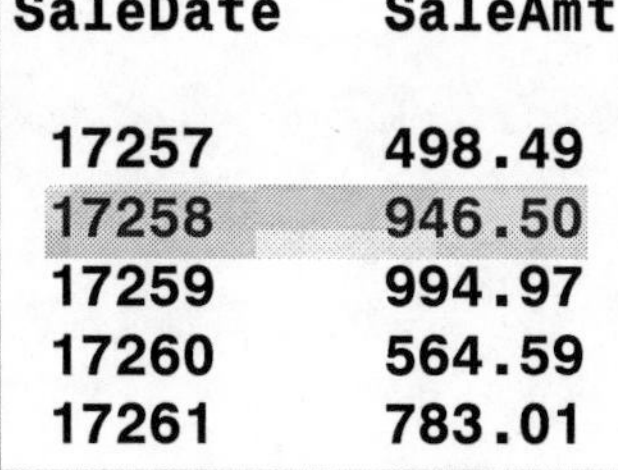

SaleDate	SaleAmt
17257	498.49
17258	946.50
17259	994.97
17260	564.59
17261	783.01

```
data mnthtot;
   set orion.aprsales;
   retain Mth2Dte 0;
   Mth2Dte=Mth2Dte+SaleAmt;
run;
```

Implicit OUTPUT;
Implicit RETURN;

PDV

SaleDate	SaleAmt	R Mth2Dte
17258	946.50	1444.99

Write observation to **mnthtot**

21 ...

Execution: Create an Accumulating Variable

SaleDate	SaleAmt
17257	498.49
17258	946.50
17259	994.97
17260	564.59
17261	783.01

```
data mnthtot;
   set orion.aprsales;
   retain Mth2Dte 0;
   Mth2Dte=Mth2Dte+SaleAmt;
run;
```

Mth2Dte is not reinitialized.

PDV

SaleDate	SaleAmt	R Mth2Dte
17258	946.50	1444.99

22 ...

Execution: Create an Accumulating Variable

SaleDate	SaleAmt
17257	498.49
17258	946.50
17259	994.97
17260	564.59
17261	783.01

```
data mnthtot;
   set orion.aprsales;
   retain Mth2Dte 0;
   Mth2Dte=Mth2Dte+SaleAmt;
run;
```

Continue until EOF.

PDV

SaleDate	SaleAmt	R Mth2Dte
17258	946.50	1444.99

23

Create an Accumulating Variable

```
proc print data=mnthtot noobs;
   format SaleDate date9.;
run;
```

Partial PROC PRINT Output

SaleDate	Sale Amt	Mth2Dte
01APR2007	498.49	498.49
02APR2007	946.50	1444.99
03APR2007	994.97	2439.96
04APR2007	564.59	3004.55
05APR2007	783.01	3787.56

24

p203d02

Setup for the Poll

What happens if there are missing values for **SaleAmt**?

Open and submit **p203a02** and examine the output.

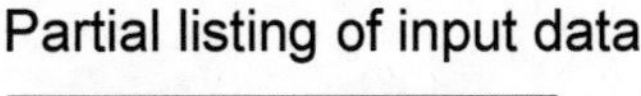

Partial listing of input data

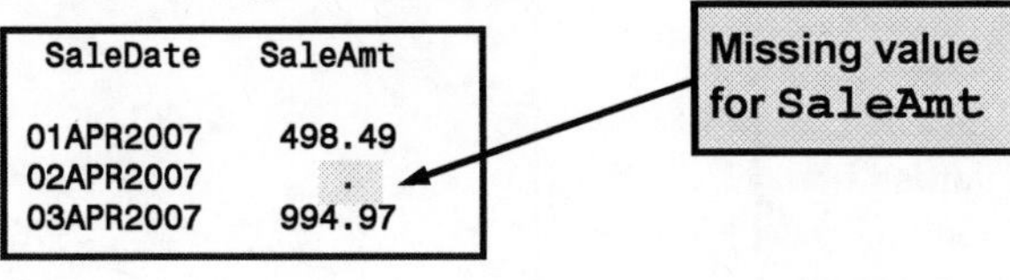

SaleDate	SaleAmt
01APR2007	498.49
02APR2007	.
03APR2007	994.97

26

3.02 Multiple Choice Poll

What effect did the missing value for **SaleAmt** have on **Mth2Dte**?

a. The missing value was ignored; **Mth2Dte** values were not affected.

b. The missing value will cause the DATA step to stop processing.

c. The missing value will cause the subsequent values for **Mth2Dte** to be set to missing.

27

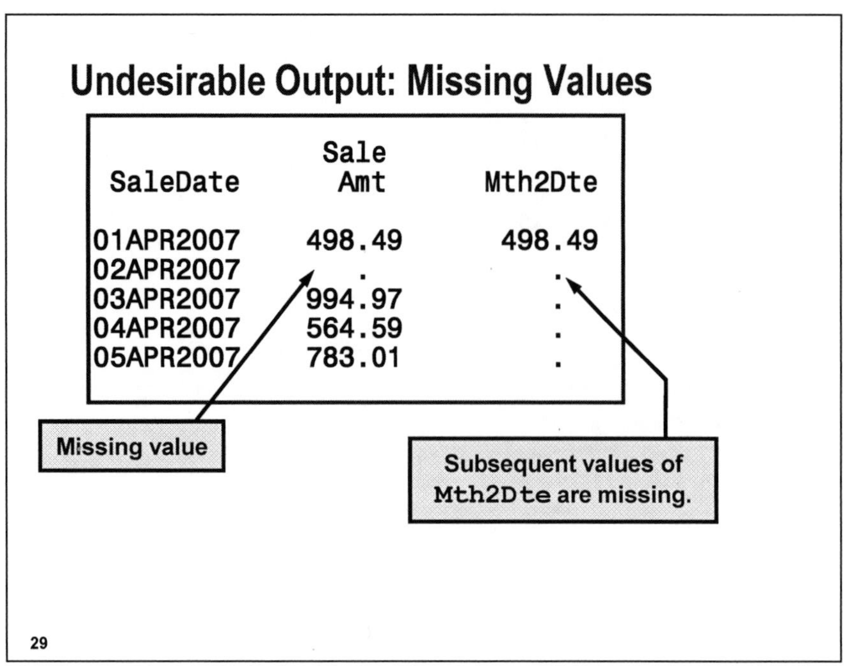

The SUM Function

A RETAIN statement along with a SUM function in an assignment statement can be used to create **Mth2Dte**.

```
retain Mth2Dte 0;
Mth2Dte=sum(Mth2Dte,SaleAmt);
```

✎ The SUM function ignores missing values.

30

The Sum Statement

When you create an accumulating variable, a better alternative is to use the sum statement.

General form of the sum statement:

variable **+** *expression*;

Example:

```
Mth2Dte+SaleAmt;
```

31

The sum statement is more efficient than a RETAIN statement along with a SUM function.

The Sum Statement – Details

The sum statement

- creates the variable on the left side of the plus sign if it does not already exist
- initializes the variable to zero before the first iteration of the DATA step
- automatically retains the variable
- adds the value of *expression* to the variable at execution
- ignores missing values.

32

The Sum Statement – Example

Use the sum statement to create **Mth2Dte**.

```
data mnthtot2;
   set work.aprsales2;
   Mth2Dte+SaleAmt;
run;
```

Specifics about **Mth2Dte**:

- Initialized to zero
- Automatically retained
- Increased by the value of **SaleAmt** for each observation
- Ignored missing values of **SaleAmt**

33 p203d03

The Sum Statement – Example

```
proc print data=mnthtot2 noobs;
   format SaleDate date9.;
run;
```

Partial PROC PRINT Output

SaleDate	SaleAmt	Mth2Dte
01APR2007	498.49	498.49
02APR2007	.	498.49
03APR2007	994.97	1493.46
04APR2007	564.59	2058.05
05APR2007	783.01	2841.06

34

Exercises

Level 1

1. Creating Accumulating Totals

The data set **orion.order_fact** contains information about orders for several years, sorted by **Order_Date**. Each observation represents one order, and **Total_Retail_Price** contains the sales value for the order.

Partial Listing of **orion.order_fact** (617 Total Observations, 12 Total Variables)

Order_ID	Order_ Date	Total_Retail_ Price
1230058123	11JAN2003	$16.50
1230080101	15JAN2003	$247.50
1230106883	20JAN2003	$28.30
1230147441	28JAN2003	$32.00
1230315085	27FEB2003	$63.60
1230333319	02MAR2003	$234.60

a. Orion Star would like to examine growth in sales during the date range of 01Nov2004 to 14Dec2004.

- Open file **p203e01**. It creates and prints a data set named **work.mid_q4** from **orion.order_fact**. The DATA step uses the following WHERE statement to read only the observations in the specified date range.

```
where '01nov2004'd <= Order_Date <= '14dec2004'd;
```

- Modify the program to create an accumulating total, **Sales2Dte**, to display the sales-to-date total.
- Also create an accumulating variable, **Num_Orders**, indicating how many orders-to-date that total represents. Each observation counts as one order.

b. Modify the PROC PRINT step to show your results.

- Display **Sales2Dte** with a DOLLAR10.2 format.
- Show only the columns **Order_ID**, **Order_Date**, **Total_Retail_Price**, **Sales2Dte**, and **Num_Orders**.

PROC PRINT Output

Orders from 01Nov2004 through 14Dec2004

Obs	Order_ID	Order_ Date	Total_Retail_ Price	Sales2Dte	Num_ Orders
1	1234033037	01NOV2004	$53.70	$53.70	1
2	1234092222	10NOV2004	$7.20	$60.90	2
3	1234133789	17NOV2004	$328.30	$389.20	3
4	1234186330	25NOV2004	$200.10	$589.30	4
5	1234198497	26NOV2004	$39.00	$628.30	5
6	1234235150	02DEC2004	$369.00	$997.30	6
7	1234247283	03DEC2004	$187.20	$1,184.50	7
8	1234255111	04DEC2004	$257.40	$1,441.90	8
9	1234279341	08DEC2004	$116.70	$1,558.60	9
10	1234301319	11DEC2004	$105.60	$1,664.20	10

Level 2

2. Creating Accumulating Totals with Conditional Logic

The data set **orion.order_fact** contains a group of orders across several years, sorted by **Order_Date**.

Partial Listing of **orion.order_fact** (617 Total Observations, 12 Total Variables)

Order_ID	Order_ Type	Order_ Date	Quantity
1230058123	1	11JAN2003	1
1230080101	2	15JAN2003	1
1230106883	2	20JAN2003	1
1230147441	1	28JAN2003	2
1230315085	1	27FEB2003	3
1230333319	2	02MAR2003	1

a. Orion Star would like to analyze 2005 data by creating accumulating totals for the number of items sold from retail, catalog, and Internet channels.

- The value of **Order_Type** indicates whether the sale was retail (=1), catalog (=2), or Internet (=3).
- Create a data set named **work.typetotals** with accumulating totals for **TotalRetail**, **TotalCatalog**, and **TotalInternet**, as described above.

  The variable **Quantity** contains the number of items sold for each order.

- For testing your program in this step, read only the first 10 observations that satisfy the WHERE statement.

  Remember to process only those rows where **Order_Date** occurs in 2005.

b. Continue testing your program by printing the results from step **a.** Print all the variables and check to make sure that the program is correctly calculating values for the accumulating totals.

PROC PRINT Output

Obs	Customer_ID	Employee_ID	Street_ID	Order_ Date	Delivery_ Date	Order_ID	Order_ Type	Product_ID
1	195	120150	1600101663	02JAN2005	02JAN2005	1234437760	1	230100600028
2	36	99999999	9260128237	11JAN2005	14JAN2005	1234534069	3	240800100026
3	183	120121	1600100760	12JAN2005	12JAN2005	1234537441	1	240100200001
4	16	99999999	3940105865	12JAN2005	14JAN2005	1234538390	2	220200300015
5	16	99999999	3940105865	17JAN2005	19JAN2005	1234588648	2	230100500101
6	16	99999999	3940105865	17JAN2005	19JAN2005	1234588648	2	230100600024
7	16	99999999	3940105865	24JAN2005	26JAN2005	1234659163	2	230100700008
8	63	99999999	9260125492	24JAN2005	25JAN2005	1234665265	2	240100100063
9	171	99999999	1600101555	29JAN2005	02FEB2005	1234709803	3	220100100304
10	183	120179	1600100760	31JAN2005	31JAN2005	1234727966	1	240700400004

Obs	Quantity	Total_Retail_ Price	CostPrice_ Per_Unit	Discount	Total Retail	Total Catalog	Total Internet
1	2	$193.40	$48.45	.	2	0	0
2	4	$525.20	$58.55	.	2	0	4
3	1	$16.00	$6.35	.	3	0	4
4	1	$115.00	$52.40	.	3	1	4
5	1	$138.70	$62.50	.	3	2	4
6	1	$76.10	$38.15	.	3	3	4
7	1	$504.20	$245.80	.	3	4	4
8	2	$48.40	$9.75	.	3	6	4
9	2	$122.60	$30.75	.	3	6	6
10	1	$13.20	$5.95	.	4	6	6

c. When the results from steps **a** and **b** are correct, do the following:

- Modify the program to read all observations satisfying the WHERE statement.
- Keep only the variables **Order_Date**, **Order_ID**, **TotalRetail**, **TotalCatalog**, and **TotalInternet**.
- Print your results with an appropriate title.

Partial PROC PRINT Output (90 Total Observations)

2005 Accumulating Totals for Each Type of Order

Obs	Order_ Date	Order_ID	Total Retail	Total Catalog	Total Internet
1	02JAN2005	1234437760	2	0	0
2	11JAN2005	1234534069	2	0	4
3	12JAN2005	1234537441	3	0	4
4	12JAN2005	1234538390	3	1	4
5	17JAN2005	1234588648	3	2	4
6	17JAN2005	1234588648	3	3	4
7	24JAN2005	1234659163	3	4	4
8	24JAN2005	1234665265	3	6	4
9	29JAN2005	1234709803	3	6	6
10	31JAN2005	1234727966	4	6	6
11	16FEB2005	1234891576	4	6	7
12	16FEB2005	1234897732	5	6	7
13	22FEB2005	1234958242	5	7	7

Level 3

3. Creating Accumulating Totals by Month

The data set **orion.order_fact** contains a group of orders across several years, sorted by **Order_Date**.

Partial Listing of **orion.order_fact** (617 Total Observations, 12 Total Variables)

Order_ID	Order_ Date	Total_Retail_ Price
1230058123	11JAN2003	$16.50
1230080101	15JAN2003	$247.50
1230106883	20JAN2003	$28.30
1230147441	28JAN2003	$32.00
1230315085	27FEB2003	$63.60
1230333319	02MAR2003	$234.60

Orion Star would like to generate the following report showing all orders in 2007 along with an accumulating total.

- The accumulating total should reset to zero at the start of each new month.
- Remember to process only those rows where **Order_Date** occurs in 2007.

Partial PROC PRINT Output

Accumulating Totals by Month in 2007

Obs	Order_ Date	Order_ID	Total_ Retail_ Price	MonthSales
1	02JAN2007	1241054779	$195.60	$195.60
2	03JAN2007	1241063739	$160.80	$356.40
3	04JAN2007	1241066216	$306.20	$662.60
4	06JAN2007	1241086052	$37.80	$700.40
5	13JAN2007	1241147641	$362.60	$1,063.00
6	23JAN2007	1241235281	$72.60	$1,135.60
7	24JAN2007	1241244297	$258.20	$1,393.80
8	24JAN2007	1241244297	$81.20	$1,475.00
9	24JAN2007	1241244297	$358.20	$1,833.20
10	25JAN2007	1241263172	$102.40	$1,935.60
11	25JAN2007	1241263172	$113.20	$2,048.80
12	28JAN2007	1241286432	$174.40	$2,223.20
13	29JAN2007	1241298131	$37.40	$2,260.60
14	05FEB2007	1241359997	$117.60	$117.60
15	07FEB2007	1241371145	$656.60	$774.20
16	07FEB2007	1241371145	$129.00	$903.20

3.2 Accumulating Totals for a Group of Data

Objectives

- Define First. and Last. processing.
- Calculate an accumulating total for groups of data.
- Use a subsetting IF statement to output selected observations.

38

Business Scenario

The SAS data set **orion.specialsals** contains information about employees working on special projects.

Partial Listing of **orion.specialsals**

Employee_ ID	Salary	Dept
110004	42000	HUMRES
110009	34000	ENGINR
110011	27000	FINANC
110036	20000	ENGINR
110037	19000	ENGINR

The **Salary** variable represents the portion of the employee's salary allocated to the project. An analyst would like to see these salary totals by department.

39

Desired Output

Create a new data set, **deptsals**, that has the total salaries for each department.

Listing of **deptsals**

```
 Dept       DeptSal

ADMIN        410000
ENGINR       163000
FINANC       318000
HUMRES       181000
SALES        373000
```

40

Processing Needed

Dept	Salary
ADMIN	20000
ADMIN	100000
ADMIN	50000
ENGINR	25000
ENGINR	20000
ENGINR	23000
ENGINR	27000
FINANC	10000
FINANC	12000

DeptSal

Step 1: Sort the data by Dept.

41

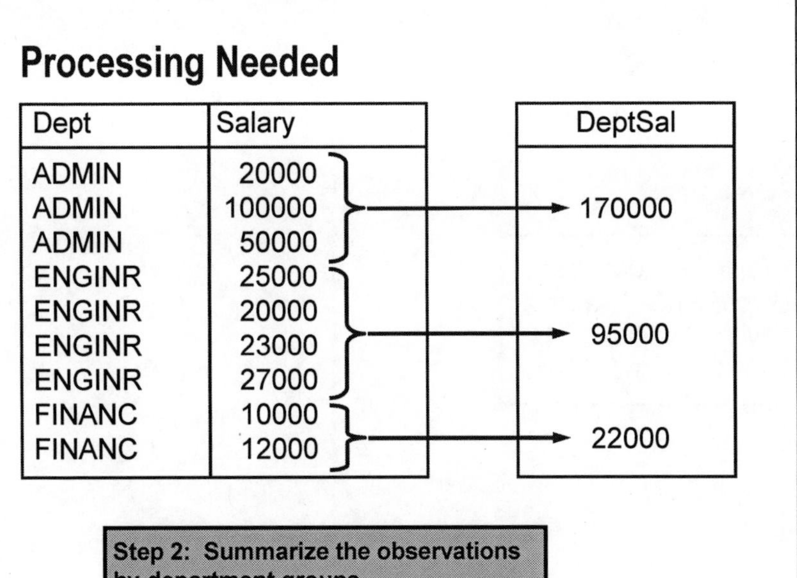

Processing Needed

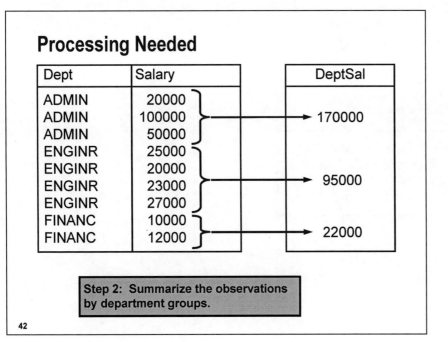

Dept	Salary	DeptSal
ADMIN	20000	
ADMIN	100000	170000
ADMIN	50000	
ENGINR	25000	
ENGINR	20000	
ENGINR	23000	95000
ENGINR	27000	
FINANC	10000	
FINANC	12000	22000

Step 2: Summarize the observations by department groups.

42

3.03 Multiple Choice Poll

How often do you work with data that needs to be processed by groups?

a. All the time
b. Regularly
c. Not often

44

The SORT Procedure (Review)

You can rearrange the observations into groups using the SORT procedure.

General form of a PROC SORT step:

```
PROC SORT DATA=input-SAS-data-set
              <OUT=output-SAS-data-set>;
     BY <DESCENDING> BY-variable ...;
RUN;
```

45

The SORT procedure

- rearranges the observations in a data set
- can sort on multiple variables
- can create a SAS data set that is a sorted copy of the input SAS data set
- replaces the input data set by default.

BY-Group Processing

The BY statement in the DATA step enables SAS to process data in groups.

General form of a BY statement in a DATA step:

```
DATA output-SAS-data-set;
     SET input-SAS-data-set;
     BY BY-variable ...;
     <additional SAS statements>
RUN;
```

46

When a BY statement is used with a SET statement, the data must be sorted by the BY variable(s) or have an index based on the BY variable(s).

BY-Group Processing

This is a good start for the SAS program ...

```
proc sort data=orion.specialsals
          out=salsort;
   by Dept;
run;

data deptsals(keep=Dept DeptSal);
   set salsort;
   by Dept;
   <additional SAS statements>
run;
```

Step 1: Sort by Dept

Step 2: Process by Dept groups

...but you need some way to identify the beginning and end of each department's group of observations.

47

First. and Last. Values

A BY statement in a DATA step creates two temporary variables for each variable listed in the BY statement.

General form of the First. and Last. variables:

> **First**.*BY-variable*
> **Last**.*BY-variable*

- The First. variable has a value of 1 for the *first* observation in a BY group; otherwise, it equals 0.
- The Last. variable has a value of 1 for the *last* observation in a BY group; otherwise, it equals 0.

48

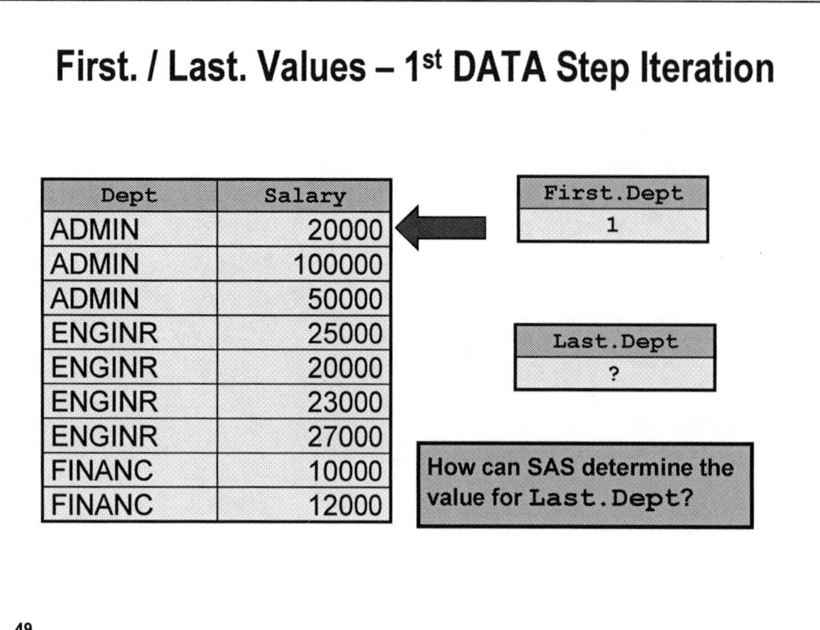
First. / Last. Values – 1st DATA Step Iteration
Dept
Salary
ADMIN
20000
ADMIN
100000
ADMIN
50000
ENGINR
25000
ENGINR
20000
ENGINR
23000
ENGINR
27000
FINANC
10000
FINANC
12000
First.Dept
1
Last.Dept
?
How can SAS determine the value for Last.Dept?
49
...

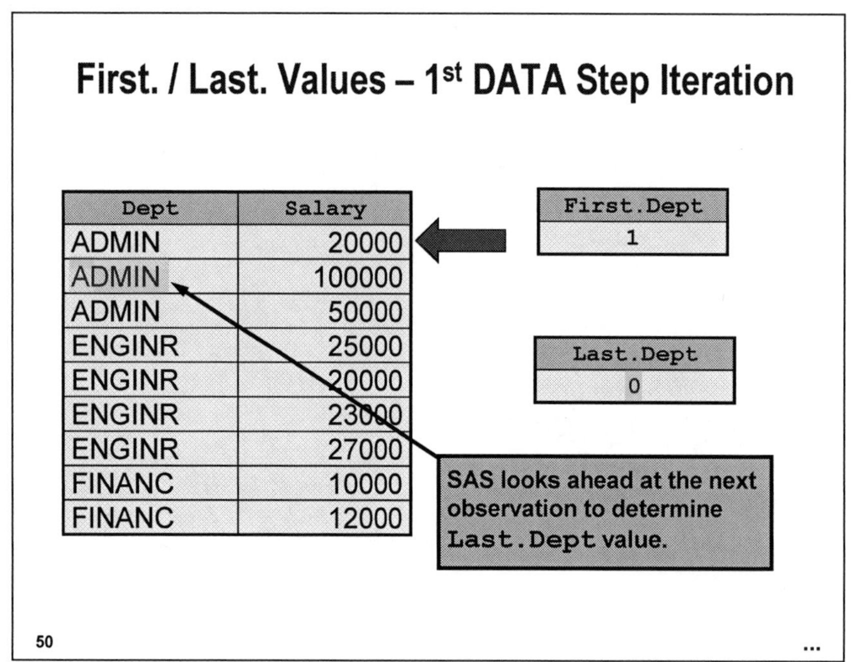
First. / Last. Values – 1st DATA Step Iteration
Dept
Salary
ADMIN
20000
ADMIN
100000
ADMIN
50000
ENGINR
25000
ENGINR
20000
ENGINR
23000
ENGINR
27000
FINANC
10000
FINANC
12000
First.Dept
1
Last.Dept
0
SAS looks ahead at the next observation to determine Last.Dept value.
50
...

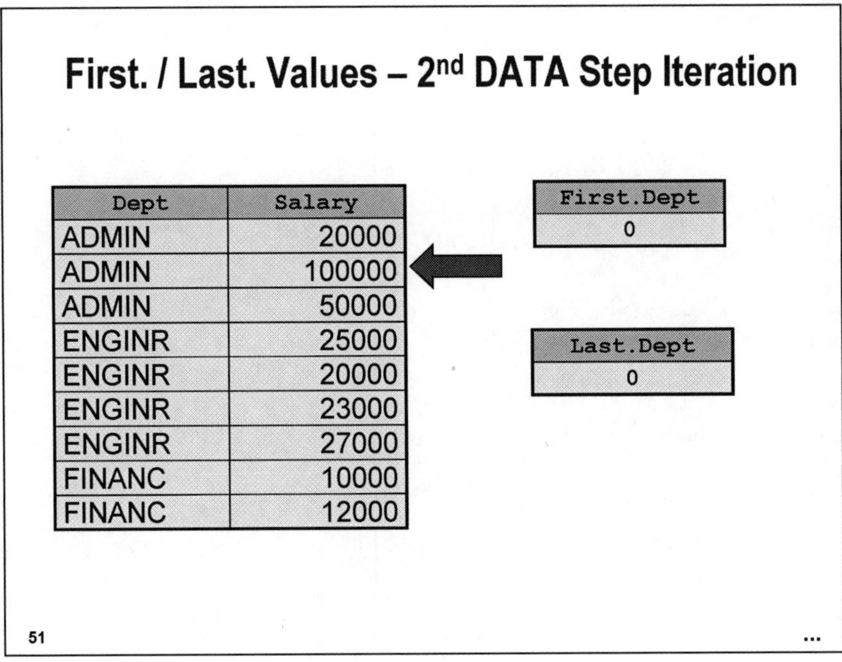
First. / Last. Values – 2nd DATA Step Iteration
Dept
Salary
ADMIN 20000
ADMIN 100000
ADMIN 50000
ENGINR 25000
ENGINR 20000
ENGINR 23000
ENGINR 27000
FINANC 10000
FINANC 12000
First.Dept
0
Last.Dept
0
51
...

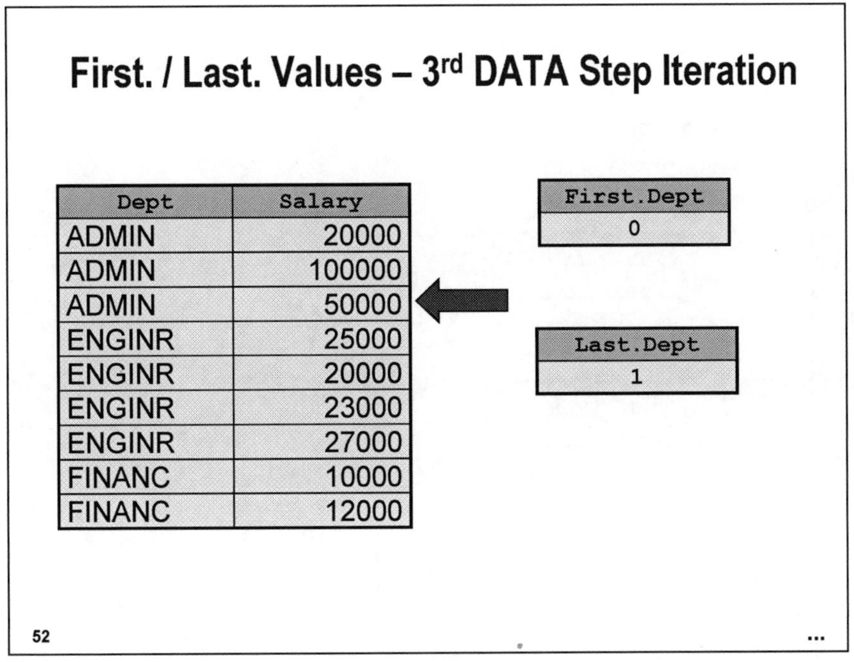
First. / Last. Values – 3rd DATA Step Iteration
Dept
Salary
ADMIN 20000
ADMIN 100000
ADMIN 50000
ENGINR 25000
ENGINR 20000
ENGINR 23000
ENGINR 27000
FINANC 10000
FINANC 12000
First.Dept
0
Last.Dept
1
52
...

First. / Last. Values – 4th DATA Step Iteration

Dept	Salary
ADMIN	20000
ADMIN	100000
ADMIN	50000
ENGINR	25000
ENGINR	20000
ENGINR	23000
ENGINR	27000
FINANC	10000
FINANC	12000

First.Dept
1

Last.Dept
0

53

3.04 Quiz

What are the values for **First.Dept** and **Last.Dept** when the DATA step is processing the observation indicated by the red arrow?

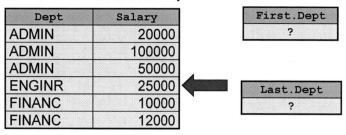

Dept	Salary
ADMIN	20000
ADMIN	100000
ADMIN	50000
ENGINR	25000
FINANC	10000
FINANC	12000

First.Dept
?

Last.Dept
?

55

What Must Happen When?

There is a three-part process for using the DATA step to summarize grouped data.

Task 1: Set the accumulating variable to zero at the start of each BY group.

Task 2: Increment the accumulating variable with a sum statement (automatically retains).

Task 3: Output only the last observation of each BY group.

57

Summarizing Data by Groups

Task 1: Set the accumulating variable to zero at the start of each BY group.

```
data deptsals(keep=Dept DeptSal);
   set SalSort;
   by Dept;
   if First.Dept then DeptSal=0;
   <additional SAS statements>
run;
```

✎ The condition is considered true when `First.Dept` has a value of 1.

58

Summarizing Data by Groups

Task 2: Increment the accumulating variable with a sum statement (automatically retains).

```
data deptsals(keep=Dept DeptSal);
   set SalSort;
   by Dept;
   if First.Dept then DeptSal=0;
   DeptSal+Salary;
   <additional SAS statements>
run;
```

59

Summarizing Data by Groups

Task 3: Output only the last observation of each BY group.

Dept	Salary	DeptSal
ADMIN	20000	20000
ADMIN	100000	120000
ADMIN	50000	170000
ENGINR	25000	25000
ENGINR	20000	45000
ENGINR	23000	68000
ENGINR	27000	95000
FINANC	10000	10000
FINANC	12000	22000

60

Subsetting IF Statement (Review)

The subsetting IF defines a condition that the observation must meet to be further processed by the DATA step.

General form of the subsetting IF statement:

IF *expression*;

- If the expression is true, the DATA step continues processing the current observation.
- If the expression is false, SAS returns to the top of the DATA step.

61

Summarizing Data by Groups

Task 3: Output only the last observation of each BY group.

```
data deptsals(keep=Dept DeptSal);
   set SalSort;
   by Dept;
   if First.Dept then DeptSal=0;
   DeptSal+Salary;
   if Last.Dept;
run;
```

62 p203d04

Summarizing Data by Groups

Partial SAS Log

```
NOTE: There were 39 observations read
      from the data set WORK.SALSORT.
NOTE: The data set WORK.DEPTSALS has 5
      observations and 2 variables.
```

63

Summarizing Data by Groups

```
proc print data=deptsals noobs;
run;
```

PROC PRINT Output

Dept	DeptSal
ADMIN	410000
ENGINR	163000
FINANC	318000
HUMRES	181000
SALES	373000

64

3.05 Multiple Answer Poll

What must happen in the DATA step to summarize data by groups? (Circle all that apply.)

a. Sort the input data.
b. Set the accumulating variable to zero at the start of each BY group.
c. Increment the accumulating variable.
d. Output only the last observation of each BY group.

66

Business Scenario

Each employee listed in **orion.projsals** is assigned to a special project. A business analyst would like to see the salary totals from each department for each special project.

Partial Listing of **orion.projsals**

Employee_ ID	Salary	Proj	Dept
110004	42000	EZ	HUMRES
110009	34000	WIN	ENGINR
110011	27000	WIN	FINANC
110036	20000	WIN	ENGINR
110037	19000	EZ	ENGINR
110048	19000	EZ	FINANC
110077	27000	CAP1	ADMIN
110097	20000	EZ	ADMIN
110107	31000	EZ	ENGINR

68

Business Scenario – Desired Output

Create a new data set, **pdsals**, that shows the number of employees and salary totals from each department for each special project.

Partial Listing of **pdsals**

Proj	Dept	Dept Sal	Num Emps
CAP1	ADMIN	70000	2
EZ	ADMIN	83000	3
EZ	ENGINR	109000	4
EZ	FINANC	122000	3
EZ	HUMRES	178000	5
NGEN	ADMIN	37000	2

69

Sorting by Project and Department

This is similar to the previous business scenario except that now the data must be sorted by multiple BY variables.

Sort the data by **Proj** and **Dept**:

- **Proj** is the primary sort variable.
- **Dept** is the secondary sort variable.

```
proc sort data=orion.projsals
          out=projsort;
   by Proj Dept;
run;
```

70 p203d05

Sorting by Project and Department

```
proc print data=projsort noobs;
   var Proj Dept Salary;
run;
```

Partial PROC PRINT Output

Proj	Dept	Salary
CAP1	ADMIN	27000
CAP1	ADMIN	43000
EZ	ADMIN	20000
EZ	ADMIN	31000
EZ	ADMIN	32000
EZ	ENGINR	19000

71

p203d05

Multiple BY Variables

The DATA step must include both **Proj** and **Dept** in the BY statement.

```
data pdsals;
   set projsort;
   by Proj Dept;
   <additional SAS statements>
run;
```

How does the DATA step set First. and Last. values for multiple BY variables?

72

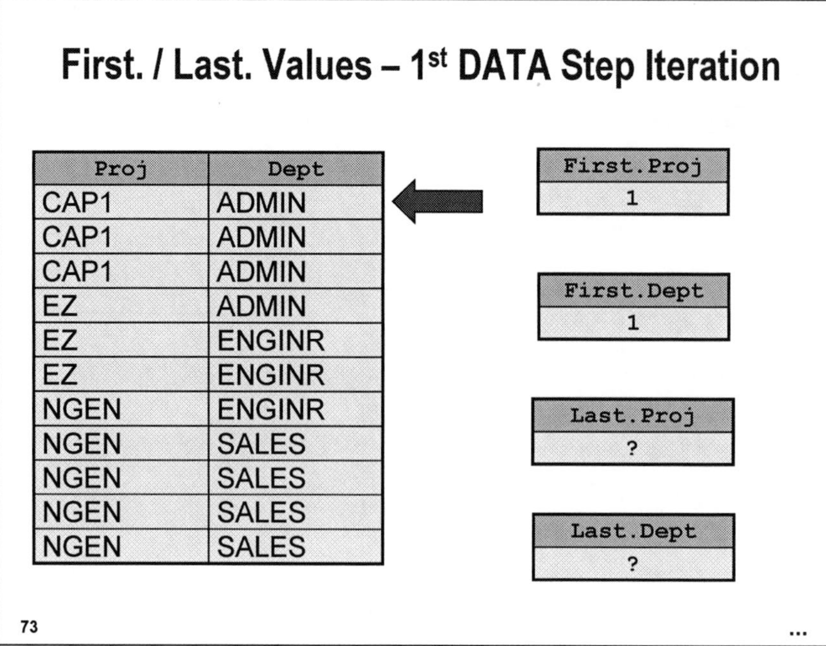
First. / Last. Values – 1st DATA Step Iteration
Proj
Dept
CAP1
ADMIN
CAP1
ADMIN
CAP1
ADMIN
EZ
ADMIN
EZ
ENGINR
EZ
ENGINR
NGEN
ENGINR
NGEN
SALES
NGEN
SALES
NGEN
SALES
NGEN
SALES
First.Proj
1
First.Dept
1
Last.Proj
?
Last.Dept
?
73
...

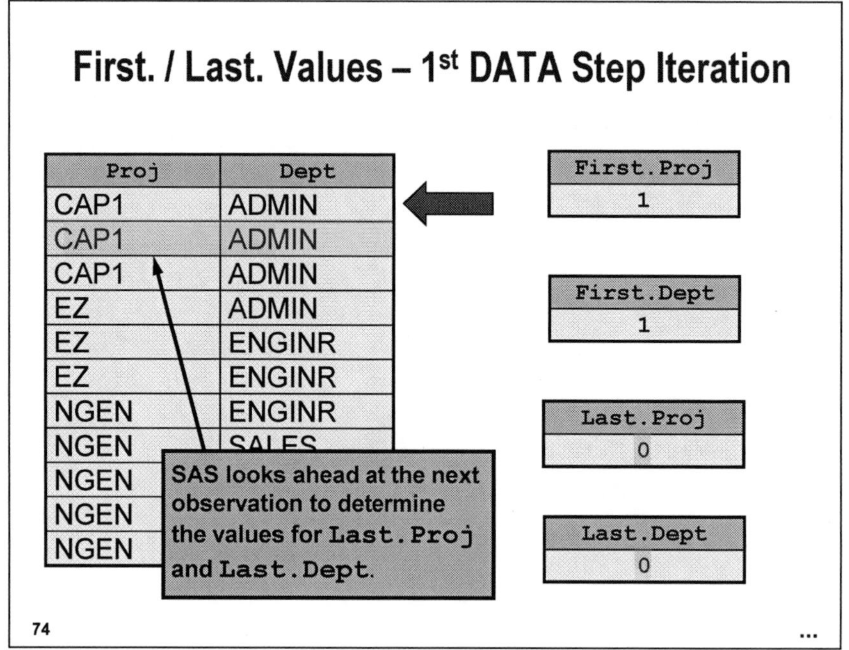
First. / Last. Values – 1st DATA Step Iteration
Proj
Dept
CAP1
ADMIN
CAP1
ADMIN
CAP1
ADMIN
EZ
ADMIN
EZ
ENGINR
EZ
ENGINR
NGEN
ENGINR
NGEN
NGEN
NGEN
NGEN
SAS looks ahead at the next observation to determine the values for Last.Proj and Last.Dept.
First.Proj
1
First.Dept
1
Last.Proj
0
Last.Dept
0
74
...

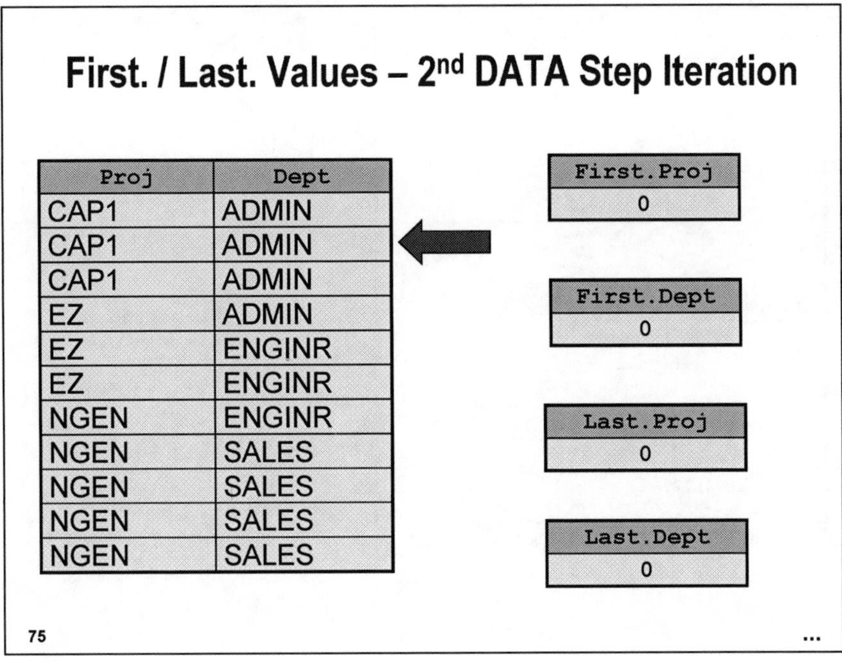
First. / Last. Values – 2nd DATA Step Iteration
Proj
Dept
CAP1 ADMIN
CAP1 ADMIN
CAP1 ADMIN
EZ ADMIN
EZ ENGINR
EZ ENGINR
NGEN ENGINR
NGEN SALES
NGEN SALES
NGEN SALES
NGEN SALES
First.Proj
0
First.Dept
0
Last.Proj
0
Last.Dept
0
75
...

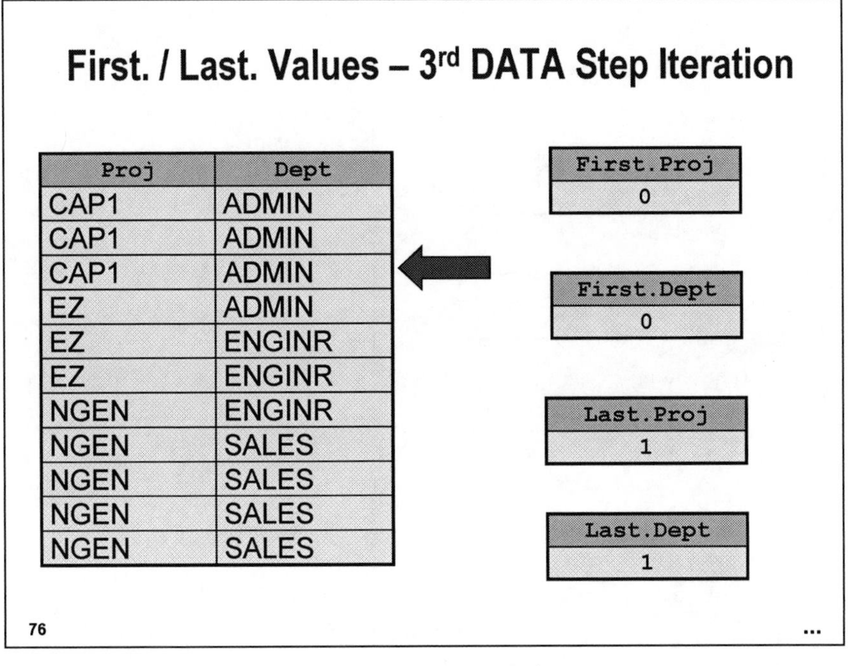
First. / Last. Values – 3rd DATA Step Iteration
Proj
Dept
CAP1 ADMIN
CAP1 ADMIN
CAP1 ADMIN
EZ ADMIN
EZ ENGINR
EZ ENGINR
NGEN ENGINR
NGEN SALES
NGEN SALES
NGEN SALES
NGEN SALES
First.Proj
0
First.Dept
0
Last.Proj
1
Last.Dept
1
76
...

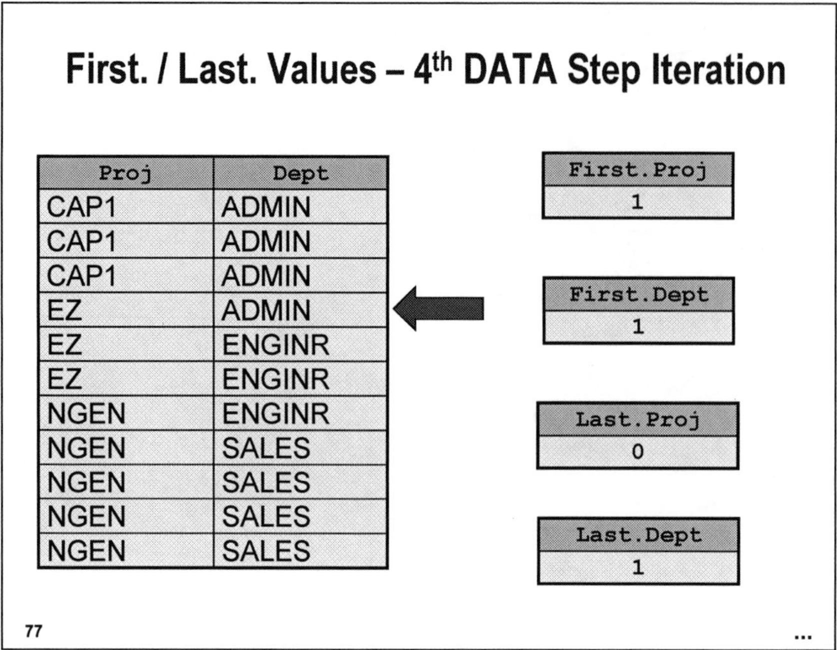
First. / Last. Values – 4th DATA Step Iteration
Proj
Dept
CAP1
ADMIN
CAP1
ADMIN
CAP1
ADMIN
EZ
ADMIN
EZ
ENGINR
EZ
ENGINR
NGEN
ENGINR
NGEN
SALES
NGEN
SALES
NGEN
SALES
NGEN
SALES
First.Proj
1
First.Dept
1
Last.Proj
0
Last.Dept
1
77
...

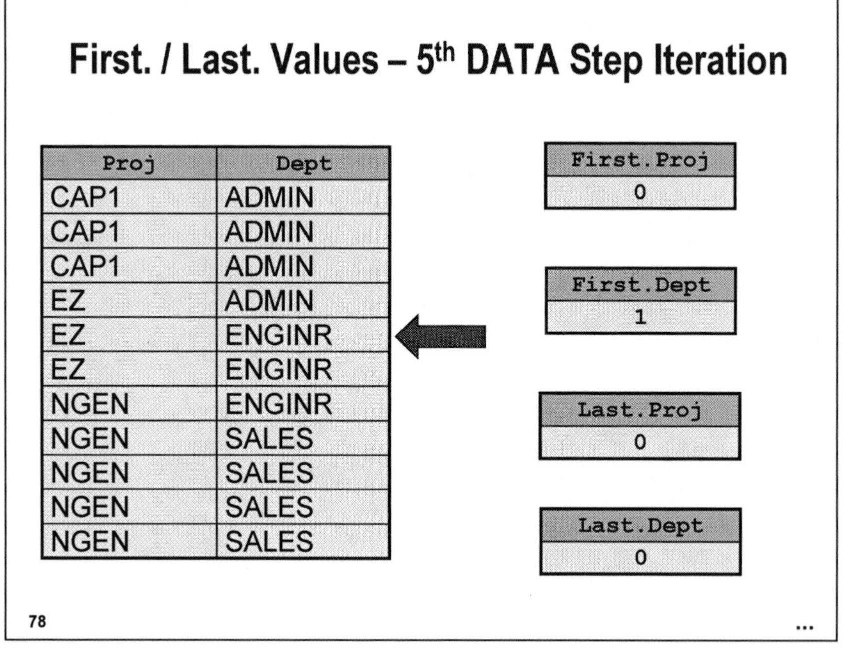
First. / Last. Values – 5th DATA Step Iteration
Proj
Dept
CAP1
ADMIN
CAP1
ADMIN
CAP1
ADMIN
EZ
ADMIN
EZ
ENGINR
EZ
ENGINR
NGEN
ENGINR
NGEN
SALES
NGEN
SALES
NGEN
SALES
NGEN
SALES
First.Proj
0
First.Dept
1
Last.Proj
0
Last.Dept
0
78
...

3.06 Quiz

What are the values for First. and Last. variables when the DATA step is processing the observation indicated by the red arrow?

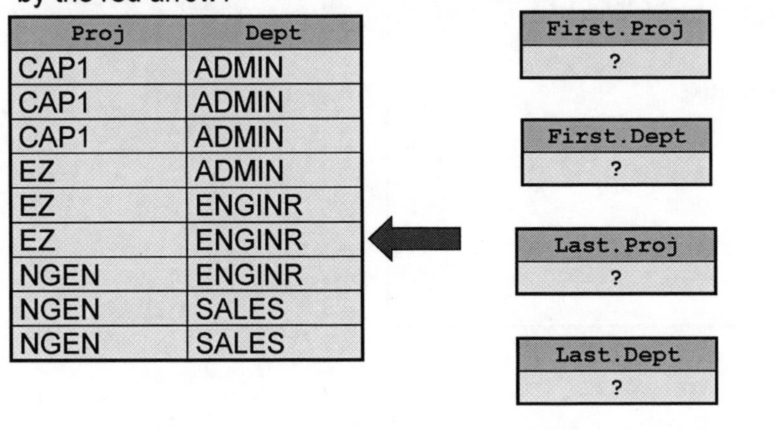

Proj	Dept
CAP1	ADMIN
CAP1	ADMIN
CAP1	ADMIN
EZ	ADMIN
EZ	ENGINR
EZ	ENGINR
NGEN	ENGINR
NGEN	SALES
NGEN	SALES

80

First. and Last. for Multiple BY Variables

When you use more than one variable in the BY statement, `Last.`*BY-variable*=1 for the **primary variable** forces `Last.`*BY-variable*=1 for the **secondary variable(s)**.

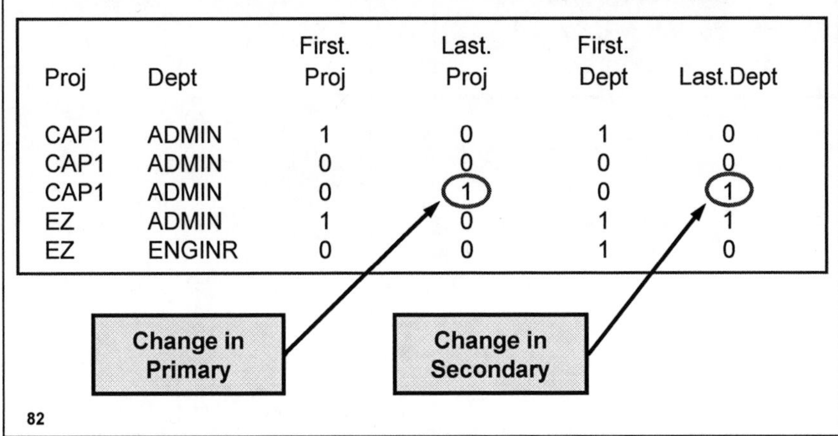

Proj	Dept	First. Proj	Last. Proj	First. Dept	Last.Dept
CAP1	ADMIN	1	0	1	0
CAP1	ADMIN	0	0	0	0
CAP1	ADMIN	0	1	0	1
EZ	ADMIN	1	0	1	1
EZ	ENGINR	0	0	1	0

82

Multiple BY Variables

Here is the complete DATA step:

```
data pdsals(keep=Proj Dept
                 DeptSal NumEmps);
   set projsort;
   by Proj Dept;
   if First.Dept then do;
      DeptSal=0;
      NumEmps=0;
   end;
   DeptSal+Salary;
   NumEmps+1;
   if Last.Dept;
run;
```

83 p203d05

Multiple BY Variables

Partial SAS Log

```
NOTE: There were 39 observations read
      from the data set WORK.PROJSORT.
NOTE: The data set WORK.PDSALS has 14
      observations and 4 variables.
```

84

Multiple BY Variables

```
proc print data=pdsals noobs;
run;
```

Partial PROC PRINT Output

Proj	Dept	Dept Sal	Num Emps
CAP1	ADMIN	70000	2
EZ	ADMIN	83000	3
EZ	ENGINR	109000	4
EZ	FINANC	122000	3

85

p203d05

Exercises

Level 1

4. Summarizing Data Using the DATA Step

The data set **orion.order_summary** contains information about sales in a particular year for each customer, separated by month. For a given customer, there might be some months that he did not place an order.

Partial Listing of **orion.order_summary** (101 Total Observations)

```
                          Order_
           Customer_ID     Month     Sale_Amt

                     5         5       478.00
                     5         6       126.80
                     5         9        52.50
                     5        12        33.80
                    10         3        32.60
                    10         4       250.80
                    10         5        79.80
```

a. Sort the input data set, **orion.order_summary**, by **Customer_ID**. Use the OUT= option to avoid overwriting the original data set. Name the output data set **work.sumsort**.

b. Create a new data set showing a total sales value for each customer.
   - Name the new data set **work.customers**.
   - Name the new variable **Total_Sales**. This variable contains the total of sales across all months for each customer.

c. Print your result.
   - Display **Total_Sales** with a DOLLAR11.2 format.
   - Add an appropriate title.

Partial PROC PRINT Output (37 Total Observations)

```
              Total Sales to each Customer

           Obs     Customer_ID     Total_Sales

             1               5         $691.10
             2              10       $3,479.09
             3              11          $78.20
             4              12         $253.20
             5              18          $29.40
             6              24         $358.80
             7              27       $1,093.60
             8              31       $1,777.60
```

Level 2

5. Summarizing and Grouping Data Using the DATA Step

The data set **orion.order_qtrsum** contains information about sales in a particular year for each customer, separated by month.

- For a given customer, there might be some months (and quarters) that the customer did not place an order.
- The variable **Order_Qtr** contains the appropriate quarter.

Partial Listing of **orion.order_qtrsum** (101 Total Observations)

Customer_ID	Order_ Qtr	Order_ Month	Sale_Amt
69	4	10	3.2
70187	4	11	8.2
10	2	6	12.2
70079	4	10	14.6
70165	3	7	16.6
92	1	3	16.9
41	3	8	17.6
171	2	4	19.1
41	2	5	19.9
69	3	9	23.5
49	4	12	24.8

The data set is not sorted by **Customer_ID** and **Order_Qtr**.

a. Create a data set named **work.qtrcustomers** that summarizes sales based on customer and quarter.

- The variable **Total_Sales** should contain the total sales for each quarter within each **Customer_ID** value.
- Create a variable named **Num_Months** that counts the total months within each quarter that the customer had an order.

b. Print your results.

- Display **Total_Sales** with a DOLLAR11.2 format.
- Add an appropriate title.

Partial PROC PRINT Output (74 Total Observations)

Total Sales to each Customer for each Quarter

Obs	Customer_ID	Order_ Qtr	Total_Sales	Num_ Months
1	5	2	$604.80	2
2	5	3	$52.50	1
3	5	4	$33.80	1
4	10	1	$32.60	1
5	10	2	$342.80	3
6	10	3	$1,065.79	2
7	10	4	$2,037.90	2
8	11	3	$78.20	1
9	12	1	$117.60	1

6. (Optional) Summarizing Data and Conditional Output

The data set **orion.usorders04** contains a group of orders from U.S. customers.

Partial Listing of **orion.usorders04** (83 Total Observations, 9 Total Variables)

Order_ID	Customer_ID	Customer_Name	Order_ Type	Total_Retail_ Price
1241054779	24	Robyn Klem	3	$195.60
1241063739	89	Wynella Lewis	1	$160.80
1241286432	27	Cynthia Mccluney	3	$174.40
1241359997	12	David Black	1	$117.60
1241461856	18	Tonie Asmussen	1	$29.40
1241623505	24	Robyn Klem	3	$46.90
1241652707	27	Cynthia Mccluney	3	$140.70
1241686210	10	Karen Ballinger	1	$32.60
1241715610	92	Lendon Celii	1	$16.90
1241731828	31	Cynthia Martinez	1	$41.50
1241731828	31	Cynthia Martinez	1	$22.70
1241895594	56	Roy Siferd	1	$13.50
1241895594	56	Roy Siferd	1	$24.40
1241930625	27	Cynthia Mccluney	3	$56.30
1241930625	27	Cynthia Mccluney	3	$58.70

a. Orion Star wants to reward customers who spent $100 or more through any particular sales channel (retail, catalog, or Internet).

- Create three data sets: **work.discount1**, **work.discount2**, and **work.discount3**.
- The value of **Order_Type** indicates whether the sale was retail (=1), catalog (=2), or Internet (=3).
- The variable **Total_Retail_Price** contains the amount that the customer spent on each individual order.
- Create a variable named **TotSales** to hold the total sales to each customer by order type.

- Output to each of the three data sets based on the following table:

Customer spent $100 or more in…	Output to…
Retail orders	**work.discount1**
Catalog orders	**work.discount2**
Internet orders	**work.discount3**

A given customer can output to more than one data set if he spent $100 or more in retail orders and the same in Internet orders, for example.

- Keep the variables **Customer_ID**, **Customer_Name**, and **TotSales**.
- Verify that the data sets **work.discount1**, **work.discount2**, and **work.discount3** have 8, 2, and 5 observations, respectively.

b. Print your results from **work.discount1**.

- Format **TotSales** with a DOLLAR11.2 format.
- Add an appropriate title.

PROC PRINT Output

```
                    Customers Spending $100 or more in Retail Orders

                    Customer_ID    Customer_Name            TotSales

                              5    Sandrina Stephano         $213.10
                             10    Karen Ballinger         $3,479.09
                             12    David Black               $253.20
                             31    Cynthia Martinez        $1,322.30
                             45    Dianne Patchin            $700.28
                             89    Wynella Lewis             $602.00
                             90    Kyndal Hooks              $221.70
                             92    Lendon Celii              $177.40
```

Level 3

7. Identifying Extreme Values in Each Group of Data

The data set **orion.customer_dim** contains information about Orion Star customers.

Partial Listing of **orion.customer_dim** (77 Total Observations, 11 Total Variables)

Customer_ID	Customer_Name	Customer_Type	Customer_ BirthDate
4	James Kvarniq	Orion Club members low activity	27JUN1974
5	Sandrina Stephano	Orion Club Gold members medium activity	09JUL1979
9	Cornelia Krahl	Orion Club Gold members medium activity	27FEB1974
10	Karen Ballinger	Orion Club members high activity	18OCT1984
11	Elke Wallstab	Orion Club members high activity	16AUG1974
12	David Black	Orion Club members medium activity	12APR1969
13	Markus Sepke	Orion Club Gold members low activity	21JUL1988
16	Ulrich Heyde	Internet/Catalog Customers	16JAN1939
17	Jimmie Evans	Orion Club members medium activity	17AUG1954
18	Tonie Asmussen	Orion Club members low activity	02FEB1954

Use First./Last. processing to create the report below. Show data on the oldest and youngest customers for each **Customer_Type**.

- The variable **o_ID** is the **Customer_ID** value of the oldest customer and **y_ID** is the **Customer_ID** value of the youngest customer for each group.
- Create a variable named **agerange** to indicate the spread between these oldest and youngest customers.
- Use **Customer_BirthDate**, rather than **Customer_Age**, for all age determinations because this is more accurate.

PROC PRINT Output

Oldest and Youngest Customers of each Customer Type

Customer_Type	oldest	youngest	o_ID	y_ID	agerange
Internet/Catalog Customers	08JUL1934	18AUG1969	29	54655	35.1
Orion Club members high activity	28SEP1934	24OCT1986	89	46966	52.1
Orion Club members medium activity	20JAN1934	16SEP1988	70059	2806	54.7
Orion Club Gold members high activity	16JAN1934	25JUL1984	50	39	50.5
Orion Club Gold members low activity	19DEC1969	21JUL1988	70201	13	18.6
Orion Club Gold members medium activity	16MAY1949	09JUL1979	215	5	30.1
Orion Club members low activity	14APR1939	18JUN1984	70108	75	45.2

There are several ways to obtain the number of years between two dates. Two possible techniques are dividing days by 365.25 or using the YRDIF function.

3.3 Chapter Review

Chapter Review

1. What statement prevents SAS from reinitializing the values in a variable?

2. Describe the effect on `Total_Salary` if it is used in this statement: `Total_Salary + Salary;`

3. If a data set is not sorted, can it be used as the input data set for BY-group processing?

88

continued...

Chapter Review

4. What statement in the DATA step enables BY-group processing?

5. In BY-group processing, two temporary variables are created for each variable listed in the BY statement. What are the names of the temporary variables?

6. What are the possible values for those temporary variables?

7. Is there ever a case where the values for the First.BY-variable and the Last.BY-variable can both be 1?

91

3.4 Solutions

Solutions to Exercises

1. **Creating Accumulating Totals**

   a. Orion Star would like to examine growth in sales during the date range of 01Nov2004 to 14Dec2004.

```
data work.mid_q4;
   set orion.order_fact;
   where '01nov2004'd <= Order_Date <= '14dec2004'd;
   Sales2Dte+Total_Retail_Price;
   Num_Orders+1;
run;
```

   b. Print your results.

```
title 'Orders from 01Nov2004 through 14Dec2004';
proc print data=work.mid_q4;
   format Sales2Dte dollar10.2;
   var Order_ID Order_Date Total_Retail_Price Sales2Dte Num_Orders;
run;
title;
```

2. **Creating Accumulating Totals with Conditional Logic**

   a. Orion Star would like to analyze 2005 data by creating accumulating totals for the number of items sold from retail, catalog, and Internet channels.

```
data work.typetotals;
   set orion.order_fact (obs=10);
   where year(Order_Date)=2005;
   /* There are equivalent WHERE statements that would work */
   if Order_Type=1 then TotalRetail+Quantity;
   else if Order_Type=2 then TotalCatalog+Quantity;
   else if Order_Type=3 then TotalInternet+Quantity;
run;
```

   b. Continue testing your program by printing the results from step **a**. Print all the variables and check to make sure that the program is correctly calculating values for the accumulating totals.

```
proc print data=work.typetotals;
run;
```

c. When the results from steps **a** and **b** look correct:

```
data work.typetotals;
   set orion.order_fact;
   where year(Order_Date)=2005;
   /* There are equivalent WHERE statements that would work */
   if Order_Type=1 then TotalRetail+Quantity;
   else if Order_Type=2 then TotalCatalog+Quantity;
   else if Order_Type=3 then TotalInternet+Quantity;
   keep Order_ID Order_Date TotalRetail
        TotalCatalog TotalInternet;
run;

title '2005 Accumulating Totals for Each Type of Order';
proc print data=work.typetotals;
run;
title;
```

3. **Creating Accumulating Totals by Month**

   Orion Star would like to generate the following report showing all orders in 2007 along with an accumulating total.

```
data work.monthtotals;
   set orion.order_fact;
   where year(Order_Date)=2007;
   retain rmonth;
   if month(Order_Date) ne rmonth then do;
      MonthSales=0;
      rmonth=month(Order_Date);
   end;
   monthsales+Total_Retail_Price;
   keep Order_ID Order_Date MonthSales Total_Retail_Price;
run;


title 'Accumulating Totals by Month in 2007';
proc print data=work.monthtotals;
   format Total_Retail_Price MonthSales dollar10.2;
run;
title;
```

4. Summarizing Data Using the DATA Step

a. Sort the input data set, **orion.order_summary**, by **Customer_ID**. Use the OUT=option to avoid overwriting the original data set. Name the output data set **work.sumsort**.

```
proc sort data=orion.order_summary out=work.sumsort;
   by Customer_ID;
run;
```

b. Create a new data set showing a total sales value for each customer.

```
data work.customers;
   set work.sumsort;
   by Customer_ID;
   if first.Customer_ID then Total_Sales=0;
   Total_Sales+Sale_Amt;
   if last.Customer_ID;
   keep Customer_ID Total_Sales;
run;
```

c. Print your result.

```
title 'Total Sales to each Customer';
proc print data=work.customers;
   format Total_Sales dollar11.2;
run;
title;
```

5. Summarizing Data Using the DATA Step

a. Create a data set named **work.qtrcustomers** that summarizes sales based on customer and quarter.

```
proc sort data=orion.order_qtrsum out=work.custsort;
   by Customer_ID Order_Qtr;
run;

data work.qtrcustomers;
   set work.custsort;
   by Customer_ID Order_Qtr;
   if first.Order_Qtr=1 then do;
      Total_Sales=0;
    Num_Months=0;
   end;
   Total_Sales+Sale_Amt;
   Num_Months+1;
   if last.Order_Qtr=1;
   keep Customer_ID Order_Qtr Total_Sales Num_Months;
run;
```

b. Print your results.

```
title 'Total Sales to each Customer for each Quarter';
proc print data=work.qtrcustomers;
   format Total_Sales dollar11.2;
run;
title;
```

6. (Optional) Summarizing Data and Conditional Output

a. Orion Star wants to reward customers who spent $100 or more through any particular sales channel (retail, catalog, or Internet).

```
proc sort data=orion.usorders04 out=work.usorders04;
  by Customer_ID Order_Type;
run;

data work.discount1 work.discount2 work.discount3;
  set work.usorders04;
  by Customer_ID Order_Type;
  if first.Order_Type=1 then TotSales=0;
  TotSales+Total_Retail_Price;
  if last.Order_Type=1 and TotSales >= 100 then do;
    if Order_Type=1 then output discount1;
   else if Order_Type=2 then output discount2;
   else if Order_Type=3 then output discount3;
  end;
  keep Customer_ID Customer_Name TotSales;
run;
```

b. Print your results from **work.discount1**.

```
title 'Customers Spending $100 or more in Retail Sales';
proc print data=work.discount1 noobs;
  format TotSales dollar11.2;
run;
title;
```

7. Identifying Extreme Values in Each Group of Data

Use First./Last. processing to create the report below. Show data on the oldest and youngest customers for each **Customer_Type**.

```
proc sort data=orion.customer_dim out=work.customers;
   by Customer_Type;
run;

data work.agecheck;
   set work.customers;
   by Customer_Type;
   retain oldest youngest o_ID y_ID;
   if first.Customer_Type=1 then do;
      oldest=Customer_BirthDate;
    youngest=Customer_BirthDate;
    o_ID=Customer_ID;
    y_ID=Customer_ID;
   end;
   if Customer_BirthDate < oldest then do;
      o_ID=Customer_ID;
      oldest=Customer_BirthDate;
   end;
   else if Customer_BirthDate > youngest then do;
      y_ID=Customer_ID;
      youngest=Customer_BirthDate;
   end;
   if last.Customer_Type=1 then do;
      agerange=(youngest-oldest)/365.25;
    output;
   end;
   keep Customer_Type oldest youngest o_ID y_ID agerange;
run;

title 'Oldest and Youngest Customers of each Customer Type';
proc print data=work.agecheck noobs;
   format oldest youngest date9. agerange 5.1;
run;
title;
```

Alternate Solution:

```
proc sort data=orion.customer_dim out=work.customers;
   by Customer_Type Customer_BirthDate;
run;

data work.agecheck;
   set work.customers;
   by Customer_Type;
   /* Could instead use: by Customer_Type Customer_BirthDate;
      In this DATA step, either BY statement works. */
   retain oldest youngest o_ID y_ID;
   if first.Customer_Type=1 then do;
      o_ID=Customer_ID;
    oldest=Customer_BirthDate;
   end;
   /* Having sorted also on Customer_BirthDate, we know the first
   customer in each BY group will be the oldest (have the
   smallest SAS date value for a Birthday). */
   if last.Customer_Type=1 then do;
      y_ID=Customer_ID;
    youngest=Customer_BirthDate;
      agerange=(youngest-oldest)/365.25;
    output;
    end;
   /* Similar story: last in each BY group will be the youngest. */
   keep Customer_Type oldest youngest o_ID y_ID agerange;
run;

title 'Oldest and Youngest Customers of each Customer Type';
proc print data=work.agecheck noobs;
   format oldest youngest date9. agerange 5.1;
run;
title;
```

Solutions to Student Activities (Polls/Quizzes)

3.01 Quiz – Correct Answer

Open and submit the program in p203a01. Does this program create the correct values for **Mth2Dte**?

```
data mnthtot;
   set orion.aprsales;
   Mth2Dte=Mth2Dte+SaleAmt;
run;
```

Partial Listing of **mnthtot**

SaleDate	Sale Amt	Mth2Dte
01APR2007	498.49	.
02APR2007	946.50	.
03APR2007	994.97	.
04APR2007	564.59	.

No, the program creates Mth2Dte with all missing values.

8

p203a01

3.02 Multiple Choice Poll – Correct Answer

What effect did the missing value for **SaleAmt** have on **Mth2Dte**?

a. The missing value was ignored; **Mth2Dte** values were not affected.

b. The missing value will cause the DATA step to stop processing.

c. The missing value will cause the subsequent values for **Mth2Dte** to be set to missing. (circled)

28

3.04 Quiz – Correct Answer

What are the values for `First.Dept` and `Last.Dept` when the DATA step is processing the observation indicated by the red arrow?

Dept	Salary
ADMIN	20000
ADMIN	100000
ADMIN	50000
ENGINR	25000
FINANC	10000
FINANC	12000

First.Dept
1

Last.Dept
1

`First.Dept` and `Last.Dept` are both 1. This will happen when a group is composed of a single observation.

56

3.05 Multiple Answer Poll – Correct Answer

What must happen in the DATA step to summarize data by groups? (Circle all that apply.)

a. Sort the input data.
(b.) Set the accumulating variable to zero at the start of each BY group.
(c.) Increment the accumulating variable.
(d.) Output only the last observation of each BY group.

Choice a. does not apply because sorting is done with PROC SORT, not in the DATA step.

67

3.06 Quiz – Correct Answer

What are the values for First. and Last. variables when the DATA step is processing the observation indicated by the red arrow?

Proj	Dept
CAP1	ADMIN
CAP1	ADMIN
CAP1	ADMIN
EZ	ADMIN
EZ	ENGINR
EZ	ENGINR
NGEN	ENGINR
NGEN	SALES
NGEN	SALES

First.Proj
0

First.Dept
0

Last.Proj
1

Last.Dept
1

81

Solutions to Chapter Review

Chapter Review Answers

1. What statement prevents SAS from reinitializing the values in a variable?

   Either the RETAIN statement or the sum statement prevents SAS from reinitializing the values in a variable.

2. Describe the effect on `Total_Salary` if it is used in this statement: `Total_Salary + Salary;`

   `Total_Salary` is

   - **initialized to zero**
   - **automatically retained**
   - **increased by the value of `Salary` for each observation.**

89

continued...

Chapter Review Answers

3. If a data set is not sorted, can it be used as the input data set for BY-group processing?

   No, BY-group processing depends on the input data set being sorted.

90

continued...

Chapter Review Answers

4. What statement in the DATA step enables BY-Group processing?

   The BY statement enables BY-group processing.

5. In BY-group processing, two temporary variables are created for each variable listed in the BY statement. What are the names of the temporary variables?

   First.BY-variable and Last.BY-variable where the BY-variable is the name of the variable used in the BY statement

92

continued...

Chapter Review Answers

6. What are the possible values for those temporary variables?

   The First. variable has a value of 1 for the first observation in a BY group; otherwise, it equals 0.

   The Last. variable has a value of 1 for the last observation in a BY group; otherwise, it equals 0.

7. Is there ever a case where the values for the First.BY-variable and the Last.BY-variable can both be 1?

   Yes, this happens when a BY group is composed of a single observation.

93

Chapter 4 Reading Raw Data Files

4.1 Reading Raw Data Files with Formatted Input....................4-3

Exercises....................4-20

4.2 Controlling When a Record Loads....................4-24

Exercises....................4-49

4.3 Additional Techniques for List Input (Self-Study)....................4-52

4.4 Chapter Review....................4-74

4.5 Solutions....................4-75

Solutions to Exercises....................4-75

Solutions to Student Activities....................4-78

Solutions to Chapter Review....................4-82

4.1 Reading Raw Data Files with Formatted Input

Objectives

- Read raw data in fixed columns using formatted input.

3

Business Scenario – Read the Offers File

The **offers.dat** raw data file contains information about discount offers. Create a SAS data set named **discounts** from the raw data.

Layout: offers.dat

Description	Column
Customer Type	1- 4
Offer Date	5-12
Item Group	14-21
Discount	22-24

Partial offers.dat

```
         1    1    2    2
1---5----0----5----0----5
104012/02/07 Outdoors15%
202010/07/07 Golf      7%
103009/22/07 Shoes    10%
103009/22/07 Clothes  10%
202007/08/07 Clothes  15%
203007/08/07 Clothes  25%
```

4

Business Scenario – Desired Output

The **discounts** data set should have one observation per input record.

Partial Listing of **discounts**

Cust_ type	Offer_dt	Item_gp	Discount
1040	02DEC2007	Outdoors	0.15
2020	07OCT2007	Golf	0.07
1030	22SEP2007	Shoes	0.10
1030	22SEP2007	Clothes	0.10
	.		
	.		
3010	17MAY2007	Clothes	0.15

5

4.01 Multiple Choice Poll

For your work, how often do you need to read raw data files?

a. All the time
b. Occasionally
c. Very rarely
d. Never

7

The DATA Step to Read Raw Data (Review)

To read raw data, the DATA step includes DATA, INFILE, and INPUT statements.

```
DATA output-SAS-data-set;
     INFILE 'raw-data-file-name';
     INPUT specifications;
     <additional SAS statements>
RUN;
```

8

<table>
<tr><th>Statement</th><th>Description</th></tr>
<tr><td>DATA output-SAS-data-set;</td><td>The DATA statement begins a DATA step and provides the name of the SAS data set being created.

output-SAS-data-set can refer to a temporary or permanent data set.</td></tr>
<tr><td>INFILE 'raw-data-file-name';</td><td>The INFILE statement identifies the physical name of the raw data file to read with an INPUT statement.

'raw-data-file-name' is the physical name that the operating environment uses to access the file of raw data.

Examples:
<table>
<tr><td>Windows</td><td><code>infile 's:\workshop\offers.dat';</code></td></tr>
<tr><td>UNIX</td><td><code>infile '/users/userid/offers.dat';</code></td></tr>
<tr><td>z/OS (OS/390)</td><td><code>infile 'userid.workshop.rawdata(offers)';</code></td></tr>
</table>
The PAD option can be useful for reading variable-length records typically found in Windows and UNIX environments. See SAS Help and Documentation for more information about the PAD option.</td></tr>
<tr><td>INPUT specifications;</td><td>The INPUT statement describes the arrangement of values in the raw data file and assigns input values to the corresponding SAS variables.</td></tr>
</table>

4.02 Quiz

Use SAS Help to navigate to Starting with Raw Data: The Basics.

Click the **Contents** tab and select:
- ⇨ **SAS Products**
  - ⇨ **Base SAS**
    - ⇨ **Step-by-Step Programming with Base SAS Software**
      - ⇨ **Getting Your Data into Shape**
        - ⇨ **Starting with Raw Data: The Basics**

Page to Introduction to Raw Data and review this section. What are the three styles of input?

10

Which Input Style to Choose?

Column input, formatted input, and list input are all styles of writing INPUT statement specifications.

Style	Used for Reading
Column Input	Standard data in fixed columns
Formatted Input	Standard and nonstandard data in fixed columns
List Input	Standard and nonstandard data separated by blanks or some other delimiter

12

Standard and Nonstandard Data (Review)

- *Standard data* is data that SAS can read without any special instructions.

  Examples of standard numeric data:

  58 -23 67.23 00.99 5.67E5 1.2E-2

- *Nonstandard data* is any data that SAS cannot read without special instructions.

  Examples of nonstandard numeric data:

  5,823 15% $67.23 01/12/1999 12MAY2006

13

The following are the only acceptable characters in a standard numeric field:

```
0 1 2 3 4 5 6 7 8 9 . E e D d - +
```

Leading or trailing blanks are also acceptable.

E, **e**, **D**, and **d** represent exponential notation in a standard numeric field. For example, **3E5** is an alternative way of writing **300000**.

Examples of nonstandard character data include preserving leading blanks in character values, hexadecimal characters, and values surrounded by matching quotation marks.

4.03 Quiz

Which style of INPUT statement specification should you choose to read the **offers.dat** raw data file?

Partial offers.dat

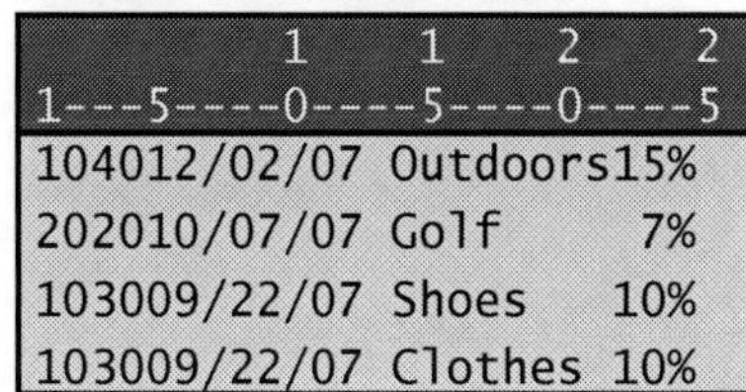

```
         1    1    2    2
1---5----0----5----0----5
104012/02/07 Outdoors15%
202010/07/07 Golf     7%
103009/22/07 Shoes   10%
103009/22/07 Clothes 10%
```

15

Reading Data Using Formatted Input

General form of the INPUT statement with formatted input:

INPUT *pointer-control variable informat* . . . ;

Formatted input is used to read data values by

- moving the input pointer to the starting position of the field
- naming the variable
- specifying an informat.

Example:

```
input @5 FirstName $10.;
```

17

Reading Data Using Formatted Input

Column pointer controls:

@n moves the pointer to column *n*.

+n moves the pointer *n* positions.

An informat specifies the following:

- the width of the input field
- how to read data values stored in the field

18

To move the pointer *n* positions backward, use +(-*n*).

SAS informats have the following form:

<$>*informat*<w>.<d>

where

$	indicates a character informat.
informat	names the SAS informat or user-defined informat.
w	specifies the number of columns to read in the input data.
.	is a required delimiter.

SAS Informat Examples

Examples of informats showing the raw data values and the converted SAS numeric values:

Informat	Raw Data Value	SAS Data Value
$8.	Outdoors	Outdoors
5.	12345	12345
COMMA7. DOLLAR7.	$12,345	12345
COMMAX7. DOLLARX7.	$12.345	12345
EUROX7.	€12.345	12345
PERCENT3.	15%	.15

19

The following table gives a brief definition for each of the informats. Complete information can be found in SAS OnlineDoc.

Informat	Definition
$*w*.	reads standard character data.
w.d	reads standard numeric data.
COMMA*w.d* DOLLAR*w.d*	reads nonstandard numeric data and removes embedded commas, blanks, dollar signs, percent signs, and dashes.
COMMAX*w.d* DOLLARX*w.d*	operates like COMMA*w.d* and DOLLAR*w.d*, but reverses the role of the decimal point and comma. This convention is common in many European countries.
EUROX*w.d*	reads nonstandard numeric data and removes embedded characters in European currency.
PERCENT*w.d*	operates like COMMA*w.d* but divides the number by 100 if it is followed by a percent sign (%).

✎ If the *d* is not specified, it defaults to 0. So, COMMA7. and COMMA7.0 are equivalent.

✎ DOLLAR*w.d* is an alias for COMMA*w.d*, and DOLLARX*w.d* is an alias for COMMAX*w.d*

✎ More information about EUROX*w.d* is available through SAS Help and Documentation.

SAS Date Informat Examples

Examples of date informats showing the nonstandard raw data values and the converted SAS numeric values:

Informat	Raw Data Value	SAS Date Value
MMDDYY6.	010160	0
MMDDYY8.	01/01/60	0
MMDDYY10.	01/01/1960	0
DDMMYY6.	311260	365
DDMMYY8.	31/12/60	365
DDMMYY10.	31/12/1960	365
DATE7.	31DEC59	-1
DATE9.	31DEC1959	-1

20

The ANYDTDTE*w.* informat can be used to read data that has a variety of date forms. More information about ANYDTDTE*w.* is available in SAS Help and Documentation.

Business Scenario – Continued

Use formatted input to create a SAS data set named **`discounts`** from the raw data in **`offers.dat`**.

Layout: `offers.dat`

Description	Column
Customer Type	1- 4
Offer Date	5-12
Item Group	14-21
Discount	22-24

Partial `offers.dat`

```
         1    1    2    2
1---5----0----5----0----5
104012/02/07 Outdoors15%
202010/07/07 Golf     7%
103009/22/07 Shoes   10%
103009/22/07 Clothes 10%
202007/08/07 Clothes 15%
203007/08/07 Clothes 25%
```

21

Write INPUT Specifications

Identify the starting position, variable name, and informat for each input field.

```
input @1 Cust_type 4.
```

Layout: offers.dat

Description	Column
Customer Type	1- 4
Offer Date	5-12
Item Group	14-21
Discount	22-24

Partial offers.dat

```
         1    1    2    2
1---5----0----5----0----5
104012/02/07 Outdoors15%
202010/07/07 Golf      7%
103009/22/07 Shoes    10%
103009/22/07 Clothes  10%
202007/08/07 Clothes  15%
203007/08/07 Clothes  25%
```

22

4.04 Quiz

Continue writing the INPUT statement to read Offer Date. (Hint: Use the MMDDYY8. informat.)

```
input @1 Cust_type 4.
          ?
```

Layout: offers.dat

Description	Column
Customer Type	1- 4
Offer Date	5-12
Item Group	14-21
Discount	22-24

Partial offers.dat

```
         1    1    2    2
1---5----0----5----0----5
104012/02/07 Outdoors15%
202010/07/07 Golf      7%
103009/22/07 Shoes    10%
103009/22/07 Clothes  10%
202007/08/07 Clothes  15%
203007/08/07 Clothes  25%
```

24

Reading Data Using Formatted Input

This SAS program uses formatted input to read the raw data file in **offers.dat**.

```
data work.discounts;
   infile 'offers.dat';
   input @1 Cust_type 4.
         @5 Offer_dt mmddyy8.
         @14 Item_gp $8.
         @22 Discount percent3.;
run;
```

26

p204d01

Compilation: Formatted Input

```
data work.discounts;
   infile 'offers.dat';
   input @1 Cust_type 4.
         @5 Offer_dt mmddyy8.
         @14 Item_gp $8.
         @22 Discount percent3.;
run;
```

Input Buffer

```
                  1                   2
1 2 3 4 5 6 7 8 9 0 1 2 3 4 5 6 7 8 9 0 1 2 3 4 5
```

PDV

Cust_type N 8	Offer_dt N 8	Item_gp $ 8	Discount N 8

27

...

Execution: Formatted Input

```
data work.discounts;
   infile 'offers.dat';
   input @1 Cust_type 4.
         @5 Offer_dt mmddyy8.
         @14 Item_gp $8.
         @22 Discount percent3.;
run;
```

Initialize PDV

Input Buffer

1	2	3	4	5	6	7	8	9	10	1	2	3	4	5	6	7	8	9	20	1	2	3	4	5

PDV

Cust_type N 8	Offer_dt N 8	Item_gp $ 8	Discount N 8
.	.		.

28 ...

Execution: Formatted Input

```
data work.discounts;
   infile 'offers.dat';
   input @1 Cust_type 4.
         @5 Offer_dt mmddyy8.
         @14 Item_gp $8.
         @22 Discount percent3.;
run;
```

Specify input data file

Input Buffer

1	2	3	4	5	6	7	8	9	10	1	2	3	4	5	6	7	8	9	20	1	2	3	4	5

PDV

Cust_type N 8	Offer_dt N 8	Item_gp $ 8	Discount N 8
.	.		.

29 ...

Execution: Formatted Input

```
data work.discounts;
   infile 'offers.dat';
   input @1 Cust_type 4.
         @5 Offer_dt mmddyy8.
         @14 Item_gp $8.
         @22 Discount percent3.;
run;
```

Load input buffer

Input Buffer

1	2	3	4	5	6	7	8	9	10	11	12	13	14	15	16	17	18	19	20	21	22	23	24	25
1	0	4	0	1	2	/	0	2	/	0	7		O	u	t	d	o	o	r	s	1	5	%	

PDV

Cust_type N 8	Offer_dt N 8	Item_gp $ 8	Discount N 8
.	.		.

30 ...

Execution: Formatted Input

```
data work.discounts;
   infile 'offers.dat';
   input @1 Cust_type 4.
         @5 Offer_dt mmddyy8.
         @14 Item_gp $8.
         @22 Discount percent3.;
run;
```

Load first value into the PDV

Input Buffer

1	2	3	4	5	6	7	8	9	10	11	12	13	14	15	16	17	18	19	20	21	22	23	24	25
1	0	4	0	1	2	/	0	2	/	0	7		O	u	t	d	o	o	r	s	1	5	%	

PDV

Cust_type N 8	Offer_dt N 8	Item_gp $ 8	Discount N 8
1040	.		.

31 ...

Execution: Formatted Input

```
data work.discounts;
   infile 'offers.dat';
   input @1 Cust_type 4.
         @5 Offer_dt mmddyy8.
         @14 Item_gp $8.
         @22 Discount percent3.;
run;
```

Load second value into the PDV

Input Buffer

```
                    1                   2
1 2 3 4 5 6 7 8 9 0 1 2 3 4 5 6 7 8 9 0 1 2 3 4 5
1 0 4 0 1 2 / 0 2 / 0 7   O u t d o o r s 1 5 %
```

PDV

Cust_type N 8	Offer_dt N 8	Item_gp $ 8	Discount N 8
1040	17502		.

32 ...

Execution: Formatted Input

```
data work.discounts;
   infile 'offers.dat';
   input @1 Cust_type 4.
         @5 Offer_dt mmddyy8.
         @14 Item_gp $8.
         @22 Discount percent3.;
run;
```

Load third value into the PDV

Input Buffer

```
                    1                   2
1 2 3 4 5 6 7 8 9 0 1 2 3 4 5 6 7 8 9 0 1 2 3 4 5
1 0 4 0 1 2 / 0 2 / 0 7   O u t d o o r s 1 5 %
```

PDV

Cust_type N 8	Offer_dt N 8	Item_gp $ 8	Discount N 8
1040	17502	Outdoors	.

33 ...

Execution: Formatted Input

```
data work.discounts;
   infile 'offers.dat';
   input @1 Cust_type 4.
         @5 Offer_dt mmddyy8.
         @14 Item_gp $8.
         @22 Discount percent3.;
run;
```

Load fourth value into the PDV

Input Buffer

```
                    1                   2
1 2 3 4 5 6 7 8 9 0 1 2 3 4 5 6 7 8 9 0 1 2 3 4 5
1 0 4 0 1 2 / 0 2 / 0 7   O u t d o o r s 1 5 %
```

PDV

Cust_type N 8	Offer_dt N 8	Item_gp $ 8	Discount N 8
1040	17502	Outdoors	.15

34 ...

Execution: Formatted Input

```
data work.discounts;
   infile 'offers.dat';
   input @1 Cust_type 4.
         @5 Offer_dt mmddyy8.
         @14 Item_gp $8.
         @22 Discount percent3.;
run;
```

Implicit OUTPUT;
Implicit RETURN;

Input Buffer

```
                    1                   2
1 2 3 4 5 6 7 8 9 0 1 2 3 4 5 6 7 8 9 0 1 2 3 4 5
1 0 4 0 1 2 / 0 2 / 0 7   O u t d o o r s 1 5 %
```

PDV

Cust_type N 8	Offer_dt N 8	Item_gp $ 8	Discount N 8
1040	17502	Outdoors	.15

35 ...

Execution: Formatted Input

```
data work.discounts;
   infile 'offers.dat';
   input @1 Cust_type 4.
         @5 Offer_dt mmddyy8.
         @14 Item_gp $8.
         @22 Discount percent3.;
run;
```

Continue until EOF

Input Buffer

1	2	3	4	5	6	7	8	9	10	1	2	3	4	5	6	7	8	9	20	1	2	3	4	5
3	0	1	0	0	5	/	1	7	/	0	7		C	l	o	t	h	e	s		1	5	%	

PDV

Cust_type N 8	Offer_dt N 8	Item_gp $ 8	Discount N 8
3010	17303	Clothes	.15

36

Read Discount Offers File – Output

```
proc print data=work.discounts noobs;
run;
```

Partial PROC PRINT Output

SAS Date Values

Cust_ type	Offer_dt	Item_gp	Discount
1040	17502	Outdoors	0.15
2020	17446	Golf	0.07
1030	17431	Shoes	0.10
1030	17431	Clothes	0.10
	.		
	.		
3010	17303	Clothes	0.15

37

Read Discount Offers File – Output

```
proc print data=work.discounts noobs;
   format Offer_dt date9.;
run;
```

Partial PROC PRINT Output

```
 Cust_
  type     Offer_dt     Item_gp     Discount

  1040    02DEC2007     Outdoors      0.15
  2020    07OCT2007     Golf          0.07
  1030    22SEP2007     Shoes         0.10
  1030    22SEP2007     Clothes       0.10
              .
              .
  3010    17MAY2007     Clothes       0.15
```

38

The FORMAT statement can also be used in the DATA step to permanently associate the DATE9. format with `Offer_dt`.

Exercises

Level 1

1. Using Formatted Input

The raw data file **sales1.dat** has employee information for the Australian and U.S. sales staff. The record layout is shown in the table below:

Layout for **sales1.dat**

	Field Description	Starting Column	Length of Field	Data Type
➡	Employee ID	1	6	Numeric
	First Name	8	12	Character
➡	Last Name	21	18	Character
	Gender	40	1	Character
➡	Job Title	43	20	Character
➡	Salary	64	8	Numeric $100,000
	Country	73	2	Character 'ZAU' or 'US'
	Birth Date	76	10	Numeric mm/dd/yyyy
➡	Hire Date	87	10	Numeric mm/dd/yyyy

a. Create a new SAS data set named **sales_staff** that contains the fields indicated by arrows in the layout table.

b. Print **sales_staff** and add an appropriate title.

Partial PROC PRINT Output (165 Total Observations)

```
                    Australian and US Sales Staff


   Employee_                                                       Hire_
      ID        Last_Name           Job_Title           Salary      Date

    120102      Zhou              Sales Manager         108255     10744
    120103      Dawes             Sales Manager          87975      5114
    120121      Elvish            Sales Rep. II          26600      5114
    120122      Ngan              Sales Rep. II          27475      6756
    120123      Hotstone          Sales Rep. I           26190     17440
    120124      Daymond           Sales Rep. I           26480     17226
```

Level 2

2. Using Formatted Input and the Subsetting IF Statement

The raw data file **sales1.dat** has employee information for the Australian and U.S. sales staff. The record layout is shown in the table below:

Layout for **sales1.dat**

	Field Description	Starting Column	Length of Field	Data Type
➡	Employee ID	1	6	Numeric
	First Name	8	12	Character
➡	Last Name	21	18	Character
	Gender	40	1	Character
➡	Job Title	43	20	Character
➡	Salary	64	8	Numeric $100,000
➡	Country	73	2	Character 'AU' or 'US'
	Birth Date	76	10	Numeric mm/dd/yyyy
➡	Hire Date	87	10	Numeric mm/dd/yyyy

a. Create two SAS data sets from the raw data file, and base them on the country of the trainee.

- Name the data sets **US_trainees** and **AU_trainees**. For this exercise, a trainee is anyone that has the job title of Sales Rep. I
- Each data set should contain the fields indicated by arrows in the layout table.
- Write only U.S. trainees to the **US_trainees** data set and only Australian trainees to the **AU_trainees** data set. Do **not** keep the **Country** variable in the output data sets.

b. Print both of the data sets with appropriate titles.

Partial PROC PRINT Output for **AU_trainees** (21 Total Observations)

```
                          Australian Trainees

  Employee_                                                Hire_
     ID         Last_Name        Job_Title       Salary     Date

   120123       Hotstone        Sales Rep. I      26190    17440
   120124       Daymond         Sales Rep. I      26480    17226
   120130       Lyon            Sales Rep. I      26955    17287
   120131       Surawski        Sales Rep. I      26910    17167
   120136       Leyden          Sales Rep. I      26605    17198
   120138       Duckett         Sales Rep. I      25795    17348
```

Partial PROC PRINT Output for **US_trainees** (42 Total Observations)

```
                              US Trainees

  Employee_                                                Hire_
     ID         Last_Name        Job_Title       Salary     Date

   121023       Fuller          Sales Rep. I      26010    17287
   121028       Smades          Sales Rep. I      26585    17471
   121029       Mcelwee         Sales Rep. I      27225    17501
   121030       Areu            Sales Rep. I      26745    17198
   121036       Mesley          Sales Rep. I      25965    17440
   121038       Anstey          Sales Rep. I      25285    17379
   121044       Abbott          Sales Rep. I      25660    17379
```

Level 3

3. **Using a Text String with Column Pointer Controls**

   - The raw data file **seminar.dat** contains comments and ratings from participants at a seminar given to Orion Star sales staff.
   - The data file contains one line for each participant:
     - The first 15 characters are reserved for the name of the participant (if given).
     - There can be a comment of up to 60 characters.
     - There will be the text Rating: immediately followed by a numeric score from 1 to 5.

Listing of **seminar.dat**

```
J. Mitchell         Very Well done!  Rating:5
Amy Jung            Rating:4
Carl Heisman        Rating:4
Linda Deal          Not enough give aways  Rating:3
Gabrielle Heron     Nice! Rating:4
                    Not helpful at all Rating:2
Kyle Patterson      Very good. Need more like it  Rating:5
```

   a. Create a new SAS data set named **seminar_ratings** that contains the names of the participants and the ratings that were given.

   b. Print the data set and give it an appropriate title.

PROC PRINT Output

```
          Names and Ratings

   Obs    Name                   Rating

    1     J. Mitchell              5
    2     Amy Jung                 4
    3     Carl Heisman             4
    4     Linda Deal               3
    5     Gabrielle Heron          4
    6                              2
    7     Kyle Patterson           5
```

4.2 Controlling When a Record Loads

Objectives

- Read a raw data file with multiple records per observation.
- Read a raw data file with mixed record types.
- Subset from a raw data file with mixed record types.

42

Business Scenario – Read Contacts Data

The raw data file **Address.dat** contains name, mailing address, and phone information.

Partial **Address.dat**

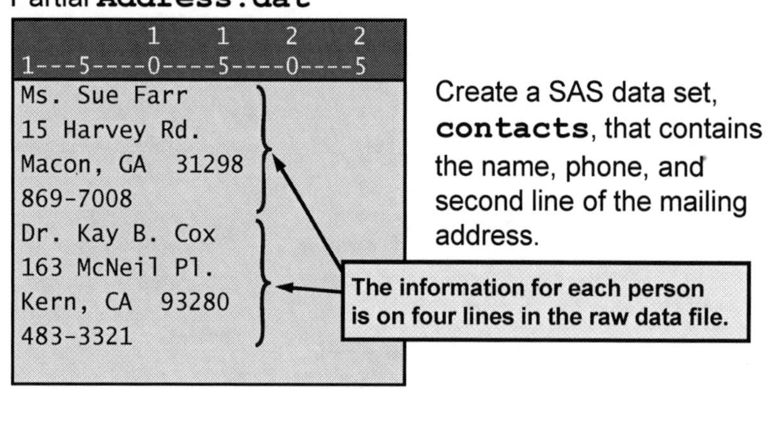

Create a SAS data set, **contacts**, that contains the name, phone, and second line of the mailing address.

43

Business Scenario – Desired Output

The **contacts** data set should have one observation per person.

Partial Listing of **contacts**

```
   FullName           Address2            Phone

Ms. Sue Farr      Macon, GA  31298      869-7008
Dr. Kay B. Cox    Kern, CA  93280       483-3321
Mr. Ron Mason     Miami, FL  33054      589-9030
Ms. G. H. Ruth    Munger, MI  48747     754-3582
```

44

Multiple INPUT Statements

By default, SAS loads a new record into the input buffer when it encounters an INPUT statement.

You can have multiple INPUT statements in one DATA step.

```
DATA SAS-data-set;
     INFILE 'raw-data-file-name';
     INPUT specifications;
     INPUT specifications;
     <additional SAS statements>
RUN;
```

Each INPUT statement ends with a semicolon.

45

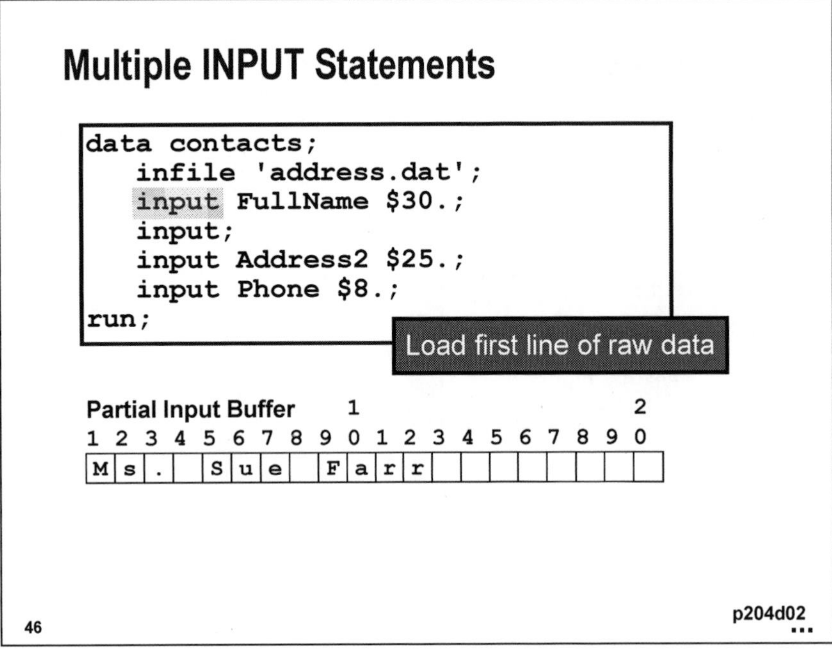
Multiple INPUT Statements
data contacts;
infile 'address.dat';
input FullName $30.;
input;
input Address2 $25.;
input Phone $8.;
run;
Load first line of raw data
Partial Input Buffer
1 2 3 4 5 6 7 8 9 0 1 2 3 4 5 6 7 8 9 0
M s .   S u e   F a r r
46
p204d02

By default, SAS begins reading each new line of raw data at position 1 of the input buffer, so having @1 in the INPUT statement is not necessary.

Multiple INPUT Statements

```
data contacts;
   infile 'address.dat';
   input FullName $30.;
   input;
   input Address2 $25.;
   input Phone $8.;
run;
```

Load second line of raw data

Partial Input Buffer

1	2	3	4	5	6	7	8	9	10	11	12	13	14	15	16	17	18	19	20
1	5		H	a	r	v	e	y		R	d	.							

Even though no variables are listed, the INPUT statement will still load the raw data line into the input buffer.

47

Multiple INPUT Statements

```
data contacts;
   infile 'address.dat';
   input FullName $30.;
   input;
   input Address2 $25.;
   input Phone $8.;
run;
```

Load third line of raw data

Partial Input Buffer

1	2	3	4	5	6	7	8	9	10	1	2	3	4	5	6	7	8	9	20
M	a	c	o	n	,		G	A		3	1	2	9	8					

48 ...

Multiple INPUT Statements

```
data contacts;
   infile 'address.dat';
   input FullName $30.;
   input;
   input Address2 $25.;
   input Phone $8.;
run;
```

Load fourth line of raw data

Partial Input Buffer

1	2	3	4	5	6	7	8	9	10	1	2	3	4	5	6	7	8	9	20
8	6	9	-	7	0	0	8												

49

Multiple INPUT Statements

Partial SAS Log

```
NOTE: 48 records were read from the infile 'address.dat'.
      The minimum record length was 18.
      The maximum record length was 30.
NOTE: The data set WORK.CONTACTS has 12 observations
      and 3 variables.
```

50

Multiple INPUT Statements

```
proc print data=contacts noobs;
run;
```

Partial PROC PRINT Output

```
      FullName            Address2             Phone

   Ms. Sue Farr       Macon, GA  31298      869-7008
   Dr. Kay B. Cox     Kern, CA  93280       483-3321
   Mr. Ron Mason      Miami, FL  33054      589-9030
   Ms. G. H. Ruth     Munger, MI  48747     754-3582
```

51

Line Pointer Controls

You can also use line pointer controls to control when SAS loads a new record.

```
DATA SAS-data-set;
     INFILE 'raw-data-file-name' ;
     INPUT specifications /
       specifications;
     <additional SAS statements>
RUN;
```

SAS loads the next record when it encounters a forward slash.

52

Line Pointer Controls

```
data contacts;
   infile 'address.dat';
   input FullName $30. / /
         Address2 $25. /
         Phone $8. ;
run;
```

Load first line of raw data

Partial Input Buffer

1	2	3	4	5	6	7	8	9	10	11	12	13	14	15	16	17	18	19	20
M	s	.		S	u	e		F	a	r	r								

53 p204d03

Line Pointer Controls

```
data contacts;
   infile 'address.dat';
   input FullName $30. / /
         Address2 $25. /
         Phone $8. ;
run;
```

Load second line of raw data

Partial Input Buffer

1	2	3	4	5	6	7	8	9	10	11	12	13	14	15	16	17	18	19	20
1	5		H	a	r	v	e	y		R	d	.							

54 ...

Line Pointer Controls

```
data contacts;
   infile 'address.dat';
   input FullName $30. / /
         Address2 $25. /
         Phone $8. ;
run;
```

Load third line of raw data

Partial Input Buffer

1	2	3	4	5	6	7	8	9	10	11	12	13	14	15	16	17	18	19	20
M	a	c	o	n	,		G	A		3	1	2	9	8					

55 ...

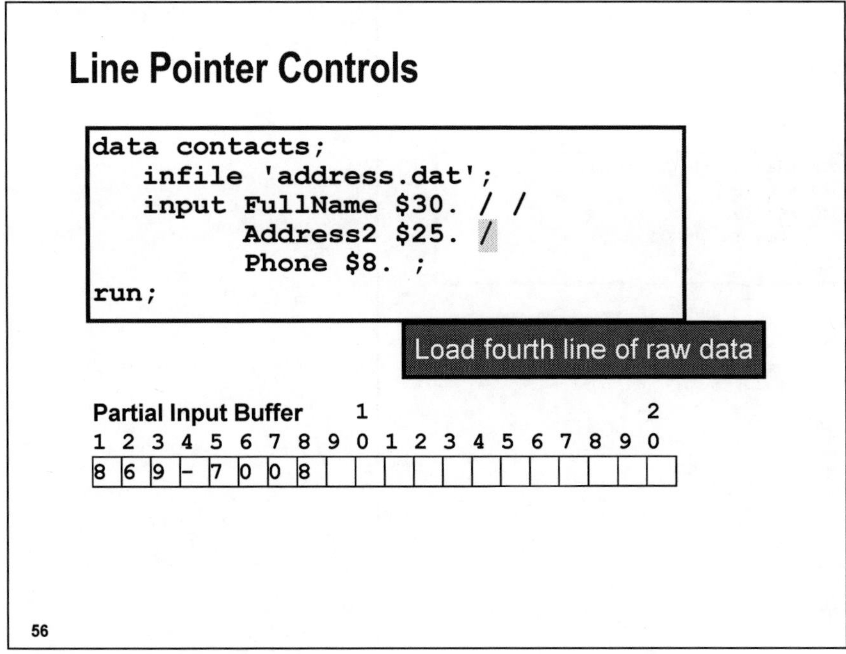

The forward slash is known as a *relative* line pointer control that moves the pointer relative to the line on which it currently positioned. There is also an *absolute* line pointer control that moves the pointer to a specific line in a group of lines. Here is an example.

```
data contacts;
   infile 'address.dat';
   input #1 FullName $30.
         #3 Address2 $25.
         #4 Phone $8.;
run;
```

See SAS Help and Documentation for more information about absolute line pointer controls.

Line Pointer Controls

Partial SAS Log

```
NOTE: 48 records were read from the infile 'address.dat'.
      The minimum record length was 18.
      The maximum record length was 30.
NOTE: The data set WORK.CONTACTS has 12 observations
      and 3 variables.
```

57

Line Pointer Controls

```
proc print data=contacts noobs;
run;
```

Partial PROC PRINT Output

FullName	Address2	Phone
Ms. Sue Farr	Macon, GA 31298	869-7008
Dr. Kay B. Cox	Kern, CA 93280	483-3321
Mr. Ron Mason	Miami, FL 33054	589-9030
Ms. G. H. Ruth	Munger, MI 48747	754-3582

58

4.05 Quiz

Using pen and paper, write an INPUT statement to read the data from the raw data file.

Raw Data

```
         1    1    2    2
1---5----0----5----0----5
10458Pine Mt. Sports
02/22/07 $2,405.50
00103RFG Textile Inc.
09/01/07 $1,095.30
24221Fifth Wheel Ltd.
06/04/07   $956.70
```

Line 1 Layout

Description	Column
Supplier Code	1- 5
Supplier Name	6-25

Line 2 Layout

Description	Column
Shipment Date	1- 8
Amount	10-18

✎ Supplier Code and Supplier Name contain character values.

60

Business Scenario – Read Top Sales Data

The raw data file, **sales.dat**, contains data about the largest sales made in the first quarter of 2007.

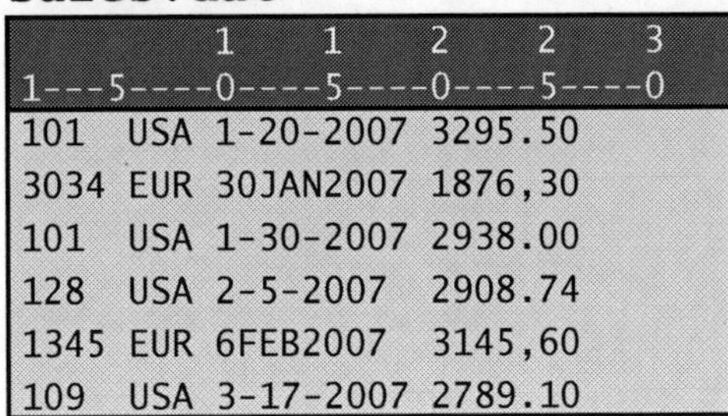

sales.dat

```
         1    1    2    2    3
1---5----0----5----0----5----0
101  USA 1-20-2007 3295.50
3034 EUR 30JAN2007 1876,30
101  USA 1-30-2007 2938.00
128  USA 2-5-2007  2908.74
1345 EUR 6FEB2007  3145,60
109  USA 3-17-2007 2789.10
```

Create a SAS data set, **salesQ1**, from the raw data in **sales.dat**.

63

Mixed Record Types

Not all records have the same format.

sales.dat

```
          1    1    2    2    3
1---5----0----5----0----5----0
101  USA 1-20-2007 3295.50
3034 EUR 30JAN2007 1876,30
101  USA 1-30-2007 2938.00
128  USA 2-5-2007  2908.74
1345 EUR 6FEB2007  3145,60
109  USA 3-17-2007 2789.10
```

The decimal places and commas are reversed for the U.S. and European sales figures, and the dates are represented differently.

64

Desired Output

Listing of **salesQ1**

Sale ID	Location	Sale Date	Amount
101	USA	17186	3295.50
3034	EUR	17196	1876.30
101	USA	17196	2938.00
128	USA	17202	2908.74
1345	EUR	17203	3145.60
109	USA	17242	2789.10

65

Mixed Record Types – First Attempt

This code is a good start to reading the mixed record types, but it gives unexpected results.

```
data salesQ1;
   infile 'sales.dat';
   input SaleID $4. @6 Location $3.;
   if Location='USA' then
      input @10 SaleDate mmddyy10.
            @20 Amount 7.;
   else if Location='EUR' then
      input @10 SaleDate date9.
            @20 Amount commax7.;
run;
```

66

p204d04

Execution: First Attempt

```
data salesQ1;
   infile 'sal
   input SaleI                 ation $3.;
   if Location='USA' then
      input @10 SaleDate mmddyy10.
            @20 Amount 7.;
   else if Location='EUR' then
      input @10 SaleDate date9.
            @20 Amount commax7.;
run;
```

Initialize PDV

Input Buffer

```
                  1                   2
1 2 3 4 5 6 7 8 9 0 1 2 3 4 5 6 7 8 9 0 1 2 3 4 5 6
```

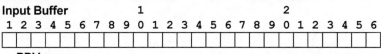

PDV

SaleID $ 4	Location $ 3	SaleDate N 8	Amount N 8
		.	.

67

...

Execution: First Attempt

```
data salesQ1;
   infile 'sales.dat';
   input SaleID $4. @6 Location $3.;
   if Location='USA' then
      input @10 SaleDate mmddyy10.
            @20 Amount 7.;
   else if Location='EUR' then
      input @10 SaleDate date9.
            @20 Amount commax7.;
run;
```

Specify input data file

Input Buffer

1	2	3	4	5	6	7	8	9	10	1	2	3	4	5	6	7	8	9	20	1	2	3	4	5	6

PDV

SaleID $ 4	Location $ 3	SaleDate N 8	Amount N 8
		.	.

68 ...

Execution: First Attempt

```
data salesQ1;
   infile 'sales.dat';
   input SaleID $4. @6 Location $3.;
   if Location='USA' then
      input @10 SaleDate mmddyy10.
            @20 Amount 7.;
   else if Location='EUR' then
      input @10 SaleDate date9.
            @20 Amount commax7.;
run;
```

Load the input buffer

Input Buffer

1	2	3	4	5	6	7	8	9	10	1	2	3	4	5	6	7	8	9	20	1	2	3	4	5	6
1	0	1			U	S	A		1	-	2	0	-	2	0	0	7		3	2	9	5	.	5	0

PDV

SaleID $ 4	Location $ 3	SaleDate N 8	Amount N 8
		.	.

69 ...

Execution: First Attempt

```
data salesQ1;
   infile 'sales.dat';
   input SaleID $4. @6 Location $3.;
   if Location='USA' then
      input @10 SaleD
            @20 Amoun
   else if Location='EUR' then
      input @10 SaleDate date9.
            @20 Amount commax7.;
run;
```

Load values into the PDV

Input Buffer

1	2	3	4	5	6	7	8	9	10	1	2	3	4	5	6	7	8	9	20	1	2	3	4	5	6
1	0	1			U	S	A		1	-	2	0	-	2	0	0	7		3	2	9	5	.	5	0

PDV

SaleID $ 4	Location $ 3	SaleDate N 8	Amount N 8
101	USA	.	.

70 ...

Execution: First Attempt

```
data salesQ1;
   infile 'sales.dat';
   input SaleID $4. @6 Location $3.;
   if Location='USA' then
      input @10 SaleDate mmddyy10.
            @20 Amount 7.;
   else if Location='EUR' then
      input @10 SaleDate date9.
            @20 Amount commax7.;
run;
```

True

Input Buffer

1	2	3	4	5	6	7	8	9	10	1	2	3	4	5	6	7	8	9	20	1	2	3	4	5	6
1	0	1			U	S	A		1	-	2	0	-	2	0	0	7		3	2	9	5	.	5	0

PDV

SaleID $ 4	Location $ 3	SaleDate N 8	Amount N 8
101	USA	.	.

71 ...

Execution: First Attempt

```
data salesQ1;
   infile 'sales.dat';
   input SaleID $4. @6 Location $3.;
   if Location='USA' then
      input @10 SaleDate mmddyy10.
            @20 Amount 7.;
   else if Location='EUR' then
      input @10 SaleDate
            @20 Amount commax7.;
run;
```

Load the input buffer

Input Buffer

1	2	3	4	5	6	7	8	9	10	11	12	13	14	15	16	17	18	19	20	21	22	23	24	25	26
3	0	3	4		E	U	R		3	0	J	A	N	2	0	0	7		1	8	7	6	,	3	0

PDV

SaleID $ 4	Location $ 3	SaleDate N 8	Amount N 8
101	USA	.	.

72 ...

Execution: First Attempt

```
data salesQ1;
   infile 'sales.dat';
   input SaleID $4. @6 Location $3.;
   if Location='USA' then
      input @10 SaleDate mmddyy10.
            @20 Amount 7.;
   else if Location='EUR' then
      input @10 SaleDate date9.
            @20 Amount commax7.;
run;
```

Invalid data message written to SAS log

Input Buffer

1	2	3	4	5	6	7	8	9	10	11	12	13	14	15	16	17	18	19	20	21	22	23	24	25	26
3	0	3	4		E	U	R		3	0	J	A	N	2	0	0	7		1	8	7	6	,	3	0

PDV

SaleID $ 4	Location $ 3	SaleDate N 8	Amount N 8
101	USA	.	.

73 ...

Execution: First Attempt

```
data salesQ1;
   infile 'sales.dat';
   input SaleID $4. @6 Location $3.;
   if Location='USA' then
      input @10 SaleDate mmddyy10.
            @20 Amount 7.;
   else if Location='EUR' then
      input @10 SaleDate
            @20 Amount c
run;
```

Implicit OUTPUT;
Implicit RETURN;

Input Buffer

1	2	3	4	5	6	7	8	9	10	1	2	3	4	5	6	7	8	9	20	1	2	3	4	5	6
3	0	3	4		E	U	R		3	0	J	A	N	2	0	0	7		1	8	7	6	,	3	0

PDV

SaleID $ 4	Location $ 3	SaleDate N 8	Amount N 8
101	USA	.	.

74 ...

Execution: First Attempt

```
data salesQ1;
   infile 'sales.dat';
   input SaleID $4. @6 Location $3.;
   if Location='USA' then
      input @10 SaleDate mmddyy10.
            @20 Amount 7.;
   else if Location='EUR' then
      input @10 SaleDate date9.
            @20 Amount commax7.;
run;
```

Continue until EOF

Input Buffer

1	2	3	4	5	6	7	8	9	10	1	2	3	4	5	6	7	8	9	20	1	2	3	4	5	6
3	0	3	4		E	U	R		3	0	J	A	N	2	0	0	7		1	8	7	6	,	3	0

PDV

SaleID $ 4	Location $ 3	SaleDate N 8	Amount N 8
101	USA	.	.

75

First Attempt – Unexpected Output

Partial SAS Log

```
NOTE: Invalid data for SaleDate in line 2 10-19.
NOTE: Invalid data for Amount in line 2 20-26.
RULE:     ----+----1----+----2----+----3----+----4----+----5----+
          3034 EUR 30JAN2007 1876,30
SaleID=101 Location=USA SaleDate=. Amount=. _ERROR_=1 _N_=1
       .
       .
NOTE: 6 records were read from the infile 'sales.dat'.
      The minimum record length was 26.
      The maximum record length was 27.
NOTE: The data set WORK.SALESQ1 has 3 observations and 4 variables.
```

76

First Attempt – Unexpected Output

```
proc print data=salesQ1 noobs;
run;
```

PROC PRINT Output

Sale ID	Location	Sale Date	Amount
101	USA	.	.
101	USA	17202	2908.74
1345	EUR	.	278910.00

To get the correct results, SAS needs some way to keep the second INPUT statement from moving to the next line of raw data.

77

The Single Trailing @

The single trailing @ holds a raw data record in the input buffer until SAS does one of the following:

- executes an INPUT statement with no trailing @
- begins the next iteration of the DATA step

General form of an INPUT statement with the single trailing @:

INPUT *specifications* ... @;

78

Normally, each INPUT statement in a DATA step reads a new data record into the input buffer. When you use a trailing @, the following occur:

- The pointer position does not change.
- No new record is read into the input buffer.
- The next INPUT statement for the same iteration of the DATA step continues to read the same record rather than a new one.

SAS releases a record held by a trailing @ when

- a null INPUT statement executes (`input;`)
- an INPUT statement without a trailing @ executes
- the next iteration of the DATA step begins.

Mixed Record Types – Correct Program

Adding the single trailing @ gives the correct output.

```
data salesQ1;
   infile 'sales.dat';
   input SaleID $4. @6 Location $3. @;
   if Location='USA' then
      input @10 SaleDate mmddyy10.
            @20 Amount 7.;
   else if Location='EUR' then
      input @10 SaleDate date9.
            @20 Amount commax7.;
run;
```

Partially stepping through the execution of the DATA step illustrates the effect of the trailing @.

79 p204d05

Execution: Correct Program

```
data salesQ1;
   infile 'sales.dat';
   input SaleID $4. @6 Location $3. @;
   if Location='USA' then
      input @10 SaleDate mmddyy10.
            @20 Amount 7.;
   else if Location='EUR' then
      input @10 SaleDate date9.
            @20 Amount commax7.;
run;
```

Load the input buffer

Input Buffer

1	2	3	4	5	6	7	8	9	10	1	2	3	4	5	6	7	8	9	20	1	2	3	4	5	6
1	0	1			U	S	A		1	-	2	0	-	2	0	0	7		3	2	9	5	.	5	0

PDV

SaleID $ 4	Location $ 3	SaleDate N 8	Amount N 8
		.	.

80 ...

Execution: Correct Program

```
data salesQ1;
   infile 'sales.dat';
   input SaleID $4. @6 Location $3. @;
   if Location='USA' then
      input @10 SaleD
            @20 Amoun
   else if Location='EUR' then
      input @10 SaleDate date9.
            @20 Amount commax7.;
run;
```

Load values into the PDV

Input Buffer

1	2	3	4	5	6	7	8	9	10	11	12	13	14	15	16	17	18	19	20	21	22	23	24	25	26
1	0	1			U	S	A		1	-	2	0	-	2	0	0	7		3	2	9	5	.	5	0

PDV

SaleID $ 4	Location $ 3	SaleDate N 8	Amount N 8
101	USA	.	.

81 ...

Execution: Correct Program

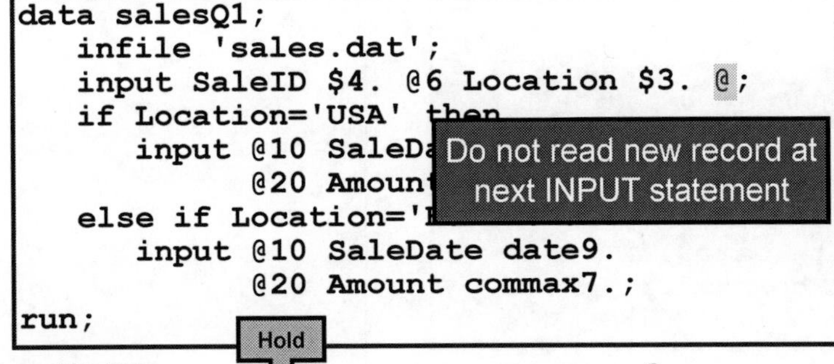

```
data salesQ1;
   infile 'sales.dat';
   input SaleID $4. @6 Location $3. @;
   if Location='USA' then
      input @10 SaleD
            @20 Amoun
   else if Location='E
      input @10 SaleDate date9.
            @20 Amount commax7.;
run;
```

Do not read new record at next INPUT statement
Hold

Input Buffer

1	2	3	4	5	6	7	8	9	10	11	12	13	14	15	16	17	18	19	20	21	22	23	24	25	26
1	0	1			U	S	A		1	-	2	0	-	2	0	0	7		3	2	9	5	.	5	0

PDV

SaleID $ 4	Location $ 3	SaleDate N 8	Amount N 8
101	USA	.	.

82 ...

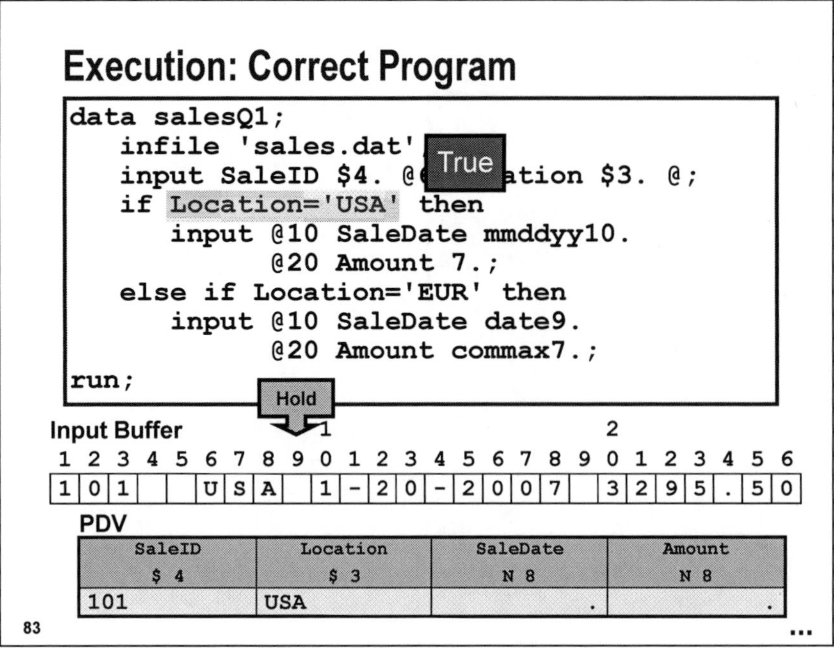
Execution: Correct Program
data salesQ1;
infile 'sales.dat';
input SaleID $4. @ ation $3. @;
True
if Location='USA' then
input @10 SaleDate mmddyy10.
@20 Amount 7.;
else if Location='EUR' then
input @10 SaleDate date9.
@20 Amount commax7.;
run;
Hold
Input Buffer
1 2
1 2 3 4 5 6 7 8 9 0 1 2 3 4 5 6 7 8 9 0 1 2 3 4 5 6
1 0 1 U S A 1 - 2 0 - 2 0 0 7 3 2 9 5 . 5 0
PDV
SaleID $ 4
Location $ 3
SaleDate N 8
Amount N 8
101
USA
.
.
83
...

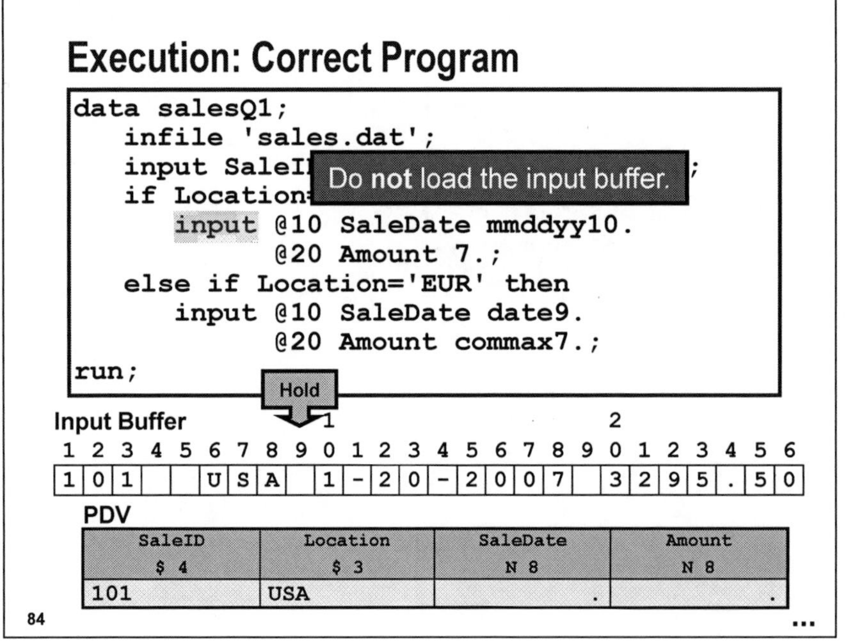
Execution: Correct Program
data salesQ1;
infile 'sales.dat';
input SaleI ;
if Location
Do not load the input buffer.
input @10 SaleDate mmddyy10.
@20 Amount 7.;
else if Location='EUR' then
input @10 SaleDate date9.
@20 Amount commax7.;
run;
Hold
Input Buffer
1 2
1 2 3 4 5 6 7 8 9 0 1 2 3 4 5 6 7 8 9 0 1 2 3 4 5 6
1 0 1 U S A 1 - 2 0 - 2 0 0 7 3 2 9 5 . 5 0
PDV
SaleID $ 4
Location $ 3
SaleDate N 8
Amount N 8
101
USA
.
.
84
...

Execution: Correct Program

```
data salesQ1;
   infile 'sales.dat';
   input SaleID $4. @6 Location $3. @;
   if Location='USA' then
      input @10 SaleDate mmddyy10.
            @20 Amount 7.;
   else if Location='EUR' then
      input @10 SaleDate date9.
            @20 Amount commax7.;
run;
```

Input Buffer

1	2	3	4	5	6	7	8	9	10	1	2	3	4	5	6	7	8	9	20	1	2	3	4	5	6
1	0	1			U	S	A		1	-	2	0	-	2	0	0	7		3	2	9	5	.	5	0

PDV

SaleID $ 4	Location $ 3	SaleDate N 8	Amount N 8
101	USA	17186	3295.50

85 ...

Execution: Correct Program

```
data salesQ1;
   infile 'sales.dat';
   input SaleID $4. @6 Location $3. @;
   if Location='USA' then
      input @10 SaleDate mmddyy10.
            @20 Amount 7.;
   else if Location='EUR' then
      input @10 SaleDate date9.
            @20 Amount commax7.;
run;
```

Continue until EOF

Input Buffer

1	2	3	4	5	6	7	8	9	10	1	2	3	4	5	6	7	8	9	20	1	2	3	4	5	6
1	0	1			U	S	A		1	-	2	0	-	2	0	0	7		3	2	9	5	.	5	0

PDV

SaleID $ 4	Location $ 3	SaleDate N 8	Amount N 8
101	USA	17186	3295.50

86

Correct Program – Output

Partial SAS Log

```
NOTE: 6 records were read from the infile 'sales.dat'.
      The minimum record length was 26.
      The maximum record length was 27.
NOTE: The data set WORK.SALESQ1 has 6 observations and 4 variables.
```

PROC PRINT Output

Sale ID	Location	Sale Date	Amount
101	USA	17186	3295.50
3034	EUR	17196	1876.30
101	USA	17196	2938.00
128	USA	17202	2908.74
1345	EUR	17203	3145.60
109	USA	17242	2789.10

87

Subsetting Mixed Record Types

Create a SAS data set, **EuropeQ1**, that contains only the European observations.

sales.dat

```
         1    1    2    2    3
1---5----0----5----0----5----0
101  USA 1-20-2007 3295.50
3034 EUR 30JAN2007 1876,30
101  USA 1-30-2007 2938.00
128  USA 2-5-2007  2908.74
1345 EUR 6FEB2007  3145,60
109  USA 3-17-2007 2789.10
```

89

Desired Output

Listing of **EuropeQ1**

Sale ID	Location	Sale Date	Amount
3034	EUR	17196	1876.3
1345	EUR	17203	3145.6

Adding a subsetting IF statement to the SAS program from the previous example produces this output.

90

4.06 Quiz

Is this the best placement for the subsetting IF statement?

```
data EuropeQ1;
   infile 'sales.dat';
   input SaleID $4. @6 Location $3. @;
   if Location='USA' then
      input @10 SaleDate mmddyy10.
            @20 Amount 7.;
   else if Location='EUR' then
      input @10 SaleDate date9.
            @20 Amount commax7.;
   if Location = 'EUR';
run;
```

92 p204d06

Placement of the Subsetting IF Statement

Generally, the most efficient place to put the subsetting IF statement is as soon as all the variables that are needed to evaluate the condition are assigned values.

```
data EuropeQ1;
   infile 'sales.dat';
   input @6 Location $3. @;
   if Location = 'EUR';
   input  @1 SaleID $4.
         @10 SaleDate date9.
         @20 Amount commax7.;
run;
```

94

p204d07

SAS releases a record held by a trailing @ when the next iteration of the DATA step begins.

Subsetting Mixed Record Types – Output

```
proc print data=EuropeQ1 noobs;
   var SaleID Location SaleDate Amount;
run;
```

PROC PRINT Output

Sale ID	Location	Sale Date	Amount
3034	EUR	17196	1876.3
1345	EUR	17203	3145.6

95

Exercises

Level 1

4. Reading Multiple Input Records per Observation

- The raw data file **sales2.dat** has employee information for the Australian and U.S. sales staff.
- Information for each employee is in three lines of raw data.
- The record layouts are shown below.

Line 1 layout

	Field Description	Starting Column	Length of Field	Data Type
➡	Employee ID	1	6	Numeric
	First Name	8	12	Character
➡	Last Name	21	18	Character

Line 2 layout

	Field Description	Starting Column	Length of Field	Data Type
➡	Job Title	1	20	Character
➡	Hire Date	22	10	Numeric mm/dd/yyyy
➡	Salary	33	8	Numeric for example, $100,000

Line 3 layout

Field Description	Starting Column	Length of Field	Data Type
Gender	1	1	Character
Birth Date	3	10	Numeric mm/dd/yyyy
Country	14	2	Character

a. Create a new SAS data set named **sales_staff2** that contains the fields indicated by arrows in the layout table.

b. Print **sales_staff2** and add an appropriate title.

Partial PROC PRINT Output (165 Total Observations)

```
                    Australian and US Sales Staff

  Employee_                                        Hire_
     ID       Last_Name         Job_Title          Date     Salary

   120102     Zhou            Sales Manager       10744     108255
   120103     Dawes           Sales Manager        5114      87975
   120121     Elvish          Sales Rep. II        5114      26600
   120122     Ngan            Sales Rep. II        6756      27475
   120123     Hotstone        Sales Rep. I        17440      26190
   120124     Daymond         Sales Rep. I        17226      26480
```

Level 2

5. Working with Mixed Record Types

- The raw data file **sales3.dat** has employee information for the Australian and U.S. Ssales staff.
- Information for each employee is in two lines of raw data.
- The record layouts are shown below.

Line 1 layout

	Field Description	Starting Column	Length of Field	Data Type
➡	Employee ID	1	6	Numeric
	First Name	8	12	Character
➡	Last Name	21	18	Character
	Gender	40	1	Character
➡	Job Title	43	20	Character

Line 2 layout for Australian employees

	Field Description	Starting Column	Length of Field	Data Type
➡	Salary	1	8	Numeric $100,000
➡	Country	10	2	Character
	Birth Date	13	10	Numeric dd/mm/yyyy
➡	Hire Date	24	10	Numeric dd/mm/yyyy

Line 2 layout for U.S. employees

	Field Description	Starting Column	Length of Field	Data Type
➡	Salary	1	8	Numeric $100,000
➡	Country	10	2	Character
	Birth Date	13	10	Numeric mm/dd/yyyy
➡	Hire Date	24	10	Numeric mm/dd/yyyy

a. Create two new SAS data sets, **US_sales** and **AU_sales**, that contain the fields indicated by arrows in the layout table. Write only U.S. employees to the **US_sales** data set and only Australian employees to the **AU_sales** data set. Do **not** include the **Country** variable in the output data sets.

> The salary and hire date values are different for Australian and U.S. employees. Be sure to use the correct informats in each INPUT statement.

b. Print both of the data sets with appropriate titles.

Partial PROC PRINT Output for **AU_sales** (63 Total Observations)

```
                   Australian Sales Staff

Employee_                                                  Hire_
   ID        Last_Name         Job_Title          Salary    Date

  120102     Zhou            Sales Manager       108255    10744
  120103     Dawes           Sales Manager        87975     5114
  120121     Elvish          Sales Rep. II        26600     5114
  120122     Ngan            Sales Rep. II        27475     6756
  120123     Hotstone        Sales Rep. I         26190    17440
  120124     Daymond         Sales Rep. I         26480    17226
  120125     Hofmeister      Sales Rep. IV        32040     6999
```

Partial PROC PRINT Output for **US_sales** (102 Total Observations)

```
                         US Sales Staff

Employee_                                                            Hire_
   ID        Last_Name           Job_Title                Salary      Date

  120261     Highpoint           Chief Sales Officer      243190     10074
  121018     Magolan             Sales Rep. II             27560      5114
  121019     Desanctis           Sales Rep. IV             31320     16223
  121020     Ridley              Sales Rep. IV             31750     15461
  121021     Farren              Sales Rep. IV             32985     12478
  121022     Stevens             Sales Rep. IV             32210     15372
  121023     Fuller              Sales Rep. I              26010     17287
  121024     Westlund            Sales Rep. II             26600     16192
```

4.3 Additional Techniques for List Input (Self-Study)

Objectives

Read delimited raw data files with any of these special characteristics:

- missing data at the end of a record
- missing data represented by consecutive delimiters
- multiple observations per record

99

Reading Delimited Data Files (Review)

Characteristics of delimited data files:

- Data values are separated by a delimiting character.
- The delimiting character can be a blank, tab, comma, or any other character.

Example: Delimited Raw Data File

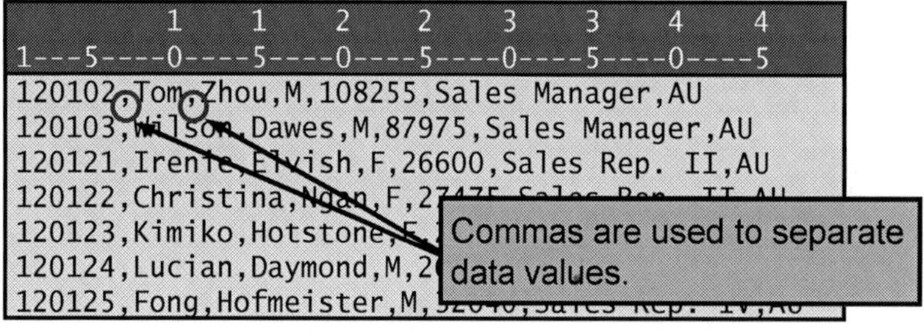

1 1 2 2 3 3 4 4
1---5----0----5----0----5----0----5----0----5
120102,Tom,Zhou,M,108255,Sales Manager,AU
120103,Wilson,Dawes,M,87975,Sales Manager,AU
120121,Irenie,Elvish,F,26600,Sales Rep. II,AU
120122,Christina,Ngan,F,2
120123,Kimiko,Hotstone,F,
120124,Lucian,Daymond,M,2
120125,Fong,Hofmeister,M,
Commas are used to separate data values.

100

Specifying the Delimiter (Review)

A blank is the default delimiter.

The DLM= options can be added to the INFILE statement to specify an alternative delimiter.

General DATA step syntax to use list input for reading comma-delimited files:

```
DATA output-SAS-data-set;
     LENGTH variable(s) $ length;
     INFILE 'raw-data-file-name' DLM=',';
     INPUT variable-1 <$>
           <variable-2 <$>...variable-n>;
     <additional SAS statements>
RUN;
```

101

Example of Reading Comma-Delimited Data

Create a SAS data set named `work.sales` from the raw data file `sales.csv`. This is a comma-delimited file and the table below lists the variables to read from each line of raw data. The values for the variables appear on the raw data lines in the order that they are listed in the table. There are more values at the end of the raw data lines, but they are not to be read as part of `work.sales`.

Variable	Type	Length for Character Variables
`Employee_ID`	Numeric	
`First_Name`	Character	12
`Last_Name`	Character	18
`Gender`	Character	1
`Salary`	Numeric	
`Job_Title`	Character	25
`Country`	Character	2

SAS Program to Create and Print **work.sales**:

```
data work.sales;
   length First_Name $ 12 Last_Name $ 18
          Gender $ 1 Job_Title $ 25
          Country $ 2;
   infile 'sales.csv' dlm=',';
   input Employee_ID First_Name $ Last_Name $
         Gender $ Salary Job_Title $ Country $;
run;

proc print data=work.sales;
   var Employee_ID First_Name Last_Name
       Gender Salary Job_Title Country;
run;
```

This program can be found in the file **p204d08**.

Partial PROC PRINT Output (165 Total Observations)

Obs	Employee_ ID	First_ Name	Last_Name	Gender	Salary	Job_Title	Country
1	120102	Tom	Zhou	M	108255	Sales Manager	AU
2	120103	Wilson	Dawes	M	87975	Sales Manager	AU
3	120121	Irenie	Elvish	F	26600	Sales Rep. II	AU
4	120122	Christina	Ngan	F	27475	Sales Rep. II	AU
5	120123	Kimiko	Hotstone	F	26190	Sales Rep. I	AU
6	120124	Lucian	Daymond	M	26480	Sales Rep. I	AU
7	120125	Fong	Hofmeister	M	32040	Sales Rep. IV	AU

Additional Techniques for List Input

Additional techniques are needed if the raw data file has any of the following special characteristics:

- missing data at the end of a record
- missing data represented by consecutive delimiters
- multiple observations per record

Each of these special cases is explored through separate business scenarios.

102

Business Scenario – Read Contact Data

The raw data file **phone.csv** contains contact names and phone numbers for Orion customers.

Create a new SAS data set, **contacts**, by reading the raw data file.

phone.csv

```
         1    1    2    2    3    3    4    4
1---5----0----5----0----5----0----5----0----5
James Kvarniq,(704) 293-8126,(701) 281-8923
Sandrina Stephano,(919) 871-7830
Cornelia Krahl,(212) 891-3241,(212) 233-5413
Karen Ballinger,(714) 344-4321
Elke Wallstab,(910) 763-5561,(910) 545-3421
```

103

Missing Values at the End of a Record

The data values in **phone.csv** are separated by commas. Each record has a contact name, then a phone number, and finally a mobile number.

phone.csv

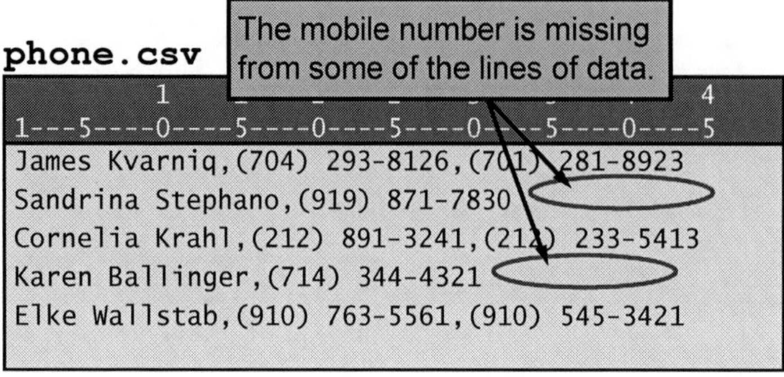
The mobile number is missing from some of the lines of data.
1 4
1---5----0----5----0----5----0----5----0----5
James Kvarniq,(704) 293-8126,(701) 281-8923
Sandrina Stephano,(919) 871-7830
Cornelia Krahl,(212) 891-3241,(212) 233-5413
Karen Ballinger,(714) 344-4321
Elke Wallstab,(910) 763-5561,(910) 545-3421

104

4.07 Quiz

Open and submit **p204a01**. Examine the SAS log. How many input records were read and how many observations were created?

```
data contacts;
   length Name $ 20 Phone Mobile $ 14;
   infile 'phone.csv' dlm=',';
   input Name $ Phone $ Mobile $;
run;

proc print data=contacts noobs;
run;
```

106 p204a01

Unexpected Results

The missing mobile phone numbers have caused unexpected results in the output.

PROC PRINT output

```
      Name                 Phone             Mobile

  James Kvarniq         (704) 293-8126    (701) 281-8923
  Sandrina Stephano     (919) 871-7830    Cornelia Krahl
  Karen Ballinger       (714) 344-4321    Elke Wallstab
```

Partial SAS Log

```
NOTE: 5 records were read from the infile 'phone.csv'.
      The minimum record length was 31.
      The maximum record length was 44.
NOTE: SAS went to a new line when INPUT statement
reached past the end of a line.
NOTE: The data set WORK.CONTACTS has 3 observations and
3 variables.
```

108

Missing Values at the End of a Record

By default, when there is missing data at the end of a row, SAS does the following:

- loads the next record to finish the observation
- writes a note to the log

109

The MISSOVER Option

The MISSOVER option prevents SAS from loading a new record when the end of the current record is reached.

General form of an INFILE statement with a MISSOVER option:

INFILE *'raw-data-file'* MISSOVER;

If SAS reaches the end of the row without finding values for all fields, variables without values are set to missing.

110

4.08 Quiz

Open **p204a02** and add the MISSOVER option to the INFILE statement. Submit the program and examine the SAS log. How many input records were read and how many observations were created?

```
data contacts;
   length Name $ 20 Phone Mobile $ 14;
   infile 'phone.csv' dlm=',';
   input Name $ Phone $ Mobile $;
run;

proc print data=contacts noobs;
run;
```

112 p204a02

Results

Adding the MISSOVER option gives the expected results.

PROC PRINT Output

```
        Name                   Phone              Mobile

James Kvarniq          (704) 293-8126     (701) 281-8923
Sandrina Stephano      (919) 871-7830
Cornelia Krahl         (212) 891-3241     (212) 233-5413
Karen Ballinger        (714) 344-4321
Elke Wallstab          (910) 763-5561     (910) 545-3421
```

Partial SAS Log

```
NOTE: 5 records were read from the infile 'phone.csv'.
      The minimum record length was 31.
      The maximum record length was 44.
NOTE: The data set WORK.CONTACTS has 5 observations and
3 variables.
```

114

Missing Values before the End of the Record

Each record in **phone2.csv** has a contact name, phone number, and a mobile number. The phone number is missing from some of the records.

Missing data is indicated by two consecutive delimiters.

phone2.csv

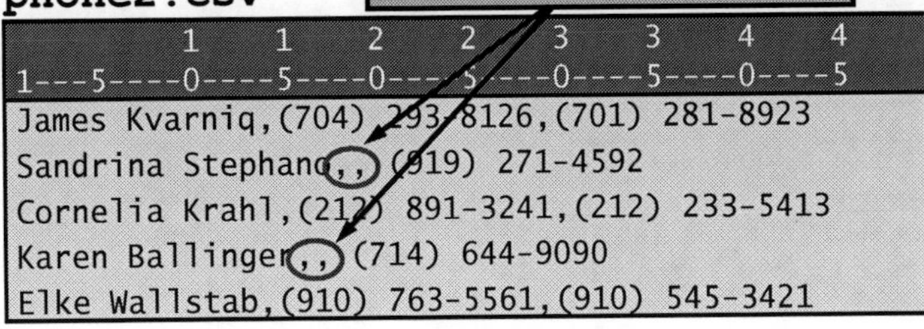

```
         1    1    2    2    3    3    4    4
1---5----0----5----0----5----0----5----0----5
James Kvarniq,(704) 293-8126,(701) 281-8923
Sandrina Stephano,,(919) 271-4592
Cornelia Krahl,(212) 891-3241,(212) 233-5413
Karen Ballinger,,(714) 644-9090
Elke Wallstab,(910) 763-5561,(910) 545-3421
```

116

4.09 Quiz

Open and submit **p204a03**. Examine the SAS log. How many input records were read and how many observations were created?

```
data contacts;
   length Name $ 20 Phone Mobile $ 14;
   infile 'phone2.csv' dlm=',';
   input Name $ Phone $ Mobile $;
run;

proc print data=contacts noobs;
run;
```

118 p204a03

Unexpected Results

The missing phone numbers have caused unexpected results in the output.

PROC PRINT Output

Name	Phone	Mobile
James Kvarniq	(704) 293-8126	(701) 281-8923
Sandrina Stephano	(919) 271-4592	Cornelia Krahl
Karen Ballinger	(714) 644-9090	Elke Wallstab

Partial SAS Log

```
NOTE: 5 records were read from the infile 'phone2.csv'.
      The minimum record length was 31.
      The maximum record length was 44.
NOTE: SAS went to a new line when INPUT statement reached
past the end of a line.
NOTE: The data set WORK.CONTACTS has 3 observations and 3
variables.
```

120

Consecutive Delimiters in List Input

By default, list input treats two or more consecutive delimiters as a single delimiter and they are not treated as a missing value.

The two consecutive commas are not being read as a missing value.

phone2.csv

```
         1    1    2    2    3    3    4    4
1---5----0----5----0----5----0----5----0----5
James Kvarniq,(704) 293-8126,(701) 281-8923
Sandrina Stephano,,(919) 271-4592
Cornelia Krahl,(212) 891-3241,(212) 233-5413
Karen Ballinger,,(714) 644-9090
Elke Wallstab,(910) 763-5561,(910) 545-3421
```

121

The DSD Option

The DSD option for the INFILE statement

- sets the default delimiter to a comma
- treats consecutive delimiters as missing values
- enables SAS to read values with embedded delimiters if the value is surrounded by quotation marks.

General form of a DSD option in an INFILE statement:

INFILE '*file-name*' DSD;

122

Using the DSD Option

Adding the DSD option will correctly read the **phone2.csv** data file.

```
data contacts;
   length Name $ 20 Phone Mobile $ 14;
   infile 'phone2.csv' dsd;
   input Name $ Phone $ Mobile $;
run;

proc print data=contacts noobs;
run;
```

✎ The DLM=',' option is no longer needed in the INFILE statement because the DSD option sets the default delimiter to a comma.

123 p204d09

Results

Adding the DSD option gives the expected results.

PROC PRINT Output

Name	Phone	Mobile
James Kvarniq	(704) 293-8126	(701) 281-8923
Sandrina Stephano		(919) 271-4592
Cornelia Krahl	(212) 891-3241	(212) 233-5413
Karen Ballinger		(714) 644-9090
Elke Wallstab	(910) 763-5561	(910) 545-3421

Partial SAS Log

```
NOTE: 5 records were read from the infile 'phone2.csv'.
      The minimum record length was 31.
      The maximum record length was 44.
NOTE: The data set WORK.CONTACTS has 5 observations and
3 variables.
```

124

Business Scenario – Read Charity Donations

The raw data file **charity.dat** contains data about donations made in 2007. The information for each donation consists of a charity ID and an amount.

Create a SAS data set, **donate07**, from the raw data in **charity.dat**.

charity.dat

```
         1    1    2    2    3
1---5----0----5----0----5----0
 AQI  495  CCI  200  CNI 249
CS  279  CU  780   DAI
875 ES  290  FFC 0  MI 745
SBA 900 V2 550 YYCR 0
```

126

Business Scenario – Desired Output

The output SAS data set should have one observation per donation.

Partial Listing of **donate07**

ID	Amount
AQI	495
CCI	200
CNI	249
CS	279
CU	780
DAI	875

127

Processing: What Is Required?

charity.dat

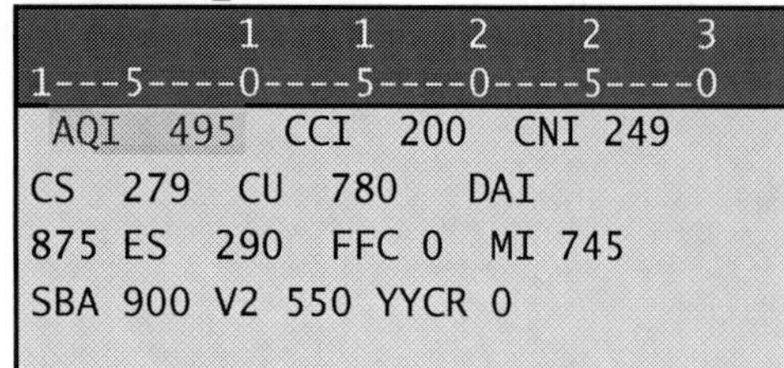
```
         1    1    2    2    3
1---5----0----5----0----5----0
 AQI  495  CCI  200  CNI 249
CS  279  CU  780   DAI
875 ES  290  FFC 0  MI 745
SBA 900 V2 550 YYCR 0
```

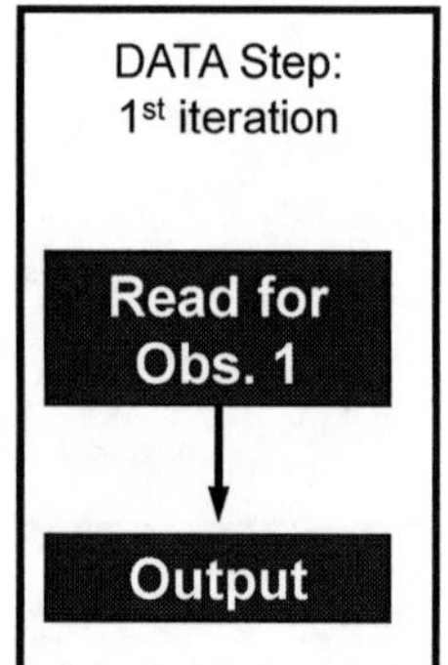

Each raw data line contains information for multiple donations.

Each iteration of the DATA step must read data for one donation.

128

Processing: What Is Required?

charity.dat

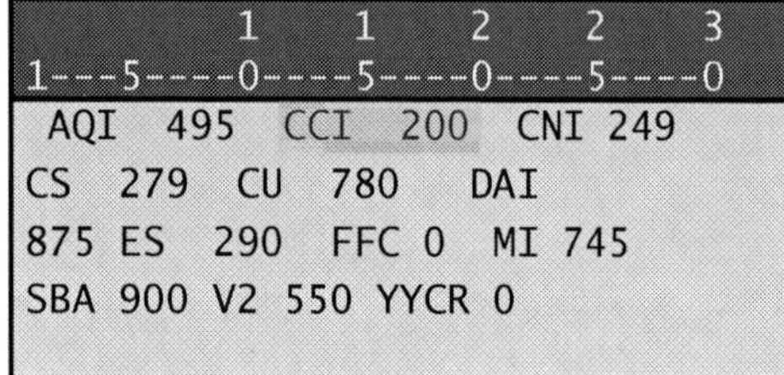
```
         1    1    2    2    3
1---5----0----5----0----5----0
 AQI  495  CCI  200  CNI 249
CS  279  CU  780   DAI
875 ES  290  FFC 0  MI 745
SBA 900 V2 550 YYCR 0
```

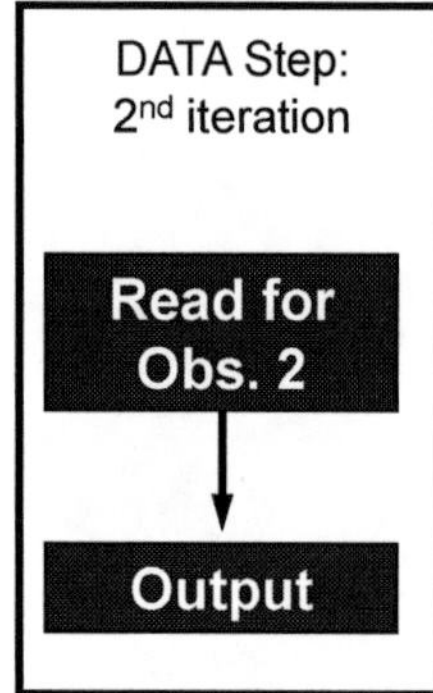

To do this kind of processing, SAS needs to use the same raw data line in several iterations of the DATA step.

129

Processing: What Is Required?

charity.dat

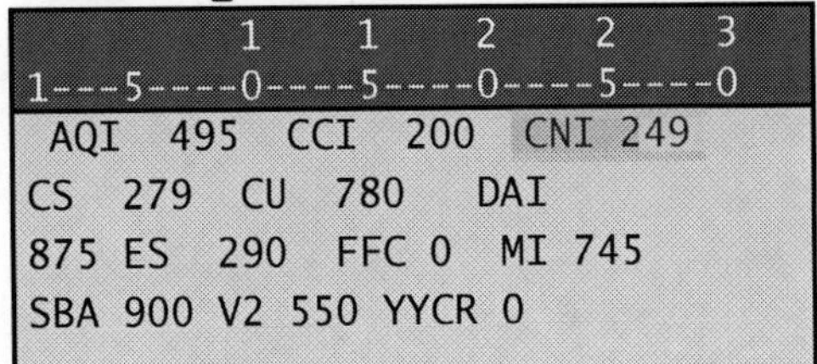

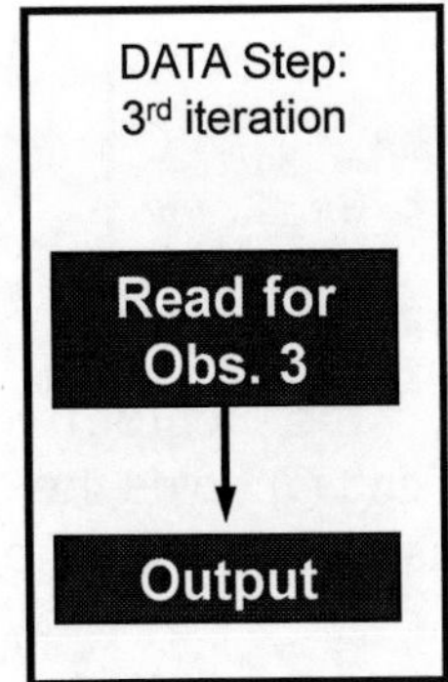

130

The Double Trailing @

The *double trailing @* holds the raw data record across iterations of the DATA step until the line pointer moves past the end of the line.

INPUT *var1 var2 var3 …* @@;

The double trailing @ should only be used with list input.

131

The Double Trailing @

```
data donate07;
   length ID $ 4;
   infile 'charity.dat';
   input ID $ Amount @@;
run;
```

Stepping through the execution of the program will illustrate how the double trailing @ holds the raw data record across iterations of the DATA step.

132

p204d10

Execution: The Double Trailing @

```
data donate07;
   length ID $ 4;
   infile 'charity.dat';
   input ID $ Amount @@;
run;
```

Initialize PDV

Input Buffer

```
                  1                   2
1 2 3 4 5 6 7 8 9 0 1 2 3 4 5 6 7 8 9 0 1 2 3 4 5 6 7 8 9
```

PDV

ID $ 4	Amount N 8
	.

133

...

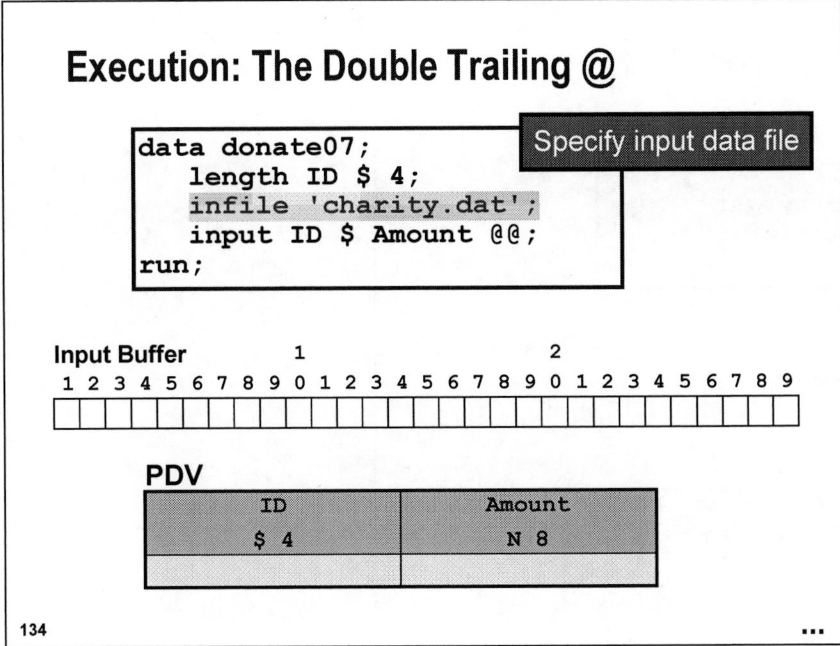
Execution: The Double Trailing @
data donate07;
length ID $ 4;
infile 'charity.dat';
input ID $ Amount @@;
run;
Specify input data file
Input Buffer
1 2
1 2 3 4 5 6 7 8 9 0 1 2 3 4 5 6 7 8 9 0 1 2 3 4 5 6 7 8 9
PDV
ID
$ 4
Amount
N 8
134
...

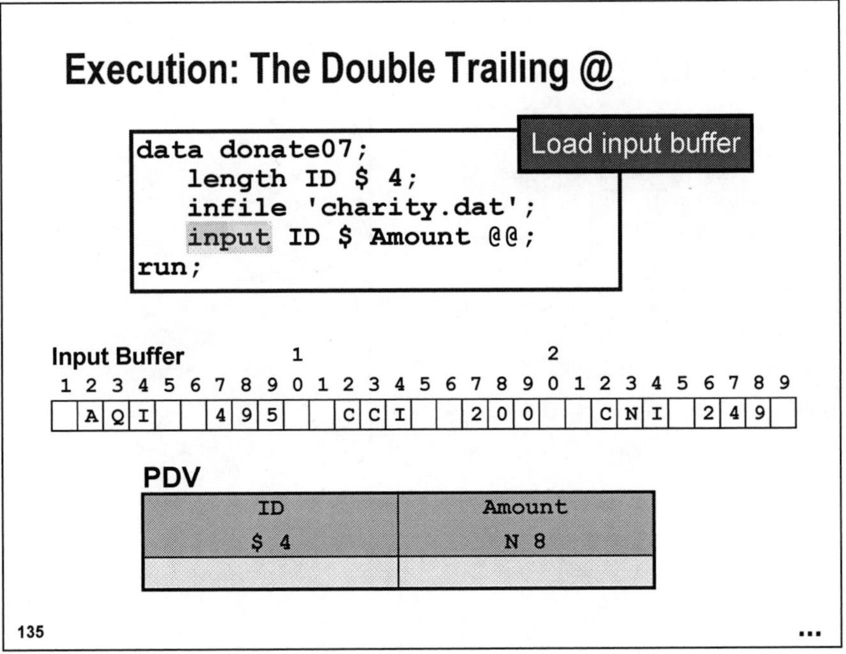
Execution: The Double Trailing @
data donate07;
length ID $ 4;
infile 'charity.dat';
input ID $ Amount @@;
run;
Load input buffer
Input Buffer
1 2
1 2 3 4 5 6 7 8 9 0 1 2 3 4 5 6 7 8 9 0 1 2 3 4 5 6 7 8 9
A Q I 4 9 5 C C I 2 0 0 C N I 2 4 9
PDV
ID
$ 4
Amount
N 8
135
...

Execution: The Double Trailing @

```
data donate07;
   length ID $ 4;
   infile 'charity.dat';
   input ID $ Amount @@;
run;
```

Input Buffer

```
          1                   2
1234567890123456789012345678 9
 AQI  495  CCI  200  CNI  249
```

PDV

ID $ 4	Amount N 8
AQI	495

136 ...

Execution: The Double Trailing @

Hold record in the input buffer

```
data donate07;
   length ID $ 4;
   infile 'charity.dat';
   input ID $ Amount @@;
run;
```

Hold

Input Buffer

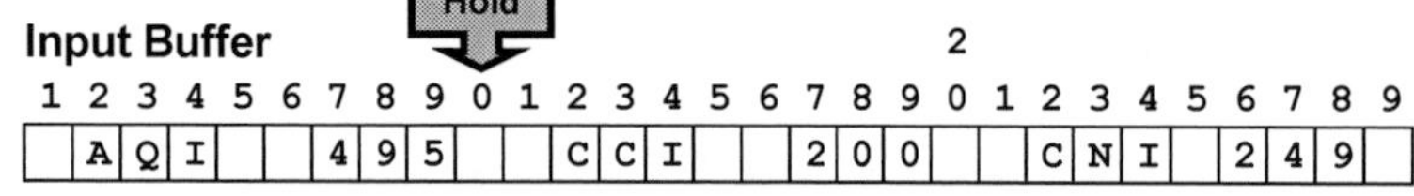

2

PDV

ID $ 4	Amount N 8
AQI	495

137 ...

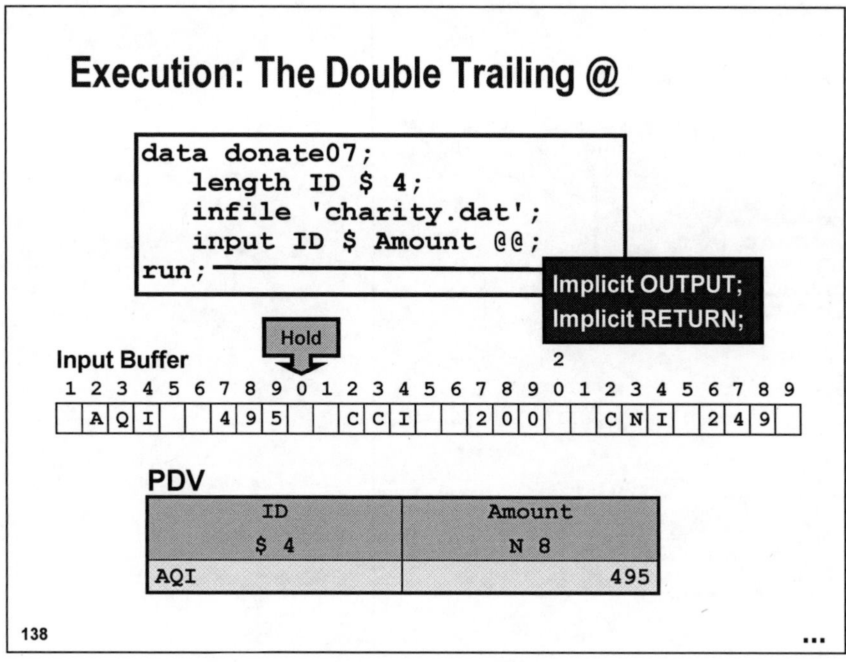
Execution: The Double Trailing @
data donate07;
length ID $ 4;
infile 'charity.dat';
input ID $ Amount @@;
run;
Implicit OUTPUT;
Implicit RETURN;
Hold
Input Buffer
2
1 2 3 4 5 6 7 8 9 0 1 2 3 4 5 6 7 8 9 0 1 2 3 4 5 6 7 8 9
A Q I 4 9 5 C C I 2 0 0 C N I 2 4 9
PDV
ID
$ 4
Amount
N 8
AQI
495
138
...

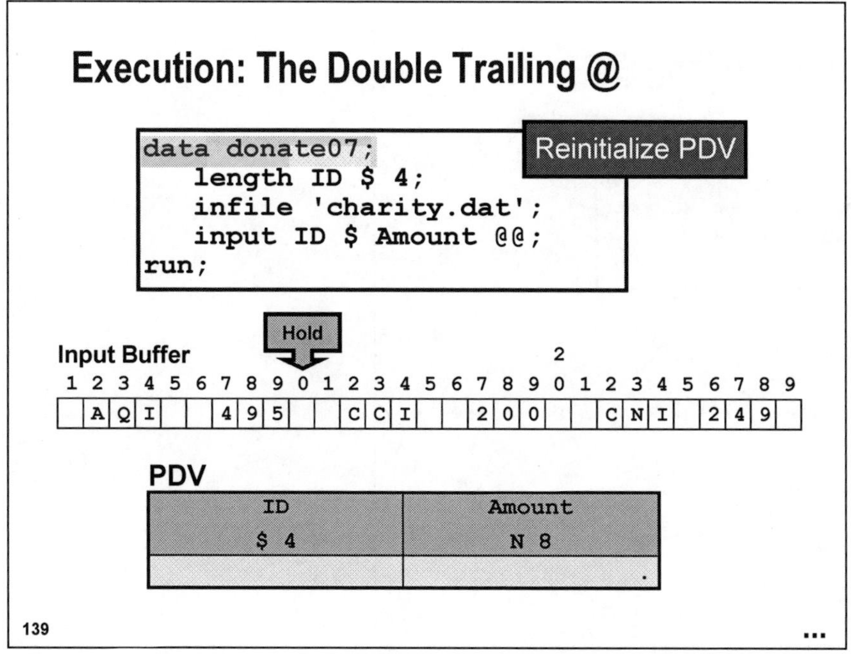
Execution: The Double Trailing @
data donate07;
length ID $ 4;
infile 'charity.dat';
input ID $ Amount @@;
run;
Reinitialize PDV
Hold
Input Buffer
2
1 2 3 4 5 6 7 8 9 0 1 2 3 4 5 6 7 8 9 0 1 2 3 4 5 6 7 8 9
A Q I 4 9 5 C C I 2 0 0 C N I 2 4 9
PDV
ID
$ 4
Amount
N 8
.
139
...

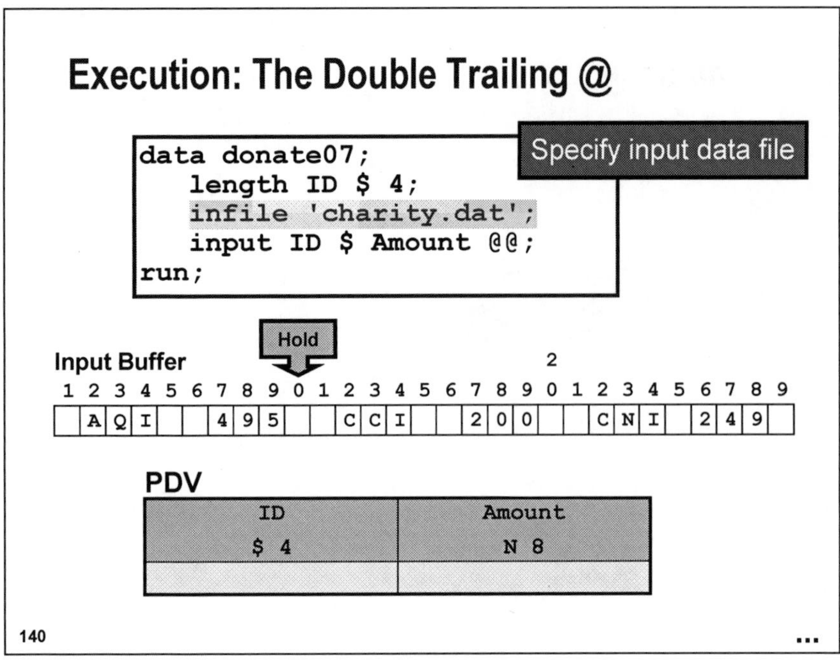
Execution: The Double Trailing @
data donate07;
length ID $ 4;
infile 'charity.dat';
input ID $ Amount @@;
run;
Specify input data file
Hold
Input Buffer
2
1 2 3 4 5 6 7 8 9 0 1 2 3 4 5 6 7 8 9 0 1 2 3 4 5 6 7 8 9
A Q I 4 9 5 C C I 2 0 0 C N I 2 4 9
PDV
ID
$ 4
Amount
N 8
140
...

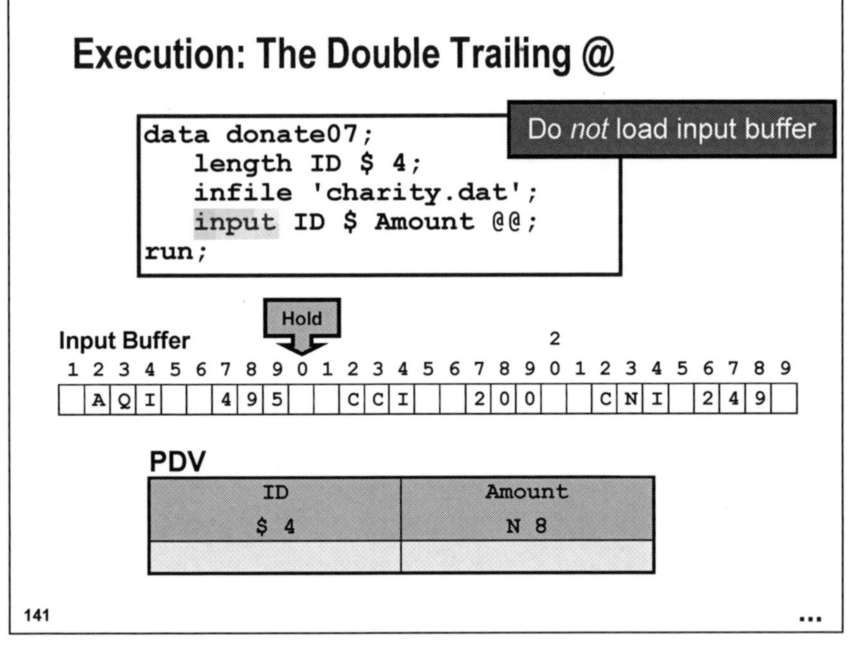
Execution: The Double Trailing @
data donate07;
length ID $ 4;
infile 'charity.dat';
input ID $ Amount @@;
run;
Do *not* load input buffer
Hold
Input Buffer
2
1 2 3 4 5 6 7 8 9 0 1 2 3 4 5 6 7 8 9 0 1 2 3 4 5 6 7 8 9
A Q I 4 9 5 C C I 2 0 0 C N I 2 4 9
PDV
ID
$ 4
Amount
N 8
141
...

Execution: The Double Trailing @

```
data donate07;
   length ID $ 4;
   infile 'charity.dat';
   input ID $ Amount @@;
run;
```

Input Buffer

```
                   1                   2
1 2 3 4 5 6 7 8 9 0 1 2 3 4 5 6 7 8 9 0 1 2 3 4 5 6 7 8 9
  A Q I     4 9 5     C C I     2 0 0     C N I   2 4 9
```

PDV

ID $ 4	Amount N 8
CCI	200

142 ...

Execution: The Double Trailing @

```
data donate07;
   length ID $ 4;
   infile 'charity.dat';
   input ID $ Amount @@;
run;
```

Hold record in the input buffer

Hold

Input Buffer

```
                   1
1 2 3 4 5 6 7 8 9 0 1 2 3 4 5 6 7 8 9 0 1 2 3 4 5 6 7 8 9
  A Q I     4 9 5     C C I     2 0 0     C N I   2 4 9
```

PDV

ID $ 4	Amount N 8
CCI	200

143 ...

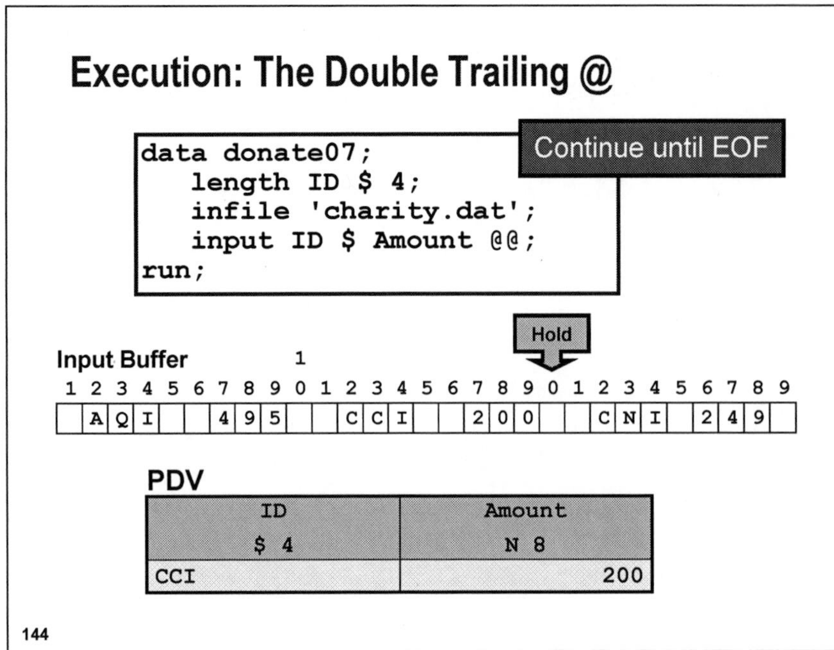

Creating Multiple Observations per Record

Partial SAS Log

```
NOTE: 4 records were read from the infile 'charity.dat'.
      The minimum record length was 23.
      The maximum record length was 28.
NOTE: SAS went to a new line when INPUT statement reached
past the end of a line.
NOTE: The data set WORK.DONATE07 has 12 observations and 2
variables.
```

The **SAS went to a new line** message is expected when a DATA step uses a double trailing @.

145

Creating Multiple Observations per Record

```
proc print data=donate07 noobs;
run;
```

Partial PROC PRINT Output

```
  ID     Amount

 AQI       495
 CCI       200
 CNI       249
 CS        279
 CU        780
 DAI       875
```

146

Single Trailing @ versus Double Trailing @

Option	Effect
@	Holds raw data record until ■ an INPUT statement with no trailing @ or ■ the next iteration of the DATA step.
@@	Holds raw data record in the input buffer until SAS reads past the end of the line.

147

The single trailing @ and the double trailing @ are mutually exclusive; they cannot and should not be used together. If both appear in the same INPUT statement, the last one specified is used. The MISSOVER option is invalid with the double trailing @.

4.4 Chapter Review

Chapter Review

1. What style of INPUT statement specification is used to read data in fixed columns?

2. In the INPUT statement, what is the symbol used to move the input pointer to a specified column?

3. What two things does the informat specify when used with formatted input?

149

continued...

Chapter Review

4. What does a forward slash (/) indicate when used in an INPUT statement?

5. In the INPUT statement, what does a trailing @ specify?

6. Generally, where is the most efficient place to put a subsetting IF statement?

151

4.5 Solutions

Solutions to Exercises

1. **Using Formatted Input**

   a. Create a new SAS data set named **sales_staff** that contains the fields highlighted in the layout table.

```
data sales_staff;
  infile 'sales1.dat';
  *infile '.workshop.rawdata(sales1)'; *MVS;
  input  @1 Employee_ID 6.
        @21 Last_Name $18.
        @43 Job_Title $20.
        @64 Salary Dollar8.
        @87 Hire_Date mmddyy10.;
run;
```

   b. Print **sales_staff** and add an appropriate title.

```
title 'Australian and US Sales Staff';
proc print data=sales_staff noobs;
run;
title;
```

2. **Using Formatted Input and the Subsetting IF Statement**

   a. Create two SAS data sets from the raw data file, and based them on the country of the trainee.

```
data AU_trainees US_trainees;
  drop Country;
  infile 'sales1.dat';
  *infile '.workshop.rawdata(sales1)'; *MVS;
  input  @1 Employee_ID 6.
        @21 Last_Name $18.
        @43 Job_Title $20.
        @64 Salary Dollar8.
        @73 Country $2.
        @87 Hire_Date mmddyy10.;
  if Job_Title = 'Sales Rep. I';
  if Country = 'AU' then output AU_trainees;
  else if Country = 'US' then output US_trainees;
run;
```

b. Print both of the data sets with appropriate titles.

```
title 'Australian Trainees';
proc print data=AU_trainees noobs;
run;

title 'US Trainees';
proc print data=US_trainees noobs;
run;
title;
```

3. Using a Text String with Column Pointer Controls

a. Create a new SAS data set named **seminar_ratings** that contains the names of the participants and the ratings that were given.

```
Data seminar_ratings;
  infile 'seminar.dat';
  *infile '.workshop.rawdata(seminar)'; *MVS;
  input Name $15.  @'Rating:' Rating 1.;
run;
```

b. Print the data set and give it an appropriate title.

```
title 'Names and Ratings';
proc print data=seminar_ratings;
  run;
title;
```

4. Reading Multiple Input Records per Observation

a. Create a new SAS data set named **sales_staff2** that contains the fields highlighted in the layout table.

```
data sales_staff2;
   infile 'sales2.dat'; *PC and UNIX;
   *infile '.workshop.rawdata(sales2)'; *z/OS Mainframe;
   input  @1 Employee_ID 6.
         @21 Last_Name $18. /
          @1 Job_Title $20.
         @22 Hire_Date mmddyy10.
         @33 Salary dollar8. /;
run;
```

Alternate Solution:

```
data sales_staff2;
   infile 'sales2.dat'; *PC and UNIX;
   *infile '.workshop.rawdata(sales2)'; *z/OS Mainframe;
   input  @1 Employee_ID 6.
         @21 Last_Name $18.;
   input  @1 Job_Title $20.
         @22 Hire_Date mmddyy10.
         @33 Salary dollar8.;
   input;
run;
```

Alternate Solution:

```
data sales_staff2;
   infile 'sales2.dat'; *PC and UNIX;
   *infile '.workshop.rawdata(sales2)'; *z/OS Mainframe;
   input  @1 Employee_ID 6.
         @21 Last_Name $18.
    #2    @1 Job_Title $20.
         @22 Hire_Date mmddyy10.
         @33 Salary dollar8.
    #3     ;
run;
```

b. Print **sales_staff2** and add an appropriate title.

```
title 'Australian and US Sales Staff';
proc print data=sales_staff2 noobs;
run;
title;
```

5. Working with Mixed Record Types

a. Create two new SAS data sets, **US_sales** and **AU_sales**, that contain the fields highlighted in the layout table.

```
data AU_sales US_sales;
  drop Country;
  infile 'sales3.dat';
  *infile '.workshop.rawdata(sales3)'; *MVS;
  input  @1 Employee_ID 6.
        @21 Last_Name $18.
        @43 Job_Title $20.;
  input @10 Country $2. @;
  if Country = 'AU' then do;
     input @1 Salary dollarx8.
          @24 Hire_Date ddmmyy10.;
     output AU_sales;
  end;
  else if Country = 'US' then do;
     input @1 Salary dollar8.
          @24 Hire_Date mmddyy10.;
     output US_sales;
  end;
run;
```

b. Print both of the data sets with appropriate titles.

```
title 'Australian Sales Staff';
proc print data=AU_sales noobs;
run;

title 'US Sales Staff';
proc print data=US_sales noobs;
run;
title;
```

Solutions to Student Activities

4.02 Quiz – Correct Answer

Use SAS Help to navigate to Starting with Raw Data: The Basics.

Click the Contents tab and select:

- ⇨ SAS Products
  - ⇨ Base SAS
    - ⇨ Step-by-Step Programming with Base SAS Software
      - ⇨ Getting Your Data into Shape
        - ⇨ Starting with Raw Data: The Basics

Page to Introduction to Raw Data and review this section. What are the three styles of input?

List, column, and formatted are the three styles of input.

11

4.03 Quiz – Correct Answer

Which style of INPUT statement specification should you choose to read the `offers.dat` raw data file?

Partial `offers.dat`

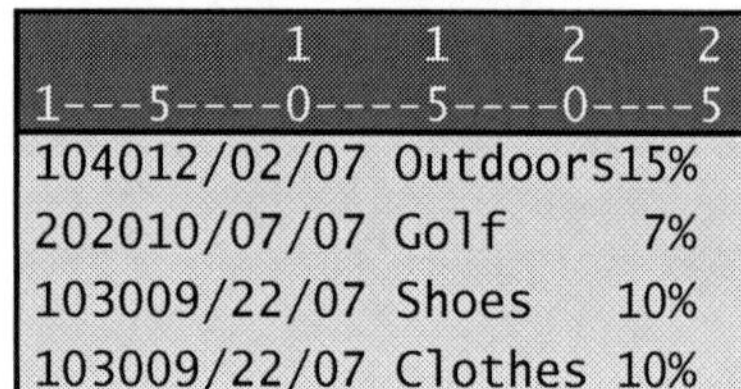

```
         1    1    2    2
1---5----0----5----0----5
104012/02/07 Outdoors15%
202010/07/07 Golf     7%
103009/22/07 Shoes   10%
103009/22/07 Clothes 10%
```

Formatted input **is the best style of INPUT statement specification to read this data.**

The `offers.dat` file is in fixed columns and has nonstandard data.

16

4.04 Quiz – Correct Answer

Continue writing the INPUT statement to read Offer Date. (Hint: Use the MMDDYY8. informat.)

```
input @1 Cust_type 4.
      @5 Offer_dt mmddyy8.
```

Layout: offers.dat

Description	Column
Customer Type	1- 4
Offer Date	5-12
Item Group	14-21
Discount	22-24

Partial offers.dat

```
          1    1    2    2
1---5----0----5----0----5
104012/02/07 Outdoors15%
202010/07/07 Golf      7%
103009/22/07 Shoes    10%
103009/22/07 Clothes 10%
202007/08/07 Clothes 15%
203007/08/07 Clothes 25%
```

25

4.05 Quiz – Correct Answer

Using pen and paper, write an INPUT statement to read the data from the raw data file.

One answer is shown here:

```
input @1 Supplier_Code $5.
      @6 Supplier_Name $20. /
      @1 Ship_Date mmddyy8.
      @10 Amount dollar9.;
```

There are other ways to correctly write the INPUT statement.

61

4.06 Quiz – Correct Answer

Is this the best placement for the subsetting IF statement?

```
data EuropeQ1;
   infile 'sales.dat';
   input SaleID $4. @6 Location $3. @;
   if Location='USA' then
      input @10 SaleDate mmddyy10.
            @20 Amount 7.;
   else if Location='EUR' then
      input @10 SaleDate date9.
            @20 Amount commax7.;
   if Location = 'EUR';
run;
```

No, the subsetting IF statement should appear as early in the DATA step as possible.

93

4.07 Quiz – Correct Answer

Open and submit **p204a01**. Examine the SAS log. How many input records were read and how many observations were created?

Five records were read from the input file, and three observations were created.

107

4.08 Quiz – Correct Answer

Open **p204a02** and add the MISSOVER option to the INFILE statement. Submit the program and examine the SAS log. How many input records were read and how many observations were created?

```
data contacts;
   length Name $ 20 Phone Mobile $ 14;
   infile 'phone.csv' dlm=',' missover;
   input Name $ Phone $ Mobile $;
run;

proc print data=contacts noobs;
run;
```

Five input records were read and five observations were created.

113 p204a02s

4.09 Quiz – Correct Answer

Open and submit **p204a03**. Examine the SAS log. How many input records were read and how many observations were created?

Five records were read from the input file and three observations were created.

119 p204a03

Solutions to Chapter Review

Chapter Review Answers

1. What style of INPUT statement specification is used to read data in fixed columns?

   Formatted input or column input

2. In the INPUT statement, what is the syntax used to move the input pointer to a specified column?

   @n* moves the pointer to column *n

3. What two things does the informat specify when used with formatted input?

   - **The width of the input field**
   - **How to read data values stored in the field**

150 *continued...*

Chapter Review Answers

4. What does a forward slash (/) indicate when used in an INPUT statement?

   It indicates that SAS should load the next record from the raw data file.

5. In the INPUT statement, what does a trailing @ specify?

   To hold the raw data record in the input buffer until SAS executes an INPUT statement with no trailing @ or the next iteration of the DATA step begins

152 *continued...*

Chapter Review Answers

6. Generally, where is the most efficient place to put a subsetting IF?

   As early in the DATA step as possible. This is as soon as all the variables that are needed to evaluate the condition in the IF statement are assigned values.

153

Chapter 5 Data Transformations

5.1 Introduction **5-3**

5.2 Manipulating Character Values (Part 1) **5-10**

Exercises 5-25

5.3 Manipulating Character Values (Part 2) **5-29**

Exercises 5-53

5.4 Manipulating Numeric Values **5-58**

Exercises 5-70

5.5 Converting Variable Type **5-73**

Exercises 5-97

5.6 Chapter Review **5-100**

5.7 Solutions **5-101**

Solutions to Exercises 5-101

Solutions to Student Activities (Polls/Quizzes) 5-108

Chapter Review Answers 5-115

5.1 Introduction

Objectives

- Review the syntax of SAS functions.
- Introduce SAS variable lists.

3

SAS Functions

SAS provides a large library of functions
for manipulating data during DATA step execution.

A SAS function is often categorized by the type of data manipulation performed:

- Array
- Character
- Date And Time
- Descriptive Statistics
- Financial
- Mathematical
- Probability
- Random Number
- Trigonometric
- Special
- State and ZIP Code

4

See SAS Help and Documentation for a complete list of functions and their syntax.

5.01 Quiz

What SAS functions have you used?

6

Syntax for SAS Functions

A *SAS function* is a routine that performs a computation and returns a value. Functions use arguments supplied by the user or by the operating environment.

General form of a SAS function call:

function-name(*argument-1*,*argument-2*,...,*argument-n*)

An *argument* can be a constant, a variable, or any SAS expression, including another function.

7

Using SAS Functions

You can use functions in DATA step statements anywhere that an expression can appear.

```
data contrib;
   set orion.employee_donations;
   Total=sum(Qtr1,Qtr2,Qtr3,Qtr4);
   if Total ge 50;
run;

proc print data=contrib noobs;
   title 'Contributions $50 and Over';
   var Employee_ID Qtr1 Qtr2 Qtr3 Qtr4
   Total;
run;
```

8

p205d01

Using SAS Functions

Partial PROC PRINT Output

Contributions $50 and Over

Employee_ID	Qtr1	Qtr2	Qtr3	Qtr4	Total
120267	15	15	15	15	60
120269	20	20	20	20	80
120271	20	20	20	20	80
120275	15	15	15	15	60
120660	25	25	25	25	100
120669	15	15	15	15	60
120671	20	20	20	20	80

9

SAS Variable Lists

An alternative to typing variables separately is to use a *SAS variable list*.

```
data contrib;
   set orion.employee_donations;
   Total=sum(of Qtr1-Qtr4);
   if Total ge 50;
run;
```

When you use a SAS variable list in a SAS function, use the keyword OF in front of the first variable name in the list.

10 p205d01

SAS Variable Lists

A SAS *variable list* is an abbreviated method of referring to a group of variable names. SAS enables you to use the following variable lists:

- Numbered range
- Name range
- Name prefix
- Special SAS name lists

11

SAS Variable Lists

Numbered range lists	`x1-xn`	specifies all variables from **x1** to **x***n* inclusive. You can begin with any number and end with any number as long as you do not violate the rules for user-supplied variable names and the numbers are consecutive.
Name range lists	`x--a`	specifies all variables ordered as they are in the program data vector, from **x** to **a** inclusive.
	`x-numeric-a`	specifies all numeric variables from **x** to **a** inclusive.
	`x-character-a`	specifies all character variables from **x** to **a** inclusive.
Name prefix lists	**REV:**	specifies all the variables that begin with **REV**, such as **REVJAN**, **REVFEB**, and **REVMAR**.
Special SAS name lists	**_ALL_**	specifies all variables that are already defined in the current DATA step.
	NUMERIC	specifies all numeric variables that are already defined in the current DATA step.
	CHARACTER	specifies all character variables that are already defined in the current DATA step.

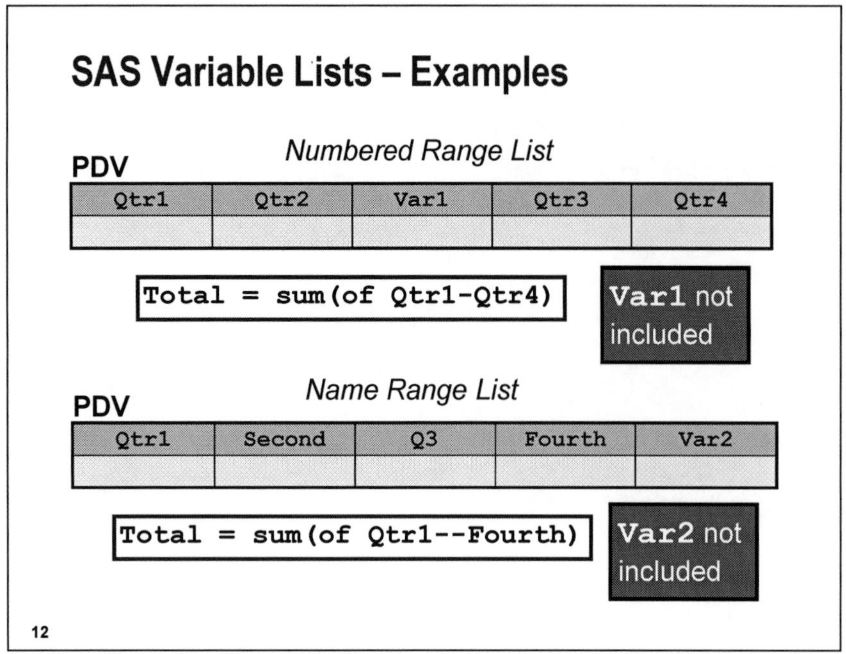

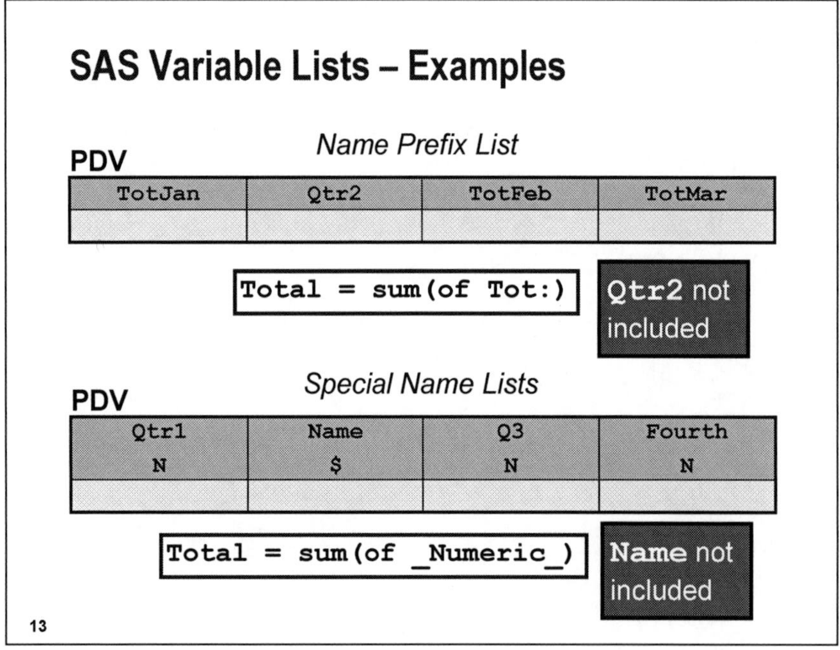

If the keyword OF is omitted from function calls that use SAS variable lists, the numbered and name range lists do not give a syntax error. Instead the lists are interpreted as expressions. For example, **`sum(Qtr1-Qtr4)`** evaluates as **`Qtr4`** subtracted from **`Qtr1`**.

5.02 Quiz

Complete the assignment statement for **Total** by using a SAS variable list and the SUM function to add the values for **Year1**, **Year2**, **Year3**, and **Year4**.

PDV

Year2	Year1	Year3	Year4	Sales

```
Total = ?
```

15

5.2 Manipulating Character Values (Part 1)

Objectives

- Use SAS functions to extract, edit, and search character values.

18

Business Scenario – Create a List of Charities

A manager in the Finance department asked for a list of all the charities that Orion Star contributes to. She would like to see the name of the charity as well as the ID code assigned to it.

Here is a sketch of the desired output:

Charity Names and ID Codes

ID	Name
AQI	Aquamissions International
CCI	Cancer Cures, Inc.
CNI	Conserve Nature, Inc.

19

Input Data

The **orion.biz_list** data set is extracted from the accounting system and contains the names of Orion Star's U.S. suppliers, charities, and consultants.

Partial Listing of **orion.biz_list**

```
Acct_
Code      Name

AEK3      ANGELA E. KEARNEY
AQI2      AQUAMISSIONS INTERNATIONAL
ATS1      A TEAM SPORTS
CBO3      CLAIRE B. OWENS
CCI2      CANCER CURES, INC.
CNI2      CONSERVE NATURE, INC.
CS1       CAROLINA SPORTS
```

20

Input Data – Details

Acct_Code is a character variable defined as length 6. Its last digit represents the type of organization: 1 denotes a supplier, 2 a charity, and 3 a consultant.

The other characters in the **Acct_Code** variable represent the ID for the organization, so the **ID** value can have as many as five characters.

Example:

Acct_Code $6	ID $5
AQI2	AQI

- 2 denotes a charity.
- AQI is the ID.

21

Input Data – Details

The name of the organization is stored as all capital letters. In the desired output, only the first letter of each word is capitalized.

Example:

Name
AQUAMISSIONS INTERNATIONAL

Change to:

Name
Aquamissions International

22

Business Scenario – Desired Results

Create a new data set, **charities**, that has the information that the finance manager would like to see.

Partial Listing of **charities**

```
         Acct_
 ID      Code      Name

AQI      AQI2      Aquamissions International
CCI      CCI2      Cancer Cures, Inc.
CNI      CNI2      Conserve Nature, Inc.
CS       CS2       Child Survivors
CU       CU2       Cuidadores Ltd.
DAI      DAI2      Disaster Assist, Inc.
```

This data set can then be used to create the manager's report.

23

The variable **Acct_Code** is in the output for learning purposes so that it can be easily compared to the **ID** variable. Otherwise, there is no need for it, and it could be dropped from the **charities** data set.

Create the List of Charities – Step 1

The first step is to subset the data based on the last character of **Acct_Code**.

Partial Listing of **orion.biz_list**

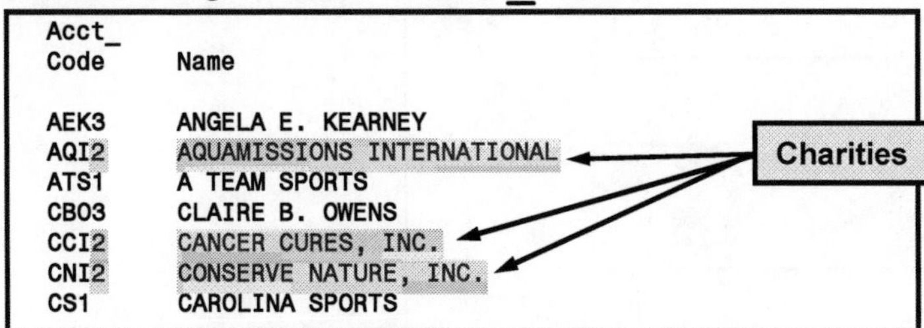
```
Acct_
Code    Name

AEK3    ANGELA E. KEARNEY
AQI2    AQUAMISSIONS INTERNATIONAL
ATS1    A TEAM SPORTS
CB03    CLAIRE B. OWENS
CCI2    CANCER CURES, INC.
CNI2    CONSERVE NATURE, INC.
CS1     CAROLINA SPORTS
```


SAS character functions make this task easy.

24

The SUBSTR Function (Right Side)

The SUBSTR function on the right side of an assignment statement is used to extract characters.

General form of the SUBSTR function:

NewVar=SUBSTR(*string,start*<,*length*>);

string	can be a character constant, variable, or expression.
start	specifies the starting position.
length	specifies the number of characters to extract. If omitted, the substring consists of the remainder of string.
NewVar	If *NewVar* is a new variable it will be created with the same length as *string*. To set a different length for *NewVar*, use a LENGTH statement prior to the assignment statement.

25

The SUBSTR function on the left side of an assignment statement is used to replace characters.

The SUBSTR Function – Example

Extract the first three characters from the value in the **Item_Code** variable and store them in **Item_Type**.

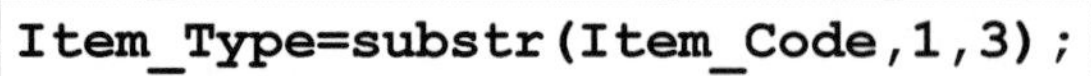

```
Item_Type=substr(Item_Code,1,3);
```

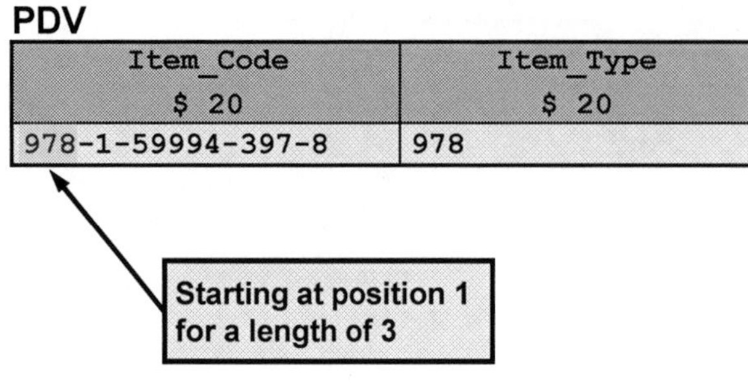

PDV
Item_Code
$ 20
Item_Type
$ 20
978-1-59994-397-8
978
Starting at position 1
for a length of 3

26

Setup for the Poll

This is the current value of **Item_Code**:

PDV
Item_Code
$ 20
978-1-59994-397-8

The SUBSTR function is a good method to extract the highlighted digits.

28

5.03 Multiple Choice Poll

Which SUBSTR function can extract the group of five numbers from the middle of the **Item_Code** value?

a. `substr(Item_Code,5,7)`
b. `substr(Item_Code,5)`
c. `substr(Item_Code,7,5)`
d. `substr(Item_Code,'mid',5)`

29

Create the List of Charities – Step 1

The last non-blank character in the **Acct_Code** value occurs in different positions for different observations.

Partial Listing of **orion.biz_list**

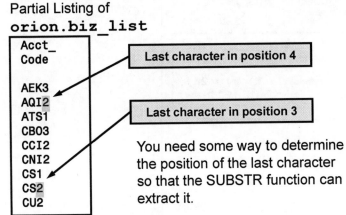

Acct_ Code
AEK3
AQI2
ATS1
CBO3
CCI2
CNI2
CS1
CS2
CU2

Last character in position 4

Last character in position 3

You need some way to determine the position of the last character so that the SUBSTR function can extract it.

31

The LENGTH Function

The LENGTH function returns the length of a non-blank character string, excluding trailing blanks.

General form of the LENGTH function:

NewVar=LENGTH(*argument*);

Example:

```
Code = 'ABCD  ';
Last_NonBlank=length(Code);
```

PDV

Code $ 6	Last_NonBlank N 8
ABCD	4

32

Create the List of Charities – Step 1

This program uses the SUBSTR and LENGTH functions to create the **charities** data set.

The LENGTH function is *nested,* or used as an argument to the SUBSTR function.

```
data charities;
  length ID $ 5;
  set orion.biz_list;
  if substr(Acct_Code,length(Acct_Code),1)='2';
  ID=substr(Acct_Code,1,length(Acct_Code)-1);
run;
```

Partially stepping through the execution for the first charity observation shows how the functions transform the data.

33 p205d02

Execution: Step 1

Read the first charity observation.

```
data charities;
  length ID $ 5;
  set orion.biz_list;
  if substr(Acct_Code,length(Acct_Code),1)='2';
  ID=substr(Acct_Code,1,length(Acct_Code)-1);
run;
```

PDV

ID $ 5	Acct_Code $ 6	Name $ 30
	AQI2	AQUAMISSIONS INTERNATIONAL

34 ...

Execution: Step 1

4

```
data charities;
  length ID $ 5;
  set orion.biz_list;
  if substr(Acct_Code,length(Acct_Code),1)='2';
  ID=substr(Acct_Code,1,length(Acct_Code)-1);
run;
```

PDV

ID $ 5	Acct_Code $ 6	Name $ 30
	AQI2	AQUAMISSIONS INTERNATIONAL

35 ...

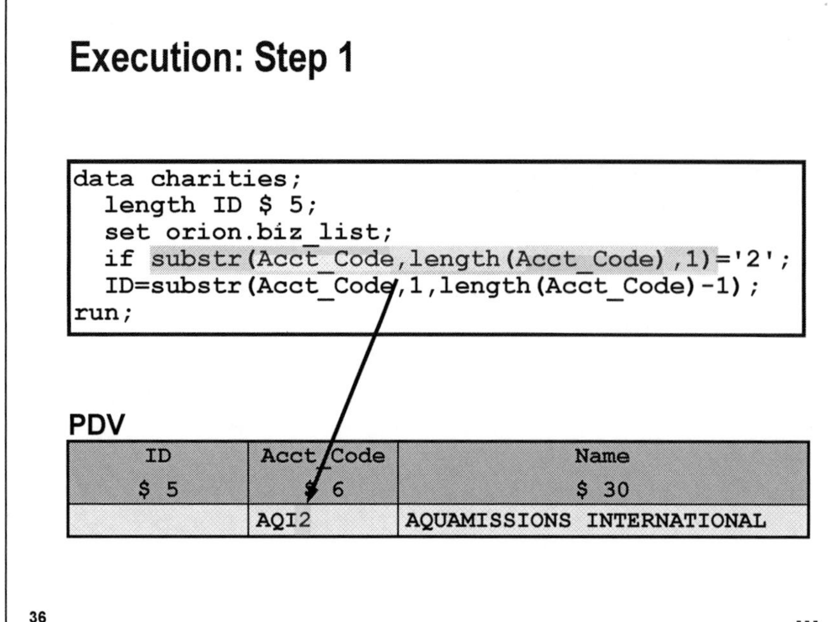
Execution: Step 1
data charities;
length ID $ 5;
set orion.biz_list;
if substr(Acct_Code,length(Acct_Code),1)='2';
ID=substr(Acct_Code,1,length(Acct_Code)-1);
run;
PDV
ID
$ 5
Acct_Code
$ 6
Name
$ 30
AQI2
AQUAMISSIONS INTERNATIONAL
36
...

Execution: Step 1

```
data charities;
  length ID $ 5;
  set orion.biz_list;
  if substr(Acct_Code,length(Acct_Code),1)='2';
  ID=substr(Acct_Code,1,length(Acct_Code)-1);
run;
```

True

PDV

ID $ 5	Acct_Code $ 6	Name $ 30
	AQI2	AQUAMISSIONS INTERNATIONAL

37 ...

Execution: Step 1

```
data charities;
  length ID $ 5;
  set orion.biz_list;
  if substr(Acct_Code,length(Acct_Code),1)='2';
  ID=substr(Acct_Code,1,length(Acct_Code)-1);
run;
```

3

PDV

ID $ 5	Acct_Code $ 6	Name $ 30
	AQI2	AQUAMISSIONS INTERNATIONAL

38 ...

Execution: Step 1

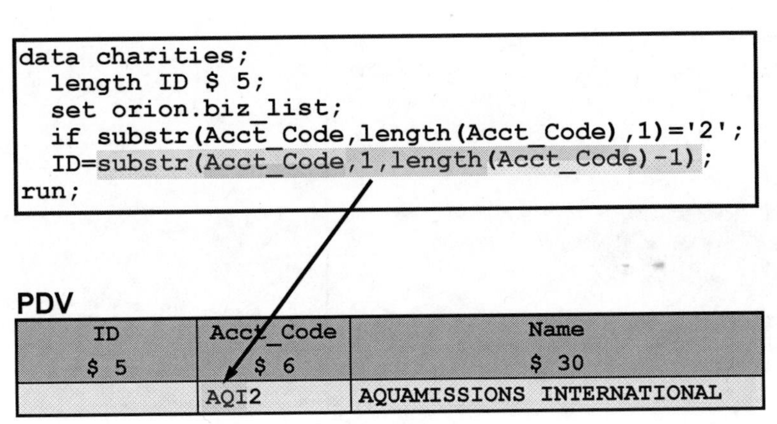
data charities;
length ID $ 5;
set orion.biz_list;
if substr(Acct_Code,length(Acct_Code),1)='2';
ID=substr(Acct_Code,1,length(Acct_Code)-1);
run;
PDV
ID
$ 5
Acct_Code
$ 6
Name
$ 30
AQI2
AQUAMISSIONS INTERNATIONAL

39 ...

Execution: Step 1

```
data charities;
  length ID $ 5;
  set orion.biz_list;
  if substr(Acct_Code,length(Acct_Code),1)='2';
  ID=substr(Acct_Code,1,length(Acct_Code)-1);
run;
```

PDV

ID $ 5	Acct_Code $ 6	Name $ 30
AQI	AQI2	AQUAMISSIONS INTERNATIONAL

40 ...

Execution: Step 1

```
data charities;
  length ID $ 5;
  set orion.biz_list;
  if substr(Acct_Code,length(Acct_Code),1)='2';
  ID=substr(Acct_Code,1,length(Acct_Code)-1);
run;
```

Implicit OUTPUT;
Implicit RETURN;

PDV

ID $ 5	Acct_Code $ 6	Name $ 30
AQI	AQI2	AQUAMISSIONS INTERNATIONAL

41

Create the List of Charities – Step 1 Complete

Listing of **charities**

```
        Acct_
  ID    Code     Name

 AQI    AQI2     AQUAMISSIONS INTERNATIONAL
 CCI    CCI2     CANCER CURES, INC.
 CNI    CNI2     CONSERVE NATURE, INC.
 CS     CS2      CHILD SURVIVORS
 CU     CU2      CUIDADORES LTD.
 DAI    DAI2     DISASTER ASSIST, INC.
 ES     ES2      EARTHSALVORS
 FFC    FFC2     FARMING FOR COMMUNITIES
 MI     MI2      MITLEID INTERNATIONAL
 SBA    SBA2     SAVE THE BABY ANIMALS
 V2     V22      VOX VICTIMAS
 YYCR   YYCR2    YES, YOU CAN RECYCLE
```

Step 2 is to transform the values in **Name** to a mix of uppercase and lowercase.

42

The PROPCASE Function

The PROPCASE function converts all words in an argument to *proper case*, in which the first letter is uppercase and the remaining letters are lowercase.

General form for the PROPCASE function:

NewVar=PROPCASE(*argument* <,*delimiter(s)*>);

argument	can be a character constant, variable, or expression.
delimiter(s)	delimiters are characters which separate words. If omitted, the default delimiters are the blank, /, - , (, ., and tab characters.
NewVar	If *NewVar* is a new variable, it is created with the same length as *argument*.

43

The PROPCASE Function

Example:

```
Name = 'SURF&LINK SPORTS';
Pname = propcase(Name);
Pname2 = propcase(Name,' &');
```

PDV

Name $ 16	Pname $ 16
SURF&LINK SPORTS	Surf&link Sports

Pname2 $ 16
Surf&Link Sports

44

5.04 Quiz

This PDV shows the current value of **Name**:

Name
HEATH*BARR*LITTLE EQUIPMENT SALES

Write an assignment statement that converts the value of **Name** to this:

Name
Heath*Barr*Little Equipment Sales

46

Create the List of Charities – Step 2

Adding an assignment statement to convert **Name** to proper case completes the **charities** data set.

```
data charities;
  length ID $ 5;
  set orion.biz_list;
  if substr(Acct_Code,length(Acct_Code),1)='2';
  ID=substr(Acct_Code,1,length(Acct_Code)-1);
  Name = propcase(Name);
run;
```

48

p205d03

Create the List of Charities – Complete

Listing of **charities**

ID	Acct_ Code	Name
AQI	AQI2	Aquamissions International
CCI	CCI2	Cancer Cures, Inc.
CNI	CNI2	Conserve Nature, Inc.
CS	CS2	Child Survivors
CU	CU2	Cuidadores Ltd.
DAI	DAI2	Disaster Assist, Inc.
ES	ES2	Earthsalvors
FFC	FFC2	Farming For Communities
MI	MI2	Mitleid International
SBA	SBA2	Save The Baby Animals
V2	V22	Vox Victimas
YYCR	YYCR2	Yes, You Can Recycle

49

Other Useful Character Functions

Function	Purpose
RIGHT(*string*)	right-aligns a character expression.
LEFT(*string*)	left-aligns a character expression.
UPCASE(*string*)	converts all letters in an argument to uppercase.
LOWCASE(*string*)	converts all letters in an argument to lowercase.
CHAR(*string,position*)	returns a single character from a specified *position* in a character *string*.

50

The CHAR function was introduced in SAS 9.2.

5.05 Quiz

Open and submit the program file **p205a01**. Find and correct the syntax error.

Listing of **p205a01**

```
data shoes;
   set orion.product_list;
   if substr(right(Product_Name,33,13))=
      'Running Shoes';
run;
```

Check the log for the corrected program. How many observations and variables are in the **shoes** data set?

52

Exercises

Level 1

1. Extracting Characters Based on Position

The data set **orion.au_salesforce** has employee data for the Sales branch in Australia.

Partial Listing of **orion.au_salesforce** (63 Total Observations, 9 Total Variables)

```
                       First_
          Employee_ID  Name         Last_Name      Job_Title

               120102  Tom          Zhou         Sales Manager
               120103  Wilson       Dawes        Sales Manager
               120121  Irenie       Elvish       Sales Rep. II
               120122  Christina    Ngan         Sales Rep. II
               120123  Kimiko       Hotstone     Sales Rep. I
               120124  Lucian       Daymond      Sales Rep. I
```

a. Orion Star wants to create user ID codes for logging onto the Australian Sales intranet site.

- Each user ID will consist of the first letter of the first name, the final letter of the first name, and the first four letters of the last name.
- All these letters should be lowercase.
- As a first step to doing this, extract these letters and change their case.
- Create a new data set named **work.codes**.
- Create three new variables named **FCode1**, **FCode2**, and **LCode**. As described above, these variables should contain the following:

Variable Name	Value
FCode1	First letter of **First_Name**
FCode2	Final letter of **First_Name**
LCode	First four letters of **Last_Name**

Remember to make these new values lowercase too.

There are several ways to approach getting the final letter of **First_Name**. For one of those ways, you need to know that the length of **First_Name** is 12 characters.

b. Print the resulting data set.

- Include only the variables **First_Name**, **FCode1**, **FCode2**, **Last_Name**, and **LCode**.
- Add an appropriate title.
- Verify your output.

Partial PROC PRINT output (63 Total Observations)

```
                         Extracted Letters for User IDs

               First_
        Obs    Name          FCode1    FCode2    Last_Name        LCode

          1    Tom             t         m       Zhou             zhou
          2    Wilson          w         n       Dawes            dawe
          3    Irenie          i         e       Elvish           elvi
          4    Christina       c         a       Ngan             ngan
          5    Kimiko          k         o       Hotstone         hots
          6    Lucian          l         n       Daymond          daym
          7    Fong            f         g       Hofmeister       hofm
          8    Satyakam        s         m       Denny            denn
          9    Sharryn         s         n       Clarkson         clar
```

Later you see techniques that can be used to combine these letters into a single character value.

Level 2

2. Extracting Characters Based on Position

The data set **orion.newcompetitors** has data on competing retail stores that recently opened near existing Orion Star locations.

Listing of **orion.newcompetitors**

```
                                     Postal_
        ID          City              Code

     AU15301W      PERTH             6002
     AU12217E      SYDNEY            2000
     CA    150     Toronto           M5V 3C6
     CA    238     Edmonton          T5T 2B2
     US 356NC      charlotte         28203
     US1013CO      denver            80201
     US   12CA     San diego         92139
```

a. Orion Star would like a data set containing only the small retail stores from these observations.

- Create a new variable, **Country**, that contains the first two characters of **ID**.
- Create a new variable, **Store_Code**, that contains the other characters from the value in **ID**. Left justify the value so that there are no leading blanks.
- The first character in the value of **Store_Code** indicates the size of the store, and **1** is the code for a small retail store.
- Write a program to output only the small retail store observations.
  Hint: You might need to use a SUBSTR functions as part of a subsetting IF statement
- Make sure that the **City** values appear in proper case (as displayed below).

b. Print your results with an appropriate title.

Only show the columns **Store_Code**, **Country**, **City**, and **Postal_Code**.

PROC PRINT output (5 Total Observations)

```
              New Small-Store Competitors

  Store_                                Postal_
   Code       Country     City           Code

  15301W        AU        Perth          6002
  12217E        AU        Sydney         2000
  150           CA        Toronto        M5V 3C6
  1013CO        US        Denver         80201
  12CA          US        San Diego      92139
```

Level 3

3. Converting U.S. Postal Codes to State Names

The data set **orion.contacts** contains a list of contacts for the U.S. charities that Orion Star donates to.

Listing of **orion.contacts**

ID	Title	Name	Address1	Address2
AQI	Ms.	Farr,Sue	15 Harvey Rd.	Macon, GA 31298
CCI	Dr.	Cox,Kay B.	163 McNeil Pl.	Kern, CA 93280
CNI	Mr.	Mason,Ron	442 Glen Ave.	Miami, FL 33054
CS	Ms.	Ruth,G. H.	2491 Brady St.	Munger, MI 48747
CU	Prof.	Florentino,Helen-Ashe H.	PO Box 2253	Washington, DC 20018
DAI	Ms.	Van Allsburg,Jan F.	25 Chesire Pl.	Short Hills, NJ 07078
ES	Mr.	Laff,Stanley X.	1725 Airport Rd.	Springfield, IL 62707
FFC	Mr.	Rizen,George Q.	11234 W Hoyt St.	Chicago, IL 60612
MI	Dr.	Mitchell,Marc J.	922 Mitchell Circle	Chicago, IL 60603
SBA	Ms.	Mills,Dorothy E.	34 Clear Sky Rd.	Butte, MT 59750
V2	Dr.	Webb,Jonathan W.	1012 Hwy 54	Morrisville, NC 27560
YYCR	Mr.	Keenan,Maynard J.	1315 Green Valley Ln.	Sedona, AZ 86351

a. Create a new data set named **states** that includes the variables **ID** and **Name** as well as a new variable named **Location** that shows the full name in proper case for the state that the contact is based in.

Hint: **Address2** is 24 characters long and the last item in **Address2** is always the ZIP code. Look in the online Help for character functions that use ZIP codes as arguments.

b. Print your results.

PROC PRINT output (12 Total Observations)

ID	Name	Location
AQI	Farr,Sue	Georgia
CCI	Cox,Kay B.	California
CNI	Mason,Ron	Florida
CS	Ruth,G. H.	Michigan
CU	Florentino,Helen-Ashe H.	District of Columbia
DAI	Van Allsburg,Jan F.	New Jersey
ES	Laff,Stanley X.	Illinois
FFC	Rizen,George Q.	Illinois
MI	Mitchell,Marc J.	Illinois
SBA	Mills,Dorothy E.	Montana
V2	Webb,Jonathan W.	North Carolina
YYCR	Keenan,Maynard J.	Arizona

5.3 Manipulating Character Values (Part 2)

Objectives

- Use SAS functions to extract, edit, and search character values.

57

Business Scenario – Create Mailing List Data

The **orion.contacts** data set contains the contact information for each charity's representative.

Partial Listing of **orion.contacts**

ID	Title	Name	Address1	Address2
AQI	Ms.	Farr,Sue	15 Harvey Rd.	Macon, GA 31298
CCI	Dr.	Cox,Kay B.	163 McNeil Pl.	Kern, CA 93280
CNI	Mr.	Mason,Ron	442 Glen Ave.	Miami, FL 33054
CS	Ms.	Ruth,G. H.	2491 Brady St.	Munger, MI 48747

Address1 and **Address2** are in the correct form to use for a mailing address, but the **Title** and **Name** variables need to be combined into a new variable, **FullName**.

58

Business Scenario – Desired Output

Create a new data set, **`labels`**, that is suitable for creating mailing labels.

Partial Listing of **`labels`**

ID	FullName	Address1	Address2
AQI	Ms. Sue Farr	15 Harvey Rd.	Macon, GA 31298
CCI	Dr. Kay B. Cox	163 McNeil Pl.	Kern, CA 93280
CNI	Mr. Ron Mason	442 Glen Ave.	Miami, FL 33054
CS	Ms. G. H. Ruth	2491 Brady St.	Munger, MI 48747

59

Create Mailing List Data

Partial Listing of **`orion.contacts`**

Title	Name
Ms.	Farr,Sue
Dr.	Cox,Kay B.
Mr.	Mason,Ron
Ms.	Ruth,G. H.
Prof.	Florentino, Helen-Ashe H
Ms.	Van Allsburg, Jan F.
Mr.	Laff, Stanley X.
Mr.	Rizen, George Q.
Dr.	Mitchell, Marc J.
Ms.	Mills, Dorothy E.
Dr.	Webb, Jonathan W.
Mr.	Keenan, Maynard J.

Two steps need to be accomplished:

Step 1: Separate the last name from the first and middle names.

Step 2: Combine the title, the first and middle names, and the last name.

60

Setup for the Poll

The first step in creating the mailing list is to separate the contact's name into two parts based on the position of the comma.

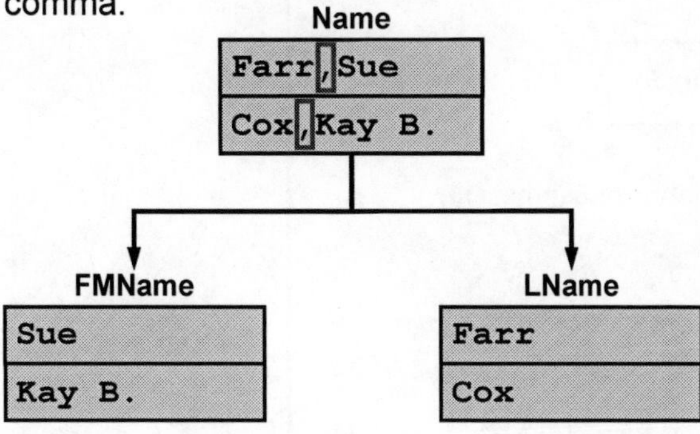

Would the SUBSTR function be appropriate for this?

62

5.06 Poll

Would the SUBSTR function be appropriate to separate the contact's name into two parts?

- ❍ Yes
- ❍ No

63

The SUBSTR function would be difficult to use because the comma is not in the same position for each value of **`Name`**. The SCAN function provides an easier way to separate the last name from the first and middle names.

The SCAN Function

The SCAN function returns the *n*th word of a character value.

General form of the SCAN function:

NewVar=SCAN(*string*,*n*<,*charlist*>);

string	can be a character constant, variable, or expression.
n	specifies the *n*th word to extract from *string*.
charlist	lists the character(s) that delimit words. If omitted, the default delimiters are as follows:

<table>
<tr><td>ASCII (PC, UNIX)</td><td>blank . < (+ | & ! $ *) ; - / , % ^</td></tr>
<tr><td>EBCDIC (z/OS)</td><td>blank . < (+ | & ! $ *) ; - / , % | ¢ ¬</td></tr>
</table>

65

The SCAN function is used to extract words from a character value when the relative order of words is known, but their starting positions are not.

The SCAN Function – Details

When you use the SCAN function,

- a missing value is returned if there are fewer than *n* words in the string
- if *n* is negative, the SCAN function selects the word in the character string starting from the end of string
- the length of the created variable is 200 bytes.

✎ A good practice is to explicitly define the length of any created variable with a LENGTH statement.

66

continued...

The SCAN Function – Details

When you use the SCAN function,

- delimiters before the first word have no effect
- any character or set of characters can serve as delimiters
- two or more contiguous delimiters are treated as a single delimiter.

67

The SCAN Function – Example

Extract the second word of **Phrase**.

```
Second=scan(Phrase,2,' ');
```

PDV

Phrase $ 21	Second $ 200
software and services	and

68

5.07 Quiz

Consider this PDV and assignment statement:

```
Second=scan(Phrase,2,',');
```

PDV

Phrase $ 28	Second $ 200
software, hardware, services	

What value will be stored in **Second**?

70

The SCAN Function – Example

Extract the second word of **Phrase** without the leading space.

```
Second=scan(Phrase,2,', ');
```

PDV

Phrase $ 28	Second $ 200
software, hardware, services	hardware

72

Setup for the Poll

Consider this DATA step:

```
data Scan_Quiz;
   Text = "New Year's Day, January 1st, 2007";
   Year = [            ?              ;]
run;
```

74 p205d05

5.08 Multiple Choice Poll

What expression completes the assignment statement to correctly extract 2007 from the **Text** variable?

a. `scan(Text,-1);`

b. `scan(Text,6);`

c. `scan(Text,6,', ');`

d. All of the above would work.

75

Create Mailing List Data

Using the SCAN function gives an easy way to separate the names for the mailing list.

```
data labels;
   set orion.contacts;
   length FMName LName $ 15;
   FMName = scan(Name,2,',');
   LName = scan(Name,1,',');
run;
```

77

p205d06

Create Mailing List Data

```
proc print data=labels noobs;
   var ID Name Title FMName LName;
run;
```

Partial PROC PRINT Output

```
ID      Name         Title    FMName    LName

AQI     Farr,Sue      Ms.     Sue       Farr
CCI     Cox,Kay B.    Dr.     Kay B.    Cox
CNI     Mason,Ron     Mr.     Ron       Mason
CS      Ruth,G. H.    Ms.     G. H.     Ruth
```

The next step is to join the values of **Title**, **FMName**, and **LName** into another variable.

78

p205d06

The CATX Function

The CATX function joins or *concatenates* character strings.

General form of the CATX function:

NewVar = CATX(*separator, string-1, … ,string-n*)

separator	Is a character string that is inserted between the concatenated *string-1,…,string-n* arguments.
string-1, …,string-n	can be a character constant, variable, or expression. Leading and trailing blanks are removed from each argument.

The size of the created variable, *NewVar*, is 200 bytes if it is not previously defined with a LENGTH statement.

79

The CATX Function – Example

Combine **FMName** and **LName** to create **FullName**.

```
FullName=catx(' ',FMName,LName);
```

PDV

FMName $ 15	LName $ 15	FullName $ 200
Sue	Farr	Sue Farr

80

Other CAT Functions

There are three other CAT functions that concatenate character strings.

Function	Details
CAT(*string-1, … ,string-n*)	does not remove leading or trailing blanks from the arguments before concatenating them.
CATS(*string-1, … ,string-n*)	removes leading and trailing blanks from the arguments.
CATT(*string-1, … ,string-n*)	removes trailing blanks from the arguments.

81

Example of CAT Functions

```
data test_cat;
   /* Each value has a leading and trailing blank */
   a = ' a ';
   b = ' b ';
   c = ' c ';
   cat_example = cat(a,b,c);
   catt_example = catt(a,b,c);
   cats_example = cats(a,b,c);
run;
```

Partial PDV Showing Concatenated Values

cat_example	catt_example	cats_example
a b c	a b c	abc

Create Mailing List Data – Finished Program

Adding an assignment statement with the CATX function completes the program.

```
data labels;
   set orion.contacts;
   length FullName $ 35 FMName LName $ 15;
   FMName = scan(Name,2,',');
   LName = scan(Name,1,',');
   FullName = catx(' ',Title,FMName,LName);
run;
```

82 p205d07

Create Mailing List Data – Finished Program

```
proc print data=labels noobs;
   var ID FullName Address1 Address2;
run;
```

Partial PROC PRINT Output

ID	FullName	Address1	Address2
AQI	Ms. Sue Farr	15 Harvey Rd.	Macon, GA 31298
CCI	Dr. Kay B. Cox	163 McNeil Pl.	Kern, CA 93280
CNI	Mr. Ron Mason	442 Glen Ave.	Miami, FL 33054
CS	Ms. G. H. Ruth	2491 Brady St.	Munger, MI 48747

83 p205d07

Concatenation Operator

The *concatenation operator* is another way to join character strings.

General form of the concatenation operator:

NewVar=string1 !! *string2*;

Example:

```
Phone = '('!!area!!') '!!Number;
```

PDV

Area $ 3	Number $ 8	Phone $ 14
919	531-0000	(919) 531-0000

The operator can also be written as two vertical bars (||) or two broken vertical bars (¦¦).

84

5.09 Quiz

Create a Favorites link to the SAS Help entry for Functions by Category.

Hint: Use the Index tab. Type the keyword **`functions`** and then select **by category** from the list.

86

Business Scenario: Data Clean Up

The Internet Sales Group accidentally used the wrong data files for the Orion Star Catalog Web site. They corrected the problem as soon as it was noticed, but some orders were created with data errors in them.

orion.clean_up has sample observations showing the problems.

89

Business Scenario: Data Clean Up

Listing of **orion.clean_up**

```
Product_ID          Product                       Order_ID

21 02 002 00003     Sunfit Trunks, Blue           1231986335
21 02 002 00003     Luci Knit Mittens, Red        1232003930
21 02 002 00004     Luci Knit mittens, Blue       1232007693
21 02 002 00004     Sunfit Trunks, aqua           1232007700
21 02 002 00005     Sunfit Trunks, Yellow         1232087464
21 02 002 00005     Lucky Knit Mittens, Black     1232092527
```

- The **Product_ID** for mittens should have 5 instead of a 2 for the third group of numbers.
- Luci is a typo; the correct word is Lucky.
- **Product_ID** values should have no internal spaces.
- All words in the **Product** value should start with a capital letter.

90

Business Scenario – Desired Output

The **correct** data set shows what the data should be.

Listing of **correct**

Product_ID	Product	Order_ID
210200200003	Sunfit Trunks, Blue	1231986335
210200500003	Lucky Knit Mittens, Red	1232003930
210200500004	Lucky Knit Mittens, Blue	1232007693
210200200004	Sunfit Trunks, Aqua	1232007700
210200200005	Sunfit Trunks, Yellow	1232087464
210200500005	Lucky Knit Mittens, Black	1232092527

91

Data Clean Up – Step 1

The first step in creating the **correct** data set is to do the following:

- Find the observations with `Mittens` as part of the **Product** value.
- Change the middle characters of the **Product_ID** values for those observations.

The FIND and SUBSTR functions are useful for this.

92

The FIND Function

The FIND function searches a target string for a specified substring.

General form of the FIND function:

Position = FIND(*string,substring<,modifiers,startpos>*);

The FIND function returns a numeric value that is

- the starting position of the first occurrence of *substring* within *string*, if *substring* is found
- 0, if *substring* is not found.

93

continued...

The FIND Function

The FIND function searches a target *string* for a specified *substring.*

General form of the FIND function:

Position = FIND(*string,substring<,modifiers,startpos>*);

Modifiers can be

- I to indicate a case-insensitive search
- T to indicate to ignore trailing blanks in the string and substring values.

startpos indicates where in the *string* to start searching for the *substring.*

94

More on modifiers and the *startpos* value:

- A modifier can be the value I or T. These two values can be combined in either order and in either case. If this argument is omitted, the search is case sensitive and trailing blanks are taken into consideration.
- The *startpos* value not only specifies the position at which the search should start but also the direction of the search. A positive value indicates a forward (right) search. A negative value indicates a backward (left) search. If this argument is omitted, the search starts at position 1 and moves forward.
- These two optional arguments can be in either order (that is, *startpos* can precede *modifier*).

The FIND Function – Example

```
data find;
   Text='AUSTRALIA, DENMARK, US';
   Pos1=find(Text,'US');
   Pos2=find(Text,' US');
   Pos3=find(Text,'us');
   Pos4=find(Text,'us','I');
   Pos5=find(Text,'us','I',10);
run;
```

PDV

Pos1
N 8

What value will SAS assign to **Pos1**?

95 p205d08

The FIND Function – Example

2

```
data find;
   Text='AUSTRALIA, DENMARK, US';
   Pos1=find(Text,'US');
   Pos2=find(Text,' US');
   Pos3=find(Text,'us');
   Pos4=find(Text,'us','I');
   Pos5=find(Text,'us','I',10);
run;
```

PDV

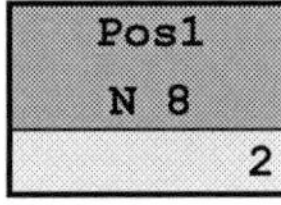

96

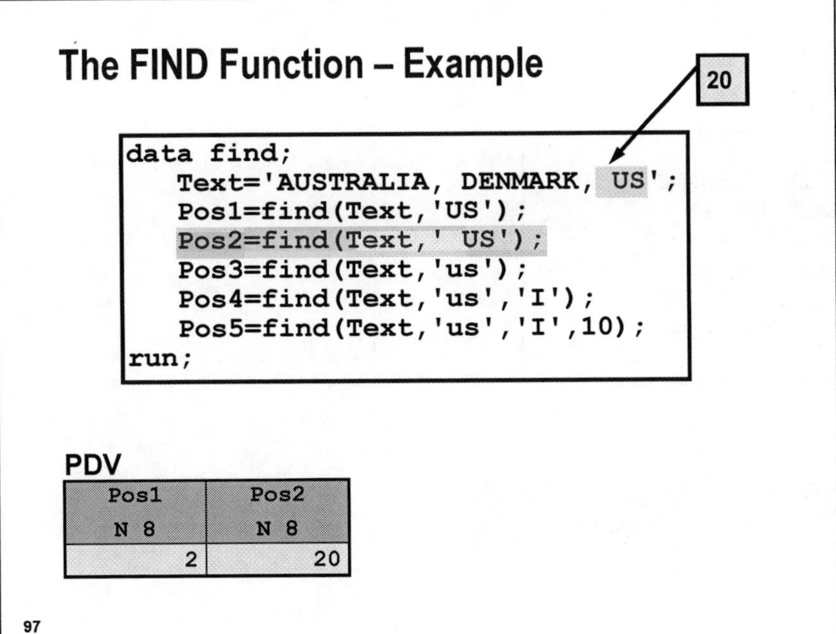
The FIND Function – Example
20
data find;
Text='AUSTRALIA, DENMARK, US';
Pos1=find(Text,'US');
Pos2=find(Text,' US');
Pos3=find(Text,'us');
Pos4=find(Text,'us','I');
Pos5=find(Text,'us','I',10);
run;
PDV
Pos1 N 8 2
Pos2 N 8 20
97

5.10 Quiz

Complete the PDV for the values for **Pos3** and **Pos4**.

```
data find;
   Text='AUSTRALIA, DENMARK, US';
   Pos1=find(Text,'US');
   Pos2=find(Text,' US');
   Pos3=find(Text,'us');
   Pos4=find(Text,'us','I');
   Pos5=find(Text,'us','I',10);
run;
```

PDV

Pos1 N 8	Pos2 N 8	Pos3 N 8	Pos4 N 8
2	20		

99

The FIND Function – Example

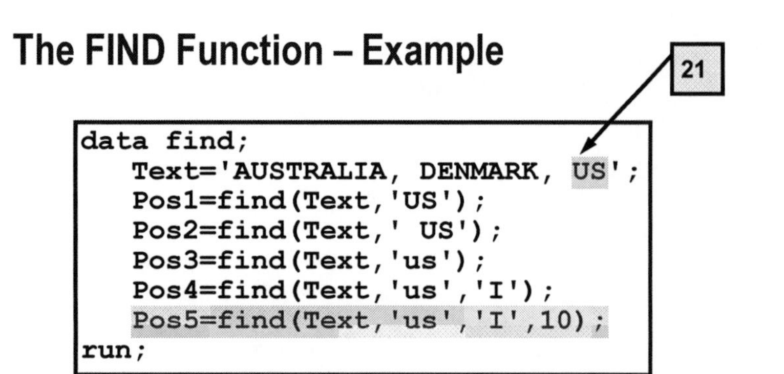


```
data find;
   Text='AUSTRALIA, DENMARK, US';
   Pos1=find(Text,'US');
   Pos2=find(Text,' US');
   Pos3=find(Text,'us');
   Pos4=find(Text,'us','I');
   Pos5=find(Text,'us','I',10);
run;
```

PDV

Pos1 N 8	Pos2 N 8	Pos3 N 8	Pos4 N 8	Pos5 N 8
2	20	0	2	21

101

The SUBSTR Function (Left Side)

This form of the SUBSTR function (left side of assignment statement) replaces characters in a character variable.

General form of the SUBSTR function (left side):

SUBSTR(*string,start*<*,length*>)=*value*;

string	specifies a character variable.
start	specifies the starting position to replace characters with the *value*.
length	specifies the number of characters to replace in *string*. If omitted, all characters from the *start* position to the end of the *string* are replaced. The length value cannot be larger than the remaining length of *string* (including trailing blanks) after *start*.

102

The SUBSTR Function (Left Side) – Example

Replace two characters starting at position 11.

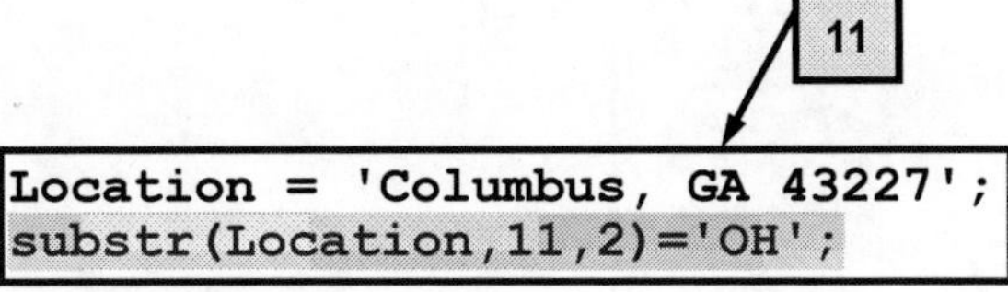

11
Location = 'Columbus, GA 43227';
substr(Location,11,2)='OH';

PDV

Location $ 18
Columbus, OH 43227

103

Data Clean Up – Step 1

Use the SUBSTR and FIND functions to change incorrect product IDs for mittens.

```
data correct;
   set orion.clean_up;
   if find(Product,'Mittens','I')>0 then do;
      substr(Product_ID,9,1) = '5';
   end;
run;

proc print data=correct noobs;
run;
```

104 p205d09

Data Clean Up – Step 1

PROC PRINT Output

```
Product_ID         Product                     Order_ID

21 02 002 00003    Sunfit Trunks, Blue         1231986335
21 02 005 00003    Luci Knit Mittens, Red      1232003930
21 02 005 00004    Luci Knit mittens, blue     1232007693
21 02 002 00004    Sunfit Trunks, aqua         1232007700
21 02 002 00005    Sunfit Trunks, Yellow       1232087464
21 02 005 00005    Lucky Knit Mittens, Black   1232092527
```

The next step is to change the error `Luci` to `Lucky`.

The TRANWRD function is the best way to do this kind of change.

105

The TRANWRD Function

The TRANWRD function replaces or removes all occurrences of a given word (or a pattern of characters) within a character string.

General form for the TRANWRD function:

NewVar=TRANWRD(*source,target,replacement*);

source	specifies the source string that you want to change.
target	specifies the string searched for in *source*.
replacement	specifies the string that replaces *target*.

106

Using the TRANWRD function to replace an existing string with a longer string might cause truncation of the resulting value if a LENGTH statement is not used.

The TRANWRD Function – Details

General form for the TRANWRD function:

```
NewVar=TRANWRD(source,target,replacement);
```

These details apply when you use the TRANWRD function:

- The TRANWRD function does not remove trailing blanks from *target* or *replacement*.
- If *NewVar* was not previously defined, it is given a length of 200.
- If the target string is not found in the source, then no replacement occurs.

107

Data Clean Up – Step 2

Use the TRANWRD function to replace all occurrences of `Luci` with `Lucky`.

```
data correct;
   set orion.clean_up;
   if find(Product,'Mittens','I') > 0 then do;
      substr(Product_ID,9,1) = '5';
      Product=Tranwrd(Product,'Luci ','Lucky ');
   end;
run;

proc print data=correct noobs;
run;
```

108

p205d10

Data Clean Up – Step 2

PROC PRINT Output

```
Product_ID          Product                        Order_ID

21 02 002 00003     Sunfit Trunks, Blue           1231986335
21 02 005 00003     Lucky Knit Mittens, Red       1232003930
21 02 005 00004     Lucky Knit mittens, blue      1232007693
21 02 002 00004     Sunfit Trunks, aqua           1232007700
21 02 002 00005     Sunfit Trunks, Yellow         1232087464
21 02 005 00005     Lucky Knit Mittens, Black     1232092527
```

For step 3, removing the embedded blanks from **Product_ID** is easy with the COMPRESS function.

109

The COMPRESS Function

The COMPRESS function removes the characters listed in the *chars* argument from the *source*.

General form for the COMPRESS function:

```
NewVar=COMPRESS(source<,chars>);
```

If no *chars* are specified, the COMPRESS function removes all blanks from the *source*.

110

The COMPRESS Function

```
ID ='20 01-005 024';
New_ID1=compress(ID);
New_ID2=compress(ID,'-');
New_ID3=compress(ID,' -');
```

PDV

ID $ 13	New_ID1 $ 13
20 01-005 024	2001-005024

New_ID2 $ 13	New_ID3 $ 13
20 01005 024	2001005024

111

Other Functions That Remove Blanks

Function	Purpose
TRIM(*string*)	removes trailing blanks from a character string.
STRIP(*string*)	removes all leading and trailing blanks from a character string.
COMPBL(*string*)	removes multiple blanks from a character string by translating each occurrence of two or more consecutive blanks into a single blank.

112

The TRIMN function is similar to the TRIM function. TRIMN returns a null string (zero blanks) if the argument is blank, while TRIM returns a blank.

The STRIP function returns a null string if the argument is blank.

By default, the length of the value returned by the COMPBL function is the same as the length of the argument.

Data Clean Up – Step 3

Use the COMPRESS and PROPCASE functions to eliminate blanks from **Product_ID** and ensure the proper case for **Product**.

```
data correct;
   set orion.clean_up;
   if find(Product,'Mittens','I') > 0 then do;
      substr(Product_ID,9,1) = '5';
      Product=tranwrd(Product,'Luci ','Lucky ');
   end;
   Product_ID = compress(Product_ID);
   Product = propcase(Product);
run;

proc print data=correct noobs;
run;
```

113

p205d11

Data Clean Up – Step 3

PROC PRINT Output

Product_ID	Product	Order_ID
210200200003	Sunfit Trunks, Blue	1231986335
210200500003	Lucky Knit Mittens, Red	1232003930
210200500004	Lucky Knit Mittens, Blue	1232007693
210200200004	Sunfit Trunks, Aqua	1232007700
210200200005	Sunfit Trunks, Yellow	1232087464
210200500005	Lucky Knit Mittens, Black	1232092527

114

Exercises

Level 1

4. Cleaning Text Data

Customer names are available in a data set named **orion.customers_ex5**:

Customer_ID	Name	Country	Gender	Birth_Date
000-000-00-0004	KVARNIQ, James	US	M	27Jun1974
Silver000-000-00-0005	STEPHANO, Sandrina	US	F	9-Jul1979
000-000-00-0009	KRAHL, Cornelia	DE	F	27Feb1974
platinum000-000-00-0010	BALLINGER, Karen	US	F	18Oct1984
000-000-00-0011	WALLSTAB, Elke	DE	F	16Aug1974
Silver000-000-00-0012	BLACK, David	US	M	12Apr1969

Use this data set to create a new data set named **names** that contains each customer's name in this format:

Mr. John B. Smith

Ms. Jane Doe

a. Write a program to create the **names** data set.

- The **names** data set should contain only three variables: **New_Name**, **Name**, and **Gender**.
- The **New_Name** variable should contain the customer's name in the new format.
  - Female names should be preceded by the honorific title Ms.
  - Male names by the title Mr.

b. Print the **names** data set.

c. Verify that your conversion efforts were successful.

Partial PROC PRINT Output (77 Total Observations)

```
Obs    New_Name                   Name                   Gender
  1    Mr. James Kvarniq          KVARNIQ, James           M
  2    Ms. Sandrina Stephano      STEPHANO, Sandrina       F
  3    Ms. Cornelia Krahl         KRAHL, Cornelia          F
  4    Ms. Karen Ballinger        BALLINGER, Karen         F
  5    Ms. Elke Wallstab          WALLSTAB, Elke           F
  6    Mr. David Black            BLACK, David             M
  7    Mr. Markus Sepke           SEPKE, Markus            M
```

5. (Optional) Searching for and Replacing Character Values

- As in the previous exercise, the data set **`orion.customers_ex5`** contains information about Orion Star customers.
- Customers who are frequent purchasers are tagged as `Silver`, `Gold`, or `Platinum`, which appears at the beginning of their **`Customer_ID`** value.
- Due to updates in the way that Orion Star designates **`Customer_ID`** values, the existing values need to be modified. Any four-digit string, for example, `-00-`, in **`Customer_ID`** should be replaced by `-15-` in the output data sets.

  a. Create three output data sets: **`work.silver`**, **`work.gold`**, and **`work.platinum`**.
  - Search **`Customer_ID`** for the values `Silver`, `Gold`, and `Platinum` and output them to the respective data set when they are found.
  - You should get 17 observations in **`work.silver`**, 2 in **`work.gold`**, and 5 in **`work.platinum`**.
  - Keep the variables **`Customer_ID`**, **`Name`**, and **`Country`** in all data sets.

  b. Print the data sets with appropriate titles.

  c. Confirm that any `-00-` was replaced by `-15-`.

  Hint: Make sure that your searches are not case sensitive!

Partial PROC PRINT Output (17 Total Observations)

```
                        Silver-Level Customers

              Customer_ID          Name                  Country

         Silver000-000-15-0005    STEPHANO, Sandrina      US
         Silver000-000-15-0012    BLACK, David            US
         Silver000-000-15-0024    KLEM, Robyn             US
```

PROC PRINT Output (2 Total Observations)

```
                        Gold-Level Customers

            Customer_ID              Name           Country

       Gold000-000-15-0027    MCCLUNEY, Cynthia      US
       Gold000-000-07-0201    BORWICK, Angel         CA
```

PROC PRINT Output (5 Total Observations)

```
                       Platinum-Level Customers

             Customer_ID            Name                     Country

     platinum000-000-15-0010    BALLINGER, Karen               US
     platinum000-000-15-0031    MARTINEZ, Cynthia              US
     platinum000-000-15-0171    BOWERMAN, Robert               AU
     platinum000-000-15-2806    VAN DEN BERG, Raedene          ZA
     platinum000-000-07-0100    YEARGAN, Wilma                 CA
```

Level 2

6. Searching Character Values and Explicit Output

- The data set **orion.employee_donations** contains information on charity contributions from Orion Star employees.
- Each employee is allowed to list either one or two charities, which are shown in the **Recipients** variable.

Partial Listing of **orion.employee_donations** (124 Total Observations, 7 Total Variables)

```
Employee_ID    Recipients

     120265    Mitleid International 90%, Save the Baby Animals 10%
     120267    Disaster Assist, Inc. 80%, Cancer Cures, Inc. 20%
     120269    Cancer Cures, Inc. 10%, Cuidadores Ltd. 90%
     120270    AquaMissions International 10%, Child Survivors 90%
     120271    Cuidadores Ltd. 80%, Mitleid International 20%
     120272    AquaMissions International 10%, Child Survivors 90%
     120275    AquaMissions International 60%, Child Survivors 40%
     120660    Disaster Assist, Inc.
     120662    Cancer Cures, Inc.
     120663    EarthSalvors 30%, Vox Victimas 70%
```

Some charity names have a comma in them.

a. Use explicit output to create a data set named **work.split**.

- The data set will have one observation for each combination of employee and charity to which he donated.
- Some employees made two contributions; therefore, they will have two observations in the output data set. These employees contain a % character in the value of **Recipients**.

Store the position where the % character was found in a variable named **PctLoc**. This can make subsequent coding easier.

- Create a variable named **Charity** with the name and percent contribution of the appropriate charity.
- Read only the first 10 observations from **orion.employee_donations** to test your program.

b. Modify the program to read the entire **orion.employee_donations** data set.

- Print only the columns **Employee_ID** and **Charity**.
- Add an appropriate title.

Partial PROC PRINT Output (212 Total Observations)

```
                        Charity Contributions for each Employee

                     Employee_ID    Charity

                          120265    Mitleid International 90%
                          120265    Save the Baby Animals 10%
                          120267    Disaster Assist, Inc. 80%
                          120267    Cancer Cures, Inc. 20%
                          120269    Cancer Cures, Inc. 10%
                          120269    Cuidadores Ltd. 90%
                          120270    AquaMissions International 10%
                          120270    Child Survivors 90%
                          120271    Cuidadores Ltd. 80%
                          120271    Mitleid International 20%
                          120272    AquaMissions International 10%
                          120272    Child Survivors 90%
                          120275    AquaMissions International 60%
                          120275    Child Survivors 40%
                          120660    Disaster Assist, Inc. 100%
                          120662    Cancer Cures, Inc. 100%
                          120663    EarthSalvors 30%
                          120663    Vox Victimas 70%
```

Level 3

7. Using Character Functions with the Input Buffer

- The raw data file **`supply.dat`** contains information on supplier IDs (up to five characters), supplier names (up to 30 characters), and the country from which that supplier ships (two characters).

Raw Data File **`supply.dat`** (52 rows total)

```
                                    50 Scandinavian Clothing A/S NO
109 Petterson AB SE
316 Prime Sports Ltd GB
755 Top Sports DK
772 AllSeasons Outdoor Clothing US
798 Sportico ES
1280 British Sports Ltd GB
1303 Eclipse Inc US
1684 Magnifico Sports PT
1747 Pro Sportswear Inc US
2963 3Top Sports US
2995 Van Dammeren International NL
```

- The keyword _INFILE_, when SAS reads from a raw data file, enables you to treat the contents of the input buffer as one long character string. This can sometimes be helpful, given the wide variety of character functions in SAS.
- Blanks appear both as delimiters and inside supplier names.

> Remember that both the SCAN and FIND functions can process backward through strings. See SAS Help and Documentation for more details on how to do this.

a. Create a data set named **`work.supplier`**.

- Use list input to obtain values for **`Supplier_ID`**.
- Utilize character functions and the _INFILE_ statement to get values for **`Supplier_Name`** and **`Country`**.

b. Print the data set with an appropriate title.

Partial PROC PRINT Output (52 Total Observations)

```
                              Supplier Information

              Supplier_
                 ID        Supplier_Name                    Country

                 50        Scandinavian Clothing A/S          NO
                 109       Petterson AB                       SE
                 316       Prime Sports Ltd                   GB
                 755       Top Sports                         DK
                 772       AllSeasons Outdoor Clothing        US
                 798       Sportico                           ES
                 1280      British Sports Ltd                 GB
                 1303      Eclipse Inc                        US
```

5.4 Manipulating Numeric Values

Objectives

- Use SAS functions to truncate numeric values.
- Use SAS functions to compute descriptive statistics of numeric values.

117

Truncation Functions

These functions truncate numeric values:

- ROUND
- CEIL
- FLOOR
- INT

118

The ROUND Function

The ROUND function returns a value rounded to the nearest multiple of the round-off unit.

General form of the ROUND function:

```
NewVar=ROUND(argument<,round-off-unit>);
```

argument	is a number or numeric expression.
round-off-unit	is numeric and positive. If *round-off-unit* is not provided, *argument* is rounded to the nearest integer.

119

The ROUND Function – Example

```
data truncate;
   NewVar1=round(12.12);
   NewVar2=round(42.65,.1);
   NewVar3=round(-6.478);
   NewVar4=round(96.47,10);
run;
```

PDV

NewVar1 N 8	NewVar2 N 8	NewVar3 N 8	NewVar4 N 8
12	42.7	-6	100

120

The ROUND Function – Example

```
data truncate;
   NewVar5=round(12.69,.25);
   NewVar6=round(42.65,.5);
run;
```

Round to the nearest multiple of .25

PDV

NewVar5 N 8	NewVar6 N 8
12.75	.

121 ...

The ROUND Function – Example

```
data truncate;
   NewVar5=round(12.69,.25);
   NewVar6=round(42.65,.5);
run;
```

Round to the nearest multiple of .5

PDV

NewVar5 N 8	NewVar6 N 8
12.75	42.5

122

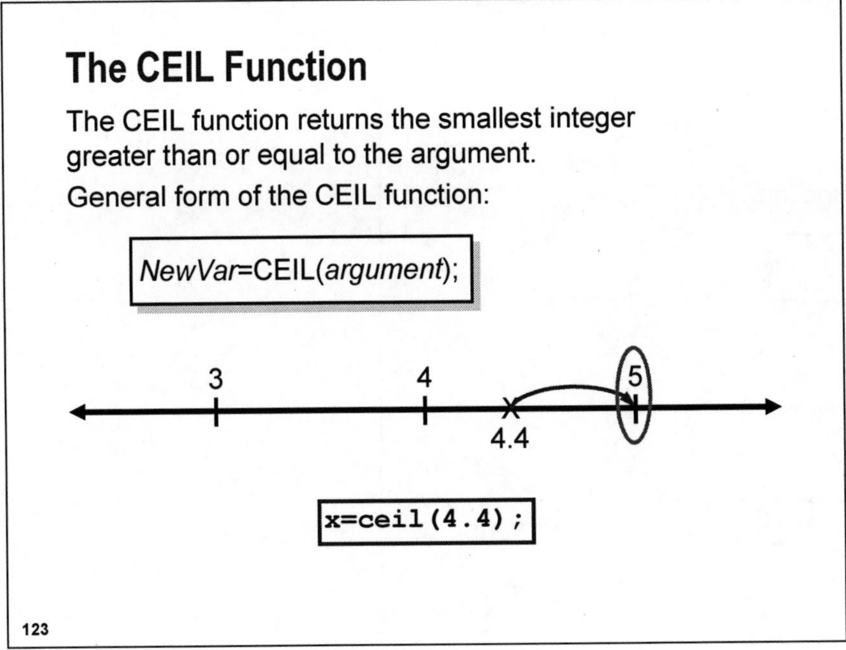

The value of *argument* is numeric.

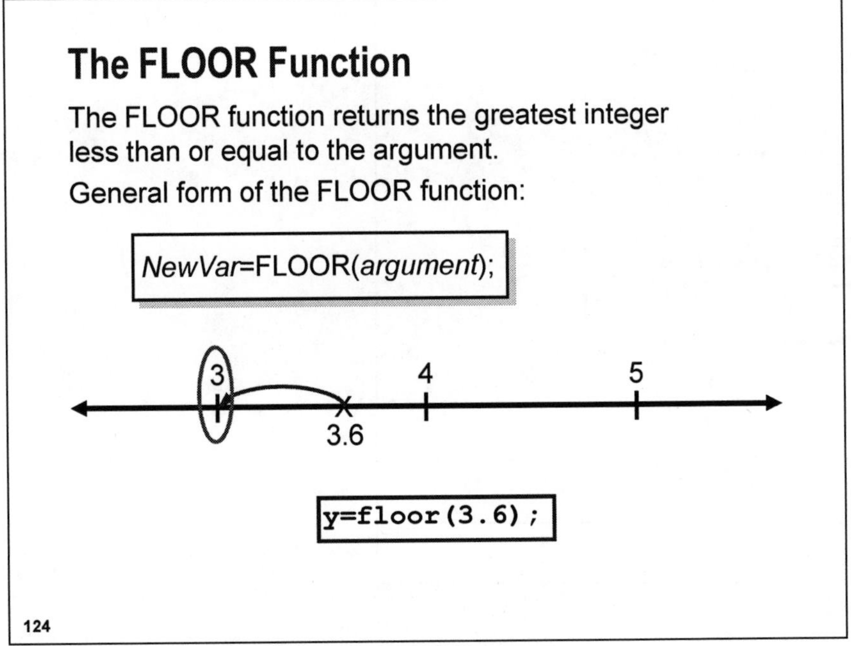

The value of *argument* is numeric.

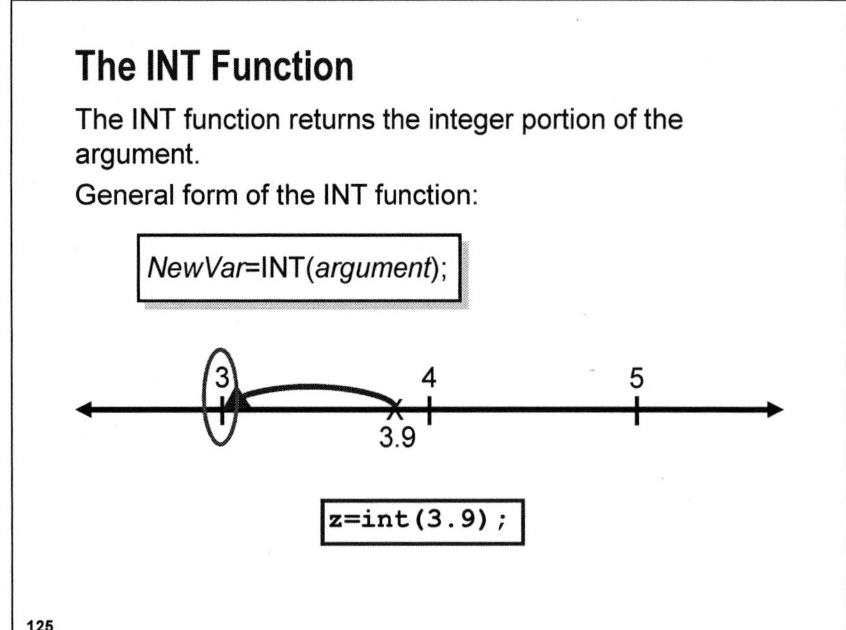
The INT Function
The INT function returns the integer portion of the argument.
General form of the INT function:
NewVar=INT(argument);
3
4
5
3.9
z=int(3.9);
125

The value of *argument* is numeric.

Truncation Functions – Example

```
data truncate;
   Var1=6.478;
   CeilVar1=ceil(Var1);
   FloorVar1=floor(Var1);
   IntVar1=int(Var1);
run;
```

PDV

Var1	CeilVar1	FloorVar1	IntVar1
6.478	7	6	6

126

Setup for the Poll

In this program, the values returned from the FLOOR and INT functions are the same.

```
data truncate;
   Var1=6.478;
   CeilVar1=ceil(Var1);
   FloorVar1=floor(Var1);
   IntVar1=int(Var1);
run;
```

PDV

Var1	CeilVar1	FloorVar1	IntVar1
6.478	7	6	6

128

5.11 Poll

Given the same value as an argument, do the INT and the FLOOR functions always return the same result?

❍ Yes

❍ No

129

Truncation Functions

Compare the values from the CEIL, FLOOR, and INT functions with a negative argument.

```
data truncate;
   Var1=-6.478;
   CeilVar1=ceil(Var1);
   FloorVar1=floor(Var1);
   IntVar1=int(Var1);
run;
```

PDV

Var1	CeilVar1	FloorVar1	IntVar1
-6.478	-6	-7	-6

131

For values greater than or equal to 0, the FLOOR and INT functions return the same value. For values less than 0, the CEIL and INT functions return the same value.

Business Scenario – Donation Statistics

Create a new data set, **donation_stats**, based on the information in **orion.employee_donations**.

For each employee, calculate the following:

- the employee's total donation for the year.
- the average donation for the quarters in which the employee made a donation. Round the average to the nearest dollar.
- the number of quarters in which the employee made a donation.

133

Business Scenario – Input and Desired Output

Partial Listing of **orion.employee_donations**

```
Obs    Employee_ID    Qtr1    Qtr2    Qtr3    Qtr4

 1       120265         .       .       .      25
 2       120267        15      15      15      15
 3       120269        20      20      20      20
 4       120270        20      10       5       .
```

Partial Listing of **donation_stats**

```
                           Avg     Num
  Employee_ID    Total      QT      Qt

     120265        25       25      1
     120267        60       15      4
     120269        80       20      4
     120270        35       12      3
```

134

Descriptive Statistics Functions

Using descriptive statistic functions will be the easiest way to calculate the values needed for **donation_stats**.

Function	Returns
SUM	Sum of arguments.
MEAN	Average of arguments.
MIN	Smallest value from arguments.
MAX	Largest value from arguments.
N	Count of non-missing arguments.
NMISS	Count of missing numeric arguments.
CMISS	Count of missing numeric or character arguments.

135

The CMISS function is new in SAS 9.2.

Descriptive Statistics Functions

These functions all share the same general syntax:

function-name(*argument-1*,*argument-2*,...,*argument-n*)

- *argument-1* through *argument-n* are numeric.
- An argument can be a variable list, which is preceded by OF.
- The SUM, MEAN, MAX, and MIN functions ignore missing values in their arguments.

136

Descriptive Statistics Functions

```
data descript;
   Var1=12;
   Var2=.;
   Var3=7;
   Var4=5;
   SumVars=sum(Var1,Var2,Var3,Var4);
   AvgVars=mean(of Var1-Var4);
   MissVars=cmiss(of Var1-Var4);
run;
```

PDV

Var1	Var2	Var3	Var4
12	.	7	5

SumVars	AvgVars	MissVars
24	.	.

137 p205d12

...

Descriptive Statistics Functions

```
data descript;
   Var1=12;
   Var2=.;
   Var3=7;
   Var4=5;
   SumVars=sum(Var1,Var2,Var3,Var4);
   AvgVars=mean(of Var1-Var4);
   MissVars=cmiss(of Var1-Var4);
run;
```

PDV

Var1	Var2	Var3	Var4
12	.	7	5

SumVars	AvgVars	MissVars
24	8	.

138 ...

Descriptive Statistics Functions

```
data descript;
   Var1=12;
   Var2=.;
   Var3=7;
   Var4=5;
   SumVars=sum(Var1,Var2,Var3,Var4);
   AvgVars=mean(of Var1-Var4);
   MissVars=cmiss(of Var1-Var4);
run;
```

PDV

Var1	Var2	Var3	Var4
12	.	7	5

SumVars	AvgVars	MissVars
24	8	1

139

5.12 Multiple Choice Poll

Ord1, **Ord2**, and **Ord3** are variables that contain the sale amounts of the last three orders from a customer. Which of the following expressions can calculate the total of the two largest orders?

a. `sum(max(of Ord1-Ord3),max(of Ord1-Ord3))`
b. `sum(of Ord1-Ord3)-min(of Ord1-Ord3)`
c. `max(of Ord1-Ord3) + min(of Ord1-Ord3)`
d. None of the above

141

Business Scenario – Complete

Use the SUM, MEAN, and N functions to calculate the donation statistics.

```
data donation_stats;
   set orion.employee_donations;
   keep Employee_ID Total AvgQT NumQT;
   Total = sum(of Qtr1-Qtr4);
   AvgQT = round(Mean(of Qtr1-Qtr4));
   NumQt = n(of Qtr1-Qtr4);
run;
```

143 p205d13

Business Scenario – Complete

```
proc print data=donation_stats noobs;
   var Employee_ID Total AvgQt NumQt;
run;
```

Partial PROC PRINT Output

```
                         Avg      Num
Employee_ID    Total      QT       Qt

   120265        25       25       1
   120267        60       15       4
   120269        80       20       4
   120270        35       12       3
```

144

Exercises

Level 1

8. Calculating Statistics and Rounding

The data set **orion.orders_midyear** contains an observation for each customer, with the total retail value of the customer's monthly orders for the first half of the year.

Partial Listing of **orion.orders_midyear** (24 Total Observations)

Customer_ID	month1	month2	month3	month4	month5	month6
5	213.1	.	478.0	525.80	394.35	191.79
10	188.1	414.09	2876.9	3164.59	2373.44	169.29
11	78.2	.	.	.	.	70.38
12	135.6	.	117.6	129.36	97.02	122.04
18	.	.	29.4	32.34	24.26	.
24	93.0	265.80	.	.	.	83.70
27	310.7	782.90	.	.	.	279.63
31	1484.3	293.30	.	.	.	1335.87
34	642.5	.	86.3	94.93	71.20	578.25

a. Create a data set named **work.sale_stats** with three new variables for all months in which the customer placed an order.

- The variable **MonthAvg** should contain the average.
- The variable **MonthMax** should contain the maximum.
- The variable **MonthSum** should contain the sum of values.
- Round **MonthAvg** to the nearest integer.

Most SAS descriptive statistics functions automatically ignore missing values.

b. Print the variables **Customer_ID**, **MonthAvg**, **MonthMax**, and **MonthSum**. Add an appropriate title.

Partial PROC PRINT Output (24 Total Observations)

```
                  Statistics on Months in which the Customer Placed an Order

                                   Month        Month        Month
                   Customer_ID       Avg          Max          Sum

                             5       361       525.80      1803.04
                            10      1531      3164.59      9186.41
                            11        74        78.20       148.58
                            12       120       135.60       601.62
                            18        29        32.34        86.00
                            24       148       265.80       442.50
                            27       458       782.90      1373.23
                            31      1038      1484.30      3113.47
                            34       295       642.50      1473.18
```

Level 2

There is no level 2 exercise for this section.

Level 3

9. Calculating Statistics for Missing, Median, and Highest Values

The data set **orion.orders_midyear** contains an observation for each customer, with the total retail value of the customer's monthly orders for the first half of the year.

Partial Listing of **orion.orders_midyear** (24 Total Observations)

```
      Customer_ID     month1     month2     month3      month4      month5      month6

                5      213.1        .        478.0      525.80      394.35      191.79
               10      188.1     414.09     2876.9     3164.59     2373.44      169.29
               11       78.2        .          .           .           .         70.38
               12      135.6        .        117.6      129.36       97.02      122.04
               18         .         .         29.4       32.34       24.26         .
               24       93.0     265.80        .           .           .         83.70
               27      310.7     782.90        .           .           .        279.63
               31     1484.3     293.30        .           .           .       1335.87
               34      642.5        .         86.3       94.93       71.20      578.25
```

a. Orion Star wants to look at information on the median order and the top two months' orders, but only for frequent customers.

- Create a data set named **work.freqcustomers** that contains the requested statistics.
- Frequent customers are defined to be those who placed an order in at least five of the six months.

b. Print your results with an appropriate title.

> The *median* of a set of values is the middle or central value. For example, the median of {1, 200, 3} is the value 3. If the set has an even number of values, the median is the midpoint between the two middle values.

> Consult the SAS documentation, as needed, to learn more about functions that can generate the desired results. It might be particularly useful to look at "Functions and CALL Routines by Category" in the *SAS Language Dictionary.*

PROC PRINT Output

```
                              Month Statistics on Frequent Customers

                                                                                          Month_
                                                                        Month_   Month_    2nd
Customer_ID  month1  month2  month3   month4   month5   month6   Median  Highest  Highest

      5  213.10      .     478.0   525.80   394.35  191.790   394.35   525.80   478.00
     10  188.10  414.09   2876.9  3164.59  2373.44  169.290  1393.77  3164.59  2876.90
     12  135.60      .     117.6   129.36    97.02  122.040   122.04   135.60   129.36
     34  642.50      .      86.3    94.93    71.20  578.250    94.93   642.50   578.25
     41  134.00  119.20    313.0   344.30   258.23  120.600   196.11   344.30   313.00
     45  443.88  216.20     40.2    44.22    33.17  399.492   130.21   443.88   399.49
     90   33.60  110.20    396.9   436.59   327.44   30.240   218.82   436.59   396.90
     92   16.90      .     160.5   176.55   132.41   15.210   132.41   176.55   160.50
    171   73.99  534.60   1241.4  1365.54  1024.16   66.591   779.38  1365.54  1241.40
```

5.5 Converting Variable Type

Objectives

- Explain the automatic conversion that SAS uses to convert values between data types.
- Explicitly convert values between data types.

148

Business Scenario – Convert HR Data

Orion Star recently acquired a small marketing firm and needs to convert the firm's personnel data into a data set that can be easily transferred into Orion's HR system.

The data set **orion.convert** has a sample of the marketing firm's personnel data.

Listing of **orion.convert**

ID $ 5	GrossPay $ 6	Code N 8	Mobile $ 8	Hired $ 10
36	52,000	303	393-0956	04/13/2004
48	32,000	919	770-8292	08/25/2006
52	49,000	301	449-5239	06/08/2005

149

Business Scenario – Desired Output

Store the converted personnel data in **hrdata**.

Listing of **hrdata**

EmpID N 8	GrossPay N 8	Bonus N 8	Phone $ 14	HireDate N 8
11036	52000	5200	(303) 393-0956	16174
11048	32000	3200	(919) 770-8292	17038
11052	49000	4900	(301) 449-5239	16595

- 11000 is added to **ID** to create **EmpID**. (This avoids conflicts with existing Orion Star Employee IDs.)
- **GrossPay** is the only variable name being kept.
- **Bonus** is a retention bonus and is 10% of **GrossPay**.

150

continued...

Business Scenario – Desired Output

Store the converted personnel data in **hrdata**.

Listing of **hrdata**

EmpID N 8	GrossPay N 8	Bonus N 8	Phone $ 14	HireDate N 8
11036	52000	5200	(303) 393-0956	16174
11048	32000	3200	(919) 770-8292	17038
11052	49000	4900	(301) 449-5239	16595

- **Phone** is a combination of **Code** and **Mobile**.
- **HireDate** is a SAS date value.

151

Data Conversion

For this business scenario, SAS needs to convert one data type to another.

Character-to-Numeric

- The character values in **`ID`**, **`GrossPay`**, and **`Hired`** need to be transformed into numeric values.

Numeric-to-Character

- The numeric values in **`Code`** need to be transformed into character values before being concatenated with the values in **`Mobile`**.

152

Data Conversion

Data types can be converted two ways:

- *automatically* by allowing SAS to do it for you.
- *explicitly* with these functions:

INPUT	character-to-numeric conversion
PUT	numeric-to-character conversion

153

Automatic Character-to-Numeric Conversion

What will happen when the character values of **ID** are used in an arithmetic expression?

```
data hrdata;
   keep EmpID;
   set orion.convert;
   EmpID = ID + 11000;
run;
```

154

p205d14

Automatic Character-to-Numeric Conversion

Partial Log

```
28   data hrdata;
29      keep EmpID;
30      set orion.convert;
31      EmpID = ID + 11000;
32   run;

NOTE: Character values have been converted to numeric values at
the places given by:
      (Line):(Column).
      31:11
NOTE: There were 3 observations read from the data set
ORION.CONVERT.
NOTE: The data set WORK.HRDATA has 3 observations and 1
variables.
```

155

Automatic Character-to-Numeric Conversion

```
proc print data=hrdata noobs;
run;
```

PROC PRINT Output

```
EmpID

11036
11048
11052
```

The automatic conversion worked great for **ID**. Now see what happens with **GrossPay**.

156

Automatic Character-to-Numeric Conversion

What happens when the character values of **GrossPay** are used in an arithmetic expression?

```
data hrdata;
   keep GrossPay Bonus;
   set orion.convert;
   Bonus = GrossPay * .10;
run;
```

157

p205d15

Automatic Character-to-Numeric Conversion

```
proc print data=hrdata noobs;
run;
```

PROC PRINT Output

```
Gross
Pay         Bonus

52,000        .
32,000        .
49,000        .
```

Why did the automatic conversion not work for the values of **GrossPay**?

158

Automatic Character-to-Numeric Conversion

SAS automatically converts a character value to a numeric value when the character value is used in a numeric context, such as the following:

- assignment to a numeric variable
- an arithmetic operation
- logical comparison with a numeric value
- a function that takes numeric arguments

159

The WHERE statement and the WHERE= data set option do not perform any automatic conversion in comparisons.

Automatic Character-to-Numeric Conversion

The automatic conversion

- uses the *w.* informat
- produces a numeric missing value from a character value that does not conform to standard numeric notation (digits with optional decimal point and/or leading sign and/or E-notation).

160

Automatic Character-to-Numeric Conversion

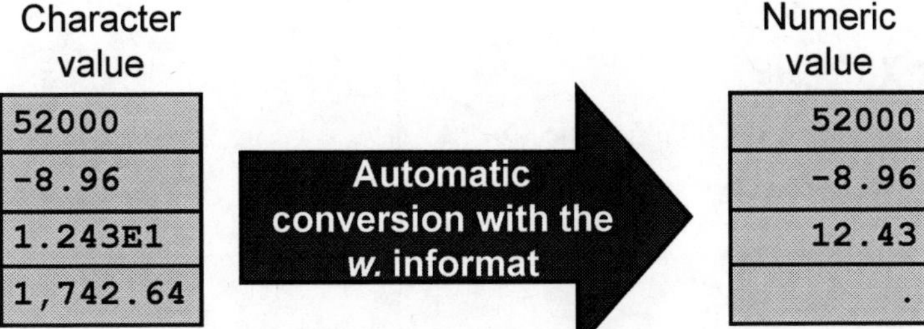

- The values in **GrossPay** contained commas, which could not be converted by the *w.* informat, so **GrossPay** was assigned a missing value.
- To explicitly convert the values in **GrossPay**, use the INPUT function.

161

The INPUT Function

The INPUT function returns the value produced when the source is read with a specified informat.

General form of the INPUT function:

NumVar=INPUT(*source*,*informat*);

source	contains a SAS character expression
informat	is the SAS informat to apply to the *source*.

✎ No conversion messages are written to the log by the INPUT function.

162

If you use the INPUT function to create a variable not previously defined, the type and length of the variable is defined by the informat.

The INPUT Function – Example

This DATA step shows examples of the INPUT function.

```
data conversions;
   CVar1='32000';
   CVar2='32.000';
   CVar3='03may2008';
   CVar4='030508';
   NVar1=input(CVar1,5.);
   NVar2=input(CVar2,commax6.);
   NVar3=input(CVar3,date9.);
   NVar4=input(CVar4,ddmmyy6.);
run;
```

163 p205d16

The INPUT Function – Example

```
proc contents data=conversions;
run;
```

Partial PROC CONTENTS Output

Alphabetic List of Variables and Attributes

#	Variable	Type	Len
1	CVar1	Char	5
2	CVar2	Char	6
3	CVar3	Char	9
4	CVar4	Char	6
5	NVar1	Num	8
6	NVar2	Num	8
7	NVar3	Num	8
8	NVar4	Num	8

164

The INPUT Function – Example

```
proc print data=conversions noobs;
run;
```

PROC PRINT Output

CVar1	CVar2	CVar3	CVar4	NVar1	NVar2	NVar3	NVar4
32000	32.000	03may2008	030508	32000	32000	17655	17655

165

5.13 Quiz

Fill in the missing expression in the DATA step below. The expression should calculate **TotalValue** by multiplying **SharePrice** by **MyShares**.

```
data Input_Quiz;
   SharePrice = "$130.25";
   MyShares = 125;
   TotalValue =                    ?

run;
```

167

Explicit Character-to-Numeric Conversion

Continue with the business scenario by creating the variables **EmpID**, **Bonus**, and **HireDate**.

Use the INPUT function to explicitly convert character values to numeric.

```
data hrdata;
   keep EmpID GrossPay Bonus HireDate;
   set orion.convert;
   EmpID = input(ID,5.)+11000;
   Bonus = input(GrossPay,comma6.)*.10;
   HireDate = input(Hired,mmddyy10.);
run;
```

169 p205d18

Explicit Character-to-Numeric Conversion

```
proc print data=hrdata noobs;
   var EmpID GrossPay Bonus HireDate;
run;
```

PROC PRINT Output

SAS date values

EmpID	Gross Pay	Bonus	Hire Date
11036	52,000	5200	16174
11048	32,000	3200	17038
11052	49,000	4900	16595

170

Explicit Character-to-Numeric Conversion

```
proc print data=hrdata noobs;
  var EmpID GrossPay Bonus HireDate;
  format HireDate mmddyy10.;
run;
```

PROC PRINT Output

EmpID	Gross Pay	Bonus	HireDate
11036	52,000	5200	04/13/2004
11048	32,000	3200	08/25/2006
11052	49,000	4900	06/08/2005

What data type is **GrossPay**?

171

Converting a Variable to Another Data Type

```
proc contents data=hrdata;
run;
```

Partial PROC CONTENTS Output

```
Alphabetic List of Variables and Attributes

   #    Variable     Type    Len

   3    Bonus        Num       8
   2    EmpID        Num       8
   1    GrossPay     Char      6
   4    HireDate     Num       8
```

How can you convert **GrossPay** to a numeric variable with the same name?

172

5.14 Quiz

Will this statement convert **GrossPay** to numeric?

```
GrossPay=input(GrossPay,comma6.);
```

Open and run the program **p205a02**. Did **GrossPay** become a numeric variable?

174

Converting a Variable to Another Data Type

```
GrossPay=input(GrossPay,comma6.);
```

This assignment statement does **not** change **GrossPay** from a character variable to a numeric variable.

A variable is character or numeric. After the variable's type is established, it cannot be changed.

By following three steps, you can create a new variable with the same name and a different type.

176

Converting a Variable to Another Data Type

Step 1: Use the RENAME= data set option to rename the variable that you want to convert.

```
data hrdata;
   set orion.convert(rename=(GrossPay=
                             CharGross));
run;
```

General form of the RENAME data set option:

SAS-data-set(RENAME=(*old-name*=*new-name*))

177

old-name specifies the variable that you want to rename.

new-name specifies the new name of the variable. It must be a valid SAS name.

The new name of the variable that you want to convert is arbitrary. In this example, the existing variable is renamed **CharGross** to emphasize that a character variable is being converted.

To rename more than one variable from the same data set, separate the variables that you want to rename with a space. For example, to rename not only **GrossPay**, but also **ID**, use the following statement:

```
set orion.convert(rename=(GrossPay=CharGross ID=IDNum));
```

Converting a Variable to Another Data Type

Step 2: Use the INPUT function in an assignment statement to create a new variable with the original name of the variable that you renamed.

```
data hrdata;
   set orion.convert(rename=(GrossPay=
                              CharGross));
   GrossPay=input(CharGross,comma6.);
run;
```

178

Converting a Variable to Another Data Type

Step 3: Use a DROP= data set option in the DATA statement to exclude the original variable from the output SAS data set.

```
data hrdata(drop=CharGross);
   set orion.convert(rename=(GrossPay=
                              CharGross));
   GrossPay=input(CharGross,comma6.);
run;
```

The compilation for this program shows the PDV being created with a numeric **GrossPay** variable.

179 p205d19

Converting a Variable: Compilation

```
data hrdata(drop=CharGross);
   set orion.convert(rename=(GrossPay=
                              CharGross));
   GrossPay=input(CharGross,comma6.);
run;
```

Partial PDV

ID $ 5	CharGross $ 6	Hired $ 7

180 ...

Converting a Variable: Compilation

```
data hrdata(drop=CharGross);
   set orion.convert(rename=(GrossPay=
                              CharGross));
   GrossPay=input(CharGross,comma6.);
run;
```

Partial PDV

ID $ 5	CharGross $ 6	Hired $ 7	GrossPay N 8

181 ...

Converting a Variable: Compilation

```
data hrdata(drop=CharGross);
   set orion.convert(rename=(GrossPay=
                              CharGross));
   GrossPay=input(CharGross,comma6.);
run;
```

Partial PDV

ID	CharGross	Hired	GrossPay
$ 5	D $ 6	$ 7	N 8

182

Continue with the Business Scenario

The **orion.convert** data set contains a numeric variable **Code** (area code) and a character variable **Mobile** (mobile telephone number). Create a character variable, **Phone**, that contains the area code in parentheses followed by the mobile telephone number.

For the first try at creating the **Phone** variable, let SAS automatically handle the conversion.

184

Automatic Numeric-to-Character Conversion

Partial list of `orion.convert`

Code N 8	Mobile $ 8
303	393-0956
919	770-8292
301	449-5239

```
data hrdata;
   keep Phone Code Mobile;
   set orion.convert;
   Phone='(' !! Code !! ') ' !! Mobile;
run;
```

SAS automatically converts the numeric values in **Code** into character values.

185 p205d20

Automatic Numeric-to-Character Conversion

Partial Log

```
14   data hrdata;
15     keep Phone Code Mobile;
16     set orion.convert;
17     Phone='(' !! Code !! ') ' !! Mobile;
18   run;

NOTE: Numeric values have been converted to character values
    at the places given by:
      (Line):(Column).
      17:16
NOTE: There were 3 observations read from the data set
    ORION.CONVERT.
NOTE: The data set WORK.HRDATA has 3 observations and 3
    variables.
```

186

Automatic Numeric-to-Character Conversion

```
proc print data=hrdata noobs;
run;
```

PROC PRINT Output

```
Code    Mobile              Phone

 303    393-0956    (        303) 393-0956
 919    770-8292    (        919) 770-8292
 301    449-5239    (        301) 449-5239
```

Why did SAS insert the extra blanks before the area code?

187

Automatic Numeric-to-Character Conversion

SAS automatically converts a numeric value to a character value when the numeric value is used in a character context, such as

- assignment to a character variable
- a concatenation operation
- a function that accepts character arguments.

188

The WHERE statement and the WHERE= data set option do not perform any automatic conversion in comparisons.

Automatic Numeric-to-Character Conversion

The automatic conversion

- uses the BEST12. format
- right-aligns the resulting character value.

Numeric value: 8 bytes

303

Automatic conversion with BEST12. format

Character value: 12 bytes

303

9 leading blanks

189

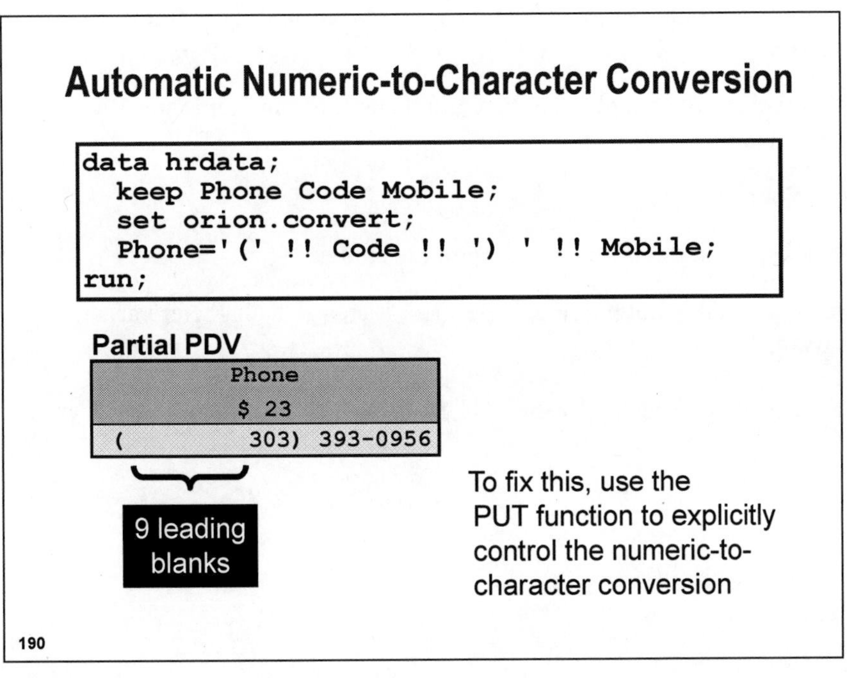
Automatic Numeric-to-Character Conversion
data hrdata;
keep Phone Code Mobile;
set orion.convert;
Phone='(' !! Code !! ') ' !! Mobile;
run;
Partial PDV
Phone
$ 23
(303) 393-0956
9 leading blanks
To fix this, use the PUT function to explicitly control the numeric-to-character conversion
190

The PUT Function

The PUT function writes values with a specific format.

```
CharVar=PUT(source,format);
```

The PUT function returns the value produced when *source* is written with *format*.

191

source identifies the SAS variable or constant whose value you want to reformat. This argument can be character or numeric.

format contains the SAS format that you want applied to the variable or constant that is specified in the source. It must agree with the source in type.

The PUT function always returns a character string.

Numeric formats right-align the results. Character formats left-align the results.

If you use the PUT function to create a variable not previously defined, it creates a character variable with a length equal to the format width.

No conversion messages are written to the log by the PUT function.

The PUT Function – Example

This DATA step shows examples of the PUT function.

```
data conversion;
   NVar1=614;
   NVar2=55000;
   NVar3=366;
   CVar1=put(NVar1,3.);
   CVar2=put(NVar2,dollar7.);
   CVar3=put(NVar3,date9.);
run;
```

192

p205d21

The PUT Function – Example

```
proc contents data=conversion varnum;
run;
```

The VARNUM option in the PROC CONTENTS statement prints a list of the variables by their logical position in the data set.

Partial PROC CONTENTS Output

Variables in Creation Order

#	Variable	Type	Len
1	NVar1	Num	8
2	NVar2	Num	8
3	NVar3	Num	8
4	CVar1	Char	3
5	CVar2	Char	7
6	CVar3	Char	9

193

The PUT Function – Example

```
proc print data=conversion noobs;
run;
```

PROC PRINT Output

NVar1	NVar2	NVar3	CVar1	CVar2	CVar3
614	55000	366	614	$55,000	01JAN1961

194

Explicit Numeric-to-Character Conversion

```
data hrdata;
   keep Phone Code Mobile;
   set orion.convert;
   Phone='(' !! put(Code,3.) !! ') '
            !! Mobile;
run;
```

Partial Log

```
data hrdata;
  keep Phone Code Mobile;
  set orion.convert;
  Phone='(' !! put(Code,3.) !! ') ' !! Mobile;
run;

NOTE: The data set WORK.HRDATA has 3 observations
      and 3 variables.
```

195 p205d22

Explicit Numeric-to-Character Conversion

```
proc print data=hrdata noobs;
run;
```

PROC PRINT Output

```
Code    Mobile       Phone

 303    393-0956     (303) 393-0956
 919    770-8292     (919) 770-8292
 301    449-5239     (301) 449-5239
```

196

The CAT Functions and Numeric Conversion

The CAT family of functions converts any numeric argument to a character string by using the BEST12. format and then removing any leading blanks. No note is written to the log.

This assignment statement using CAT:

```
Phone=cat('(',Code,') ',Mobile);
```

gives equivalent results to this statement:

```
Phone='(' !! put(Code,3.) !! ') ' !! Mobile;
```

Now you can write the complete SAS program to convert the personnel data.

197

Convert HR Data – Complete Program

```
data hrdata;
   keep EmpID GrossPay Bonus Phone HireDate;
   set orion.convert(rename=(GrossPay=
                             CharGross));
   EmpID = input(ID,5.)+11000;
   GrossPay = input(CharGross,comma6.);
   Bonus = GrossPay*.10;
   HireDate = input(Hired,mmddyy10.);
   Phone=cat('(',Code,') ',Mobile);
run;

proc print data=hrdata noobs;
   var EmpID GrossPay Bonus Phone HireDate;
   format HireDate mmddyy10.;
run;
```

198

p205d23

Convert HR Data – Complete Program

PROC PRINT Output

```
           Gross
  EmpID     Pay     Bonus        Phone            HireDate

  11036    52000     5200    (303) 393-0956     04/13/2002
  11048    32000     3200    (919) 770-8292     08/25/1998
  11052    49000     4900    (301) 449-5239     06/08/2001
```

199

Exercises

Level 1

10. Using the PUT and INPUT Functions

The data set **orion.shipped** contains details about each product shipped to one of Orion Star's retail outlets in 2007.

Partial Listing of **orion.shipped**

```
  Product_ID      Ship_Date     Quantity      Price

240800200021     05JAN2007          2        $42.45
240800200035     04JAN2007          6        $12.15
240200100225     04JAN2007          2        $77.85
210200500002     09JAN2007          3         $5.70
```

Partial PROC CONTENTS Output for **orion.shipped**

```
          Variables in Creation Order

 #     Variable       Type    Len    Format

 1     Product_ID     Num       8
 2     Ship_Date      Num       8    DATE9.
 3     Quantity       Num       8
 4     Price          Char      7
```

An analyst at Orion Star has written a SAS program to calculate the total price of the items shipped and create a comment that includes the ship date. Unfortunately, the SAS program is giving unexpected results.

a. Open and submit the program, **p205e10.sas**.

b. View the unexpected results.

Partial PROC PRINT of Unexpected Results

```
  Product_ID      Ship_Date     Quantity      Price          Comment            Total

240800200021     05JAN2007          2        $42.45     Shipped on 17171          .
240800200035     04JAN2007          6        $12.15     Shipped on 17170          .
240200100225     04JAN2007          2        $77.85     Shipped on 17170          .
210200500002     09JAN2007          3         $5.70     Shipped on 17175          .
```

c. Modify the program to generate the expected results.

Partial PROC PRINT of Desired Results

Product_ID	Ship_Date	Quantity	Price	Comment	Total
240800200021	05JAN2007	2	$42.45	Shipped on 01/05/2007	$84.90
240800200035	04JAN2007	6	$12.15	Shipped on 01/04/2007	$72.90
240200100225	04JAN2007	2	$77.85	Shipped on 01/04/2007	$155.70
210200500002	09JAN2007	3	$5.70	Shipped on 01/09/2007	$17.10

- Look above at the PROC CONTENTS output for **orion.shipped**.
- Notice that **Ship_Date** is numeric with a permanently assigned DATE9. format. It needs to be converted into a character value using the MMDDYY10. format.
- Notice that **Price** is character. It needs to be converted into a numeric value using the COMMA7.2 or DOLLAR7.2 informat.
- Use functions to convert the values of **Ship_Date** and **Price** to get the desired results.

Level 2

11. Changing a Variable's Data Type

The data set **orion.US_newhire** contains information about newly hired employees.

Partial Listing of **orion.US_newhire**

ID	Telephone	Birthday
120-012-40-4928	5467887	05DEC1968
120-012-83-3816	6888321	03MAY1965
120-341-44-0781	9418123	23NOV1972
120-423-01-7721	7839191	28JUN1967

Partial PROC CONTENTS Output of **orion.US_newhire**

Variables in Creation Order

#	Variable	Type	Len
1	ID	Char	15
2	Telephone	Num	8
3	Birthday	Char	9

a. Create a new data set from **orion.US_newhire**.

- Name the new data set **US_converted**.
- Remove the embedded dashes in **ID**.
- Convert **ID** to a numeric value.
- Convert **Telephone** to character and place a – (hyphen/dash) between the third and forth digits.
- Convert **Birthday** to a SAS date value.

b. Print **US_converted** with an appropriate title and use PROC CONTENTS to check the variables types.

Partial PROC PRINT of **US_converted** (10 Total Observations)

```
                 US New Hires

          ID           Telephone     Birthday

     120012404928      546-7887        3261
     120012833816      688-8321        1949
     120341440781      941-8123        4710
     120423017721      783-9191        2735
```

Partial PROC CONTENTS of **US_converted**

```
     Variables in Creation Order

 #    Variable      Type     Len

 1    ID            Num        8
 2    Telephone     Char       8
 3    Birthday      Num        8
```

5.6 Chapter Review

Chapter Review

1. Rewrite **`sum(Qtr1,Qtr2,Qtr3,Qtr4)`** to use a numbered range list in place of writing each variable's name.

2. What function is used to extract characters from a string?

3. What function converts all words in a string to have the first letter as uppercase and the remaining letters as lowercase?

4. What does the FIND function do?

202

Chapter Review

5. What function can be used to remove all occurrences of the character '-' from a string?

6. List some of the descriptive statistic functions.

7. What happens if you use a character variable with a function that takes numeric arguments?

8. What function can be used to convert a character value into a numeric value using a specified informat?

205

5.7 Solutions

Solutions to Exercises

1. **Extracting Characters Based on Position**

   a. Orion Star wants to create user ID codes for logging onto the Australian Sales intranet site.

```
data work.codes;
  set orion.au_salesforce;
  length FCode1 FCode2 $ 1 LCode $ 4;
  FCode1=lowcase(substr(First_Name,1,1));
  FCode2=lowcase(substr(First_Name,length(First_Name),1));
  LCode=lowcase(substr(Last_Name,1,4));
run;
```

   b. Print the resulting data set.

```
title 'Extracted Letters for User IDs';
proc print data=work.codes;
  var First_Name FCode1 FCode2 Last_Name LCode;
run;
title;
```

Alternate Solution:

```
data work.codes;
  set orion.au_salesforce;
  length FCode1 FCode2 $ 1 LCode $ 4;
  FCode1=lowcase(substr(First_Name,1,1));
  FCode2=lowcase(substr(right(First_Name),12,1));
  /* Note 12 is the variable length of First_Name */
  LCode=lowcase(substr(Last_Name,1,4));
run;
title 'Extracted Letters for User IDs';
proc print data=work.codes;
  var First_Name FCode1 FCode2 Last_Name LCode;
run;
title;
```

2. Extracting Characters Based on Position

a. Orion Star would like a data set containing only the small retail stores from these observations.

```
data work.small;
  set orion.newcompetitors;
  Country = substr(ID,1,2);
  Store_Code=left(substr(ID,3));
  if substr(Store_Code,1,1) = '1';
  City=propcase(City);
run;
```

b. Print your results with an appropriate title.

```
title 'New Small-Store Competitors';
proc print data=work.small noobs;
   var Store_Code Country City Postal_Code;
run;
title;
```

3. Converting U.S. Postal Codes to State Names

a. Create a new data set named **states** that includes the variables **ID** and **Name** as well as a new variable named **Location** that shows the full name in proper case for the state that the contact is based in.

```
data states;
  set orion.contacts;
  keep ID Name Location;
  Location = zipnamel(substr(right(address2),20,5));
run;
```

b. Print your results with an appropriate title.

```
proc print data=states noobs;
run;
```

4. Cleaning Text Data

a. Write a program to create the **names** data set.

```
data names;
   length New_Name $50
          FMnames $30
          Last $30;
   set orion.customers_ex5;
   FMnames = scan(Name,2,',');
   Last = propcase(scan(Name,1,','));
   if Gender="F" then New_Name=CATX(' ','Ms.',FMNames,Last);
   else if Gender="M" then New_Name=CATX(' ','Mr.',FMNames,Last);
   keep New_Name Name Gender;
run;
```

b. Print the **names** data set.

```
proc print data=names;
run;
```

5. (Optional) Searching and Replacing Character Values

a. Create three output data sets: **work.silver**, **work.gold**, and **work.platinum**.

```
data work.silver work.gold work.platinum;
   set orion.customers_ex5;
   Customer_ID=tranwrd(Customer_ID,'-00-','-15-');
   if find(Customer_ID,'Silver','I') > 0 then
        output work.silver;
   else if find(Customer_ID,'Gold','I') > 0 then
        output work.gold;
   else if find(Customer_ID,'Platinum','I') > 0 then
        output work.platinum;
   keep Name Customer_ID Country;
run;
```

b. Print the data sets with appropriate titles.

```
title 'Silver-Level Customers';
proc print data=work.silver noobs;
run;

title 'Gold-Level Customers';
proc print data=work.gold noobs;
run;

title 'Platinum-Level Customers';
proc print data=work.platinum noobs;
run;
title;
```

c. Confirm that any `-00` was replaced by `-15`.

6. Searching Character Values and Explicit Output

a. Use explicit output to create a data set named **work.split**.

```
data work.split;
   set orion.employee_donations (obs=10);
   PctLoc=find(Recipients,'%');
   /* Position in which the first '%' occurs */
   if PctLoc > 0 then do;
     Charity=substr(Recipients,1,PctLoc);
     output;
     Charity=substr(Recipients,PctLoc+3);
     output;
   end;
   /* If '%' was found, then there's more than one recipient */
   /* Use PctLoc+3 for the '%, ' before the second charity */
   else do;
     Charity=trim(Recipients)!!' 100%';
     output;
   end;
   drop PctLoc Recipients;
run;

proc print data=work.split noobs;
   var Employee_ID Charity;
run;
```

b. Modify the program to read the entire **orion.employee_donations** data set.

```
data work.split;
   set orion.employee_donations;
   PctLoc=find(Recipients,'%');
   /* Position in which the first '%' occurs */
   if PctLoc > 0 then do;
     Charity=substr(Recipients,1,PctLoc);
     output;
     Charity=substr(Recipients,PctLoc+3);
     output;
   end;
   /* If '%' was found, then there's more than one recipient */
   /* Use PctLoc+3 for the '%, ' before the second charity */
   else do;
     Charity=trim(Recipients)!!' 100%';
     output;
   end;
   drop PctLoc Recipients;
run;

title 'Charity Contributions for each Employee';
proc print data=work.split noobs;
   var Employee_ID Charity;
run;
title;
```

Alternate Solution:

```
  /* Use SCAN with '%' as a delimiter */

data work.split;
   set orion.employee_donations;
   PctLoc=find(Recipients,'%');
   /* Position in which the first '%' occurs */
   if PctLoc > 0 then do;
     Charity=scan(Recipients,1,'%')!!'%';
     output;
     Charity=substr(scan(Recipients,2,'%')!!'%',3);
     output;
   end;
   /* Because '%' is the delimiter, we must concatenate
      a '%' to the character string after the SCAN */
   else do;
     Charity=trim(Recipients)!!' 100%';
     output;
   end;
   drop PctLoc Recipients ;
run;

title 'Charity Contributions for each Employee';
proc print data=work.split noobs;
   var Employee_ID Charity;
run;
title;
```

7. Using Character Functions with the Input Buffer

a. Create a data set named **work.supplier**.

```
data work.supplier;
   length Supplier_ID $ 5 Supplier_Name $ 30 Country $ 2;
   infile 'supply.dat';
   input Supplier_ID $;
   Country=scan(_INFILE_,-1,' ');
   StartCol=find(_INFILE_,' ');
   EndCol=find(_INFILE_,' ',-999);
   /* Everything between these first and last blanks is
   the supplier name. */
   Supplier_Name=substr(_INFILE_,StartCol+1,EndCol-StartCol);
   /* Knowing where the last blank is, Country could have
   also been created using SUBSTR. */
   drop StartCol EndCol;
run;
```

b. Print the data set with an appropriate title.

```
title 'Supplier Information';
proc print data=work.supplier noobs;
run;
title;
```

8. Calculating Statistics and Rounding

a. Create a data set **work.sale_stats** with three new variables for all months in which the customer placed an order.

```
data work.sale_stats;
   set orion.orders_midyear;
   MonthAvg=round(mean(of month1-month6));
   MonthMax=max(of month1-month6);
   MonthSum=sum(of month1-month6);
run;
```

b. Print the variables **Customer_ID**, **MonthAvg**, **MonthMax**, and **MonthSum**. Add an appropriate title.

```
title 'Statistics on Months in which the Customer Placed an Order';
proc print data=work.sale_stats noobs;
   var Customer_ID MonthAvg MonthMax MonthSum;
run;
title;
```

9. Calculating Statistics for Missing, Median, and Highest Values

a. Orion Star wants to look at information on the median order and the top two months' orders, but only for frequent customers.

```
data work.freqcustomers;
   set orion.orders_midyear;
   if n(of month1-month6) >= 5;
   /* Alternative: if nmiss(of month1-month6) <= 1; */
   Month_Median=median(of month1-month6);
   Month_Highest=largest(1,of month1-month6);
   Month_2ndHighest=largest(2,of month1-month6);
run;
```

b. Print your results with an appropriate title.

```
title 'Month Statistics on Frequent Customers';
proc print data=work.freqcustomers noobs;
run;
title;
```

10. Using the PUT and INPUT Functions

Modify the program to generate the expected results.

```
data shipping_notes;
  set orion.shipped;
  length Comment $ 21;
  Comment = cat('Shipped on ',put(Ship_Date,mmddyy10.));
  Total = Quantity * input(Price,comma7.2);
run;

proc print data=shipping_notes noobs;
  format Total dollar7.2;
run;
```

11. Changing a Variable's Data Type

a. Create a new data set from **orion.US_newhire**.

```
data US_converted
     (drop=cID nTelephone cBirthday);
  set orion.US_newhire
     (rename=(ID=cID Telephone=nTelephone
              Birthday=cBirthday));
  ID = input(compress(cID,'-'),15.);
  length Telephone $ 8;
  Telephone = cat(substr(put(nTelephone,7.),1,3),
             '-',substr(put(nTelephone,7.),4));
  Birthday = input(cBirthday,date9.);
run;
```

b. Print **US_converted** with an appropriate title and use PROC CONTENTS to check the variables types.

```
title 'US New Hires';
proc print data=US_converted noobs;
run;
title;

proc contents data=US_converted varnum;
run;
```

Solutions to Student Activities (Polls/Quizzes)

5.02 Quiz – Correct Answer

Any of these assignment statements would give the correct value for **Total**.

PDV

Year2	Year1	Year3	Year4	Sales

```
Total = sum(of Year1-Year4);

Total = sum(of Year2--Year4);

Total = sum(of Year:);
```

16

5.03 Multiple Choice Poll – Correct Answer

Which SUBSTR function can extract the group of five numbers from the middle of the **Item_Code** value?

a. `substr(Item_Code,5,7)`
b. `substr(Item_Code,5)`
(c.) `substr(Item_Code,7,5)`
d. `substr(Item_Code,'mid',5)`

30

5.04 Quiz – Correct Answer

This PDV shows the current value of **Name**:

Name
HEATH*BARR*LITTLE EQUIPMENT SALES

Write an assignment statement that will convert the value of **Name** to this:

Name
Heath*Barr*Little Equipment Sales

```
Name = propcase(Name,' *');
```

The second argument to the PROPCASE function must list all the characters to use as delimiters. In this example, the space and * both need to be listed.

47

5.05 Quiz – Correct Answer

Misplaced parentheses are some of the most common syntax errors with functions.

Correctly placed

Listing of the corrected **p205a01**

```
data shoes;
  set orion.product_list;
  if substr(right(Product_Name),33,13)=
       'Running Shoes';
run;
```

After running the corrected program, the shoes data set has eight observations and five variables.

53 P205a01s

5.06 Poll – Correct Answer

Would the SUBSTR function be appropriate to separate the contact's name into two parts?

- ❍ Yes
- ❍ No (circled)

The SUBSTR function would be difficult to use because the comma is not in the same position for each value of name.

The SCAN function is a better choice to separate the last from the first and middle names.

64

5.07 Quiz – Correct Answer

Consider this PDV and assignment statement:

```
Second=scan(Phrase,2,',');
```

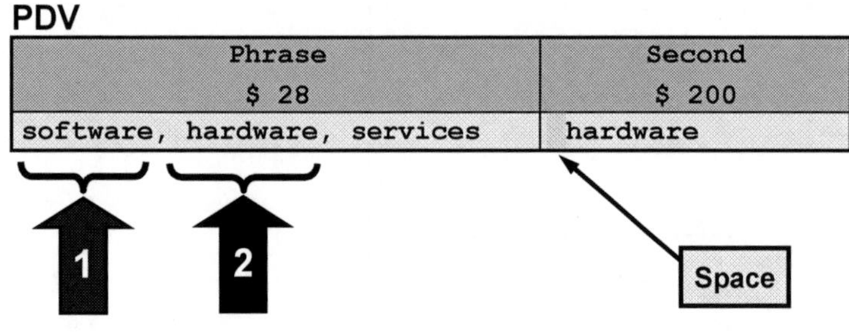

71

5.08 Multiple Choice Poll – Correct Answer

What expression completes the assignment statement to correctly extract 2007 from the **Text** variable?

a. `scan(Text,-1);`

b. `scan(Text,6);`

c. `scan(Text,6,', ');`

(d.) All of the above would work.

76

5.09 Quiz – Correct Answer

Create a Favorites link to the SAS Help entry for Functions by Category.

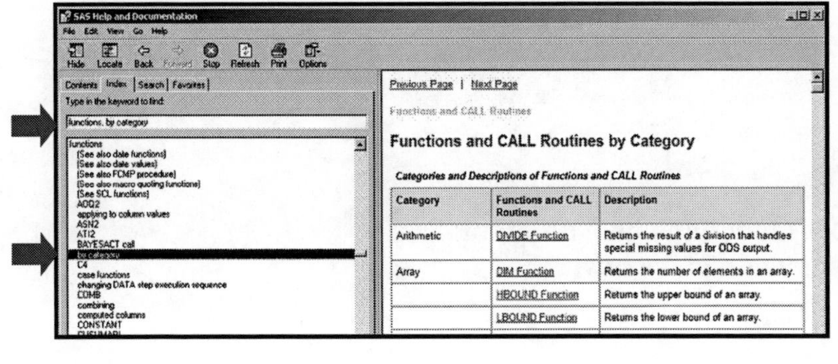

87

5.10 Quiz – Correct Answer

Complete the PDV for the values for **Pos3** and **Pos4**.

```
data find;
   Text='AUSTRALIA, DENMARK, US';
   Pos1=find(Text,'US');
   Pos2=find(Text,' US');
   Pos3=find(Text,'us');
   Pos4=find(Text,'us','I');
   Pos5=find(Text,'us','I',10);
run;
```

PDV

Pos1 N 8	Pos2 N 8	Pos3 N 8	Pos4 N 8
2	20	0	2

100

5.11 Poll – Correct Answer

Given the same value as an argument, do the INT and the FLOOR functions always return the same result?

❍ Yes

No

The INT and the FLOOR functions give different results if the argument value is negative.

130

5.12 Multiple Choice Poll – Correct Answer

Ord1, **Ord2**, and **Ord3** are variables that contain the sale amounts of the last three orders from a customer. Which of the following expressions can calculate the total of the two largest orders?

a. `sum(max(of Ord1-Ord3),max(of Ord1-Ord3))`

(b.) `sum(of Ord1-Ord3)-min(of Ord1-Ord3)`

c. `max(of Ord1-Ord3) + min(of Ord1-Ord3)`

d. None of the above

Adding the amount from all three orders and then subtracting the amount of the smallest order leaves the sum of the two largest orders.

142

5.13 Quiz – Correct Answer

Fill in the missing expression in the DATA step below. The expression should calculate **TotalValue** by multiplying **SharePrice** by **MyShares**.

```
data Input_Quiz;
   SharePrice = "$130.25";
   MyShares = 125;
   TotalValue = input(SharePrice,comma7.)*
                MyShares;
run;
```

168 p205d17

For the curious, the value stored in **TotalValue** is 16281.25.

5.14 Quiz – Correct Answer

Will this statement convert **GrossPay** to numeric?

```
GrossPay=input(GrossPay,comma6.);
```

Open and run the program **p205a02**. Did **GrossPay** become a numeric variable?

No, GrossPay remained a character variable.

175

Chapter Review Answers

Chapter Review Answers

1. Rewrite **`sum(Qtr1,Qtr2,Qtr3,Qtr4)`** to use a numbered range list in place of writing each variable's name.

   sum(of Qtr1-Qtr3)

2. What function is used to extract characters from a string?

   The SUBSTR function extracts characters from a string.

203

continued...

Chapter Review Answers

3. What function converts all words in a string to have the first letter as uppercase and the remaining letters as lowercase?

   The PROPCASE function converts all words in a string into proper case.

4. What does the FIND function do?

   The FIND function searches a target string for a specified substring.

204

Chapter Review Answers

5. What function can be used to remove all occurrences of the character '-' from a string?

   The COMPRESS function can be used.

6. List some of the descriptive statistic functions.

   SUM, MEAN, MIN, MAX, N, NMISS, and CMISS are some of the descriptive statistic functions.

7. What happens if you use a character variable with a function that takes numeric arguments?

   SAS automatically converts the character value to a numeric value using the *w.* informat.

206

continued...

Chapter Review Answers

8. What function can be used to convert a character value into a numeric value using a specified informat?

   The INPUT function uses an informat to convert a character value into a numeric value.

207

Chapter 6 Debugging Techniques

6.1 Using the PUTLOG Statement 6-3

Demonstration: Determining Logic Errors 6-12

6.2 Using the DEBUG Option 6-17

Demonstration: Identifying Logic Errors with the DATA Step Debugger 6-21

Demonstration: Setting Breakpoints 6-35

Exercises 6-42

6.3 Chapter Review 6-44

6.4 Solutions 6-45

Solutions to Exercises 6-45

Solutions to Student Activities (Polls/Quizzes) 6-48

Solutions to Chapter Review 6-50

6.1 Using the PUTLOG Statement

Objectives

- Use the PUTLOG statement in the DATA step to help identify logic errors.

3

Business Scenario

A mailing list application at Orion Star is not working properly. Use debugging techniques to identify and correct the problem.

4

Syntax Errors versus Logic Errors

- A *syntax error* occurs when program statements do not conform to the rules of the SAS language.
  - An error message is written to the log.
- A *logic error* occurs when the program statements follow the rules but the results are not correct.
  - No notes are written to the log, so logic errors are often difficult to detect.

This section focuses on identifying logic errors.

5

Mailing List Application

Using the **orion.mailing_list** data set as input, create a new data set, **us_mailing**, that includes only those observations with a United States address.

The new data set should include only the person's name, street address, city, state, and ZIP code.

6

Browse the Input Data

Partial Listing of **orion.mailing_list**

Name	Address1	Address3
Abbott, Ray	2267 Edwards Mill Rd	Miami-Dade, FL, 33135, US
Aisbitt, Sandy	30 Bingera Street	Melbourne, 2001, AU
Akinfolarin, Tameaka	5 Donnybrook Rd	Philadelphia, PA, 19145, US
Amos, Salley	3524 Calico Ct	San Diego, CA, 92116, US
Anger, Rose	744 Chapwith Rd	Philadelphia, PA, 19142, US
Anstey, David	939 Hilltop Needmore Rd	Miami-Dade, FL, 33157, US
Antonini, Doris	681 Ferguson Rd	Miami-Dade, FL, 33141, US
Apr, Nishan	105 Brack Penny Rd	San Diego, CA, 92071, US
Ardskin, Elizabeth	701 Glenridge Dr	Miami-Dade, FL, 33177, US
Areu, Jeryl	265 Fyfe Ct	Miami-Dade, Fl, 33133, US
Arizmendi, Gilbert	379 Englehardt Dr	San Diego, CA, 91950, US
Armant, Debra	10398 Crown Forest Ct	San Diego, CA, 92025, US
Armogida, Bruce	1914 Lansing St	Philadelphia, PA, 19119, US
Arruza, Fauver	265 Fyfe Ct	Miami-Dade, FL, 33133, US
Asta, Wendy	3565 Lake Park Dr	Philadelphia, PA, 19145, US
Atkins, John	6137 Blue Water Ct	Miami-Dade, FL, 33161, US
Bahlman, Sharon	24 LaTrobe Street	Sydney, 2165, AU

7

Desired Results

Partial Listing of **us_mailing**

Name	Address1	City	State	Zip
Ray Abbott	2267 Edwards Mill Rd	Miami-Dade	FL	33135
Tameaka Akinfolarin	5 Donnybrook Rd	Philadelphia	PA	19145
Salley Amos	3524 Calico Ct	San Diego	CA	92116
Rose Anger	744 Chapwith Rd	Philadelphia	PA	19142
David Anstey	939 Hilltop Needmore Rd	Miami-Dade	FL	33157
Doris Antonini	681 Ferguson Rd	Miami-Dade	FL	33141
Nishan Apr	105 Brack Penny Rd	San Diego	CA	92071
Elizabeth Ardskin	701 Glenridge Dr	Miami-Dade	FL	33177
Jeryl Areu	265 Fyfe Ct	Miami-Dade	Fl	33133
Gilbert Arizmendi	379 Englehardt Dr	San Diego	CA	91950
Debra Armant	10398 Crown Forest Ct	San Diego	CA	92025

8

The Current Program

```
data us_mailing;
   set orion.mailing_list;
   drop Address3;
   length City $ 25 State $ 2 Zip $ 5;
   if find(Address3,'US');
   Name=catx(' ',
             scan(Name,2,','),
             scan(Name,1,','));
   City=scan(Address3,1,',');
   State=scan(address3,2,',');
   Zip=scan(Address3,3,',');
run;
proc print data=us_mailing noobs;
   title 'Current Output from Program';
run;
```

9

6.01 Quiz

Open and submit **p206a01**. What errors are in the output?

```
data us_mailing;
   set orion.mailing_list;
   drop Address3;
   length City $ 25 State $ 2 Zip $ 5;
   if find(Address3,'US');
   Name=catx(' ',
             scan(Name,2,','),
             scan(Name,1,','));
   City=scan(Address3,1,',');
   State=scan(address3,2,',');
   Zip=scan(Address3,3,',');
run;
proc print data=us_mailing noobs;
   title 'Current Output from Program';
run;
```

p206a01

11

The PUTLOG Statement

The PUTLOG statement can be used in the DATA step to

- display messages in the log
- display the value(s) of one or more variables.

General form of the PUTLOG statement:

PUTLOG *<specifications>*;

There are various ways to write the *specifications*.

13

The PUTLOG statement can be used to write to the SAS log in both batch and interactive modes. The PUT statement can also be used for this purpose. Additionally, the PUT statement is used to write to an external file. If an external file is open for output, steps must be taken to ensure that debugging messages are written to the SAS log and not to the external file. See SAS documentation for more information about the PUT statement.

Use PUTLOG to Write Text to the Log

To write text to the log, use this form of the PUTLOG statement:

PUTLOG '*text*';

For example,

```
putlog 'Looking for country';
```

writes **Looking for country** to the log.

14

Use PUTLOG to Write the Value of a Variable

To write the name and value of a variable to the log, use this form of the PUTLOG statement:

PUTLOG *variable-name*=;

For example, if the value of the variable **`City`** is `San Diego`, the statement

```
putlog City=;
```

writes **`City=San Diego`** to the log.

15

Use PUTLOG to Write Formatted Values

To write the formatted value of a variable to the log, use this form of the PUTLOG statement:

PUTLOG *variable-name format-namew.*;

For example, if the value of the variable **`City`** is `Philadelphia` with a leading space, the statement

```
putlog City $quote22.;
```

writes " **`Philadelphia`**" to the log.

 The value of *w* should be wide enough to display the value of the variable and the quotation marks.

16

The format $QUOTE*w*. writes a character value in double quotation marks and preserves any leading spaces.

Use PUTLOG to Write Values of All Variables

To write the current contents of the program data vector (PDV) to the log, use this form of the PUTLOG statement:

Partial SAS Log

```
Name=Abbott, Ray Address1=2267 Edwards Mill Rd Address3=Miami-
Dade, FL, 33135, US City=  State=  Zip=  _ERROR_=0 _N_=1
Name=Aisbitt, Sandy Address1=30 Bingera Street
Address3=Melbourne, 2001, AU City=  State=  Zip=  _ERROR_=0
_N_=2
Name=Akinfolarin, Tameaka Address1=5 Donnybrook Rd
Address3=Philadelphia, PA, 19145, US City=  State=  Zip=
_ERROR_=0 _N_=3
```

17

Special Variables

The temporary variables _N_ and _ERROR_ can be helpful when you debug a DATA step.

Variable	Description	Debugging Use
_N_	The number of times that the DATA step iterated	Display debugging messages for some number of iterations of the DATA step
ERROR	Initialized to 0, set to 1 when an error occurs	Display debugging messages when an error occurs.

18

6.02 Quiz

Open the file **p206a02**. Insert statements to display the values of _N_ and _ERROR_ in the first three iterations of the DATA step. Submit and view the log.

```
data _null_;
   set orion.donate;
run;
```

20 p206a02

The END= Option

The END= option creates a temporary variable that acts as an end-of-file indicator.

- The option can be used in SET and INFILE statements.
- The variable is initialized to 0 and is set to 1 when the last observation or record is read.

General form of the END= option:

SET *SAS-data-set* END=*variable* <*options*>;

INFILE '*raw-data-file*' END=*variable* <*options*>;

22

Processing at the End of a DATA Step

Use conditional logic to check the value of the END= variable to determine if it is the last iteration of the DATA step.

```
data work.donate;
   set orion.donate end=last;
   <additional SAS statements>
   if last=1 then do;
      <additional SAS statements>
   end;
run;
```

The IF statement can also be written in this form:

```
if last then do;
```

23

Using PUTLOG with Conditional Logic

The program below displays a message in the log on the first iteration of the DATA step, and displays the contents of the PDV in the last iteration of the DATA step.

```
data _null_;
   set orion.donate end=lastObs;
   if _n_=1 then
      putlog 'First iteration';
   if lastObs then do;
      putlog 'Final values of variables:';
      putlog _all_;
   end;
run;
```

Partial SAS Log

```
First iteration
Final values of variables:
lastObs=1 Employee_ID=12447 Qtr=4 Amount=35 _ERROR_=0 _N_=16
```

24 p206d01

Determining Logic Errors

p206d02

This demonstration shows how to detect and correct logic errors using the PUTLOG statement.

1. Open and submit **p206d02**.

```
data us_mailing;
   set orion.mailing_list;
   drop Address3;
   length City $ 25 State $ 2 Zip $ 5;
   if find(Address3,'US');
   Name=catx(' ',scan(Name,2,','),scan(Name,1,','));
   City=scan(Address3,1,',');
   State=scan(address3,2,',');
   Zip=scan(Address3,3,',');
run;

proc print data=us_mailing noobs;
   title 'Current Output from Program';
run;
title;
```

Partial PROC PRINT Output

Current Output from Program

Name	Address1	City	State	Zip
Ray Abbott	2267 Edwards Mill Rd	Miami-Dade	F	3313
Tameaka Akinfolarin	5 Donnybrook Rd	Philadelphia	P	1914
Salley Amos	3524 Calico Ct	San Diego	C	9211
Rose Anger	744 Chapwith Rd	Philadelphia	P	1914
David Anstey	939 Hilltop Needmore Rd	Miami-Dade	F	3315
Doris Antonini	681 Ferguson Rd	Miami-Dade	F	3314
Nishan Apr	105 Brack Penny Rd	San Diego	C	9207
Elizabeth Ardskin	701 Glenridge Dr	Miami-Dade	F	3317
Jeryl Areu	265 Fyfe Ct	Miami-Dade	F	3313
Gilbert Arizmendi	379 Englehardt Dr	San Diego	C	9195
Debra Armant	10398 Crown Forest Ct	San Diego	C	9202

The values for `State` and `Zip` are incorrect. The SAS log does not contain any errors or warnings.

2. Insert PUTLOG statements to determine which statements execute, and to display the values of **_n_**, **State**, and **Zip**. Use the OBS= data set option to process only 10 observations.

```
data us_mailing;
   set orion.mailing_list (obs=10);
   drop Address3;
   length City $ 25 State $ 2 Zip $ 5;
   putlog _n_=;
   putlog "Looking for country";
   if find(Address3,'US') > 0;
   putlog "Found US";
   Name=catx(' ',scan(Name,2,','),scan(Name,1,','));
   City=scan(Address3,1,',');
   State=scan(address3,2,',');
   Zip=scan(Address3,3,',');
   putlog State= Zip=;

run;
```

3. Submit the code. The output from the PUTLOG statements appears in the log. The **US** observations are recognized, but the values of **State** and **Zip** are incorrect.

Partial SAS Log

```
_N_=1
Looking for country
Found US
State=F Zip=3313
_N_=2
Looking for country
_N_=3
Looking for country
Found US
State=P Zip=1914
```

4. Use the $QUOTE*w*. format in the PUTLOG statements to further examine the values of **State** and **Zip**.

By default, the PUTLOG statement writes character values with the standard character format $*w*., where *w* is the length of the character variable. The standard character format left-justifies the value and removes leading blanks.

The $QUOTE*w*. format writes the value enclosed in double quotation marks and preserves leading blanks. The closing quotation mark is displayed after the last non-blank character, so trailing blanks are not displayed.

```
data us_mailing;
   set orion.mailing_list (obs=10);
   drop Address3;
   length City $ 25 State $ 2 Zip $ 5;
   putlog _n_=;
   putlog "Looking for country";
   if find(Address3,'US') > 0;
   putlog "Found US";
   Name=catx(' ',scan(Name,2,','),scan(Name,1,','));
   City=scan(Address3,1,',');
   State=scan(address3,2,',');
   putlog state $quote4.;
   Zip=scan(Address3,3,',');
   putlog Zip $quote7.;
run;
```

5. Submit the code. The log shows that each value of **State** and **Zip** contains a leading blank.

Partial SAS Log

```
_N_=1
Looking for country
Found US
" F"
" 3313"
_N_=2
Looking for country
_N_=3
Looking for country
Found US
" P"
" 1914"
```

6. Use the LEFT function to remove leading blanks from **State** and **Zip**.

```
data us_mailing (obs=5);
   set orion.mailing_list (obs=10);
   drop Address3;
   length City $ 25 State $ 2 Zip $ 5;
   putlog _n_=;
   putlog "Looking for country";
   if find(Address3,'US') > 0;
   putlog "Found US";
   Name=catx(' ',scan(Name,2,','),scan(Name,1,','));
   City=scan(Address3,1,',');
   State=left(scan(address3,2,','));
   putlog state $quote4.;
   Zip=left(scan(Address3,3,','));
   putlog Zip $quote7.;
run;
```

7. Submit the code and check the log. The values of **State** and **Zip** are correct.

Partial SAS Log

```
_N_=1
Looking for country
Found US
"FL"
"33135"
_N_=2
Looking for country
_N_=3
Looking for country
Found US
"PA"
"19145"
```

8. Remove the OBS= option and the PUTLOG statements. Submit the code and check the log and output.

```
data us_mailing;
   set orion.mailing_list;
   drop Address3;
   length City $ 25 State $ 2 Zip $ 5;
   if find(Address3,'US') > 0;
   Name=catx(' ',scan(Name,2,','),scan(Name,1,','));
   City=scan(Address3,1,',');
   State=left(scan(address3,2,','));
   Zip=left(scan(Address3,3,','));
run;

proc print data=work.us_mailing noobs;
   title 'Corrected Output';
run;
```

Partial PROC PRINT Output

```
                                    Corrected Output

   Name                          Address1                         City        State      Zip

   Ray Abbott                    2267 Edwards Mill Rd        Miami-Dade         FL      33135
   Tameaka Akinfolarin           5 Donnybrook Rd             Philadelphia       PA      19145
   Salley Amos                   3524 Calico Ct              San Diego          CA      92116
   Rose Anger                    744 Chapwith Rd             Philadelphia       PA      19142
   David Anstey                  939 Hilltop Needmore Rd     Miami-Dade         FL      33157
   Doris Antonini                681 Ferguson Rd             Miami-Dade         FL      33141
   Nishan Apr                    105 Brack Penny Rd          San Diego          CA      92071
   Elizabeth Ardskin             701 Glenridge Dr            Miami-Dade         FL      33177
```

6.2 Using the DEBUG Option

Objectives

- Use the DEBUG option in the DATA statement to identify logic errors.
- Set breakpoints in the debugger. (Self-Study)

28

The DEBUG Option

The DEBUG option is an interactive interface to the DATA step. Commands are available to

- execute a DATA step one statement at a time
- examine the value of one or more variables
- watch one or more variables as they change in value.

General form of the DEBUG option:

DATA *data-set-name* / DEBUG;

29

DATA Step Debugger

The debugger can only be used with a DATA step, not a PROC step.

- The DEBUG option is only available in interactive mode.
- A DATA step cannot be restarted after it ends; however, the final values of variables can be examined.

30

The DATA Step Debugger Window

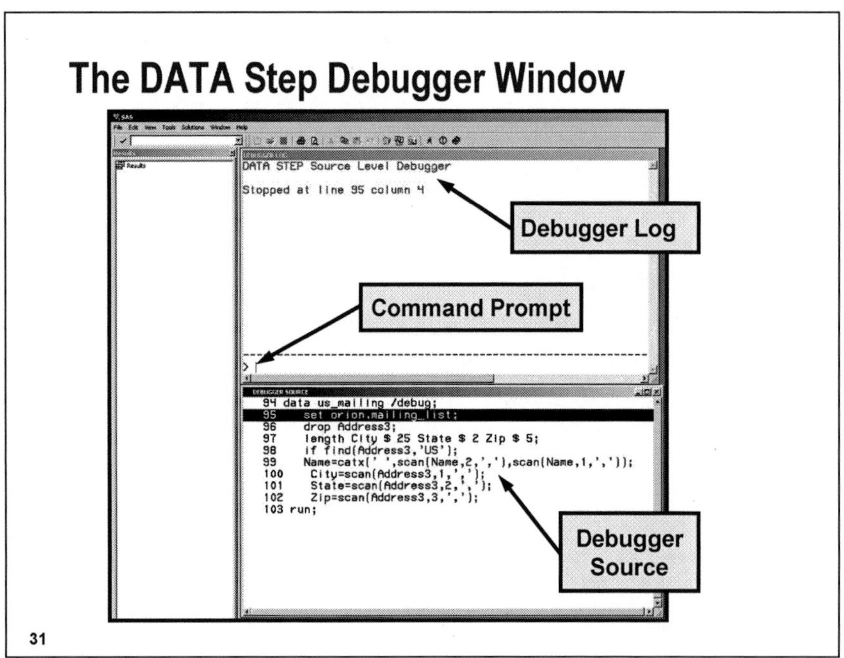

31

DEBUG Commands

Common commands used with the DEBUG option:

Command	Alias	Action
STEP	ENTER key	executes statements one at a time
EXAMINE	E variable(s)	displays the value of one or more variables
WATCH	W variable(s)	suspends execution when the value of a watched variable changes
QUIT	Q	terminates a debugger session

32

The W and E commands precede the name of the variable; for example:

```
w City
e _all_
```

DEBUG Commands

Other useful commands used with the DEBUG option:

Command	Alias	Action
LIST	L argument	displays all occurrences of the item listed in the argument L W – list watched variables
DELETE Watch	D W variable(s)	deletes the watch status of the listed variables
SET	SET	assigns a new value to the specified variable: SET variable=expression

33

Syntax:

LIST _ALL_ | WATCH

DELETE WATCH *variable(s)* | _ALL_

DATA Step Debugger Documentation

For help on the DATA Step Debugger, select **SAS Products** ⇨ **Base SAS** ⇨ **SAS 9.2 Language Reference: Dictionary** ⇨ **Appendixes** ⇨ **DATA Step Debugger**.

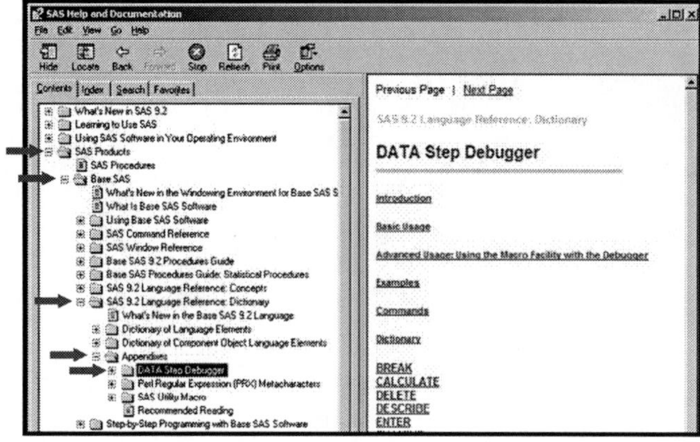

34

6.03 Quiz

Use the SAS Help facility to locate DATA Step Debugger examples. In the first example, what command is used to examine data values after the first iteration?

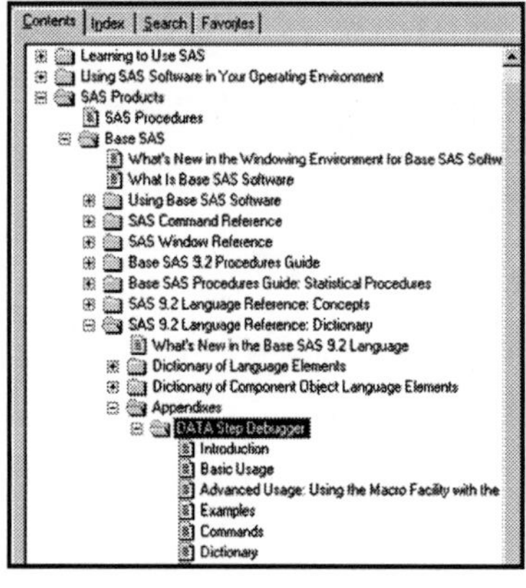

36

Identifying Logic Errors with the DATA Step Debugger

p206d03

1. Open and submit **p206d03**. The program generates incorrect results.

```
data us_mailing;
   set orion.mailing_list;
   drop Address3;
   length City $ 25 State $ 2 Zip $ 5;
   if find(Address3,'US');
   Name=catx(' ',scan(Name,2,','),scan(Name,1,','));
   City=scan(Address3,1,',');
   State=scan(address3,2,',');
   Zip=scan(Address3,3,',');
run;

proc print data=us_mailing noobs;
   title 'Current Output from Program';
run;
title;
```

Partial PROC PRINT Output

```
                          Current Output from Program

Name                    Address1                  City           State    Zip

Ray Abbott              2267 Edwards Mill Rd      Miami-Dade       F      3313
Tameaka Akinfolarin     5 Donnybrook Rd           Philadelphia     P      1914
Salley Amos             3524 Calico Ct            San Diego        C      9211
Rose Anger              744 Chapwith Rd           Philadelphia     P      1914
David Anstey            939 Hilltop Needmore Rd   Miami-Dade       F      3315
Doris Antonini          681 Ferguson Rd           Miami-Dade       F      3314
```

The values of **State** and **Zip** are incorrect.

2. Add the DEBUG option to the DATA statement.

```
data us_mailing /debug;
   set orion.mailing_list;
   drop Address3;
   length City $ 25 State $ 2 Zip $ 5;
   if find(Address3,'US');
   Name=catx(' ',scan(Name,2,','),scan(Name,1,','));
   City=scan(Address3,1,',');
   State=scan(address3,2,',');
   Zip=scan(Address3,3,',');
run;
```

3. Submit the DATA step. The DATA Step Debugger opens.

   Resize the windows if necessary so that you can see the Debugger Log window, the Debugger Source window, and the command prompt.

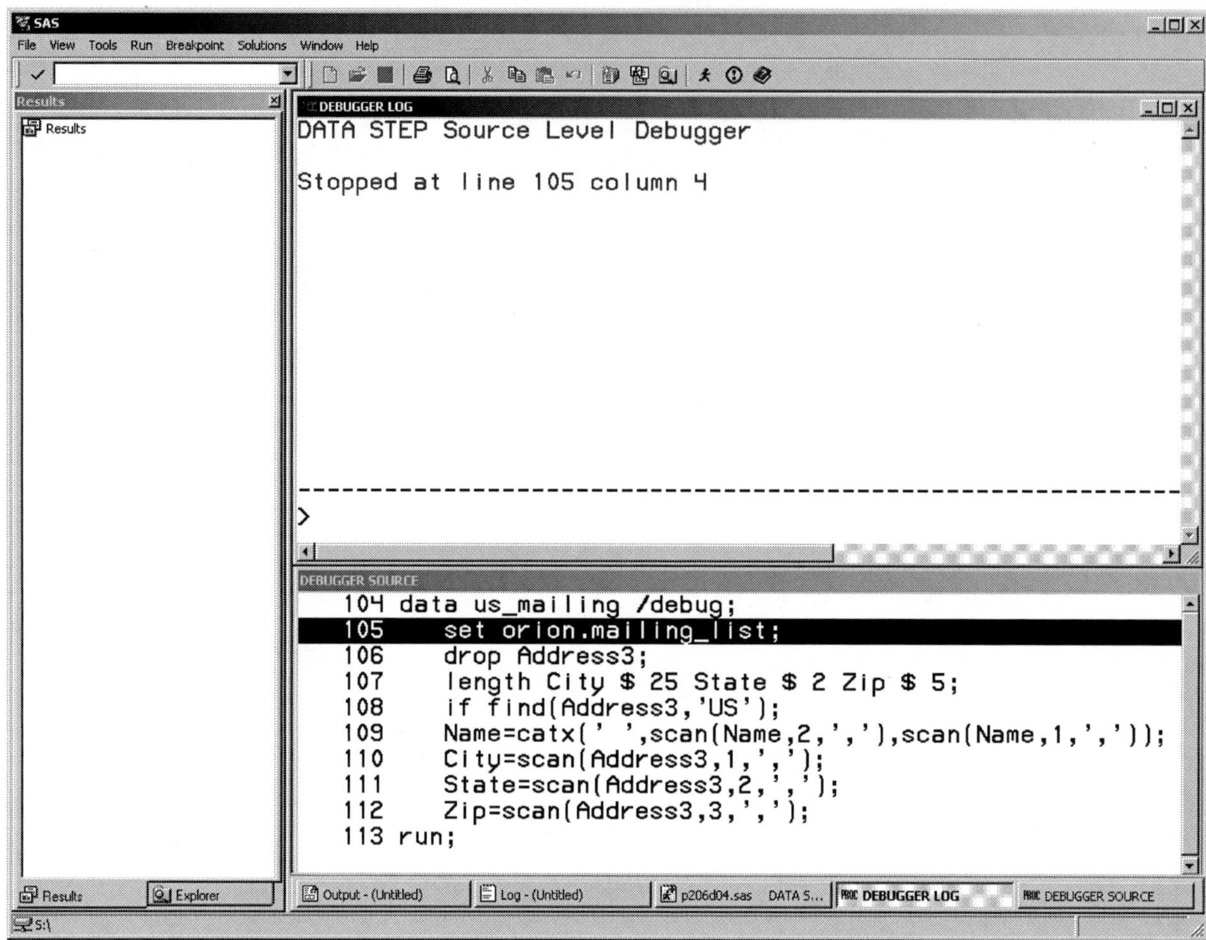

   The next statement to execute is highlighted in the Debugger Source window.

4. Be sure that the Debugger Log window is active. Press ENTER to execute the highlighted statement.

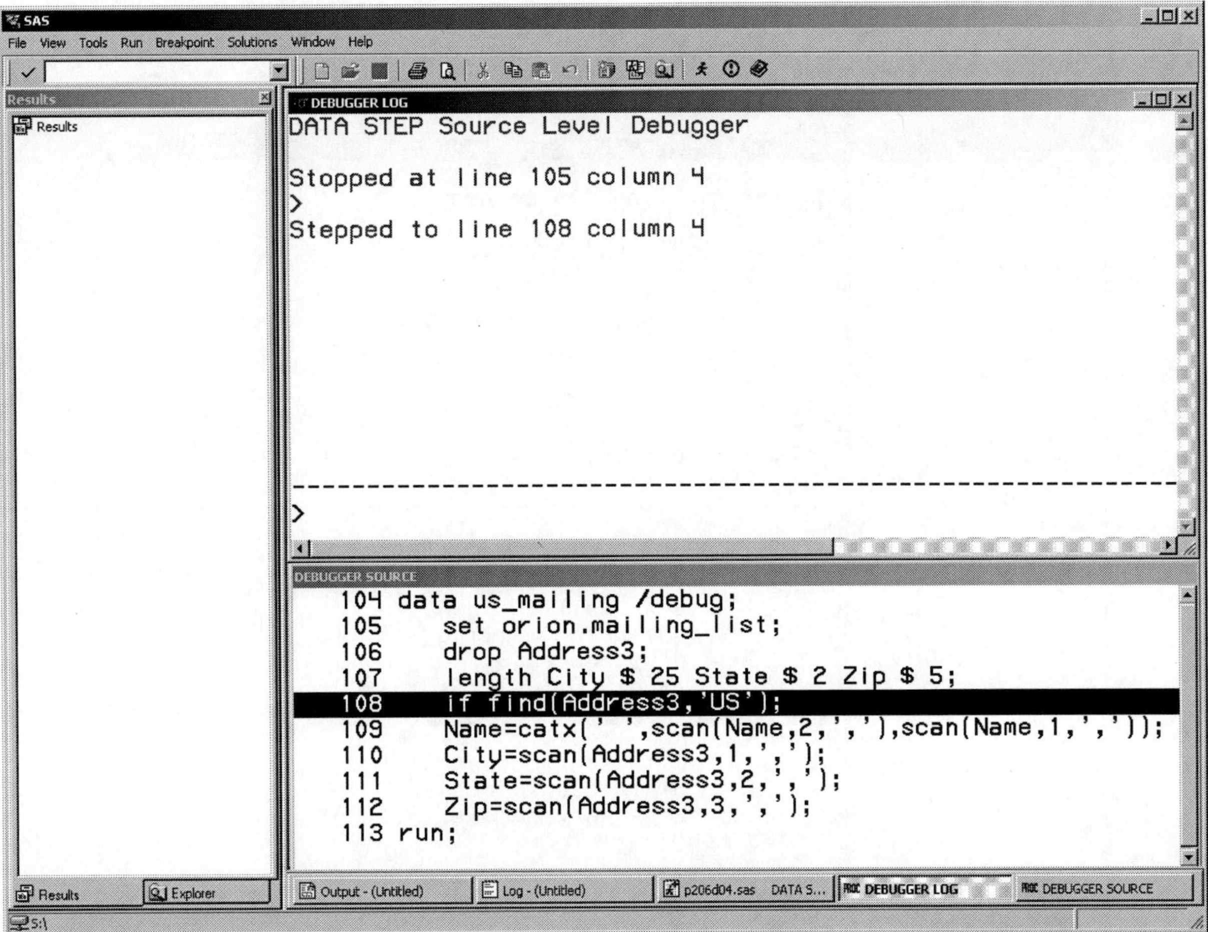

The SET statement executed and the first observation from the input data set is now in the PDV. The subsetting IF statement is highlighted and executes when you press ENTER.

5. Examine all the variables in the PDV with `e _all_`.

```
e _all_
```

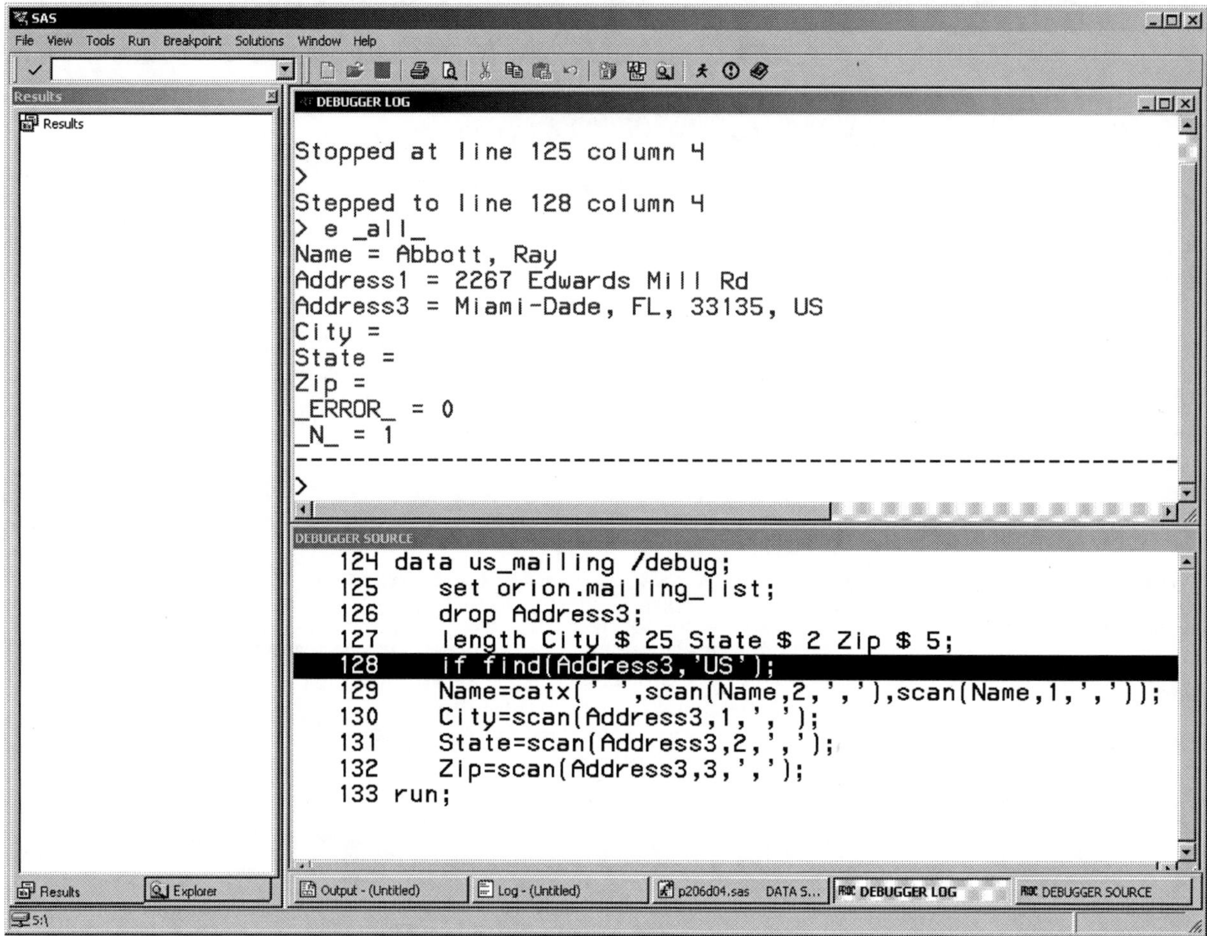

6. Press ENTER again to execute the subsetting IF statement.

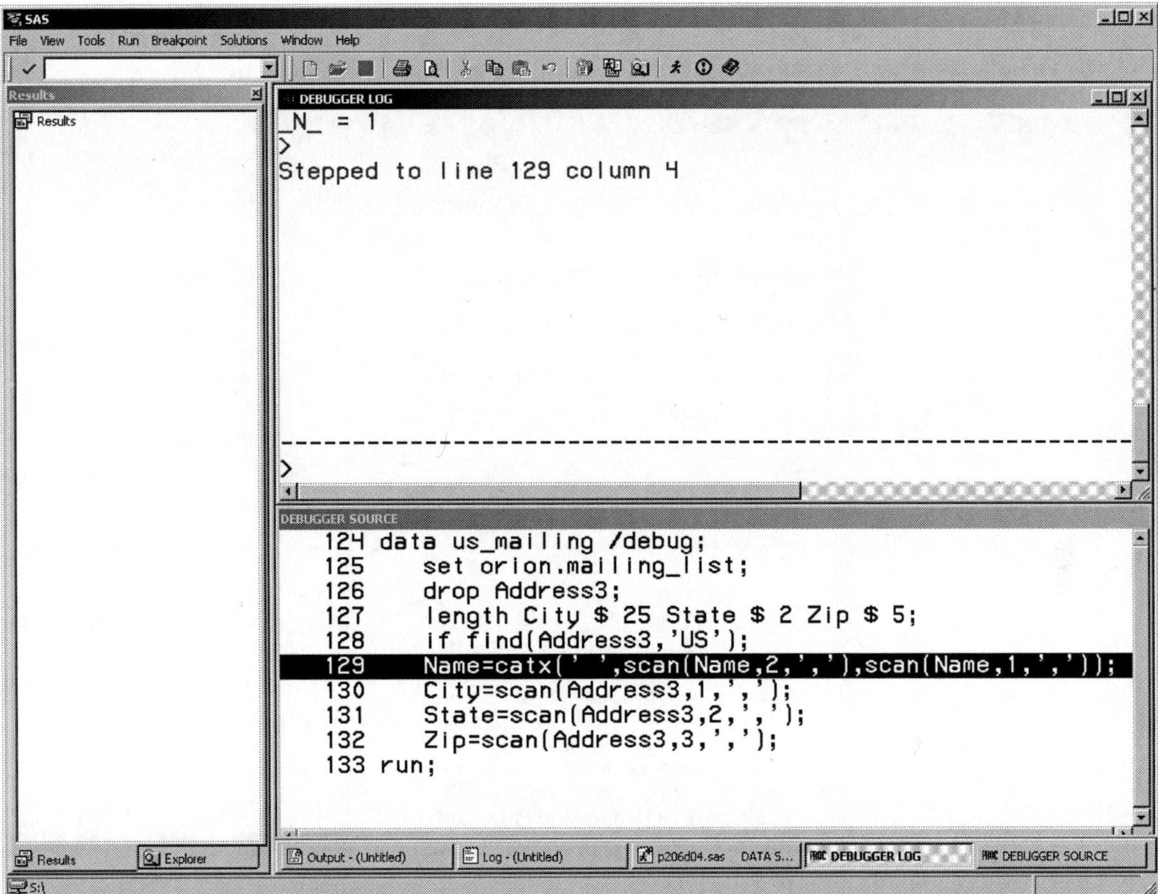

The subsetting IF expression is true, so the processing of this observation continues.

7. Press ENTER to execute the statement that restructures **Name**.

8. Press ENTER to execute the statement that extracts **City** from **Address3**.

9. Press ENTER to execute the statement that extracts **State** from **Address3**.

10. Use the EXAMINE command to examine the value of **State**.

```
e state
```

The value of **State** is displayed in the Debugger Log window. It has the value `F`.

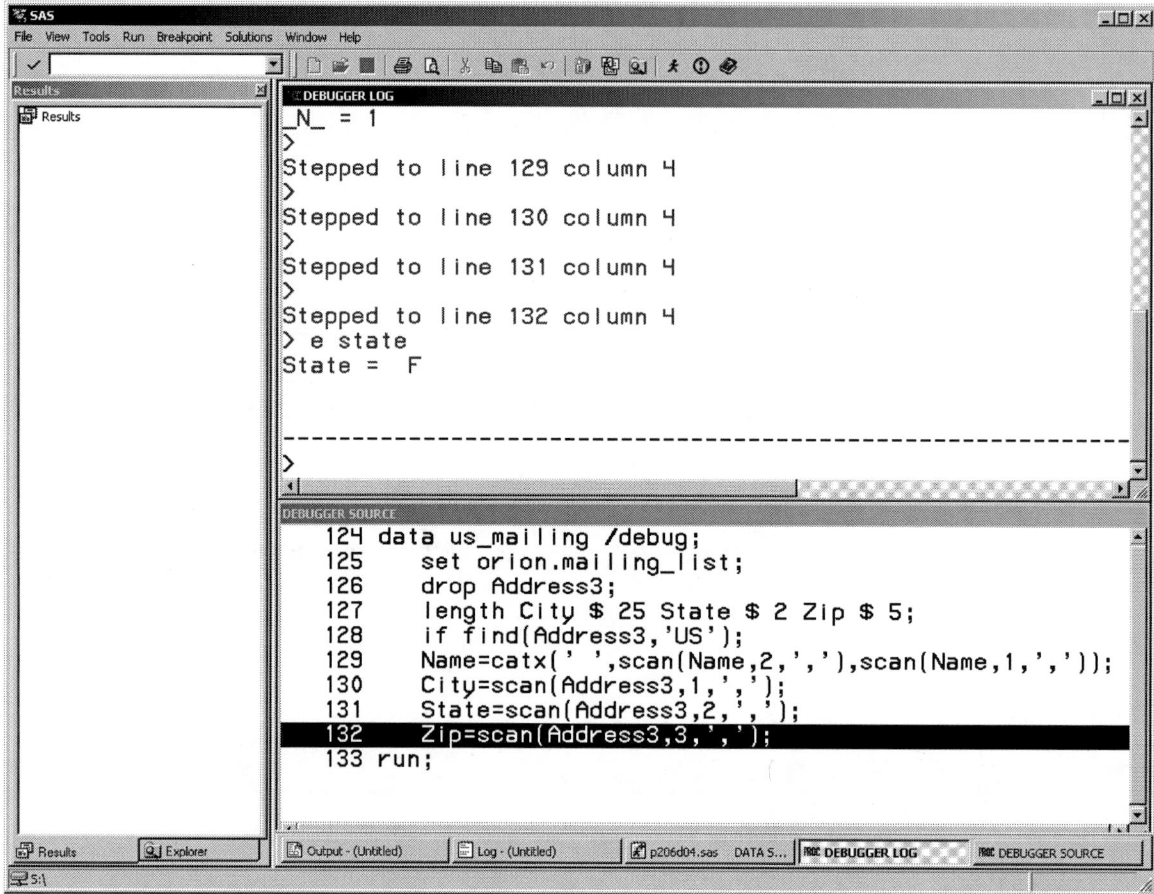

11. Use the EXAMINE command to examine the value of **Address3**.

```
e address3
```

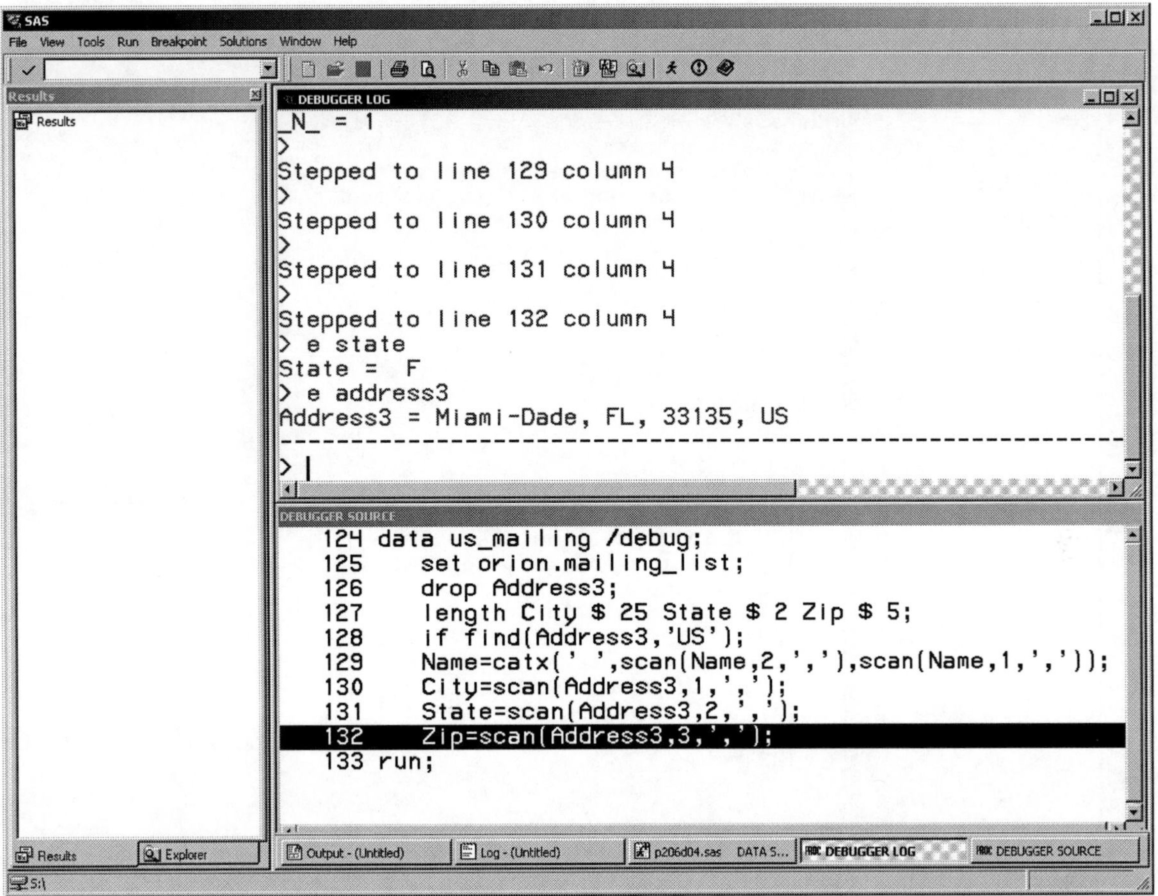

You can see that the state code is `FL` in **Address3**, but only the `F` is assigned to **State**.

12. Set a watch on **State** and **Address3**.

```
w state address3
```

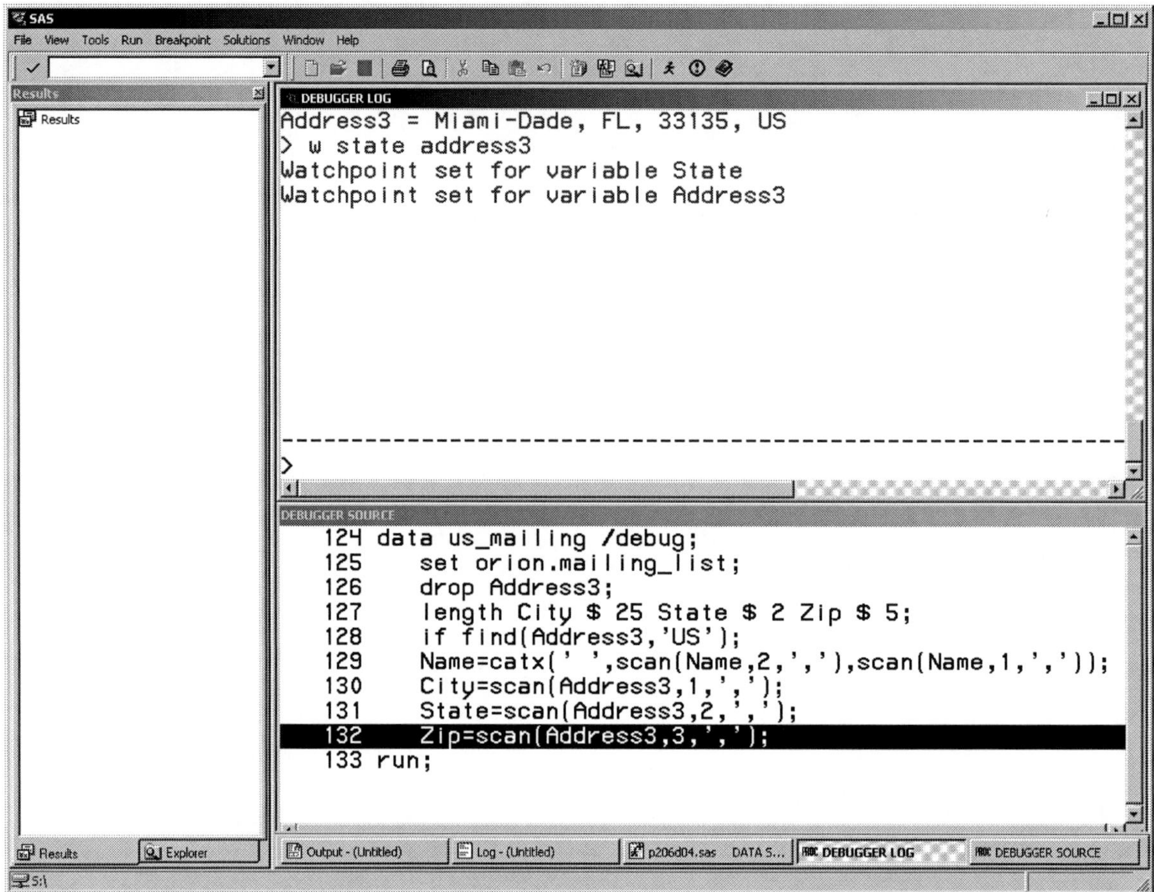

Execution is suspended when the value of a watched variable changes. Both the old and new values appear in the Debugger Log window.

13. Press ENTER repeatedly to execute the statements one at a time. Watch as the values of **Address3** and **State** change. Execute the statement that assigns a value to **State**.

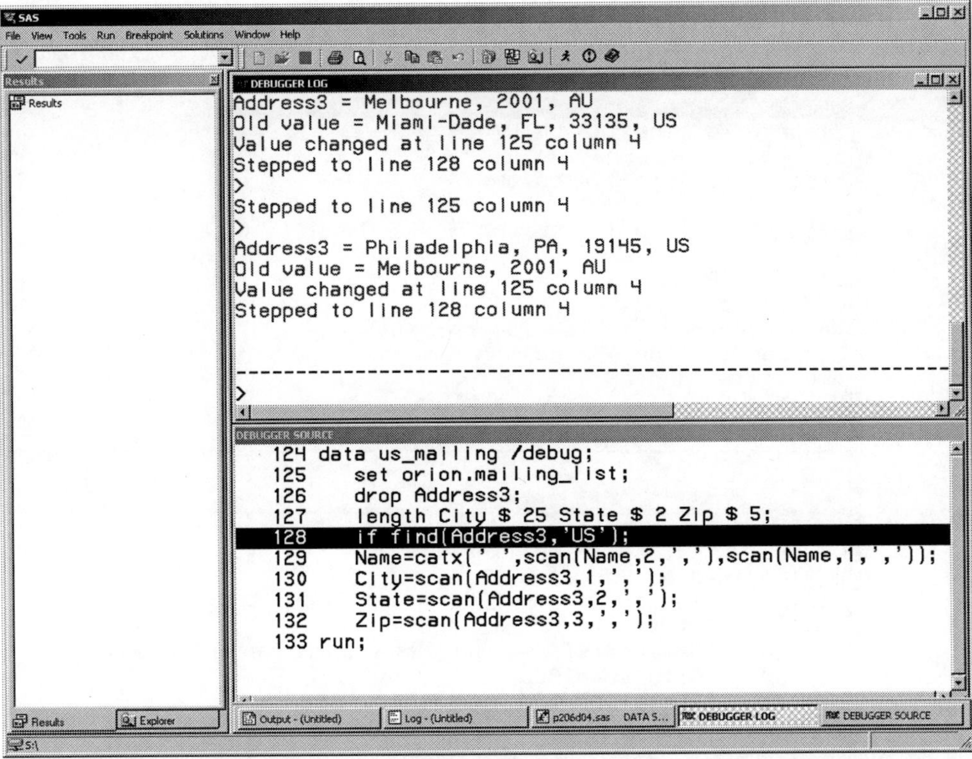

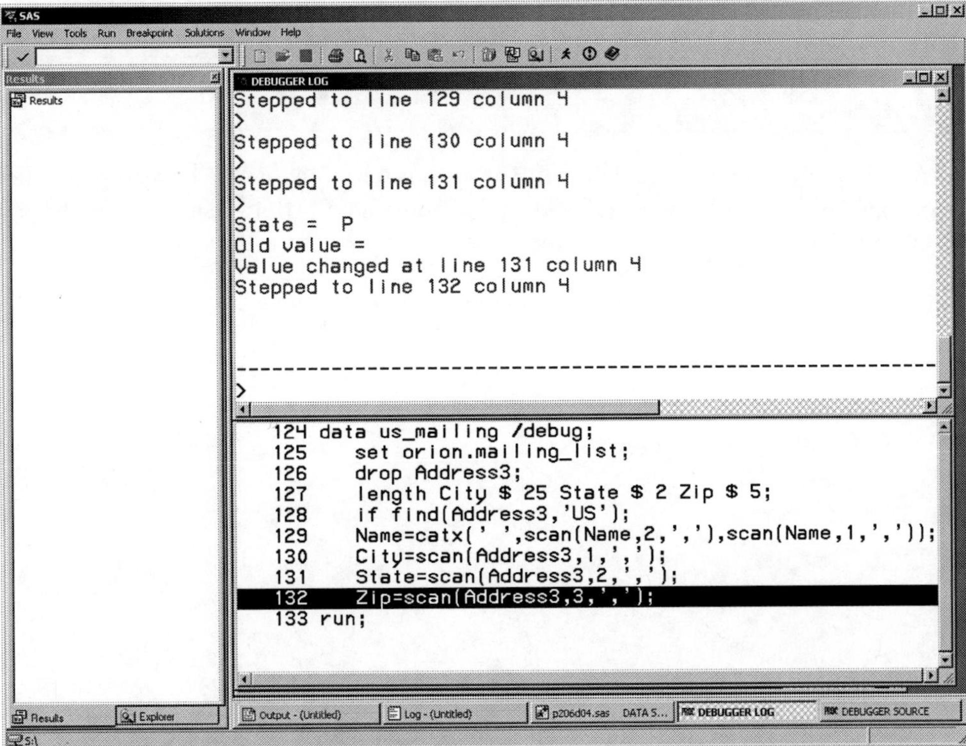

14. Use a format with the EXAMINE command to further examine the value of **`State`**.

```
e state $quote4.
```

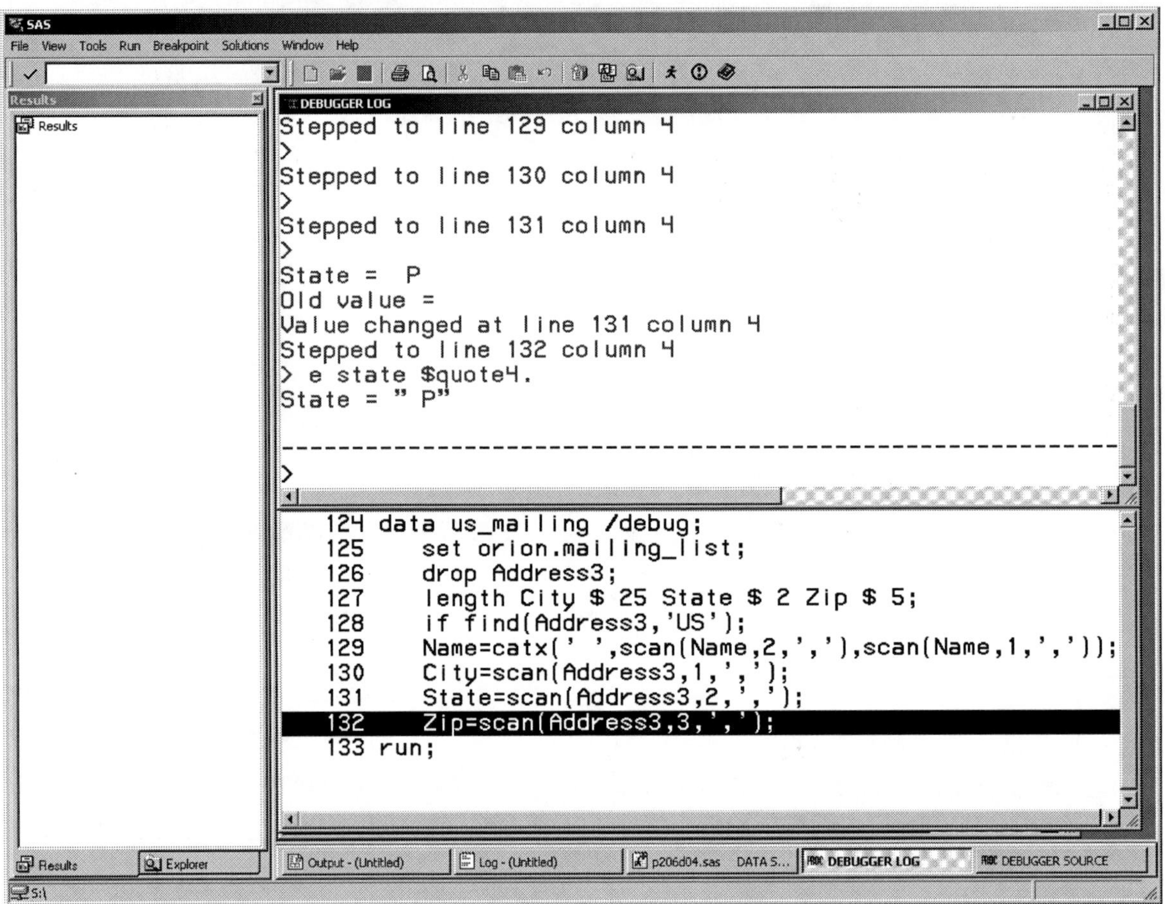

The Debugger Log window shows that the value of **`State`** has a leading blank. This is caused by the blank after the comma delimiter in **`Address3`** and can be eliminated by left-justifying the value returned by the SCAN function.

15. Press ENTER to execute the statement that assigns a value to **`Zip`**.

16. Use the EXAMINE command with the $QUOTE7. format to display the value of **Zip**.

```
e zip $quote7.
```

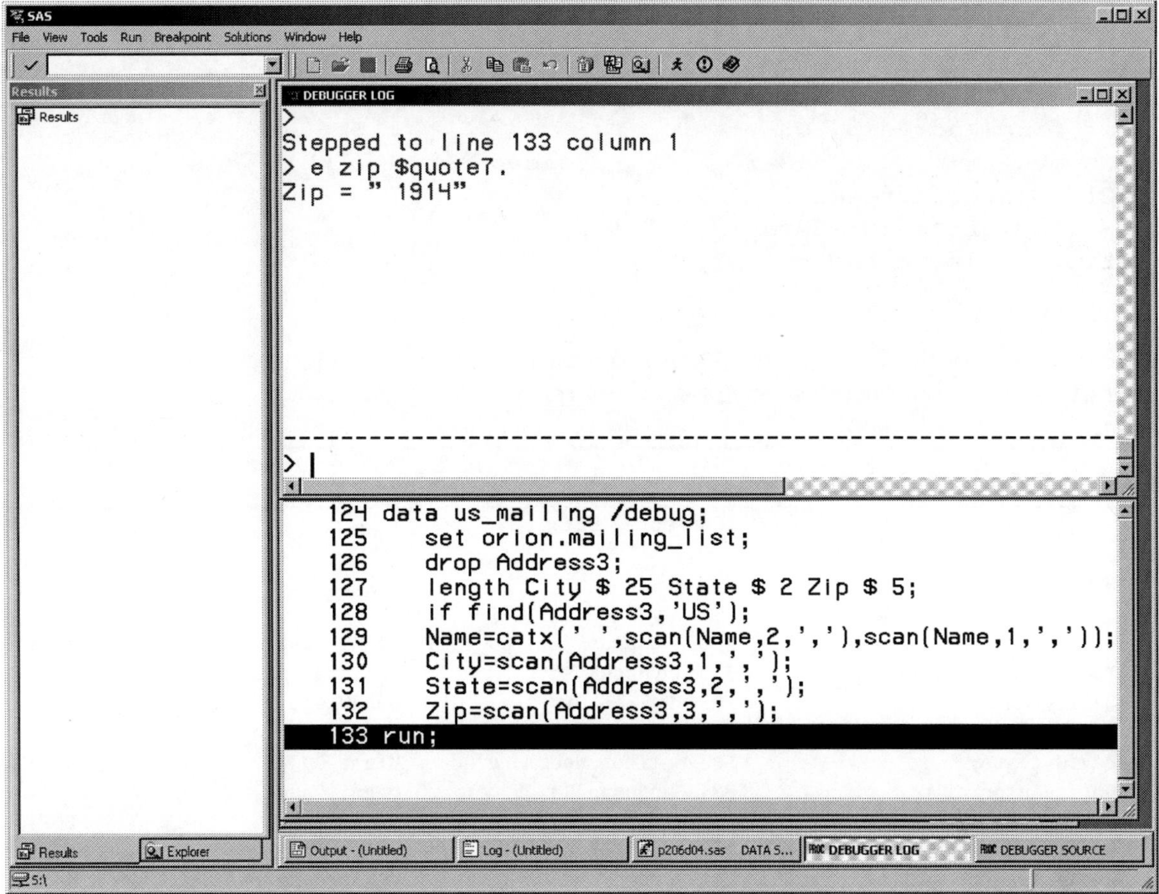

The Debugger Log shows that the value of **Zip** also has a leading blank. This can be eliminated by left-justifying the value returned by the SCAN function before assigning it to **Zip**.

17. Now that you identified the error, use the QUIT command to halt the DATA step.

```
q
```

18. Remove the DEBUG option from the DATA step and use the LEFT function to remove the leading space from **State** and **Zip**. Submit the corrected code.

```
data us_mailing;
   set orion.mailing_list;
   drop Address3;
   length City $ 25 State $ 2 Zip $ 5;
   if find(Address3,'US');
   Name=catx(' ',scan(Name,2,','),scan(Name,1,','));
   City=scan(Address3,1,',');
   State=left(scan(Address3,2,','));
   Zip=left(scan(Address3,3,','));
run;

proc print data=work.us_mailing noobs;
   title 'Corrected Output from Program';
run;
```

Partial PROC PRINT Output

Corrected Output

Name	Address1	City	State	Zip
Ray Abbott	2267 Edwards Mill Rd	Miami-Dade	FL	33135
Tameaka Akinfolarin	5 Donnybrook Rd	Philadelphia	PA	19145
Salley Amos	3524 Calico Ct	San Diego	CA	92116
Rose Anger	744 Chapwith Rd	Philadelphia	PA	19142
David Anstey	939 Hilltop Needmore Rd	Miami-Dade	FL	33157
Doris Antonini	681 Ferguson Rd	Miami-Dade	FL	33141
Nishan Apr	105 Brack Penny Rd	San Diego	CA	92071
Elizabeth Ardskin	701 Glenridge Dr	Miami-Dade	FL	33177
Jeryl Areu	265 Fyfe Ct	Miami-Dade	Fl	33133
Gilbert Arizmendi	379 Englehardt Dr	San Diego	CA	91950
Debra Armant	10398 Crown Forest Ct	San Diego	CA	92025

Setting Breakpoints (Self-Study)

A *breakpoint* is a point at which program execution is suspended, allowing the user to submit debugger commands.

- Breakpoints can be conditional or unconditional.
- Breakpoints can be in effect on every iteration of the DATA step or after a set number of iterations.
- An exclamation mark appears to the left of the line in the Debugger Source window.

Breakpoints are useful in DATA steps that iterate many times.

40

The BREAK Command (Self-Study)

General form of the BREAK command:

BREAK *location* <AFTER *count*> <WHEN *expression*> <DO *group*>

location	The number of the line at which to suspend execution.
AFTER *count*	Break after the line has been executed *count* times.
WHEN *expression*	Break when *expression* evaluates to TRUE.
DO *group*	One or more debugger commands enclosed by a DO and an END statement.

41

Sample BREAK Commands (Self-Study)

Command	Description
B 32	Set a breakpoint on line 32
B 25 after 4	Break on line 25 after it executed four times
B 7 when num=0	Break on line 7 when num=0
B 7 after 3 when num=0	Break on line 7 after it executed three times only if num=0
B 9 do; e city zip; end;	Break on line 9 and display the values of `City` and `Zip` automatically
D B 9	Delete the breakpoint on line 9

42

The GO Command (Self-Study)

The GO command resumes program execution.

General form of the GO command:

```
GO <line-number>
```

line-number	The number of the program line at which execution is to be suspended

Sample GO Commands

Command	Description
G	Resume execution at the next executable line.
G 30	Resume execution and suspend execution at line 30.

43

Setting Breakpoints

p206d04

This demonstration illustrates the use of breakpoints in the interactive debugger.

1. Open and submit **p206d04** to start the interactive debugger. Determine the line number of the RUN statement in the Debugger Source window. Submit a BREAK command to set a breakpoint at the RUN statement, using the appropriate line number. In this sample, the RUN statement is at line 62, so the command `b 62` sets a breakpoint in the RUN statement.

```
b 62
```

DEBUGGER LOG

```
DATA STEP Source Level Debugger

Stopped at line 54 column 4
> b 62
Breakpoint 1 set at line 62
-----------------------------------------------------------------------
>
```

DEBUGGER SOURCE

```
   53 data us_mailing /debug;
   54    set orion.mailing_list;
   55    drop Address3;
   56    length City $ 25 State $ 2 Zip $ 5;
   57    if find(Address3,'US');
   58    Name=catx(' ',scan(Name,2,','),scan(Name,1,','));
   59    City=scan(Address3,1,',');
   60    State=scan(Address3,2,',');
   61    Zip=scan(Address3,3,',');
!  62 run;
```

An exclamation mark displayed to the left of a line indicates that there is a breakpoint on that line.

2. Submit the **GO** command to start the DATA step. Execution suspends before executing the RUN statement due to the breakpoint.

```
G
```

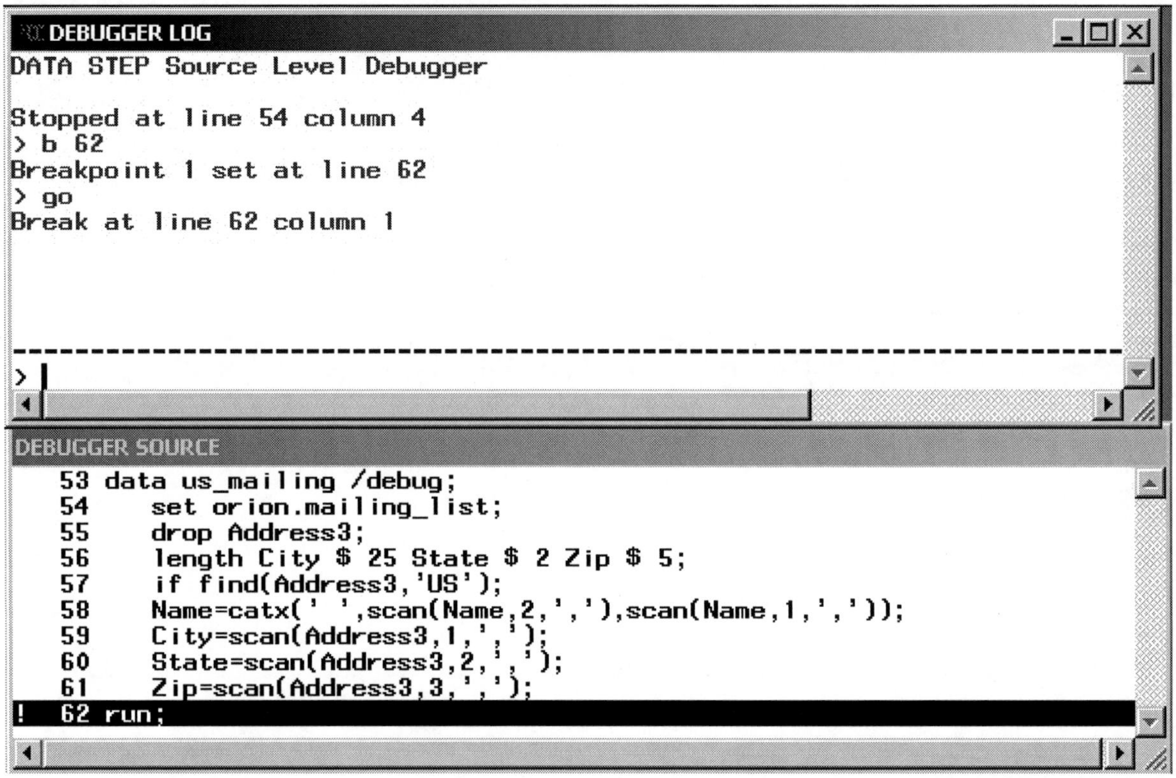

DEBUGGER LOG

```
DATA STEP Source Level Debugger

Stopped at line 54 column 4
> b 62
Breakpoint 1 set at line 62
> go
Break at line 62 column 1
--------------------------------------------------------------------------
>
```

DEBUGGER SOURCE

```
   53 data us_mailing /debug;
   54     set orion.mailing_list;
   55     drop Address3;
   56     length City $ 25 State $ 2 Zip $ 5;
   57     if find(Address3,'US');
   58     Name=catx(' ',scan(Name,2,','),scan(Name,1,','));
   59     City=scan(Address3,1,',');
   60     State=scan(Address3,2,',');
   61     Zip=scan(Address3,3,',');
!  62 run;
```

3. Submit an EXAMINE command to display the values of **State** and **Zip**.

```
e state zip
```

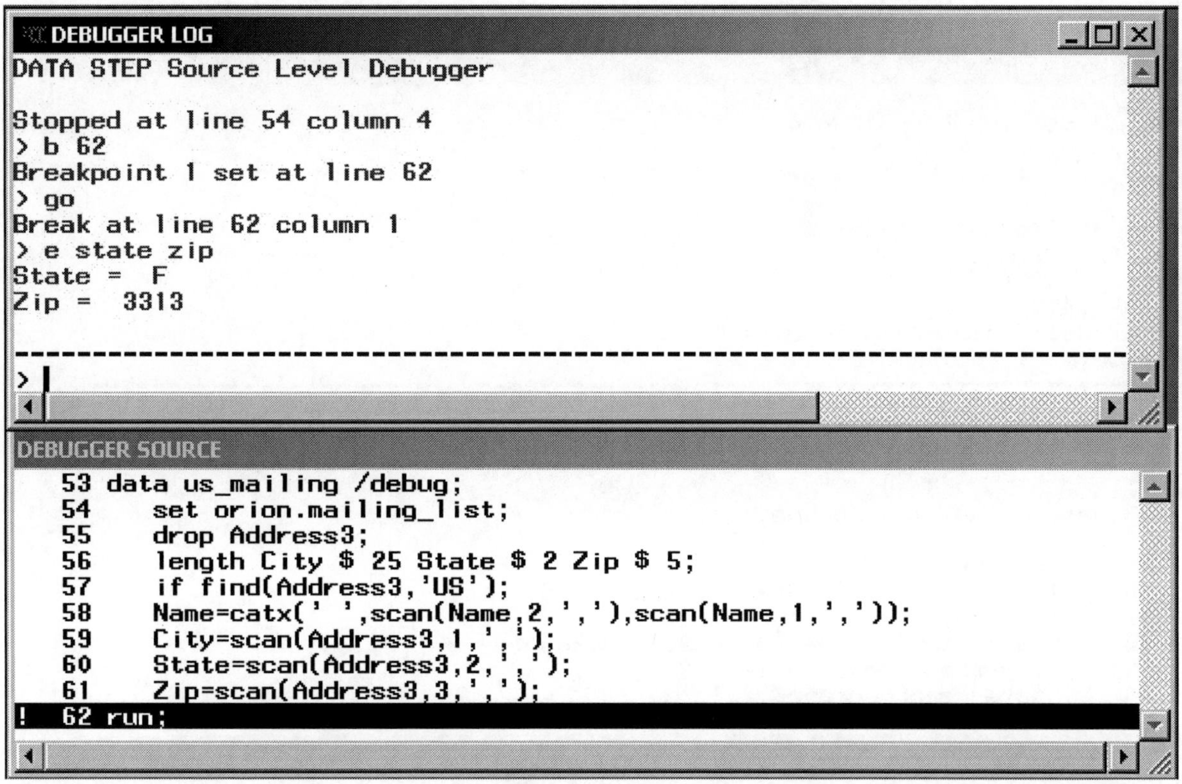

DEBUGGER LOG

```
DATA STEP Source Level Debugger

Stopped at line 54 column 4
> b 62
Breakpoint 1 set at line 62
> go
Break at line 62 column 1
> e state zip
State =  F
Zip =  3313

-----------------------------------------------------------------------
>
```

DEBUGGER SOURCE

```
   53 data us_mailing /debug;
   54    set orion.mailing_list;
   55    drop Address3;
   56    length City $ 25 State $ 2 Zip $ 5;
   57    if find(Address3,'US');
   58    Name=catx(' ',scan(Name,2,','),scan(Name,1,','));
   59    City=scan(Address3,1,',');
   60    State=scan(Address3,2,',');
   61    Zip=scan(Address3,3,',');
!  62 run;
```

The results show that **State** is only one character instead of two and **Zip** is four characters instead of five.

4. Modify the breakpoint to display the values of **State** and **Zip** when program execution reaches the RUN statement.

```
b 62 do; e state zip; end;
```

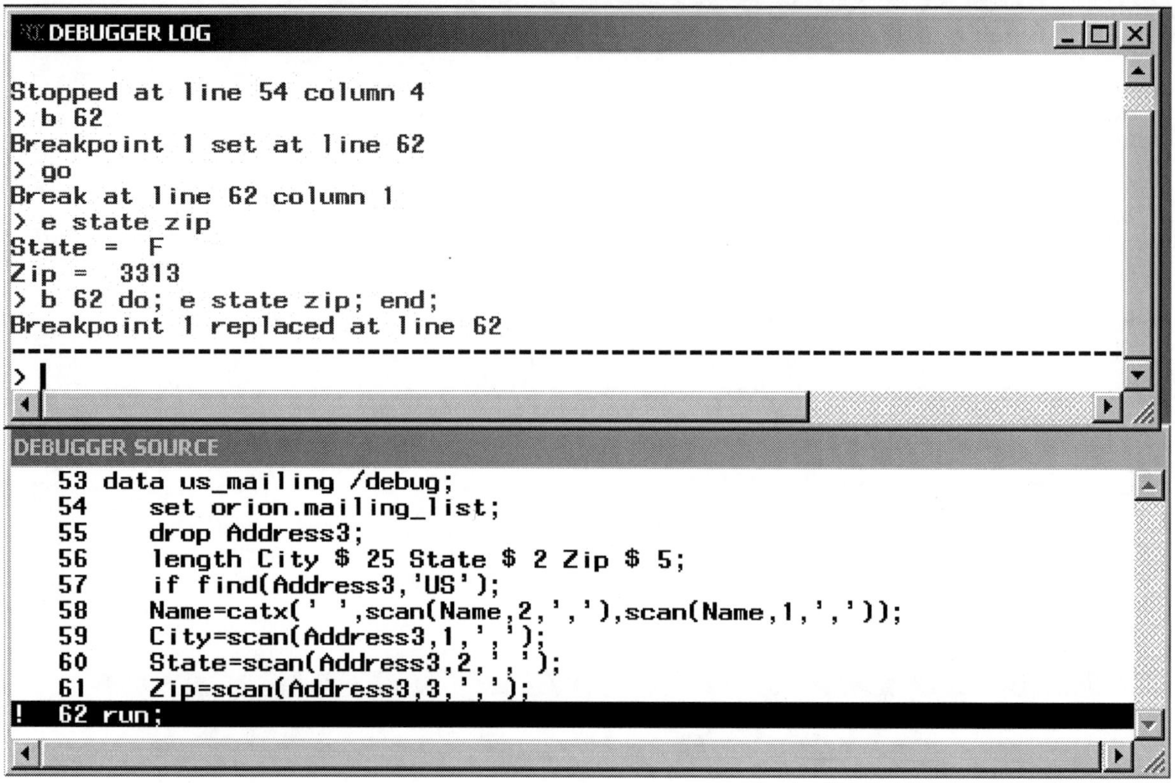

DEBUGGER LOG

```
Stopped at line 54 column 4
> b 62
Breakpoint 1 set at line 62
> go
Break at line 62 column 1
> e state zip
State =  F
Zip =  3313
> b 62 do; e state zip; end;
Breakpoint 1 replaced at line 62
---------------------------------------------------------------------
>
```

DEBUGGER SOURCE

```
   53 data us_mailing /debug;
   54     set orion.mailing_list;
   55     drop Address3;
   56     length City $ 25 State $ 2 Zip $ 5;
   57     if find(Address3,'US');
   58     Name=catx(' ',scan(Name,2,','),scan(Name,1,','));
   59     City=scan(Address3,1,',');
   60     State=scan(Address3,2,',');
   61     Zip=scan(Address3,3,',');
!  62 run;
```

The message in the Log indicates that the previous breakpoint was replaced. Resume execution.

```
g
```

DEBUGGER LOG

```
> go
Break at line 62 column 1
> e state zip
State =  F
Zip =  3313
> b 62 do; e state zip; end;
Breakpoint 1 replaced at line 62
> go
Break at line 62 column 1
State =  P
Zip =  1914
----------------------------------------------------------------------
>
```

DEBUGGER SOURCE

```
   53 data us_mailing /debug;
   54    set orion.mailing_list;
   55    drop Address3;
   56    length City $ 25 State $ 2 Zip $ 5;
   57    if find(Address3,'US');
   58    Name=catx(' ',scan(Name,2,','),scan(Name,1,','));
   59    City=scan(Address3,1,',');
   60    State=scan(Address3,2,',');
   61    Zip=scan(Address3,3,',');
!  62 run;
```

Execution is suspended when the breakpoint is reached, and the values of **State** and **Zip** are displayed automatically.

5. Modify the breakpoint to use a format in the EXAMINE command to get a closer look at the data values, and then submit the **Go** command twice to proceed to the next breakpoint and examine the variables.

```
b 62 do; e state $quote4. Zip $quote7.; end;
g
g
```

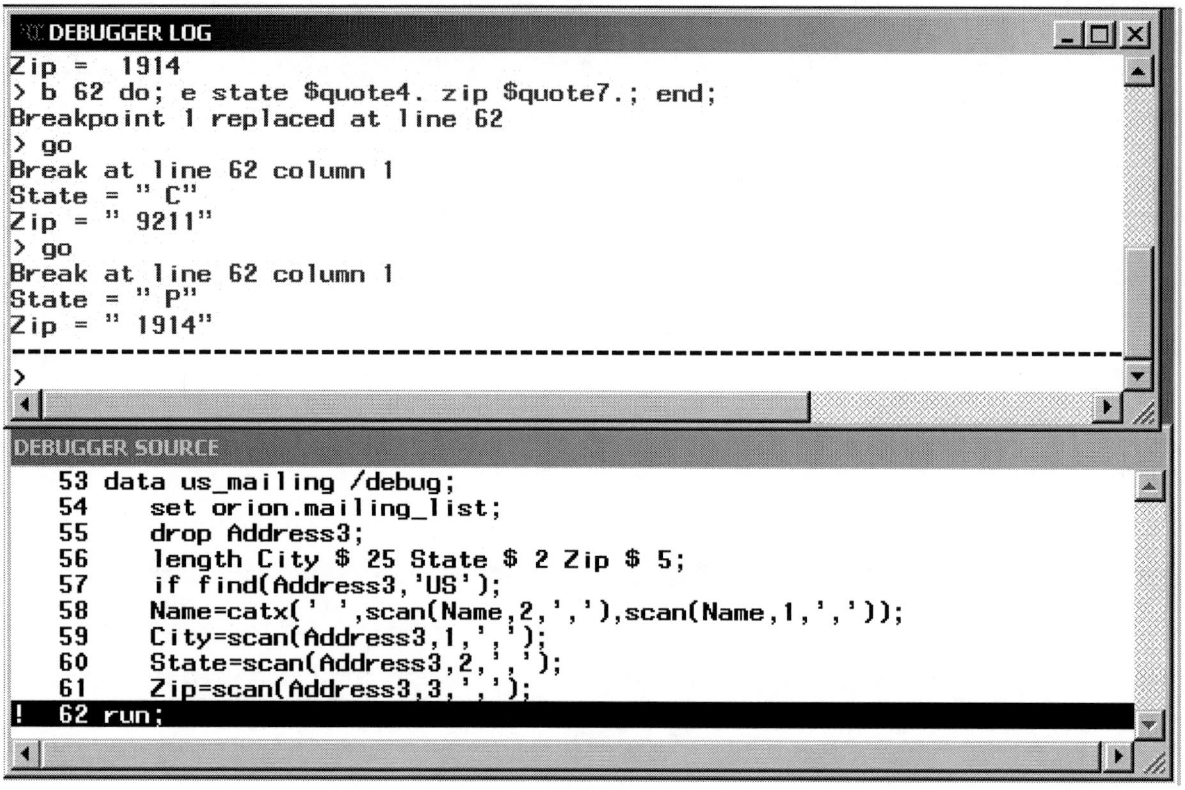

```
DEBUGGER LOG
Zip =   1914
> b 62 do; e state $quote4. zip $quote7.; end;
Breakpoint 1 replaced at line 62
> go
Break at line 62 column 1
State = " C"
Zip = " 9211"
> go
Break at line 62 column 1
State = " P"
Zip = " 1914"
---------------------------------------------------------------------------
>

DEBUGGER SOURCE
   53 data us_mailing /debug;
   54     set orion.mailing_list;
   55     drop Address3;
   56     length City $ 25 State $ 2 Zip $ 5;
   57     if find(Address3,'US');
   58     Name=catx(' ',scan(Name,2,','),scan(Name,1,','));
   59     City=scan(Address3,1,',');
   60     State=scan(Address3,2,',');
   61     Zip=scan(Address3,3,',');
!  62 run;
```

The displayed value shows that there is a leading space on both **State** and **Zip**.

6. Submit a **`Quit`** command to exit the DATA Step Debugger.

```
q
```

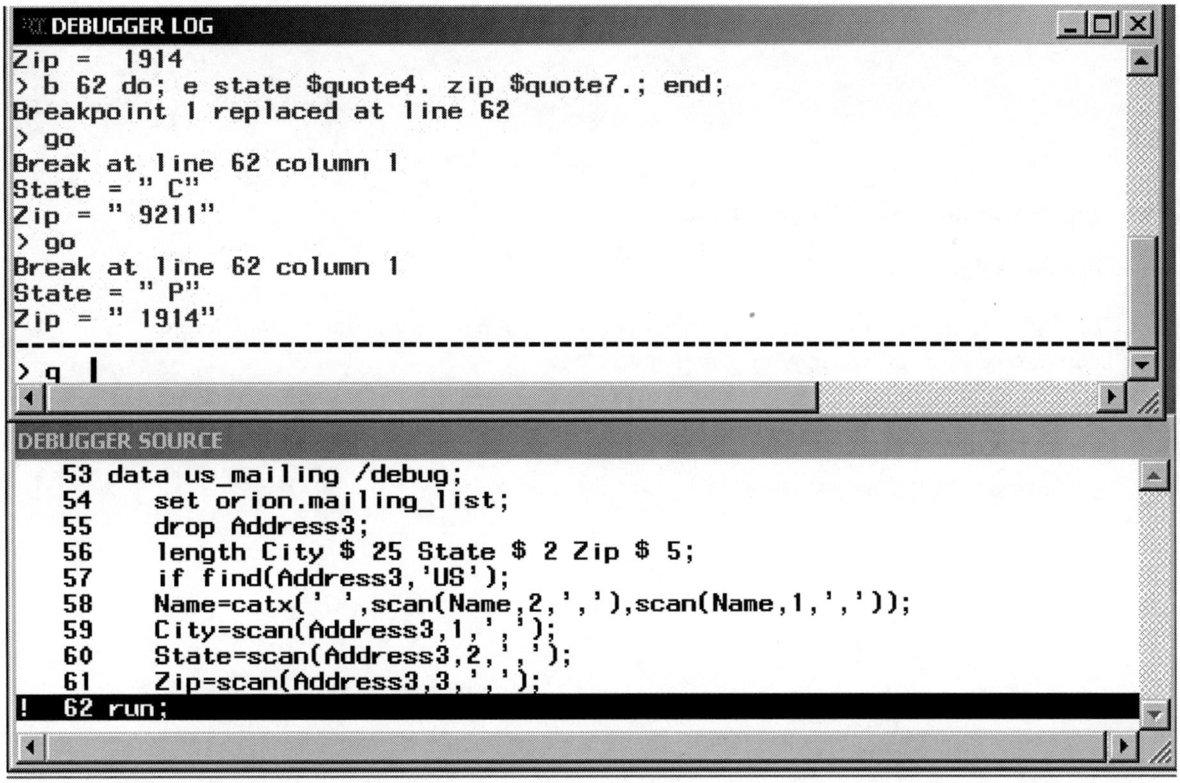

DEBUGGER LOG

```
Zip =   1914
> b 62 do; e state $quote4. zip $quote7.; end;
Breakpoint 1 replaced at line 62
> go
Break at line 62 column 1
State = " C"
Zip = " 9211"
> go
Break at line 62 column 1
State = " P"
Zip = " 1914"
-----------------------------------------------------------------------------------
> q
```

DEBUGGER SOURCE

```
   53 data us_mailing /debug;
   54     set orion.mailing_list;
   55     drop Address3;
   56     length City $ 25 State $ 2 Zip $ 5;
   57     if find(Address3,'US');
   58     Name=catx(' ',scan(Name,2,','),scan(Name,1,','));
   59     City=scan(Address3,1,',');
   60     State=scan(Address3,2,',');
   61     Zip=scan(Address3,3,',');
!  62 run;
```

✎ Multiple breakpoints can be in effect simultaneously.

The DELETE command is used to delete one or more breakpoints.

To delete a specific breakpoint:

DELETE BREAK *line-num*.

d b *line-num*

To delete all breakpoints :

DELETE BREAK _ALL_

d b
all

Exercises

Level 1

1. Debugging with the PUTLOG Statement

a. Open and submit **p206e01**.

b. Compare your results to the correct output below. Notice that your output is different. There are no error or warning messages in the log.

Correct Partial PROC PRINT Output

```
                         Total_
 Obs    Customer_ID       Sales

   1              5      691.10
   2             10     3479.09
   3             11       78.20
   4             12      253.20
   5             18       29.40
   6             24      358.80
   7             27     1093.60
   8             31     1777.60
   9             34      728.80
  10             41      566.20
```

c. Insert PUTLOG statements to check program flow, display values of variables, and so on to identify the error(s).

d. Correct the error(s), resubmit the program, and verify your results.

2. Debugging with the DEBUG Option

a. Open and submit **p206e01**.

b. Compare your results to the correct output below. Notice that your output is different. There are no error or warning messages in the log.

Correct Partial PROC PRINT Output

```
                         Total_
 Obs    Customer_ID       Sales

   1              5      691.10
   2             10     3479.09
   3             11       78.20
   4             12      253.20
   5             18       29.40
   6             24      358.80
   7             27     1093.60
   8             31     1777.60
  10             41      566.20
```

c. Use the DEBUG option to start the DATA Step Debugger in order to identify the error(s).

d. Correct the error(s), resubmit the program, and verify your results.

Level 2

3. Setting Breakpoints

- Use breakpoints in the DATA Step Debugger to debug a SAS program. Refer to the self-study section on setting breakpoints and the SAS documentation for the correct syntax and examples.

  a. Open and submit **p206e01**.

  b. Compare your results to the correct output below. Notice that your output is different. There are no error or warning messages in the log.

Correct Partial PROC PRINT Output

```
                          Total_
Obs    Customer_ID         Sales

  1              5        691.10
  2             10       3479.09
  3             11         78.20
  4             12        253.20
  5             18         29.40
  6             24        358.80
  7             27       1093.60
  8             31       1777.60
  9             34        728.80
 10             41        566.20
```

  c. Use the DATA Step Debugger to debug the program.

  d. Correct the error(s) and verify your results.

6.3 Chapter Review

Chapter Review

1. What statement can be used in the DATA step to display the value of one or more variables?

2. How can you display the values of all variables?

3. How can you know when you are processing the last input observation or record?

4. Name two special variables that can be helpful when you debug a DATA step.

46

continued...

Chapter Review

5. How do you invoke the DATA Step Debugger?

6. What shortcut can be used to execute the statements one at a time?

7. What command would you use to see the values of **`v1`** and **`v2`** every time that they change in value?

8. What command enables you to see the values of every variable in the PDV?

48

6.4 Solutions

Solutions to Exercises

1. **Debugging with the PUTLOG Statement**

   a. Open the file **p206e01** and submit it.

   b. Compare your results. Notice your output.

```
data customers;
   set orion.order_summary;
   by Customer_ID;
   if first.Customer_ID=1 then TotSales=0;
   putlog TotSales= Sale_Amt=;
   Total_Sales+Sale_Amt;
   if last.Customer_ID=1;
   keep Customer_ID Total_Sales;
run;
```

   c. Use PUTLOG statements to identify the errors.

```
data customers;
   set orion.order_summary;
   by Customer_ID;
   if first.Customer_ID=1 then TotSales=0;
   putlog TotSales= Sale_Amt=;
   Total_Sales+Sale_Amt;
   putlog Total_Sales=;
   if last.Customer_ID=1;
   keep Customer_ID Total_Sales;
run;
```

   d. Correct the error and resubmit the program.

```
data customers;
   set orion.order_summary;
   by Customer_ID;
   if first.Customer_ID=1 then Total_Sales=0;
   Total_Sales+Sale_Amt;
   if last.Customer_ID=1;
   keep Customer_ID Total_Sales;
run;

proc print data=customers;
run;
```

2. Debugging with the DEBUG Option

a. Open the file **p206e01** and submit.

```
data customers;
   set orion.order_summary;
   by Customer_ID;
   if first.Customer_ID=1 then TotSales=0;
   Total_Sales+Sale_Amt;
   if last.Customer_ID=1;
   keep Customer_ID Total_Sales;
run;
```

b. Compare your results to the correct output below. Notice that your output is different. There are no error or warning messages in the log.

c. Use the DEBUG option to identify the error.

```
data customers /debug;
   set orion.order_summary;
   by Customer_ID;
   if first.Customer_ID=1 then TotSales=0;
   Total_Sales+Sale_Amt;
   if last.Customer_ID=1;
   keep Customer_ID Total_Sales;
run;
```

Execute the program statements one at a time by pressing ENTER. The following commands might be useful to examine values of variables:

- `e TotSales`
- `e Total_Sales Sale_Amt`
- `w Total_Sales Sale_Amt`
- `w first.customer_id last.customer_id`

d. Correct the error and resubmit the program.

```
data customers;
   set orion.order_summary;
   by Customer_ID;
   if first.Customer_ID=1 then Total_Sales=0;
   Total_Sales+Sale_Amt;
   if last.Customer_ID=1;
   keep Customer_ID Total_Sales;
run;
proc print data=customers;
run;
```

3. Setting Breakpoints

a. Open the file **p206e01** and submit it.

```
data customers;
   set orion.order_summary;
   by Customer_ID;
   if first.Customer_ID=1 then TotSales=0;
   Total_Sales+Sale_Amt;
   if last.Customer_ID=1;
   keep Customer_ID Total_Sales;
run;
```

b. Compare your results to the correct output below. Notice that your output is different. There are no error or warning messages in the log.

c. Use the DATA Step Debugger to debug the program.

```
data customers /debug;
   set orion.order_summary;
   by Customer_ID;
   if first.Customer_ID=1 then TotSales=0;
   Total_Sales+Sale_Amt;
   if last.Customer_ID=1;
   keep Customer_ID Total_Sales;
run;
```

Execute the program statements one at a time by pressing ENTER. The following commands might be useful to examine values of variables.

- `b` ***`linenum`***
- `go`
- `b` ***`linenum`*** `when first.customer_id=1`
- `b` ***`linenum`*** `when first.customer_id=1 do;  e _all_;  end;`

d. Correct the error(s) and resubmit the program.

```
data customers;
   set orion.order_summary;
   by Customer_ID;
   if first.Customer_ID=1 then Total_Sales=0;
   Total_Sales+Sale_Amt;
   if last.Customer_ID=1;
   keep Customer_ID Total_Sales;
run;
proc print data=customers;
run;
```

Solutions to Student Activities (Polls/Quizzes)

6.01 Quiz – Correct Answer

The values of `State` and `Zip` are incorrect.

Current Output from Program

Name	Address1	City	State	Zip
Ray Abbott	2267 Edwards Mill Rd	Miami-Dade	F	3313
Tameaka Akinfolarin	5 Donnybrook Rd	Philadelphia	P	1914
Salley Amos	3524 Calico Ct	San Diego	C	9211
Rose Anger	744 Chapwith Rd	Philadelphia	P	1914
David Anstey	939 Hilltop Needmore Rd	Miami-Dade	F	3315
Doris Antonini	681 Ferguson Rd	Miami-Dade	F	3314
Nishan Apr	105 Brack Penny Rd	San Diego	C	9207
Elizabeth Ardskin	701 Glenridge Dr	Miami-Dade	F	3317
Jeryl Areu	265 Fyfe Ct	Miami-Dade	F	3313
Gilbert Arizmendi	379 Englehardt Dr	San Diego	C	9195
Debra Armant	10398 Crown Forest Ct	San Diego	C	9202

12

6.02 Quiz – Correct Answer

Open the file **p206a02**. Insert statements to display the values of _N_ and _ERROR_ in the first three iterations of the DATA step.

Solution

```
data _null_;
   set orion.donate;
   if _n_ <= 3 then
      putlog _n_= _error_=;
run;
```

Alternate solution

```
data _null_;
   set orion.donate (obs=3);
   putlog _n_= _error_=;
run;
```

Partial SAS Log

```
_N_=1 _ERROR_=0
_N_=2 _ERROR_=0
_N_=3 _ERROR_=0
```

Use _N_ to execute PUTLOG on the first 3 iterations of the DATA step, or use OBS= to process only 3 observations.

p206a02s

21

6.03 Quiz – Correct Answer

In the first example, what command is used to examine data values after the first iteration? **`examine _all_`**

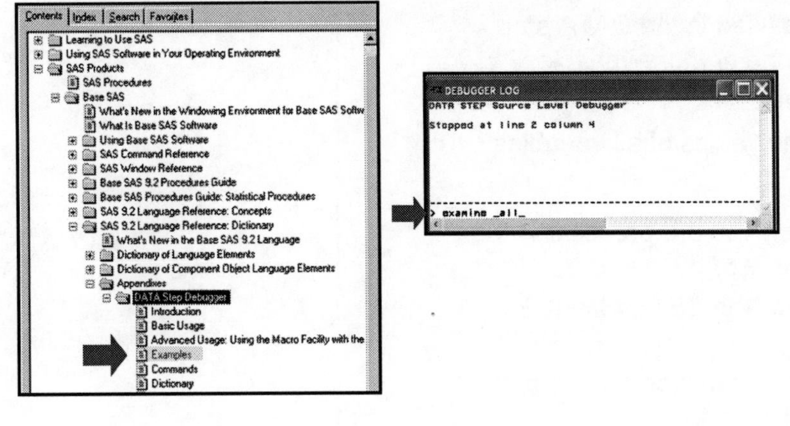

37

Solutions to Chapter Review

Chapter Review – Answers

1. What statement can be used in the DATA step to display the value of one or more variables?

   The PUTLOG statement

2. How can you display the values of all variables?

   `putlog _all_`

3. How can you know when you are processing the last input observation or record?

   Use the END= option in the SET or INFILE statement.

4. Name two special variables that can be helpful when you debug a DATA step.

   _N_ and _ERROR_

47

continued...

Chapter Review – Answers

5. How do you invoke the DATA Step Debugger?

   Use the /DEBUG option in the DATA statement.

6. What shortcut can be used to execute the statements one at a time?

   Pressing ENTER

7. What command would you use to see the values of **`v1`** and **`v2`** every time they change in value?

   `watch v1 v2` **or** **`w v1 v2`**

8. What command enables you to see the values of every variable in the PDV?.

   `e _all_`

49

Chapter 7 Processing Data Iteratively

7.1 DO Loop Processing **7-3**

Exercises 7-31

7.2 SAS Array Processing **7-34**

Exercises 7-47

7.3 Using SAS Arrays **7-52**

Exercises 7-69

7.4 Chapter Review **7-72**

7.5 Solutions **7-73**

Solutions to Exercises 7-73

Solutions to Student Activities (Polls/Quizzes) 7-79

Solutions to Chapter Review 7-83

7.1 DO Loop Processing

Objectives

- Explain iterative DO loops.
- Use DO loops to eliminate redundant code and repetitive calculations.
- Use conditional DO loops.
- Use nested DO loops.

3

Business Scenario

An Orion Star employee wants to compare the interest for yearly versus quarterly compounding on a $50,000 investment made for one year at 4.5 percent interest.

How much money will the employee accrue in each situation?

4

Repetitive Coding

```
data compound;
   Amount=50000;
   Rate=.045;
   Yearly=Amount*Rate;
   Quarterly+((Quarterly+Amount)*Rate/4);
   Quarterly+((Quarterly+Amount)*Rate/4);
   Quarterly+((Quarterly+Amount)*Rate/4);
   Quarterly+((Quarterly+Amount)*Rate/4);
run;
proc print data=compound noobs;
run;
```

PROC PRINT Output

Amount	Rate	Yearly	Quarterly
50000	0.045	2250	2288.25

5 p207d01

Repetitive Coding

What if the employee wants to determine annual and quarterly compounded interest for a period of 20 years (80 quarters)?

```
data compound;
   Amount=50000;
   Rate=.045;
     Yearly +(Yearly+Amount)*Rate;
20x  .
     .
     .
     Yearly +(Yearly+Amount)*Rate;
     Quarterly+((Quarterly+Amount)*Rate/4);
80x  .
     .
     .
     Quarterly+((Quarterly+Amount)*Rate/4);
run;
```

6

DO Loop Processing

Use DO loops to perform the repetitive calculations.

```
data compound(drop=i);
   Amount=50000;
   Rate=.045;
   do i=1 to 20;
      Yearly +(Yearly+Amount)*Rate;
   end;
   do i=1 to 80;
      Quarterly+((Quarterly+Amount)*Rate/4);
   end;
run;
```

7 p207d02

Various Forms of Iterative DO Loops

There are several forms of iterative DO loops that execute the statements between the DO and END statements repetitively.

DO *index-variable=start* **TO** *stop* <**BY** *increment*>;
   iterated SAS statements…
END;

DO *index-variable=item-1* <,…*item-n*>;
   iterated SAS statements…
END;

8

The Iterative DO Statement

General form of an iterative DO statement:

DO *index-variable=start* TO *stop* <BY *increment*>;

The values of *start*, *stop*, and *increment*

- must be numbers or expressions that yield numbers
- are established before executing the loop
- if omitted, *increment* defaults to 1.

9

start specifies the initial value of the index variable.

stop specifies the ending value of the index variable.

increment specifies a positive or negative number to control the incrementing of *index-variable.*

When *increment* is positive, *start* must be the lower bound and *stop*, if present, must be the upper bound for the loop. If *increment* is negative, *start* must be the upper bound and *stop*, if present, must be the lower bound for the loop.

Changes to the values of *stop* or *increment* made within the DO loop do not affect the number of iterations.

The Iterative DO Statement

Index-variable details:

- The *index-variable* is written to the output data set by default.
- At the termination of the loop, the value of *index-variable* is one *increment* beyond the *stop* value.

Modifying the value of *index-variable* affects the number of iterations, and might cause infinite looping or early loop termination.

10

7.01 Quiz

What are the final values of the index variables after the following DO loops execute?

The final values are highlighted.

```
do i=1 to 5;
   ...
end;                        1 2 3 4 5 6

do j=2 to 8 by 2;
   ...
end;

do k=10 to 2 by -2;
   ...
end;
```

12

The Iterative DO Statement

General form of an iterative DO statement with an *item-list*:

DO *index-variable=item-1* <,…*item-n*>;

- The DO loop is executed once for each item in the list.
- The list must be comma separated.

14

Sample DO Loops with Item Lists

Items in the list can be all numeric or all character constants, or they can be variables.

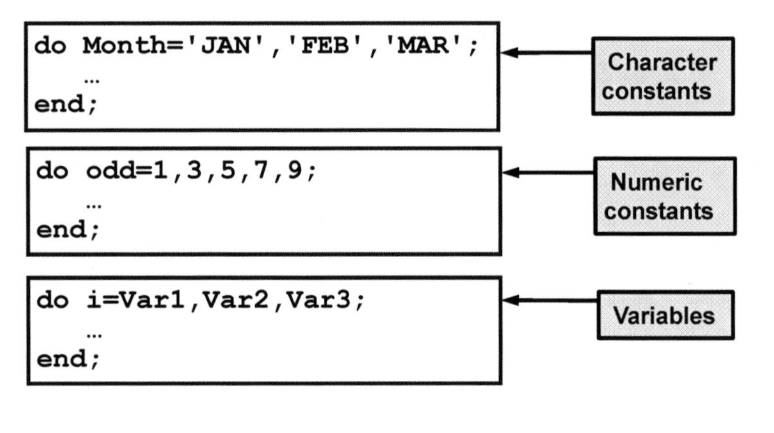
do Month='JAN','FEB','MAR';
...
end;
Character constants
do odd=1,3,5,7,9;
...
end;
Numeric constants
do i=Var1,Var2,Var3;
...
end;
Variables

15

Enclose character constants in quotation marks.

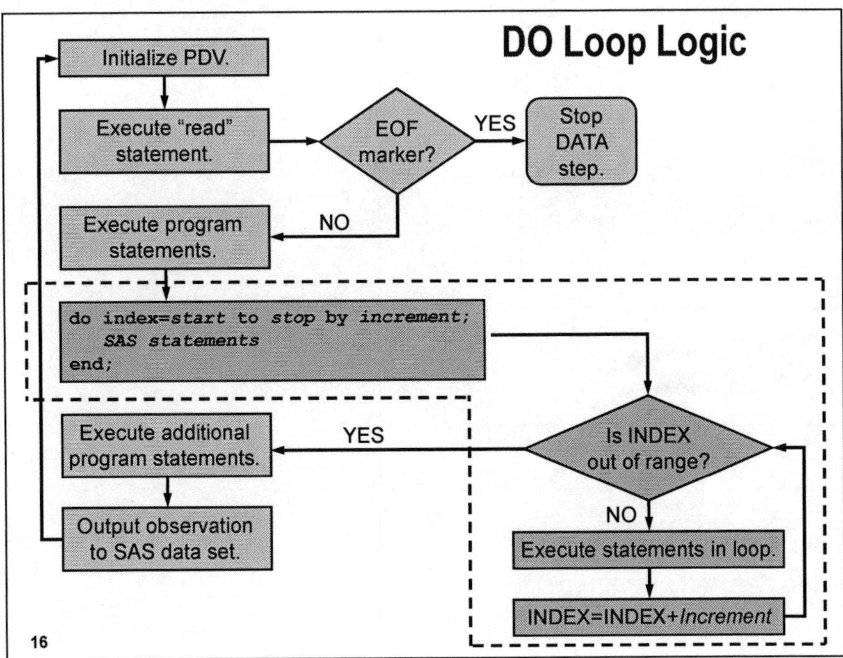

Business Scenario

On January 1 of each year, an Orion Star employee invests $5,000 in an account. Determine the value of the account after three years based on a constant annual interest rate of 4.5 percent, starting in 2008.

```
data invest;
   do Year=2008 to 2010;
      Capital+5000;
      Capital+(Capital*.045);
   end;
run;
```

p207d03

17

Execution: Performing Repetitive Calculations

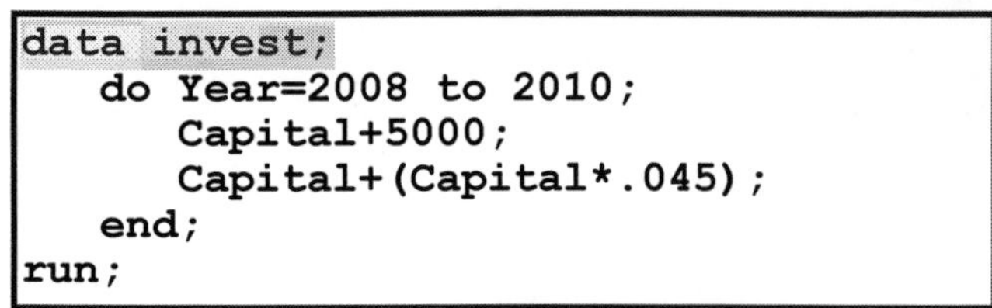

```
data invest;
   do Year=2008 to 2010;
      Capital+5000;
      Capital+(Capital*.045);
   end;
run;
```

Initialize PDV

PDV

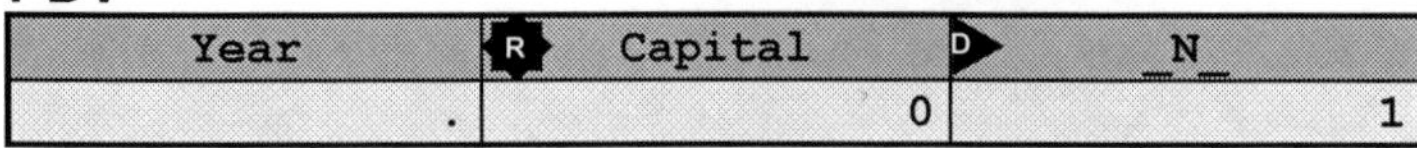

Year	R Capital	D _N_
.	0	1

Capital is used in a sum statement, so it is automatically initialized to zero and retained.

18 ...

Execution: Performing Repetitive Calculations

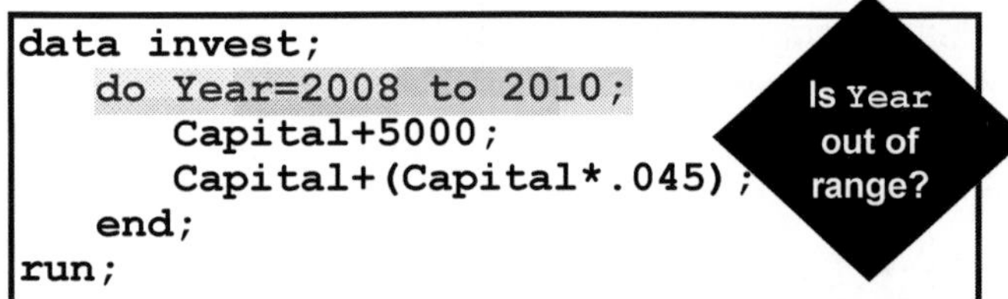

```
data invest;
   do Year=2008 to 2010;
      Capital+5000;
      Capital+(Capital*.045);
   end;
run;
```

Is Year out of range?

PDV

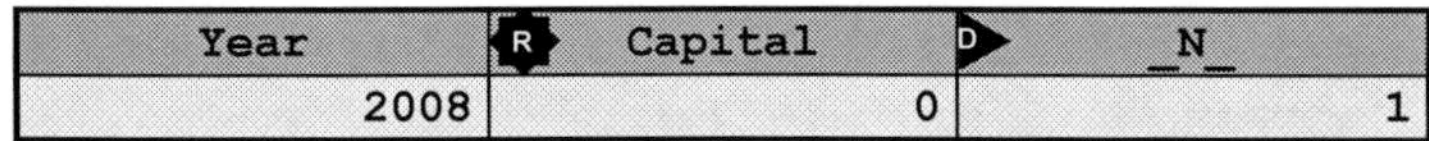

Year	R Capital	D _N_
2008	0	1

19 ...

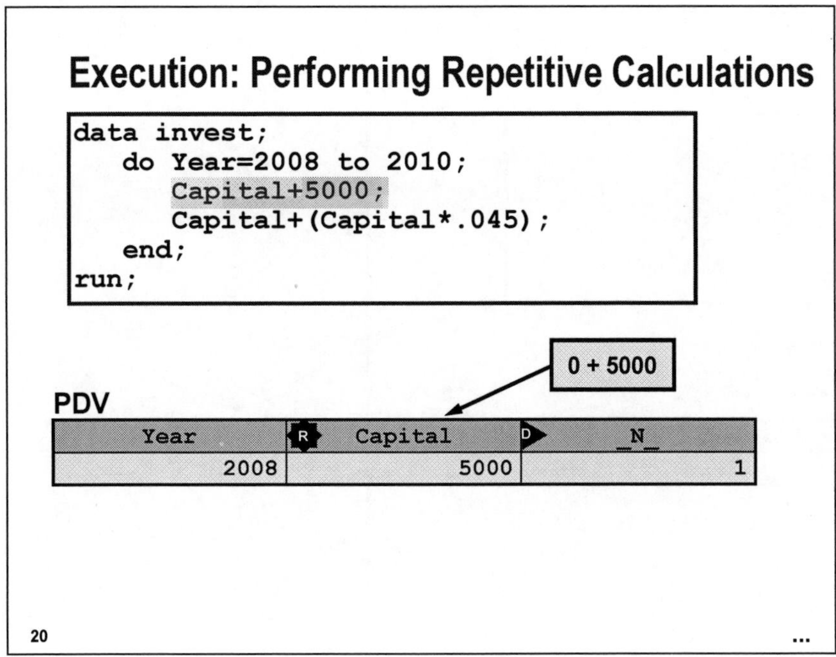
Execution: Performing Repetitive Calculations
data invest;
do Year=2008 to 2010;
Capital+5000;
Capital+(Capital*.045);
end;
run;
0 + 5000
PDV
Year
Capital
_N_
2008
5000
1
20
...

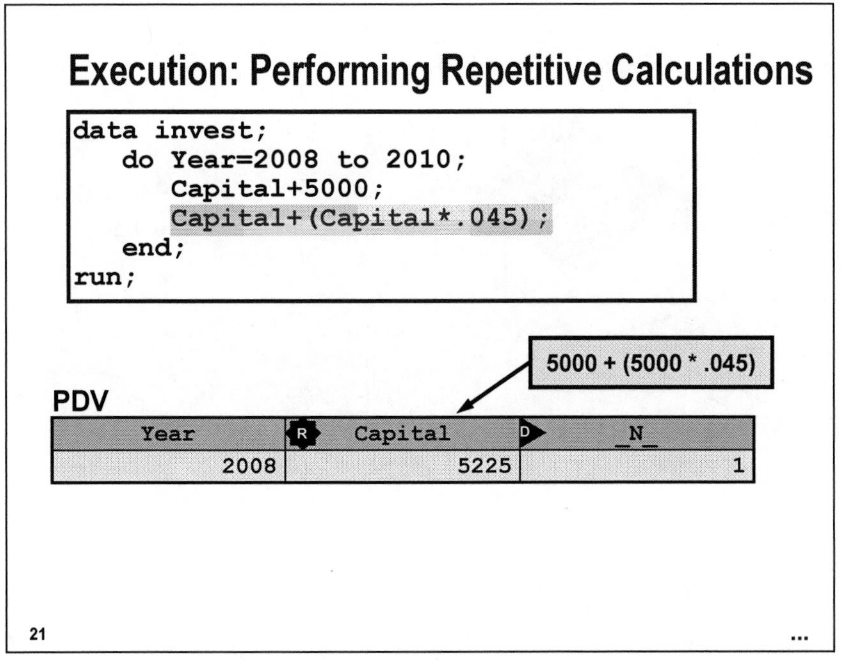
Execution: Performing Repetitive Calculations
data invest;
do Year=2008 to 2010;
Capital+5000;
Capital+(Capital*.045);
end;
run;
5000 + (5000 * .045)
PDV
Year
Capital
_N_
2008
5225
1
21
...

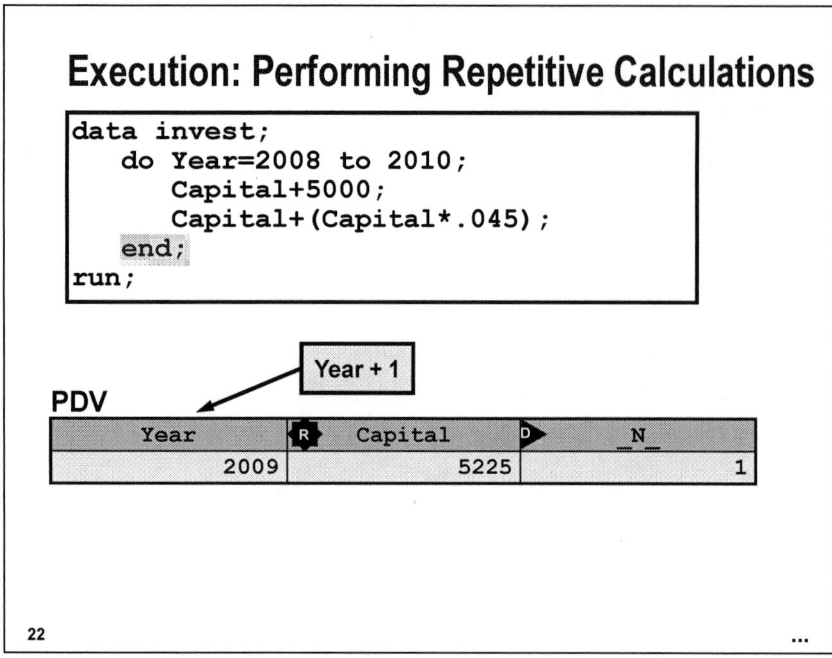
Execution: Performing Repetitive Calculations
data invest;
do Year=2008 to 2010;
Capital+5000;
Capital+(Capital*.045);
end;
run;
Year + 1
PDV
Year
Capital
_N_
2009
5225
1
22
...

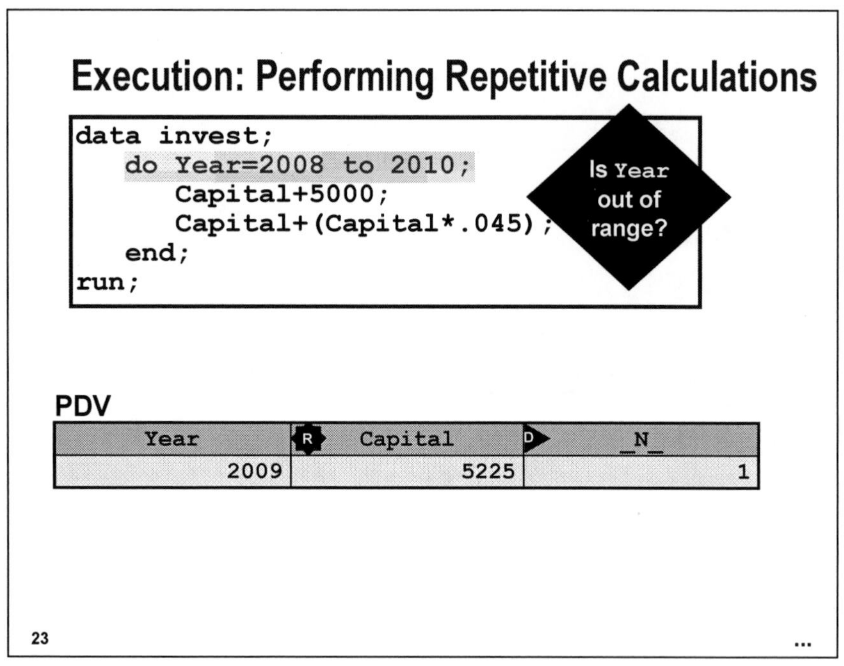
Execution: Performing Repetitive Calculations
data invest;
do Year=2008 to 2010;
Capital+5000;
Capital+(Capital*.045);
end;
run;
Is Year out of range?
PDV
Year
Capital
_N_
2009
5225
1
23
...

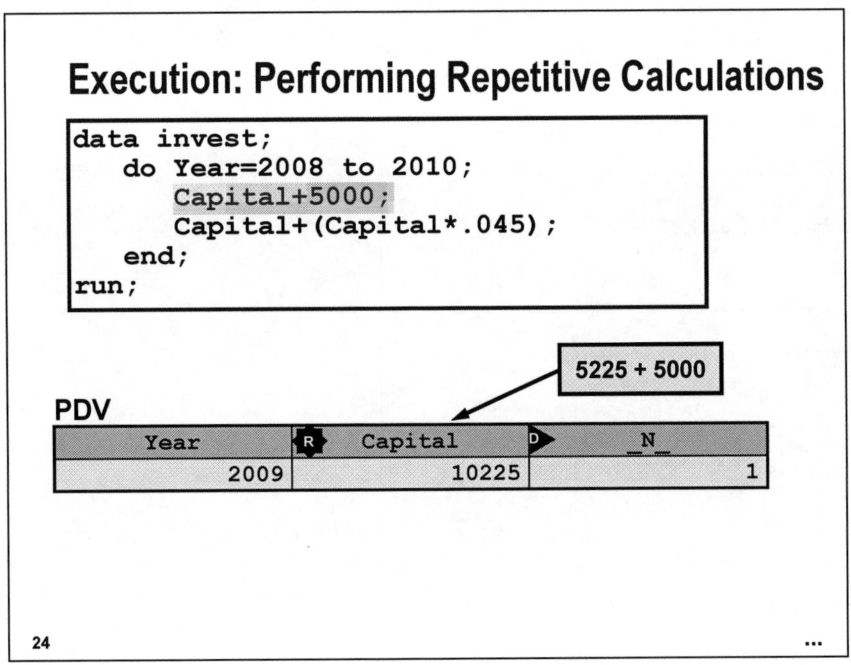
Execution: Performing Repetitive Calculations
data invest;
do Year=2008 to 2010;
Capital+5000;
Capital+(Capital*.045);
end;
run;
5225 + 5000
PDV
Year
Capital
_N_
2009
10225
1
24
...

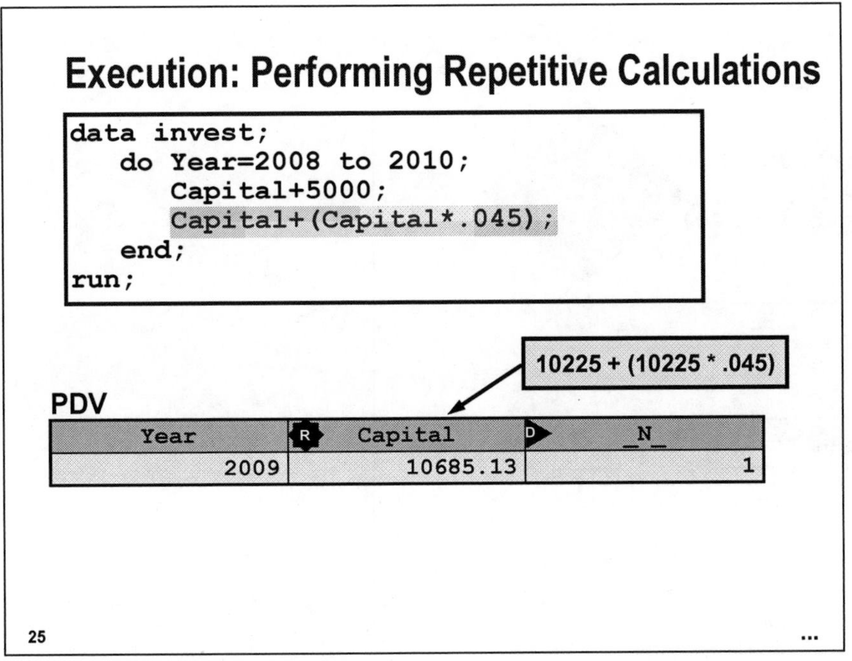
Execution: Performing Repetitive Calculations
data invest;
do Year=2008 to 2010;
Capital+5000;
Capital+(Capital*.045);
end;
run;
10225 + (10225 * .045)
PDV
Year
Capital
_N_
2009
10685.13
1
25
...

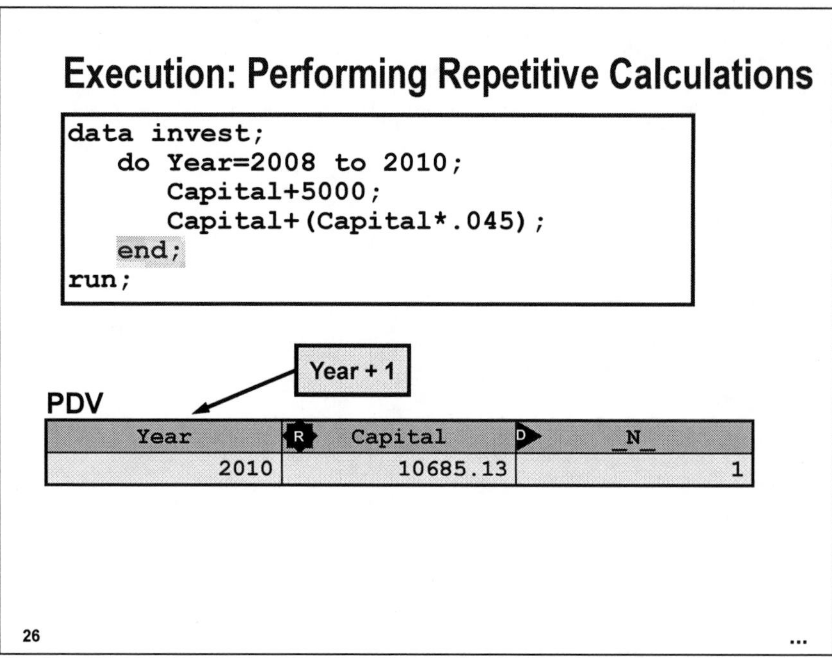

Execution: Performing Repetitive Calculations
data invest;
do Year=2008 to 2010;
Capital+5000;
Capital+(Capital*.045);
end;
run;
Year + 1
PDV
Year
R
Capital
D
_N_
2010
10685.13
1
26
...

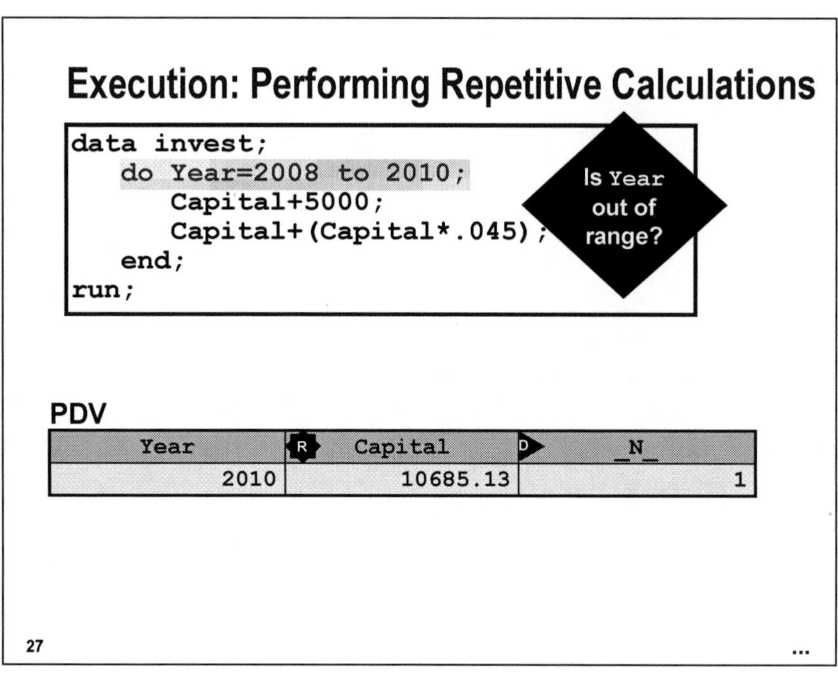

Execution: Performing Repetitive Calculations
data invest;
do Year=2008 to 2010;
Capital+5000;
Capital+(Capital*.045);
end;
run;
Is Year out of range?
PDV
Year
R
Capital
D
_N_
2010
10685.13
1
27
...

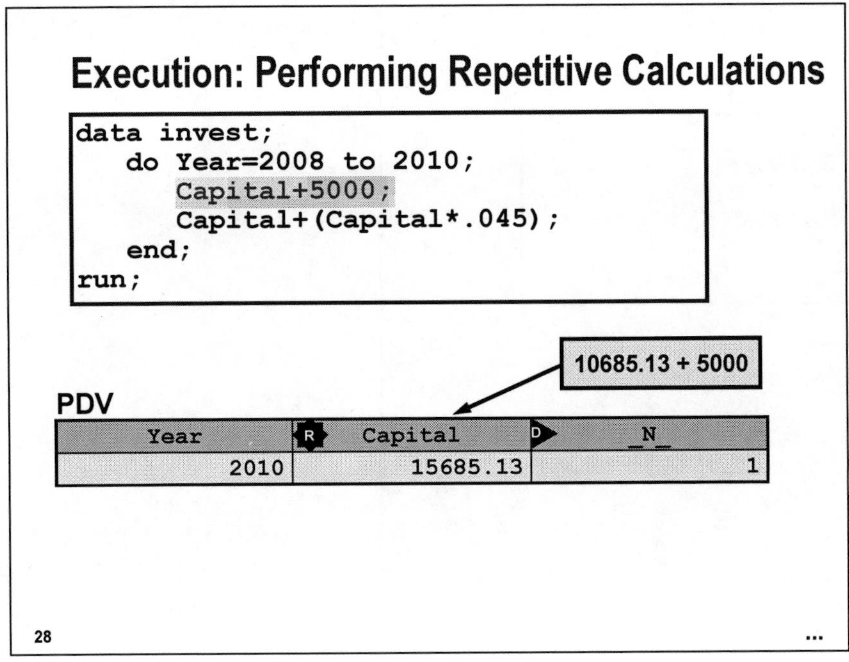
Execution: Performing Repetitive Calculations
data invest;
do Year=2008 to 2010;
Capital+5000;
Capital+(Capital*.045);
end;
run;
10685.13 + 5000
PDV
Year
R
Capital
D
_N_
2010
15685.13
1
28
...

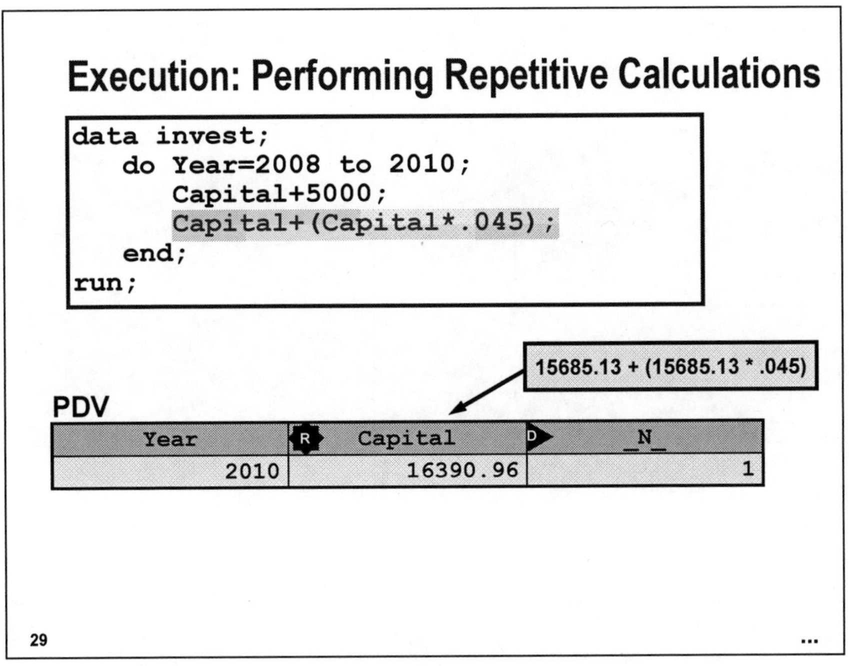
Execution: Performing Repetitive Calculations
data invest;
do Year=2008 to 2010;
Capital+5000;
Capital+(Capital*.045);
end;
run;
15685.13 + (15685.13 * .045)
PDV
Year
R
Capital
D
_N_
2010
16390.96
1
29
...

Execution: Performing Repetitive Calculations

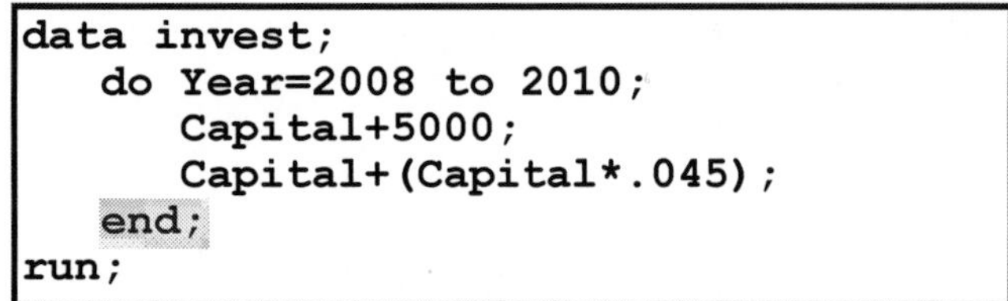

```
data invest;
   do Year=2008 to 2010;
      Capital+5000;
      Capital+(Capital*.045);
   end;
run;
```

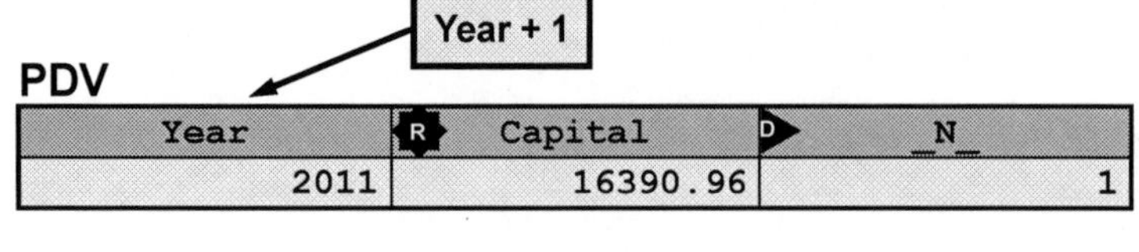

Year	Capital	_N_
2011	16390.96	1

30 ...

Execution: Performing Repetitive Calculations

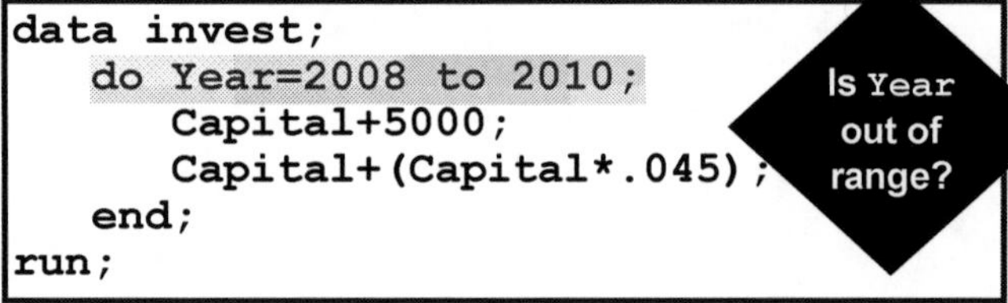

```
data invest;
   do Year=2008 to 2010;
      Capital+5000;
      Capital+(Capital*.045);
   end;
run;
```


PDV

Year	Capital	_N_
2011	16390.96	1

31 ...

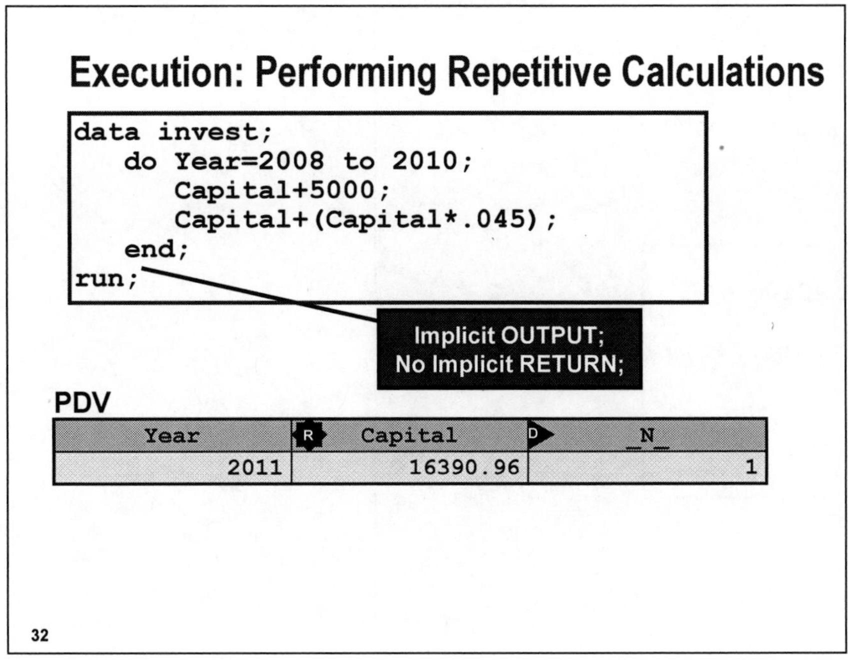

Output: Performing Repetitive Calculations

```
proc print data=invest noobs;
run;
```

PROC PRINT Output

Year	Capital
2011	16390.96

33

p207d03

7.02 Quiz

How can you generate a separate observation for each year?

```
data invest;
   do Year=2008 to 2010;
      Capital+5000;
      Capital+(Capital*.045);
   end;
run;
proc print data=invest noobs;
run;
```

35 p207a01

Business Scenario

Recall the example that forecasts the growth of several departments at Orion Star. Modify the forecasting application to use a DO loop to eliminate redundant code.

Listing of **orion.growth**

Department	Total_ Employees	Increase
Administration	34	0.25
Engineering	9	0.30
IS	25	0.10
Marketing	20	0.20
Sales	201	0.30
Sales Management	11	0.10

38

A Forecasting Application (Review)

```
data forecast;
   set orion.growth;
   Year=1;
   Total_Employees=Total_Employees*(1+Increase);
   output;
   Year=2;
   Total_Employees=Total_Employees*(1+Increase);
   output;
run;
proc print data=forecast noobs;
run;
```

What if you want to forecast growth over the next six years?

39 p207d04

Use a DO Loop to Reduce Redundant Code

```
data forecast;
   set orion.growth;
   do Year=1 to 6;
      Total_Employees=
         Total_Employees*(1+Increase);
      output;
   end;
run;

proc print data=forecast noobs;
run;
```

40 p207d05

Output

Partial PROC PRINT Output

Department	Total_ Employees	Increase	Year
Administration	42.500	0.25	1
Administration	53.125	0.25	2
Administration	66.406	0.25	3
Administration	83.008	0.25	4
Administration	103.760	0.25	5
Administration	129.700	0.25	6
Engineering	11.700	0.30	1
Engineering	15.210	0.30	2
Engineering	19.773	0.30	3
Engineering	25.705	0.30	4
Engineering	33.416	0.30	5
Engineering	43.441	0.30	6
IS	27.500	0.10	1

41

7.03 Quiz

What stop value would you use in the DO loop to determine the number of years that it would take for the Engineering department to exceed 75 people?

```
data forecast;
   set orion.growth;
   do Year=1 to 6;
      Total_Employees=
         Total_Employees*(1+Increase);
      output;
   end;
run;
proc print data=forecast noobs;
run;
```

43 p207d05

Conditional Iterative Processing

You can use DO WHILE and DO UNTIL statements to stop the loop when a condition is met rather than when the loop executed a specific number of times.

 To avoid infinite loops, be sure that the specified condition will be met.

45

The DO WHILE Statement

The DO WHILE statement executes statements in a DO loop repetitively while a condition is true.

General form of the DO WHILE loop:

DO WHILE (*expression*);
    <additional SAS statements>
END;

The value of *expression* is evaluated at the **top** of the loop.

The statements in the loop never execute if *expression* is initially false.

46

The DO UNTIL Statement

The DO UNTIL statement executes statements in a DO loop repetitively until a condition is true.

General form of the DO UNTIL loop:

```
DO UNTIL (expression);
     <additional SAS statements>
END;
```

The value of *expression* is evaluated at the **bottom** of the loop.

The statements in the loop are executed at least once.

 Although the condition is placed at the top of the loop, it is evaluated at the bottom of the loop.

47

Business Scenario

Determine the number of years that it would take for an account to exceed $1,000,000 if $5,000 is invested annually at 4.5 percent.

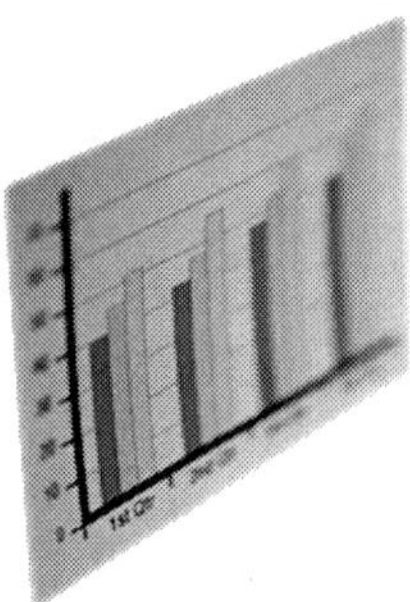

48

Using the DO UNTIL Statement

```
data invest;
   do until(Capital>1000000);
      Year+1;
      Capital+5000;
      Capital+(Capital*.045);
   end;
run;

proc print data=invest noobs;
   format Capital dollar14.2;
run;
```

PROC PRINT Output

Capital	Year
$1,029,193.17	52

49

p207d06

7.04 Quiz

How can you generate the same result with a DO WHILE statement?

```
data invest;
   do until(Capital>1000000);
      Year+1;
      Capital+5000;
      Capital+(Capital*.045);
   end;
run;

proc print data=invest noobs;
   format capital dollar14.2;
run;
```

51

p207a02

Iterative DO Loop with a Conditional Clause

You can combine DO WHILE and DO UNTIL statements with the iterative DO statement.

General form of the iterative DO loop with a conditional clause:

DO *index-variable=start* TO *stop* <BY *increment*>
    WHILE | UNTIL (*expression*);
    <*additional SAS statements*>
END;

✎ This is one method of avoiding an infinite loop in a DO WHILE or DO UNTIL statements.

53

Using DO UNTIL with an Iterative DO Loop

Determine the value of the account again. Stop the loop if 30 years is reached or more than $250,000 is accumulated.

```
data invest;
   do Year=1 to 30 until(Capital>250000);
      Capital+5000;
      Capital+(Capital*.045);
   end;
run;
proc print data=invest noobs;
   format capital dollar14.2;
run;
```

PROC PRINT Output

Year	Capital
27	$264,966.67

In a DO UNTIL loop, the condition is checked **before** the index variable is incremented.

54 p207d07

Using DO WHILE with an Iterative DO Loop

Determine the value of the account again, but this time use a DO WHILE statement.

```
data invest;
   do Year=1 to 30 while(Capital<=250000);
      Capital+5000;
      Capital+(Capital*.045);
   end;
run;
proc print data=invest noobs;
   format capital dollar14.2;
run;
```

In a DO WHILE loop, the condition is checked **after** the index variable is incremented.

PROC PRINT Output

Year	Capital
28	$264,966.67

55

p207d07

Nested DO Loops

Nested DO loops are loops within loops.

- Be sure to use different index variables for each loop.
- Each DO statement must have a corresponding END statement.
- The inner loop executes completely for each iteration of the outer loop.

DO index-variable-1=*start* TO *stop* <BY *increment*>;
    DO *index-variable-2=start* TO *stop* <BY *increment*>;
        <*additional SAS statements*>
    END;
END;

56

Business Scenario

Create one observation per year for five years, and show the earnings if you invest $5,000 per year with 4.5 percent annual interest compounded quarterly.

```
data invest(drop=Quarter);
   do Year=1 to 5;
      Capital+5000;
      do Quarter=1 to 4;
         Capital+(Capital*(.045/4));
      end;
      output;
   end;
run;

proc print data=invest noobs;
run;
```

5x 4x

57

p207d08

Output: Nested DO Loops

PROC PRINT Output

Year	Capital
1	5228.83
2	10696.95
3	16415.32
4	22395.39
5	28649.15

58

7.05 Quiz

How can you generate one observation for each quarterly amount?

```
data invest(drop=Quarter);
   do Year=1 to 5;
      Capital+5000;
      do Quarter=1 to 4;
         Capital+(Capital*(.045/4));
      end;
      output;
   end;
run;

proc print data=invest noobs;
run;
```

60 p207a03

Business Scenario

Compare the final results of investing $5,000 a year for five years in three different banks that compound interest quarterly. Assume that each bank has a fixed interest rate, stored in the **orion.banks** data set.

Listing of **orion.banks**

Name	Rate
Carolina Bank and Trust	0.0318
State Savings Bank	0.0321
National Savings and Trust	0.0328

62

Using Nested DO Loops with a SET Statement

```
data invest(drop=Quarter Year);
   set orion.banks;
   Capital=0;
   do Year=1 to 5;
      Capital+5000;
      do Quarter=1 to 4;
         Capital+(Capital*(Rate/4));
      end;
   end;
run;
```

3x 5x 4x

There are three observations in **orion.banks**. Therefore, there will be three iterations of the DATA step. **Capital** must be set to zero on each iteration of the DATA step.

63 p207d09

Execution: Nested DO Loops

```
data invest(drop=Quarter Year);
   set orion.banks;
   Capital=0;
   do Year=1 to 5;
      Capital+5000;
      do Quarter=1 to 4;
         Capital+(Capital*(Rate/4));
      end;
   end;
run;
```

First Iteration

0.0318

Partial PDV

Name	Rate	_N_
Carolina Bank and Trust	0.0318	1

64 ...

Execution: Nested DO Loops

```
data invest(drop=Quarter Year);
   set orion.banks;
   Capital=0;
   do Year=1 to 5;
      Capital+5000;
      do Quarter=1 to 4;
         Capital+(Capital*(Rate/4));
      end;
   end;
run;
```

Second Iteration

0.0321

Partial PDV

Name	Rate	_N_
State Savings Bank	0.0321	2

65 ...

Execution: Nested DO Loops

```
data invest(drop=Quarter Year);
   set orion.banks;
   Capital=0;
   do Year=1 to 5;
      Capital+5000;
      do Quarter=1 to 4;
         Capital+(Capital*(Rate/4));
      end;
   end;
run;
```

Third Iteration

0.0328

Partial PDV

Name	Rate	_N_
National Savings and Trust	0.0328	3

66

Output: Nested DO Loops

```
proc print data=invest noobs;
run;
```

PROC PRINT Output

```
Name                          Rate      Capital

Carolina Bank and Trust       0.0318    27519.69
State Savings Bank            0.0321    27544.79
National Savings and Trust    0.0328    27603.47
```

67

Exercises

Level 1

1. **Performing Computations with DO Loops**

The Orion Star Payroll department must project total employee costs (wages, retirement benefits, and medical benefits) through future years, based on assumed increases.

a. Open the file **p207e01** and make the following changes:

- Insert a DO loop containing statements to calculate the estimated values of **Wages**, **Retire**, and **Medical**.

  – Use **Start** and **Stop** to control the values of the index variable, **Year**.

- Assume the estimated annual increase shown in the table below. For example, to calculate **Wages**, use this formula:

```
wages = wages * 1.06;
```

Variable	Current Value	Estimated Annual Increase
Wages	$12,874,000	6.0%
Retire	1,765,000	1.4%
Medical	649,000	9.5%

- Create another variable, **Total_Cost**, as the sum of that year's **Wages**, **Retire**, and **Medical** values.
- Output one observation for each year.

b. Print and verify your results.

PROC PRINT Output

```
Obs    Year            Wages             Retire           Medical        Total_Cost

  1    2009    13,646,440.00       1,789,710.00        710,655.00     16,146,805.00
  2    2010    14,465,226.40       1,814,765.94        778,167.23     17,058,159.57
  3    2011    15,333,139.98       1,840,172.66        852,093.11     18,025,405.76
  4    2012    16,253,128.38       1,865,935.08        933,041.96     19,052,105.42
  5    2013    17,228,316.09       1,892,058.17      1,021,680.94     20,142,055.20
  6    2014    18,262,015.05       1,918,546.99      1,118,740.63     21,299,302.67
  7    2015    19,357,735.95       1,945,406.64      1,225,020.99     22,528,163.59
  8    2016    20,519,200.11       1,972,642.34      1,341,397.99     23,833,240.44
  9    2017    21,750,352.12       2,000,259.33      1,468,830.80     25,219,442.24
 10    2018    23,055,373.25       2,028,262.96      1,608,369.72     26,692,005.93
```

The results above were generated on January 10, 2008. Your values for **Year** might differ.

c. Corporate income for last year was $50,000,000. Income is projected to increase at one percent per year.

Modify the previous program so that the DO loop stops when the year's total costs exceed the year's income.

d. Print **Year**, **Income**, and **Total_Cost** and verify that total costs exceed income after 26 observations.

PROC PRINT Output

Obs	Year	Income	Total_Cost
1	2009	50,500,000.00	16,146,805.00
2	2010	51,005,000.00	17,058,159.57
3	2011	51,515,050.00	18,025,405.76
4	2012	52,030,200.50	19,052,105.42
5	2013	52,550,502.51	20,142,055.20
6	2014	53,076,007.53	21,299,302.67
7	2015	53,606,767.61	22,528,163.59
8	2016	54,142,835.28	23,833,240.44
9	2017	54,684,263.63	25,219,442.24
10	2018	55,231,106.27	26,692,005.93
11	2019	55,783,417.33	28,256,519.13
12	2020	56,341,251.51	29,918,944.75
13	2021	56,904,664.02	31,685,647.29
14	2022	57,473,710.66	33,563,421.13
15	2023	58,048,447.77	35,559,520.91
16	2024	58,628,932.25	37,681,694.14
17	2025	59,215,221.57	39,938,216.30
18	2026	59,807,373.78	42,337,928.49
19	2027	60,405,447.52	44,890,278.01
20	2028	61,009,502.00	47,605,361.89
21	2029	61,619,597.02	50,493,973.81
22	2030	62,235,792.99	53,567,654.57
23	2031	62,858,150.92	56,838,746.30
24	2032	63,486,732.43	60,320,451.03
25	2033	64,121,599.75	64,026,893.56
26	2034	64,762,815.75	67,973,189.29

The results above were generated on January 10, 2008. Your values for **Year** might differ.

Level 2

2. Using an Iterative DO Statement with a Conditional Clause

Orion's income last year was $50,000,000 and expenses totaled $38,750,000. Income is projected to increase at one percent per year and expenses are expected to increase at two percent per year.

a. Create a SAS data set named **work.expenses** that contains each year's projected income and expenses.

- Use an iterative DO statement with a conditional clause.
- Stop the loop when expenses exceed income or after 30 years, whichever comes first.

b. Print the results and format **`Income`** and **`Expenses`** with a dollar sign and two decimal places.

Hint: Recall that an iterative DO statement with a conditional clause produces different results with DO WHILE and DO UNTIL statements. The results below were generated using a DO UNTIL statement.

PROC PRINT Output

```
Obs            Income            Expenses    Year

 1     $64,762,815.75    $64,844,951.93     26
```

Level 3

3. Using Other Loop Control Statements

Orion's income last year was $50,000,000 and expenses totaled $38,750,000. Income is projected to increase at one percent per year and expenses are expected to increase at two percent per year.

a. Use an iterative DO statement to calculate projected income and expenses for the next 75 years.

- Investigate SAS documentation for information on other loop control statements such as CONTINUE and LEAVE.
- Include the appropriate loop control statement (CONTINUE/LEAVE) to stop the loop when expenses exceed income.

b. Print the results and format the values of **`Income`** and **`Expenses`** with dollar signs and two decimal places.

Hint: Recall that the DO WHILE and DO UNTIL statements might produce different results.

PROC PRINT Output

```
Obs            Income            Expenses    Year

 1     $64,762,815.75    $64,844,951.93     26
```

7.2 SAS Array Processing

Objectives

- Explain the concepts of SAS arrays.
- Use SAS arrays to perform repetitive calculations.

71

Array Processing

You can use arrays to simplify programs that do the following:

- perform repetitive calculations
- create many variables with the same attributes
- read data
- compare variables
- perform a table lookup

72

7.06 Quiz

Do you have experience with arrays in a programming language? If so, which languages?

74

Business Scenario

The **orion.employee_donations** data set contains quarterly contribution data for each employee. Orion management is considering a 25 percent matching program. Calculate each employee's quarterly contribution, including the proposed company supplement.

Partial Listing of **orion.employee_donations**

Employee_ID	Qtr1	Qtr2	Qtr3	Qtr4
120265	.	.	.	25
120267	15	15	15	15
120269	20	20	20	20
120270	20	10	5	.
120271	20	20	20	20
120272	10	10	10	10

75

Performing Repetitive Calculations

```
data charity;
   set orion.employee_donations;
   keep employee_id qtr1-qtr4;
   Qtr1=Qtr1*1.25;
   Qtr2=Qtr2*1.25;
   Qtr3=Qtr3*1.25;
   Qtr4=Qtr4*1.25;
run;
proc print data=charity noobs;
run;
```

Partial PROC PRINT Output

Employee_ID	Qtr1	Qtr2	Qtr3	Qtr4
120265	.	.	.	31.25
120267	18.75	18.75	18.75	18.75
120269	25.00	25.00	25.00	25.00
120270	25.00	12.50	6.25	.

76 p207d10

Performing Repetitive Calculations

The four calculations cannot be replaced by a single calculation inside a DO loop because they are not identical.

```
data charity;
   set orion.employee_donations;
   keep employee_id qtr1-qtr4;
   Qtr1=Qtr1*1.25;
   Qtr2=Qtr2*1.25;
   Qtr3=Qtr3*1.25;
   Qtr4=Qtr4*1.25;
run;
proc print data=charity noobs;
run;
```

```
do i=1 to 4;
   ?
end;
```

A SAS array can be used to simplify this code.

77

Use Arrays to Simplify Repetitive Calculations

An array provides an alternate way to access values in the PDV, which simplifies repetitive calculations.

```
data charity;
   set orion.employee_donations;
   keep employee_id qtr1-qtr4;
   Qtr1=Qtr1*1.25;
   Qtr2=Qtr2*1.25;
   Qtr3=Qtr3*1.25;
   Qtr4=Qtr4*1.25;
run;
proc print data=charity noobs;
run;
```

An array can be used to access Qtr1-Qtr4.

PDV

Employee_ID	Qtr1	Qtr2	Qtr3	Qtr4

78

What Is a SAS Array?

A *SAS array*

- is a temporary grouping of SAS variables that are arranged in a particular order
- is identified by an *array name*
- must contain all numeric or all character variables
- exists only for the duration of the current DATA step
- is **not** a variable.

79

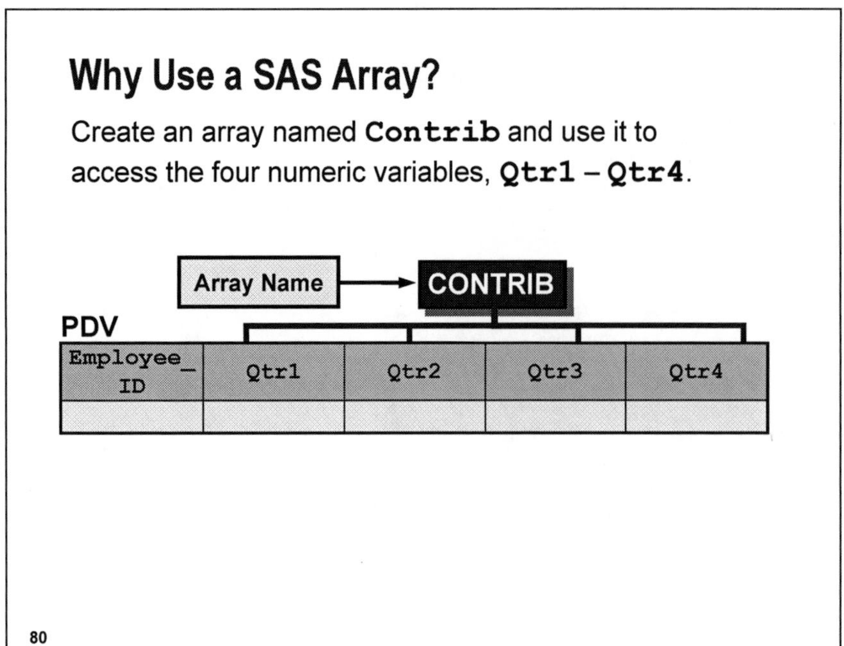

SAS arrays are different from arrays in many other programming languages. In SAS, an array is **not** a data structure. It is simply a convenient way of temporarily identifying a group of variables.

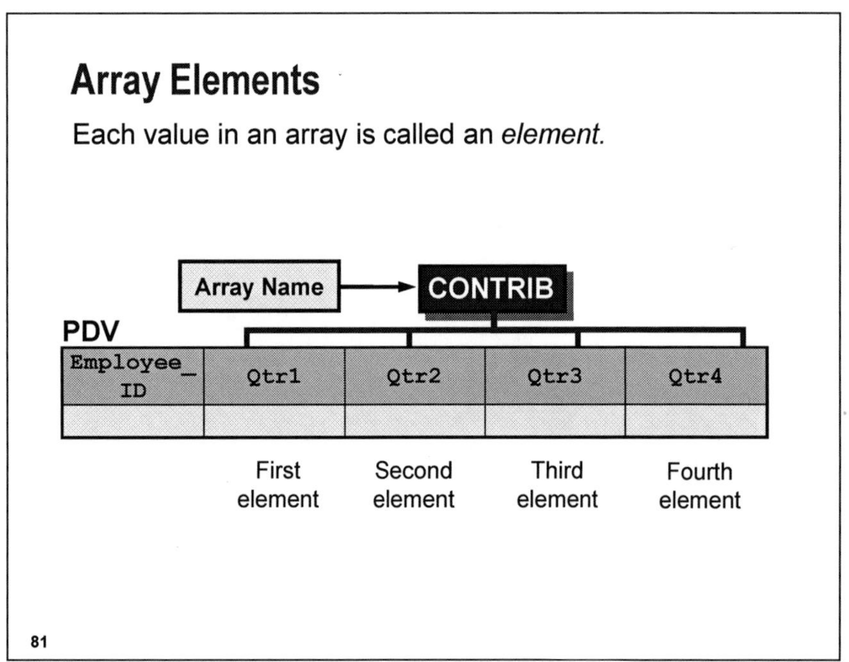

Referencing Array Elements

Each element is identified by a *subscript* that represents its position in the array. When you use an *array reference*, the corresponding value is substituted for the reference.

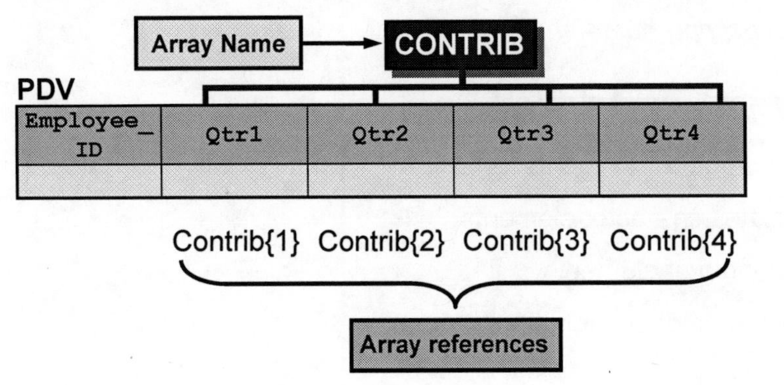

82

The ARRAY Statement

The ARRAY statement is a compile-time statement that defines the elements in an array. The elements are created if they do not already exist in the PDV.

ARRAY *array-name {subscript}* <$> <*length*>
<*array-elements*>;

{subscript}	the number of elements
$	indicates character elements
length	the length of elements
array-elements	the names of elements

83

array-name	specifies the name of the array.
{subscript}	describes the number and arrangement of elements in the array by using an asterisk, a number, numbers separated by commas (for multi-dimensional arrays), or a range of numbers. The *subscript* is enclosed in braces (**{ }**). Brackets (**[ ]**) and parentheses (**( )**) are also allowed.
$	indicates that the elements in the array are character elements. The dollar sign is not necessary if the elements in the array were previously defined as character elements.
length	specifies the length of elements in the array that were not previously assigned a length.
array-elements	names the elements that make up the array. Array elements can be listed in any order.

Array references cannot be used in compile-time statements such as LABEL, FORMAT, DROP, KEEP, or LENGTH statements.

If you use a function name as the name of the array, SAS treats parenthetical references that involve the name as array references, not function references, for the duration of the DATA step.

Defining an Array

The following ARRAY statement defines an array, **Contrib**, to access the four quarterly contribution variables.

```
array Contrib{4} qtr1 qtr2 qtr3 qtr4;
```

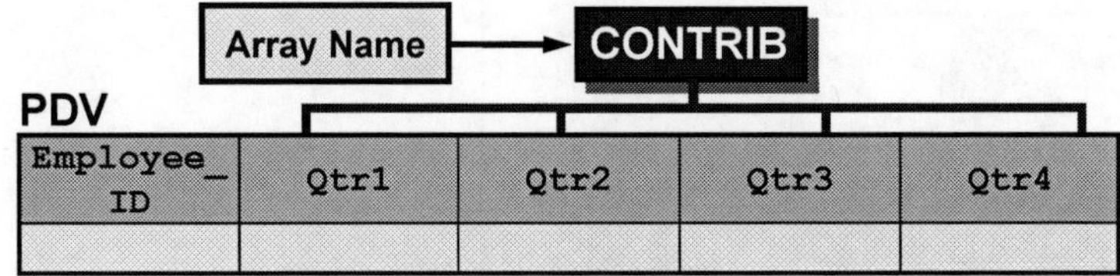

Contrib{1} Contrib{2} Contrib{3} Contrib{4}

84

The four variables, **Qtr1**, **Qtr2**, **Qtr3**, and **Qtr4**, can now be referenced via the array name **Contrib**, with an appropriate subscript.

Defining an Array

An alternate syntax uses an asterisk instead of a subscript. SAS determines the subscript by counting the variables in the element-list. The element-list must be included.

```
array Contrib{*} qtr1 qtr2 qtr3 qtr4;
```

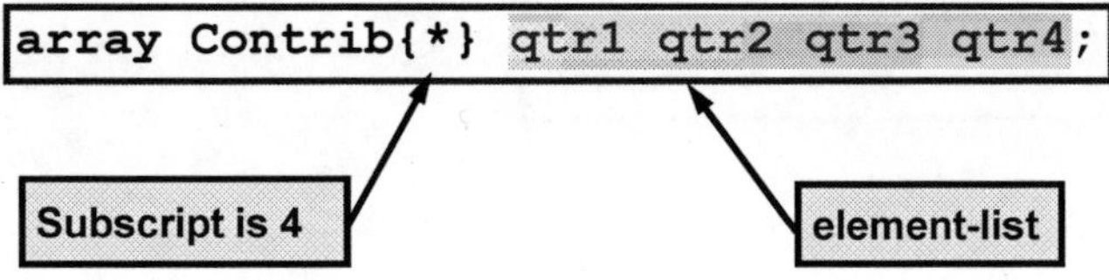

The alternate syntax is often used when the array elements are defined with a SAS variable list.

```
array Contrib{*} qtr:;
```

85

You can use special SAS name lists to reference variables that were previously defined in the same DATA step. The _CHARACTER_ variable lists character values only. The _NUMERIC_ variable lists numeric values only.

Avoid using the _ALL_ special SAS name list to reference variables, because the elements in an array must be either all character or all numeric values.

Defining an Array

Variables that are elements of an array do not need the following:

- to have similar, related, or numbered names
- to be stored sequentially
- to be adjacent

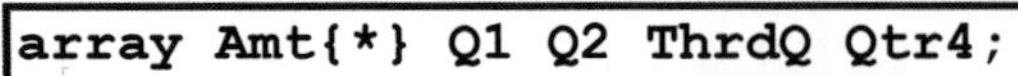

```
array Amt{*} Q1 Q2 ThrdQ Qtr4;
```

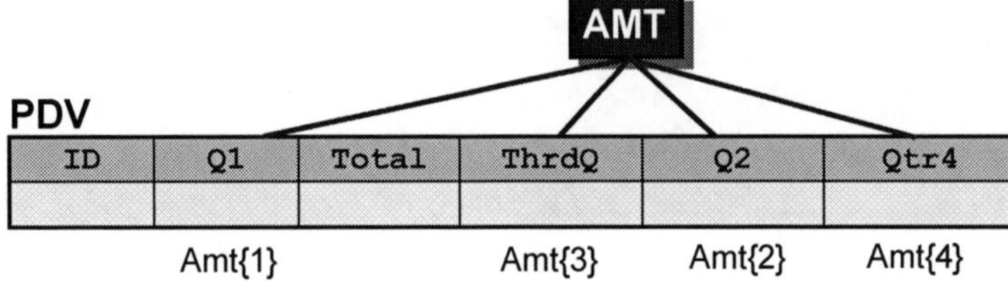

86

7.07 Quiz

Open and submit **p207a04**. View the log to determine the cause of the error.

```
data charity(keep=employee_id qtr1-qtr4);
   set orion.employee_donations;
   array Contrib1{3} qtr1-qtr4;
   array Contrib2{5} qtr:;
   /* additional SAS statements */
run;
```

88 p207a04

Using a DO Loop to Process an Array

Array processing often occurs within an iterative DO loop in the following form:

DO *index-variable*=1 TO *number-of-elements-in-array*;
<*additional SAS statements*>
END;

To reference an element, the *index-variable* is often used as a subscript:

```
array-name{index-variable}
```

90

To process particular elements of an array, specify those elements as the range of the iterative DO statement.

By default, SAS includes *index-variable* in the output data set. Use a DROP or KEEP statement or the DROP= or KEEP= data set option to prevent the index variable from being written to your output data set.

Using a DO Loop to Process an Array

```
data charity;
   set orion.employee_donations;
   keep employee_id qtr1-qtr4;
   array Contrib{4} qtr1-qtr4;
   do i=1 to 4;
      Contrib{i}=Contrib{i}*1.25;
   end;
run;
```

The index variable, **i**, is not written to the output data set because it is not listed in the KEEP statement.

91 p207d11

First Iteration of the DO Loop

```
data charity;
   set orion.employee_donations;
   keep employee_id qtr1-qtr4;
   array Contrib{4} qtr1-qtr4;
   do i=1 to 4;
      Contrib{i}=Contrib{i}*1.25;
   end;
run;
```

when i=1

```
Contrib{1}=Contrib{1}*1.25;
```

```
Qtr1=Qtr1*1.25;
```

92

...

Second Iteration of the DO Loop

```
data charity;
   set orion.employee_donations;
   keep employee_id qtr1-qtr4;
   array Contrib{4} qtr1-qtr4;
   do i=1 to 4;
      Contrib{i}=Contrib{i}*1.25;
   end;
run;
```

when i=2

```
Contrib{2}=Contrib{2}*1.25;
```

```
Qtr2=Qtr2*1.25;
```

93

...

Third Iteration of the DO Loop

```
data charity;
   set orion.employee_donations;
   keep employee_id qtr1-qtr4;
   array Contrib{4} qtr1-qtr4;
   do i=1 to 4;
      Contrib{i}=Contrib{i}*1.25;
   end;
run;
```

when i=3

```
Contrib{3}=Contrib{3}*1.25;
```

```
Qtr3=Qtr3*1.25;
```

94 ...

Fourth Iteration of the DO Loop

```
data charity;
   set orion.employee_donations;
   keep employee_id qtr1-qtr4;
   array Contrib{4} qtr1-qtr4;
   do i=1 to 4;
      Contrib{i}=Contrib{i}*1.25;
   end;
run;
```

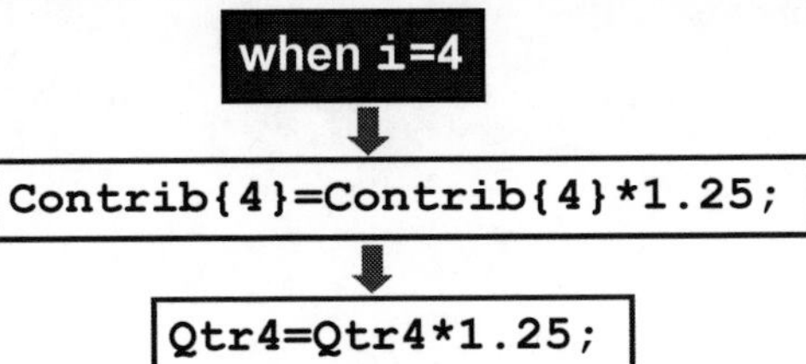
when i=4
Contrib{4}=Contrib{4}*1.25;

```
Qtr4=Qtr4*1.25;
```

95

Output: Using a Do Loop to Process an Array

```
proc print data=charity noobs;
run;
```

Partial PROC PRINT Output

Employee_ID	Qtr1	Qtr2	Qtr3	Qtr4
120265	.	.	.	31.25
120267	18.75	18.75	18.75	18.75
120269	25.00	25.00	25.00	25.00
120270	25.00	12.50	6.25	.
120271	25.00	25.00	25.00	25.00
120272	12.50	12.50	12.50	12.50
120275	18.75	18.75	18.75	18.75
120660	31.25	31.25	31.25	31.25
120662	12.50	.	6.25	6.25

96

Exercises

Level 1

4. Using Arrays for Repetitive Computations

Monthly customer order data for the first half of the year is stored in the data set **orion.orders_midyear**. The Orion Star Sales manager is considering a five-percent price decrease next year. He (the manager) wants to see how such a discount would affect this year's income.

Partial Listing of **orion.orders_midyear**

Obs	Customer_ID	Month1	Month2	Month3	Month4	Month5	Month6
1	5	213.10	.	478.0	525.80	394.35	191.79
2	10	188.10	414.09	2876.9	3164.59	2373.44	169.29
3	11	78.20	.	.	.	.	70.38
4	12	135.60	.	117.6	129.36	97.02	122.04
5	18	.	.	29.4	32.34	24.26	.
6	24	93.00	265.80	.	.	.	83.70
7	27	310.70	782.90	.	.	.	279.63
8	31	1484.30	293.30	.	.	.	1335.87
9	34	642.50	.	86.3	94.93	71.20	578.25
10	41	134.00	119.20	313.0	344.30	258.23	120.60
11	45	443.88	216.20	40.2	44.22	33.17	399.49
12	49	24.80	.	.	.	.	22.32

a. Create a data set, **discount_sales**, to reflect the five-percent discount.
- Create an array, **Mon**, to access **Month1** through **Month6**.
- Use a DO loop to adjust each customer's monthly data. Apply the five-percent discount.

b. Print the resulting data set and verify your results.
- Add an appropriate title.
- Use the DOLLAR. format for the monthly sales amounts.

PROC PRINT Output (24 Total Observations)

Monthly Sales with 5% Discount

Customer_ID	Month1	Month2	Month3	Month4	Month5	Month6
5	$202.45	.	$454.10	$499.51	$374.63	$182.20
10	$178.70	$393.39	$2,733.06	$3,006.36	$2,254.77	$160.83
11	$74.29	.	.	.	.	$66.86
12	$128.82	.	$111.72	$122.89	$92.17	$115.94
18	.	.	$27.93	$30.72	$23.04	.
24	$88.35	$252.51	.	.	.	$79.52
27	$295.17	$743.76	.	.	.	$265.65
31	$1,410.09	$278.64	.	.	.	$1,269.08

Level 2

5. Using Arrays for Repetitive Computations

Monthly customer order data for the first half of the year is stored in the data set **orion.orders_midyear**. Orion Star Sales management is considering a 10-percent price decrease during the first three months of the upcoming year. Management wants to see how such a discount would affect this year's sales.

Partial Listing of **orion.orders_midyear**

Customer_ID	Month1	Month2	Month3	Month4	Month5	Month6
5	213.10	.	478.0	525.80	394.35	191.79
10	188.10	414.09	2876.9	3164.59	2373.44	169.29
11	78.20	.	.	.	.	70.38
12	135.60	.	117.6	129.36	97.02	122.04
18	.	.	29.4	32.34	24.26	.
24	93.00	265.80	.	.	.	83.70
27	310.70	782.90	.	.	.	279.63
31	1484.30	293.30	.	.	.	1335.87
34	642.50	.	86.3	94.93	71.20	578.25

a. Create a data set, **special_offer**, including the 10-percent discount in months 1 through 3.

- Create an array, **Mon**, to access **Month1** through **Month3**.
- Use a DO loop to adjust each customer's monthly data to include the 10-percent discount (**Month1** through **Month3** only).
- Create three new variables:
  - **Total_Sales** – the total of current sales over the six months
  - **Projected_Sales** – the total of the adjusted sales over the six months (including the three discounted months)
  - **Difference** – the difference between **Total_Sales** and **Projected_Sales**
- Keep only the new variables: **Total_Sales**, **Projected_Sales**, and **Difference**.

b. Print the resulting data set and verify your results.

- Suppress the session start date, page number, and observation column.
- Add an appropriate title.
- Use the SUM statement to display a total for the **Difference** variable.
- Use the DOLLAR. format for all variables.

PROC PRINT Output

```
              Total Sales with 10% Discount in First Three Months

                          Total_     Projected_
                           Sales        Sales       Difference

                       $1,803.04    $1,733.93          $69.11
                       $9,186.41    $8,838.50         $347.91
                         $148.58      $140.76           $7.82
                         $601.62      $576.30          $25.32
                          $86.00       $83.06           $2.94
                         $442.50      $406.62          $35.88
                       $1,373.23    $1,263.87         $109.36
                       $3,113.47    $2,935.71         $177.76
                       $1,473.18    $1,400.30          $72.88
                       $1,289.33    $1,232.71          $56.62
                       $1,177.16    $1,107.13          $70.03
                          $47.12       $44.64           $2.48
                         $928.07      $869.99          $58.08
                          $37.90       $34.11           $3.79
                       $1,027.85      $992.71          $35.14
                          $47.85       $45.18           $2.67
                         $925.42      $851.76          $73.66
                       $1,334.97    $1,280.90          $54.07
                         $501.57      $483.83          $17.74
                         $697.60      $627.84          $69.76
                       $4,306.28    $4,121.28         $185.00
                         $147.10      $132.39          $14.71
                         $177.84      $171.76           $6.08
                       $1,518.95    $1,467.02          $51.93
                                                   ==========
                                                    $1,550.74
```

Level 3

6. Terminating a DATA Step

Monthly order data for the first half of the year is stored in the **orion.orders_midyear** data set. This data set is updated monthly and can contain data for one to 12 months.

Partial Listing of **orion.orders_midyear**

Obs	Customer_ID	Month1	Month2	Month3	Month4	Month5	Month6
1	5	213.10	.	478.0	525.80	394.35	191.79
2	10	188.10	414.09	2876.9	3164.59	2373.44	169.29
3	11	78.20	.	.	.	.	70.38
4	12	135.60	.	117.6	129.36	97.02	122.04
5	18	.	.	29.4	32.34	24.26	.
6	24	93.00	265.80	.	.	.	83.70
7	27	310.70	782.90	.	.	.	279.63
8	31	1484.30	293.30	.	.	.	1335.87
9	34	642.50	.	86.3	94.93	71.20	578.25
10	41	134.00	119.20	313.0	344.30	258.23	120.60
11	45	443.88	216.20	40.2	44.22	33.17	399.49
12	49	24.80	.	.	.	.	22.32

a. Orion Star decided to create a Frequent Shopper Program (FSP). The company wants to invite customers who placed orders in 50% of the months to date (assuming at least three months of data exist for that year), and who spent at least $1000 since the beginning of the year.

- Open the input data set and verify that it contains at least three months of data.
- If there is less than three months, write a message to the SAS log and stop the DATA step immediately.
- If there are at least three months of data in the data set, create an array, **Mon**, to access the **Month*n*** variables, regardless of how many **Month*n*** variables exist in the data set.
  Hint: Consider using a SAS Variable List to list the array elements.
- Use a DO loop to examine each customer's data to determine if the customer qualifies for the Frequent Shopper Program.
- Create a new data set, **fsp**, which contains an observation for each qualifying customer.
- Use the report below to determine which variables to drop or keep.

Hint: Use SAS documentation to investigate the use of the STOP statement and the DIM function.

b. Print the resulting data set with an appropriate title and formats, and verify your results.

PROC PRINT Output

```
    orion.orders_midyear: Frequent Shoppers

                                  Total_
                                  Order_     Months_
 Obs      Customer_ID             Amount     Ordered

   1                5         $1,803.04         5
   2               10         $9,186.41         6
   3               27         $1,373.23         3
   4               31         $3,113.47         3
   5               34         $1,473.18         5
   6               41         $1,289.33         6
   7               45         $1,177.16         6
   8               65         $1,027.85         3
   9               90         $1,334.97         6
  10              171         $4,306.28         6
  11              908         $1,518.95         3
```

c. Test your program using **`orion.orders_qtr1`**.

PROC PRINT Output

```
      orion.orders_qtr1: Frequent Shoppers

                                  Total_
                                  Order_     Months_
 Obs      Customer_ID             Amount     Ordered

   1               10         $3,479.09         3
   2               27         $1,093.60         2
   3               31         $1,777.60         2
   4              171         $1,849.99         3
   5             2806         $1,506.90         3
```

d. Test your program using **`orion.orders_two_months`**.

Partial SAS Log

```
Insufficient data for Frequent Shopper Program
NOTE: There were 1 observations read from the data set ORION.ORDERS_TWO_MONTHS.
NOTE: The data set WORK.FSP has 0 observations and 3 variables.
NOTE: DATA statement used (Total process time):

1066
1067  title 'orion.orders_two_months: Frequent Shoppers ';
1068  proc print data=fsp;
1069     format total_order_amount dollar10.2;
1070  run;

NOTE: No observations in data set WORK.FSP.
```

7.3 Using SAS Arrays

Objectives

- Use arrays as arguments to SAS functions.
- Explain array functions.
- Use arrays to create new variables.
- Use arrays to perform a table lookup.

100

Using an Array as a Function Argument

The program below passes an array to the SUM function.

```
data test;
   set orion.employee_donations;
   array val{4} qtr1-qtr4;
   Tot1=sum(of qtr1-qtr4);
   Tot2=sum(of val{*});
run;
proc print data=test;
   var employee_id tot1 tot2;
run;
```

The array is passed as if it were a variable list.

Partial PROC PRINT Output

Obs	Employee_ID	Tot1	Tot2
1	120265	25	25
2	120267	60	60
3	120269	80	80

101 p207d13

The DIM Function

The DIM function returns the number of elements in an array. This value is often used as the stop value in a DO loop.

General form of the DIM function:

DIM(*array_name*)

```
array Contrib{*} qtr:;
num_elements=dim(Contrib);

do i=1 to num_elements;
   Contrib{i}=Contrib{i}*1.25;
end;
run;
```

102

The HBOUND function returns the upper bound of an array. The LBOUND function returns the lower bound of an array. The following DO loop processes every element in an array:

```
do i=lbound(items) to hbound(items);
   *process items{i};
end;
```

In most arrays, subscripts range from 1 to *n*, where *n* is the number of elements in the array. The value 1 is a convenient lower bound; thus, you do not need to specify the lower bound. However, specifying both bounds is useful when the array dimensions have a beginning point other than 1. For example, the following ARRAY statement defines an array of 10 elements, with subscripts ranging from 5 to 14.

```
array items{5:14} n5-n14;
```

The DIM Function

A call to the DIM function can be used in place of the stop value in the DO loop.

```
data charity;
   set orion.employee_donations;
   keep employee_id qtr1-qtr4;
   array Contrib{*} qtr:;
   do i=1 to dim(Contrib);
      Contrib{i}=Contrib{i}*1.25;
   end;
run;
```

103 p207d12

Using an Array to Create Numeric Variables

An ARRAY statement can be used to create new variables in the program data vector.

```
array discount{4} discount1-discount4;
```

If `discount1-discount4` do not exist in the PDV, they are created.

```
array Pct{4};
```

Four new variables are created:

PDV

Pct1 N 8	Pct2 N 8	Pct3 N 8	Pct4 N 8

105

Using an Array to Create Character Variables

Define an array named **Month** to create six variables to hold character values with a length of 10.

```
array Month{6} $ 10;
```

PDV

Month1 $ 10	Month2 $ 10	Month3 $ 10	Month4 $ 10	Month5 $ 10	Month6 $ 10

106

Business Scenario

Using **orion.employee_donations** as input, calculate the percentage that each quarterly contribution represents of the employee's total annual contribution. Create four new variables to hold the percentages.

Partial Listing of **orion.employee_donations**

Employee_ID	Qtr1	Qtr2	Qtr3	Qtr4
120265	.	.	.	25
120267	15	15	15	15
120269	20	20	20	20
120270	20	10	5	.
120271	20	20	20	20
120272	10	10	10	10

107

Creating Variables with Arrays

```
data percent(drop=i);
   set orion.employee_donations;
   array Contrib{4} qtr1-qtr4;
   array Percent{4};
   Total=sum(of contrib{*});
   do i=1 to 4;
      percent{i}=contrib{i}/total;
   end;
run;
```

The second ARRAY statement creates four numeric variables: **Percent1**, **Percent2**, **Percent3**, and **Percent4**.

108 p207d14

The first ARRAY statement uses the existing variables **Qtr1**, **Qtr2**, **Qtr3**, and **Qtr4**. In that ARRAY statement, a numbered range SAS Variable List is used.

Output: Creating Variables with Arrays

```
proc print data=percent noobs;
   var Employee_ID percent1-percent4;
   format percent1-percent4 percent6.;
run;
```

Partial PROC PRINT Output

Employee_ID	Percent1	Percent2	Percent3	Percent4
120265	.	.	.	100%
120267	25%	25%	25%	25%
120269	25%	25%	25%	25%
120270	57%	29%	14%	.
120271	25%	25%	25%	25%
120272	25%	25%	25%	25%
120275	25%	25%	25%	25%
120660	25%	25%	25%	25%
120662	50%	.	25%	25%
120663	.	.	100%	.
120668	25%	25%	25%	25%

109

The PERCENT*w.d* format multiplies values by 100, formats them in the same way as the BEST*w.d* format, and adds a percent sign (%) to the end of the formatted value. Negative values are enclosed in parentheses. The PERCENT*w.d* format provides room for a percent sign and parentheses, even if the value is not negative.

Business Scenario

Using **orion.employee_donations** as input, calculate the difference in each employee's contribution from one quarter to the next.

Partial Listing of **orion.employee_donations**

Employee_ID	Qtr1	Qtr2	Qtr3	Qtr4
120265	.	.	.	25
120267	15	15	15	15
120269	20	20	20	20
120270	20	10	5	.
120271	20	20	20	20
120272	10	10	10	10

First difference: Qtr2 – Qtr1
Second difference: Qtr3 – Qtr2
Third difference: Qtr4 – Qtr3

110

7.08 Quiz

How many ARRAY statements would you use to calculate the difference in each employee's contribution from one quarter to the next?

Partial Listing of **orion.employee_donations**

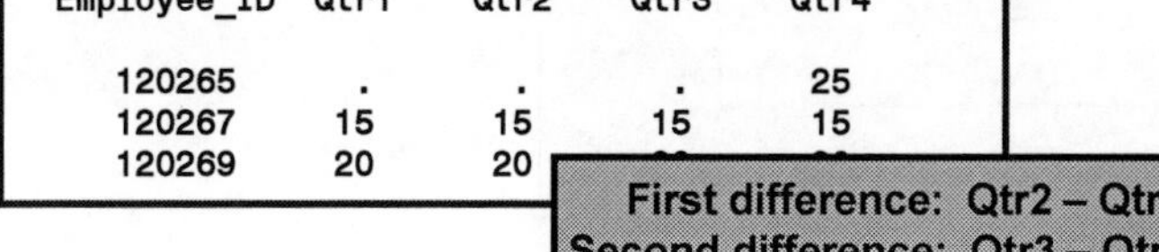

Employee_ID	Qtr1	Qtr2	Qtr3	Qtr4
120265	.	.	.	25
120267	15	15	15	15
120269	20	20		

First difference: Qtr2 – Qtr1
Second difference: Qtr3 – Qtr2
Third difference: Qtr4 – Qtr3

112

Creating Variables with Arrays

```
data change;
   set orion.employee_donations;
   drop i;
   array Contrib{4} Qtr1-Qtr4;
   array Diff{3};
   do i=1 to 3;
      Diff{i}=Contrib{i+1}-Contrib{i};
   end;
run;
```

The **Contrib** array refers to existing variables. The **Diff** array creates three variables: **Diff1**, **Diff2**, and **Diff3**.

114

p207d15

Creating Variables with Arrays

```
data change;
   set orion.employee_donations;
   drop i;
   array Contrib{4} Qtr1-Qtr4;
   array Diff{3};
   do i=1 to 3;
      Diff{i}=Contrib{i+1}-Contrib{i};
   end;
run;
```

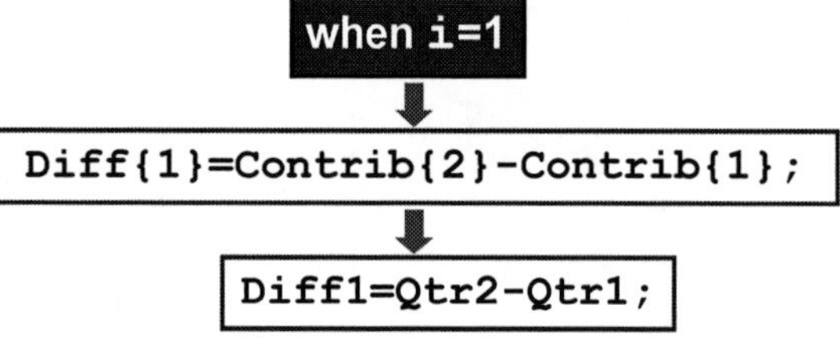

115

...

Creating Variables with Arrays

```
data change;
   set orion.employee_donations;
   drop i;
   array Contrib{4} Qtr1-Qtr4;
   array Diff{3};
   do i=1 to 3;
      Diff{i}=Contrib{i+1}-Contrib{i};
   end;
run;
```

when i=2

```
Diff{2}=Contrib{3}-Contrib{2};
```

```
Diff2=Qtr3-Qtr2;
```

116 ...

Creating Variables with Arrays

```
data change;
   set orion.employee_donations;
   drop i;
   array Contrib{4} Qtr1-Qtr4;
   array Diff{3};
   do i=1 to 3;
      Diff{i}=Contrib{i+1}-Contrib{i};
   end;
run;
```

when i=3

```
Diff{3}=Contrib{4}-Contrib{3};
```

```
Diff3=Qtr4-Qtr3;
```

117

Creating Variables with Arrays

```
proc print data=change noobs;
   var Employee_ID Diff1-Diff3;
run;
```

Partial PROC PRINT Output

Employee_ID	Diff1	Diff2	Diff3
120265	.	.	.
120267	0	0	0
120269	0	0	0
120270	-10	-5	.
120271	0	0	0
120272	0	0	0
120275	0	0	0
120660	0	0	0
120662	.	.	0

118

Assigning Initial Values to an ARRAY

The ARRAY statement has an option to assign initial values to the array elements.

General form of an ARRAY statement:

ARRAY *array-name* {*subscript*} <$> <*length*>
<*array-elements*> <(*initial-value-list*)>;

Example:

```
array Target{5} (50,100,125,150,200);
```

Use commas or spaces to separate values in the list.

120

(*initial-value-list*) lists the initial values for the corresponding array elements. The values for elements can be numbers or character strings. Character strings must be enclosed in quotation marks.

Elements and values are matched by position. If there are more array elements than initial values, the remaining array elements are assigned missing values and SAS issues a warning.

Assigning Initial Values to an ARRAY

When an *initial-value-list* is specified, all elements behave as if they were named in a RETAIN statement. This is often used to create a *lookup table*, that is, a list of values to refer to during DATA step processing.

```
array Target{5} (50,100,125,150,200);
```

PDV

R Target1 N 8	R Target2 N 8	R Target3 N 8	R Target4 N 8	R Target5 N 8
50	100	125	150	200

121

Business Scenario

Read **orion.employee_donations** to determine the difference between employee contributions and the quarterly goals of $10, $20, $20, and $15. Use a lookup table to store the quarterly goals.

```
data compare(drop=i Goal1-Goal4);
   set orion.employee_donations;
   array Contrib{4} Qtr1-Qtr4;
   array Diff{4};
   array Goal{4} (10,20,20,15);
   do i=1 to 4;
      Diff{i}=Contrib{i}-Goal{i};
   end;
run;
```

122 p207d16

This is an example of a simple table lookup program.

Compilation: What Variables Are Created?

```
data compare(drop=i Goal1-Goal4);
   set orion.employee_donations;
   array Contrib{4} Qtr1-Qtr4;
   array Diff{4};
   array Goal{4} (10,20,20,15);
   do i=1 to 4;
      Diff{i}=Contrib{i}-Goal{i};
   end;
run;
```

Partial PDV

Employee_ ID	Qtr1	Qtr2	Qtr3	Qtr4

123 ...

Compilation: What Variables Are Created?

```
data compare(drop=i Goal1-Goal4);
   set orion.employee_donations;
   array Contrib{4} Qtr1-Qtr4;
   array Diff{4};
   array Goal{4} (10,20,20,15);
   do i=1 to 4;
      Diff{i}=Contrib{i}-Goal{i};
   end;
run;
```

No variables created

Partial PDV

Employee_ ID	Qtr1	Qtr2	Qtr3	Qtr4

124 ...

Compilation: What Variables Are Created?

```
data compare(drop=i Goal1-Goal4);
   set orion.employee_donations;
   array Contrib{4} Qtr1-Qtr4;
   array Diff{4};
   array Goal{4} (10,20,20,15);
   do i=1 to 4;
      Diff{i}=Contrib{i}-Goal{i};
   end;
run;
```

Partial PDV

Employee_ ID	Qtr1	Qtr2	Qtr3	Qtr4	Diff1

Diff2	Diff3	Diff4

125 ...

Compilation: What Variables Are Created?

```
data compare(drop=i Goal1-Goal4);
   set orion.employee_donations;
   array Contrib{4} Qtr1-Qtr4;
   array Diff{4};
   array Goal{4} (10,20,20,15);
   do i=1 to 4;
      Diff{i}=Contrib{i}-Goal{i};
   end;
run;
```

Partial PDV

Employee_ ID	Qtr1	Qtr2	Qtr3	Qtr4	Diff1

Diff2	Diff3	Diff4	Goal1	Goal2	Goal3	Goal4

126 ...

Compilation: What Variables Are Created?

```
data compare(drop=i Goal1-Goal4);
   set orion.employee_donations;
   array Contrib{4} Qtr1-Qtr4;
   array Diff{4};
   array Goal{4} (10,20,20,15);
   do i=1 to 4;
      Diff{i}=Contrib{i}-Goal{i};
   end;
run;
```

Partial PDV

Employee_ ID	Qtr1	Qtr2	Qtr3	Qtr4	Diff1

Diff2	Diff3	Diff4	Goal1	Goal2	Goal3	Goal4	i

127 ...

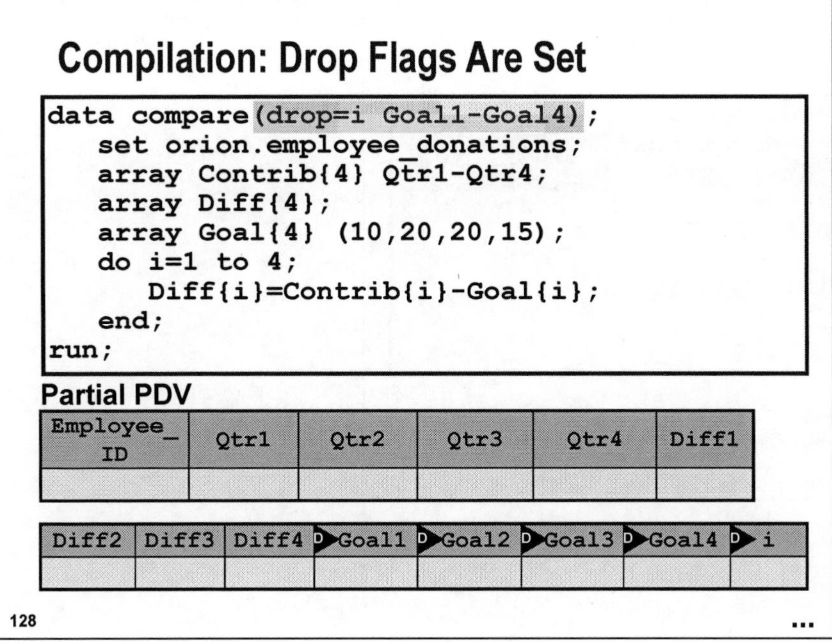
Compilation: Drop Flags Are Set
data compare(drop=i Goal1-Goal4);
set orion.employee_donations;
array Contrib{4} Qtr1-Qtr4;
array Diff{4};
array Goal{4} (10,20,20,15);
do i=1 to 4;
Diff{i}=Contrib{i}-Goal{i};
end;
run;
Partial PDV
Employee_ ID
Qtr1
Qtr2
Qtr3
Qtr4
Diff1
Diff2
Diff3
Diff4
D Goal1
D Goal2
D Goal3
D Goal4
D i
128
...

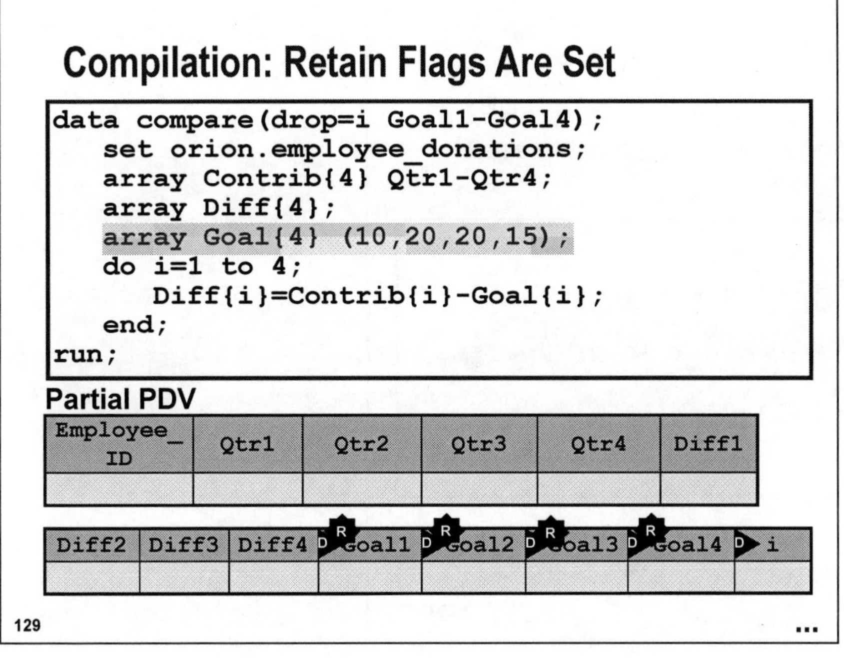
Compilation: Retain Flags Are Set
data compare(drop=i Goal1-Goal4);
set orion.employee_donations;
array Contrib{4} Qtr1-Qtr4;
array Diff{4};
array Goal{4} (10,20,20,15);
do i=1 to 4;
Diff{i}=Contrib{i}-Goal{i};
end;
run;
Partial PDV
Employee_ ID
Qtr1
Qtr2
Qtr3
Qtr4
Diff1
Diff2
Diff3
Diff4
D R Goal1
D R Goal2
D R Goal3
D R Goal4
D i
129
...

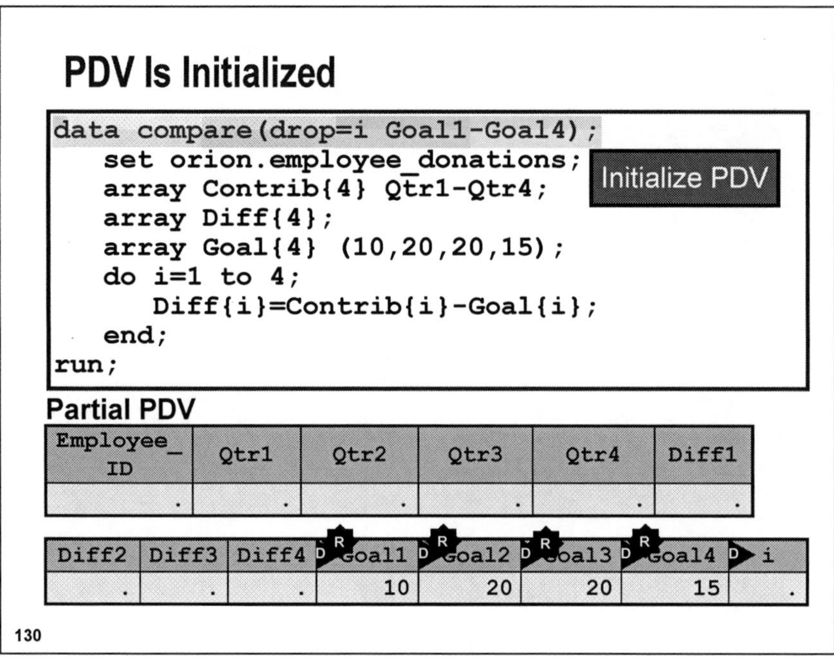
PDV Is Initialized
data compare(drop=i Goal1-Goal4);
set orion.employee_donations;
array Contrib{4} Qtr1-Qtr4;
array Diff{4};
array Goal{4} (10,20,20,15);
do i=1 to 4;
Diff{i}=Contrib{i}-Goal{i};
end;
run;
Initialize PDV
Partial PDV
Employee_ ID
Qtr1
Qtr2
Qtr3
Qtr4
Diff1
Diff2
Diff3
Diff4
D R Goal1
D R Goal2
D R Goal3
D R Goal4
D i
10
20
20
15
130

Creating a Temporary Lookup Table

You can use the keyword _TEMPORARY_ in an ARRAY statement to indicate that the elements are not needed in the output data set.

```
data compare(drop=i);
   set orion.employee_donations;
   array Contrib{4} Qtr1-Qtr4;
   array Diff{4};
   array Goal{4} _temporary_ (10,20,20,15);
   do i=1 to 4;
      Diff{i}=Contrib{i}-Goal{i};
   end;
run;
```

131 p207d17

Arrays of temporary elements are useful when the only purpose for creating an array is to perform a calculation. To preserve the result of the calculation, assign it to a variable.

Output: Creating a Temporary Lookup Table

```
proc print data=compare noobs;
   var employee_id diff1-diff4;
run;
```

Partial PROC PRINT Output

Employee_ID	Diff1	Diff2	Diff3	Diff4
120265	.	.	.	10
120267	5	-5	-5	0
120269	10	0	0	5
120270	10	-10	-15	.
120271	10	0	0	5
120272	0	-10	-10	-5
120275	5	-5	-5	0

What can be done to ignore missing values?

132

The SUM Function Ignores Missing Values

The SUM function ignores missing values. It can be used to calculate the difference between the quarterly contribution and the corresponding goal.

```
data compare(drop=i);
   set orion.employee_donations;
   array Contrib{4} Qtr1-Qtr4;
   array Diff{4};
   array Goal{4} _temporary_ (10,20,20,15);
   do i=1 to 4;
      Diff{i}=sum(Contrib{i},-Goal{i});
   end;
run;
```

133 p207d18

Output: Lookup Table Application

```
proc print data=compare noobs;
   var employee_id diff1-diff4;
run;
```

Partial PROC PRINT Output

Employee_ID	Diff1	Diff2	Diff3	Diff4
120265	-10	-20	-20	10
120267	5	-5	-5	0
120269	10	0	0	5
120270	10	-10	-15	-15
120271	10	0	0	5
120272	0	-10	-10	-5
120275	5	-5	-5	0

The missing values were handled as if no contribution were made for that quarter.

134

7.09 Quiz

Using pencil and paper, write an ARRAY statement to define a temporary lookup table named **Country** with three elements, each two characters long. Initialize the elements to AU, NZ, and US. Refer to the syntax below.

ARRAY *array-name* {*subscript*} <$> <*length*>
<*array-elements*> <(*initial-value-list*)>;

136

Exercises

Level 1

7. Using an Array for Table Lookup

The manager of the Sales department wants to identify preferred customers for an upcoming promotion. Use the **orion.orders_midyear** data set and a lookup table to create a new data set, **preferred_cust**.

Partial Listing of **orion.orders_midyear**

Customer_ID	Month1	Month2	Month3	Month4	Month5	Month6
5	213.10	.	478.0	525.80	394.35	191.79
10	188.10	414.09	2876.9	3164.59	2373.44	169.29
11	78.20	.	.	.	.	70.38
12	135.60	.	117.6	129.36	97.02	122.04
18	.	.	29.4	32.34	24.26	.
24	93.00	265.80	.	.	.	83.70
27	310.70	782.90	.	.	.	279.63
31	1484.30	293.30	.	.	.	1335.87
34	642.50	.	86.3	94.93	71.20	578.25
41	134.00	119.20	313.0	344.30	258.23	120.60
45	443.88	216.20	40.2	44.22	33.17	399.49

a. Open the file **p207e07** and make the following changes:

- Create a temporary lookup table, **Target**, to hold the target sales amount for each month:
  200, 400, 300, 100, 100, 200
- Create new variables, **Over1**, **Over2**, …,**Over6**, to hold the amount that a customer spent above the corresponding month's target.
- Use a DO loop to calculate the values of **Over1** through **Over6** when the corresponding month's sales amount exceeds the target. Note: If the sales did not exceed the target for a given month, then do not perform this calculation.
- Store the sum of **Over1** through **Over6** in another new variable, **Total_Over**.
- Write an observation only if **Total_Over** is greater than 500.
- The new data set should only include **Customer_ID**, **Over1** through **Over6**, and **Total_Over**.

b. Print the new data set and verify your results.

PROC PRINT Output

Customer_ID	Over1	Over2	Over3	Over4	Over5	Over6	Total_ Over
5	13.1	.	178.0	425.80	294.35	.	911.25
10	.	14.09	2576.9	3064.59	2273.44	.	7929.02
27	110.7	382.90	.	.	.	79.63	573.23
31	1284.3	.	.	.	.	1135.87	2420.17
34	442.5	.	.	.	.	378.25	820.75
65	.	.	51.4	286.54	189.91	.	527.85
90	.	.	96.9	336.59	227.44	.	660.93
171	.	134.60	941.4	1265.54	924.16	.	3265.70
908	.	.	219.3	471.23	328.42	.	1018.95

Level 2

8. Using a Character Array for Table Lookup

The Public Safety Department at Orion Star wants all employees to be aware of the new policies and procedures regarding customer incidents in their retail stores.

- Each employee must participate in Web-based training and then take a multiple-choice test that consists of 10 questions.
- Each question has five choices (A-E).
- The test results from each testing session are entered into the SAS data set **orion.test_answers** as shown below.
- Each observation in **orion.test_answers** contains a single person's answers.

Listing of **orion.test_answers**

Employee_ ID	Q1	Q2	Q3	Q4	Q5	Q6	Q7	Q8	Q9	Q10
121044	A	C	C	B	D	E	D	B	B	A
120145	B	C	C		E	E	D	B	A	A
120761	A	C	C	B	D	D	E	B	B	C
120656	B	C	C	A	D	B	B	C	A	D
121107	A	C	C	B	E	E	D	B	B	A
121038	B	C	C	B	D	D	D	B	B	A
120273	C	C	C	B	E	E	E	B	B	A
120759	A	C	C	B	E	E	D	B	B	A
120798		A	C	B	D	D	D	B	B	A
121030	C	C	C	C	E	E	D	B	B	B
121017	B	B	E	B	E	E	D	B	B	A
121062	A	C	C	B	E	E	D	B	B	A
121119	C	C	C	B	E	E	D	B	B	A
120812	A	C	C	B	E	E	E	B	B	A
120756	A	C	C	B	E	E	D	B	B	A

- The correct answers for the questions are shown below:

Question:	1	2	3	4	5	6	7	8	9	10
Answer:	A	C	C	B	E	E	D	B	B	A

a. Read **`orion.test_answers`** and determine whether each person passed or failed the test.

- Compute a variable **`Score`** that contains the total correct answers for each person.

  Create a temporary array for the answer key.

- If an employee scores 7 or higher, write the observation to a data set named **`passed`**.
- If an employee scores less than 7, write the observation to a data set named **`failed`**.

b. Print the **`passed`** data set to verify that it contains 12 observations.

PROC PRINT Output

Passed

Obs	Employee_ ID	Q1	Q2	Q3	Q4	Q5	Q6	Q7	Q8	Q9	Q10	Score
1	121044	A	C	C	B	D	E	D	B	B	A	9
2	120145	B	C	C		E	E	D	B	A	A	7
3	121107	A	C	C	B	E	E	D	B	B	A	10
4	121038	B	C	C	B	D	D	D	B	B	A	7
5	120273	C	C	C	B	E	E	E	B	B	A	8
6	120759	A	C	C	B	E	E	D	B	B	A	10
7	121030	C	C	C	C	E	E	D	B	B	B	7
8	121017	B	B	E	B	E	E	D	B	B	A	7
9	121062	A	C	C	B	E	E	D	B	B	A	10
10	121119	C	C	C	B	E	E	D	B	B	A	9
11	120812	A	C	C	B	E	E	E	B	B	A	9
12	120756	A	C	C	B	E	E	D	B	B	A	10

c. Print the **`failed`** data set to verify that it contains three observations.

PROC PRINT Output

Failed

Obs	Employee_ ID	Q1	Q2	Q3	Q4	Q5	Q6	Q7	Q8	Q9	Q10	Score
1	120761	A	C	C	B	D	D	E	B	B	C	6
2	120656	B	C	C	A	D	B	B	C	A	D	2
3	120798		A	C	B	D	D	D	B	B	A	6

7.4 Chapter Review

Chapter Review

1. An iterative DO loop must have a stop value? True or False?

2. A DO WHILE statement tests the condition at the ___________and a DO UNTIL statement tests the condition at the ______.

3. A _______ will always execute at least once, but a _______ might never execute.

4. What is the out of range value for this DO loop?
```
do year=2000 to year(today());
```

140

continued...

Chapter Review

5. A single array can contain both numeric and character elements. True or False?

6. What is wrong with the following array definition?
```
array value{5} v1-v6;
```

7. Write a DO statement to process every element in the following array: `array num{*} n:;`

8. What keyword causes a lookup table to be stored in memory instead of in the PDV ?

142

7.5 Solutions

Solutions to Exercises

1. **Performing Computations with DO Loops**

   a. Open the file **p207e01** and modify it.

```
data future_expenses;
   drop start stop;
   Wages=12874000;
   Retire=1765000;
   Medical=649000;
   start=year(today())+1;
   stop=start+9;
   do Year=start to stop;
      wages = wages * 1.06;
      retire=retire*1.014;
      medical=medical *1.095;
      Total_Cost=sum(wages,retire,medical);
      output;
   end;
run;
```

Alternate Solution:

```
data future_expenses;
   Wages=12874000;
   Retire=1765000;
   Medical=649000;
   do Year=year(today())+1 to year(today())+10;
      wages = wages * 1.06;
      retire=retire*1.014;
      medical=medical *1.095;
      Total_Cost= sum(wages,retire,medical);
      output;
   end;
run;
```

   b. Print the new data set and verify your results.

```
proc print data=future_expenses;
   format wages retire medical total_cost comma14.2;
   var year wages retire medical total_cost;
run;
```

c. Modify the previous program to stop when the year's total costs exceed the year's income.

```
data income_expenses;
   Wages=12874000;
   Retire=1765000;
   Medical=649000;
   Income=50000000;
   Year=year(today())+1;
   do until (Total_Cost > Income);
      wages = wages * 1.06;
      retire=retire*1.014;
      medical=medical *1.095;
      Total_Cost= sum(wages,retire,medical);
      Income=Income *1.01;
      output;
      year+1;
   end;
run;
```

d. Print **Year**, **Total_Cost**, and **Income**.

```
proc print data=income_expenses;
   format total_cost income comma14.2;
   var year income total_cost;
run;
```

2. Using an Iterative DO Loop with a Conditional Clause

a. Create a data set, **work.expenses**, that contains each year's projected income and expenses.

```
data expenses;
   Income= 50000000;
   Expenses = 38750000;
   do Year=1 to 30 until (Expenses > Income);
      income+(income * .01);
      expenses+(expenses * .02);
   end;
run;
```

b. Print the new data set.

```
proc print data=expenses;
   format income expenses dollar15.2;
run;
```

3. **Using Other Loop Control Statements**

   a. Use an iterative DO statement to calculate projected income and expenses for the next 75 years.

```
data expenses;
   Income= 50000000;
   Expenses = 38750000;
   do Year=1 to 75;
      income +(income * .01);
      expenses+(expenses * .02);
      if expenses > income then leave;
   end;
run;
```

   b. Print the results.

```
proc print data=expenses;
   format income expenses dollar14.2;
run;
```

4. **Using Arrays for Repetitive Computations**

   a. Create a data set, **discount_sales**, to reflect the five-percent discount.

```
data discount_sales;
   set orion.orders_midyear;
   array mon{*} month1-month6;
   drop i;
   do i=1 to 6;
      mon{i} = mon{i} *.95;
   end;
run;
```

   b. Print the new data set.

```
title 'Monthly Sales with 5% Discount';
proc print data=discount_sales noobs;
   format month1-month6 dollar10.2;
run;
title;
```

5. **Using Arrays for Repetitive Calculations**

   a. Create a data set, **special_offer**, to reflect the 10-percent discount in months 1 through 3.

```
data special_offer;
   set orion.orders_midyear;
   array mon{*} month1-month3;
   keep Total_Sales Projected_Sales Difference;
   Total_Sales=sum(of month1-month6);
   do i=1 to 3;
      mon{i} = mon{i} *.90;
   end;
   Projected_Sales=sum(of month1-month6);
   Difference=Total_Sales-Projected_Sales;
run;
```

b. Print the new data set.

```
options nodate nonumber;
title 'Total Sales with 10% Discount in First Three Months';
proc print data=special_offer noobs;
   format total_sales projected_sales difference dollar10.2;
   sum difference;
run;
title;
```

6. **Terminating a DATA Step**

   a. Create a new data set, **fsp**, containing customers that qualify for the Frequent Shopper Program. Use **orion.orders_midyear** as input.

```
data fsp;
   set orion.orders_midyear;
   keep Customer_ID Months_Ordered Total_Order_Amount;
   array amt{*} month:;
   if dim(amt) < 3 then do;
      put 'Insufficient data for Frequent Shopper Program';
      stop;
   end;
   Total_Order_Amount=0;
   Months_Ordered=0;
   do i=1 to dim(amt);
      if amt{i} ne . then Months_Ordered+1;
      Total_Order_Amount+amt{i};
   end;
   if Total_Order_Amount>1000 and Months_Ordered >= (dim(amt))/2;
run;
```

   b. Print the new data set.

```
title 'orion.orders_midyear: Frequent Shoppers ';
proc print data=fsp;
   format total_order_amount dollar10.2;
run;
title;
```

c. Test your program using **orion.orders_qtr1**.

```
data fsp;
   set orion.orders_qtr1;
   keep Customer_ID Months_Ordered Total_Order_Amount;
   array amt{*} month:;
   if dim(amt) < 3 then do;
      put 'Insufficient data for Frequent Shopper Program';
      stop;
   end;
   Total_Order_Amount=0;
   Months_Ordered=0;
   do i=1 to dim(amt);
      if amt{i} ne . then Months_Ordered+1;
      Total_Order_Amount+amt{i};
   end;
   if Total_Order_Amount>1000 and Months_Ordered >= (dim(amt))/2;
run;
title 'orion.orders_qtr1: Frequent Shoppers ';
proc print data=fsp;
   format total_order_amount dollar10.2;
run;
title;
```

d. Test your program using **orion.orders_two_months**.

```
data fsp;
   set orion.orders_two_months;
   keep Customer_ID Months_Ordered Total_Order_Amount;
   array amt{*} month:;
   if dim(amt) < 3 then do;
      put 'Insufficient data for Frequent Shopper Program';
      stop;
   end;
   Total_Order_Amount=0;
   Months_Ordered=0;
   do i=1 to dim(amt);
      if amt{i} ne . then Months_Ordered+1;
      Total_Order_Amount+amt{i};
   end;
   if Total_Order_Amount>1000 and Months_Ordered >= (dim(amt))/2;
run;
title 'orion.orders_two_months: Frequent Shoppers ';

proc print data=fsp;
   format total_order_amount dollar10.2;
run;
title;
```

7. Using an Array for Table Lookup

a. Open **p207e07** and modify the program to create the **preferred_cust** data set using a lookup table.

```
data preferred_cust;
   set orion.orders_midyear;
   array Mon{6} Month1-Month6;
   keep Customer_ID Over1-Over6 Total_Over;
   array Over{6};
   array Target{6} _temporary_ (200,400,300,100,100,200);
   do i=1 to 6;
      if Mon{i} > Target{i} then
         Over{i} = Mon{i} - Target{i};
   end;
   Total_Over=sum(of Over{*});
   if Total_Over > 500;
run;
```

b. Print the new data set.

```
proc print data=preferred_cust noobs;
run;
```

8. Using a Character Array for Table Lookup

a. Read **orion.test_answers** and determine whether each person passed or failed a safety test.

```
data passed failed;
   set orion.test_answers;
   drop i;
   array Response{10} Q1-Q10;
   array Answer{10} $ 1 _temporary_ ('A','C','C','B','E',
                                     'E','D','B','B','A');
   Score=0;
   do i=1 to 10;
      if Answer{i}=Response{i} then Score+1;
   end;
   if Score ge 7 then output passed;
   else output failed;
run;
```

b. Print the **passed** data set.

```
title 'Passed';
proc print data=passed;
run;
title;
```

c. Print the **failed** data set.

```
title 'Failed';
proc print data=failed;
run;
title;
```

Solutions to Student Activities (Polls/Quizzes)

7.01 Quiz – Correct Answer

What are the final values of the index variables after the following DO statements execute?

The final values are highlighted.

```
do i=1 to 5;
   ...
end;                        1 2 3 4 5 6

do j=2 to 8 by 2;
   ...
end;                        2 4 6 8 10

do k=10 to 2 by -2;
   ...
end;                        10 8 6 4 2 0
```

13

7.02 Quiz – Correct Answer

How can you generate a separate observation for each year? **Place an explicit OUTPUT statement inside the DO loop.**

```
data invest;
   do Year=2008 to 2010;
      Capital+5000;
      Capital+(Capital*.045);
      output;
   end;
run;
proc print data=invest noobs;
run;
```

PROC PRINT Output

Year	Capital
2008	5225.00
2009	10685.13
2010	16390.96

There is no observation for 2011.

36

p207a01s

7.03 Quiz – Correct Answer

What stop value would you use in the DO loop to determine the number of years it would take for the Engineering department to exceed 75 people? **Unknown.**

```
data forecast;
   set orion.growth;
   do Year=1 to 6;
      Total_Employees=
         Total_Employees*(1+Increase);
      output;
   end;
run;
proc print data=forecast noobs;
run;
```

Use *conditional iterative processing* to stop a loop when a condition is met.

44 p207d05

7.04 Quiz – Correct Answer

How could you generate the same result with a DO WHILE statement? **Change the DO UNTIL statement to a DO WHILE statement and modify the condition.**

```
data invest;
   do while(Capital<=1000000);
      Year+1;
      Capital+5000;
      Capital+(Capital*.045);
   end;
run;

proc print data=invest noobs;
   format capital dollar14.2;
run;
```

52 p207a02s

7.05 Quiz – Correct Answer

How can you generate one observation for each quarterly amount? **Move the OUTPUT statement to the inner loop and do not drop Quarter.**

```
data invest;
   do Year=1 to 5;
      Capital+5000;
      do Quarter=1 to 4;
         Capital+(Capital*(.045/4));
         output;
      end;
   end;
run;
proc print data=invest
run;
```

Partial PROC PRINT Output

Year	Capital	Quarter
1	5056.25	1
1	5113.13	2
1	5170.66	3
1	5228.83	4
2	10343.90	1
2	10460.27	2

61

p207a03s

7.07 Quiz – Correct Answer

Open and submit **p207a04**. View the log to determine the cause of the error. **The subscript and the number of elements in the list do not agree.**

```
data charity(keep=employee_id qtr1-qtr4);
   set orion.employee_donations;
   array Contrib1{3} qtr1-qtr4;
   array Contrib2{5} qtr:;
   /* additional SAS statements */
run;
```

The subscript and element-list must agree.

Partial SAS Log

```
177      array Contrib1{3} qtr1-qtr4;
ERROR: Too many variables defined for the dimension(s) specified
for the array Contrib1.
178      array Contrib2{5} qtr:;
ERROR: Too few variables defined for the dimension(s) specified
for the array Contrib2.
```

89

7.08 Quiz – Correct Answer

How many ARRAY statements would you use to calculate the difference in each employee's contribution from one quarter to the next? **Answers can vary, but one solution is to use two arrays.**

Partial Listing of **`orion.employee_donations`**

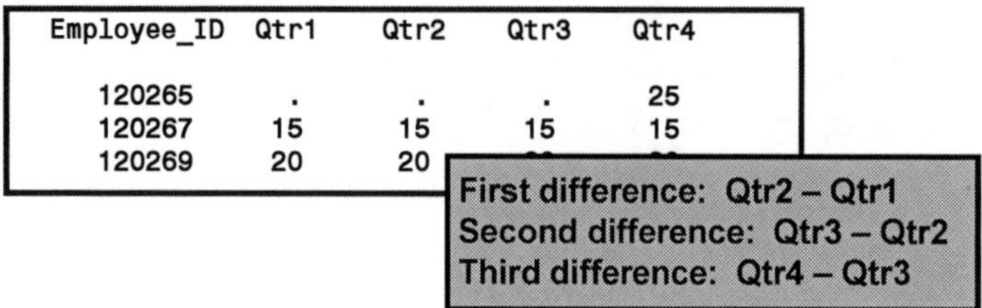

Employee_ID	Qtr1	Qtr2	Qtr3	Qtr4
120265	.	.	.	25
120267	15	15	15	15
120269	20	20		

Use one array to refer to the existing variables and a second array to create the three `Difference` variables.

113

7.09 Quiz – Correct Answer

Using pencil and paper, write an ARRAY statement to define a temporary lookup table named **`Country`** with three elements, each two characters long. Initialize the elements to AU, NZ, and US. Refer to the syntax below.

ARRAY *array-name* {*subscript*} <$> <*length*>
<*array-elements*> <(*initial-value-list*)>;

```
array Country{3} $ 2 _temporary_ ('AU','NZ','US');
```

137

Solutions to Chapter Review

Chapter Review Answers

1. An iterative DO loop must have a stop value. True or False
   False. It might have a list of values.

2. A DO WHILE statement tests the condition at the **top of the loop**, and a DO UNTIL statement tests the condition at the **bottom**.

3. A **DO UNTIL** statement will always execute at least once, but a **DO WHILE** statement might never execute.

4. What is the out of range value for this DO loop?
   ```
   do year=2000 to year(today());
   ```
   The upcoming year, so in 2009 the final value of year will be 2010.

141

continued...

Chapter Review Answers

5. A single array can contain both numeric and character elements. True or False? **False**

6. What is wrong with the following array definition?
   ```
   array value{5} v1-v6;
   ```
   The subscript and the number of items in the element list does not agree.

7. Write a DO statement to process every element in the following array: `array num{*} n:;`
   ```
   do i=1 to dim(num);
   ```

8. What keyword causes a lookup table to be stored in memory instead of in the PDV ?
   TEMPORARY

143

Chapter 8 Restructuring a Data Set

8.1 Rotating with the DATA Step 8-3

Exercises 8-24

8.2 Using the TRANSPOSE Procedure 8-28

Exercises 8-49

8.3 Chapter Review 8-52

8.4 Solutions 8-53

Solutions to Exercises 8-53

Solutions to Student Activities (Polls/Quizzes) 8-56

Solutions to Chapter Review 8-58

8.1 Rotating with the DATA Step

Objectives

- Use a DATA step with arrays and DO loop processing to restructure a data set.

3

Data Set Structure

Some data sets store all the information about one entity in a single observation. This data set structure is useful for data mining and generating reports. For convenience this is referred to as a *wide* data set.

Customer_ID	Qtr1	Qtr2	Qtr3	Qtr4	Method
134391	.	125	.	.	Cash
143561	150	79	67	15	Credit
158913	208	22	.	33	Credit

All information for Customer 143561 is in a single observation.

4

Data Set Structure

Other data sets have multiple observations per entity. Each observation typically contains a small amount of data, and missing values might or might not be stored. For convenience, this is referred to as a *narrow* data set.

Customer_ID	Period	Amount
134391	Qtr2	125
143561	Qtr1	150
143561	Qtr2	79
143561	Qtr3	67
143561	Qtr4	15
158913	Qtr1	208
158913	Qtr2	22

✎ The information for Customer 143561 is stored in four observations.

5

Why Restructure a Data Set?

Before writing a program, you need to consider the data available, the desired output, and the processing required. Sometimes restructuring the data can simplify a task.

The Sales Manager requested the following report showing customer information:

Sketch of desired report:

Customer ID	Qtr1	Qtr2	Qtr3	Qtr4	Total
134391	.	125	.	.	125
143561	150	79	67	15	311
158913	208	22	.	33	263

6

Why Restructure a Data Set?

You explore the available data and locate the following data set:

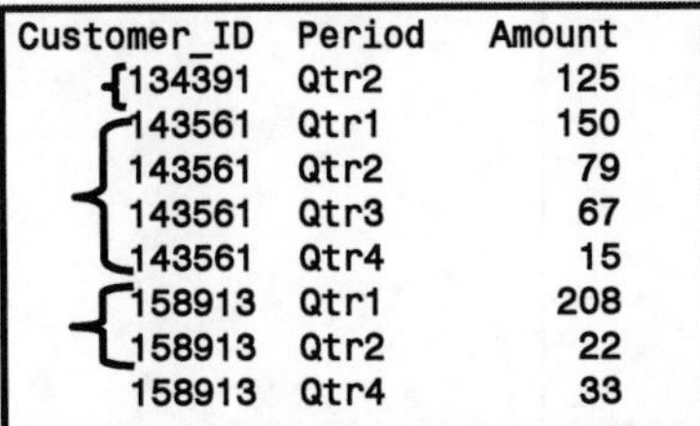

Customer_ID	Period	Amount
134391	Qtr2	125
143561	Qtr1	150
143561	Qtr2	79
143561	Qtr3	67
143561	Qtr4	15
158913	Qtr1	208
158913	Qtr2	22
158913	Qtr4	33

This data set has the required data, but the current structure would require a DATA step with First. and Last. processing.

7

Why Restructure a Data Set?

If the data set were in this form, a simple assignment statement is all that would be needed to create the new variable, `Total`.

Customer_ID	Qtr1	Qtr2	Qtr3	Qtr4
134391	.	125	.	.
143561	150	79	67	15
158913	208	22	.	33

✎ Restructuring from a narrow to a wide data set simplifies the processing.

8

8.01 Quiz

Which data set structure is more appropriate for using PROC FREQ to determine the number of charitable donations made in each of the four quarters (`Qtr1–Qtr4`)?

a.

Employee_ID	Qtr1	Qtr2	Qtr3	Qtr4
120265	.	.	.	25
120267	15	15	15	15
120269	20	20	20	20

b.

Employee_ID	Period	Amount
120265	Qtr4	25
120267	Qtr1	15
120267	Qtr2	15
120267	Qtr3	15
120267	Qtr4	15

10

Business Scenario – A Frequency Report

The Orion Payroll Manager asked for a report showing the number of Orion Star employees who made charitable donations in each quarter.

Sketch of the Desired Report

Period	Frequency
Qtr1	56
Qtr2	99
Qtr3	24
Qtr4	75

The FREQ procedure can be used to generate the desired report.

12

Business Scenario Considerations

The **`orion.employee_donations`** data set contains the needed information, but is not in the form to be easily analyzed using the FREQ procedure.

Partial Listing of **`orion.employee_donations`**

Employee_ID	Qtr1	Qtr2	Qtr3	Qtr4	Paid_By
120265	.	.	.	25	Cash or Check
120267	15	15	15	15	Payroll Deduction
120269	20	20	20	20	Payroll Deduction

✐ Changing the data set from a wide to a narrow structure can simplify this task.

13

Business Scenario Considerations

Restructure the input data set, and create a separate observation for each nonmissing quarterly contribution. The output data set, **`rotate`**, should contain only **`Employee_ID`**, **`Period`**, and **`Amount`**.

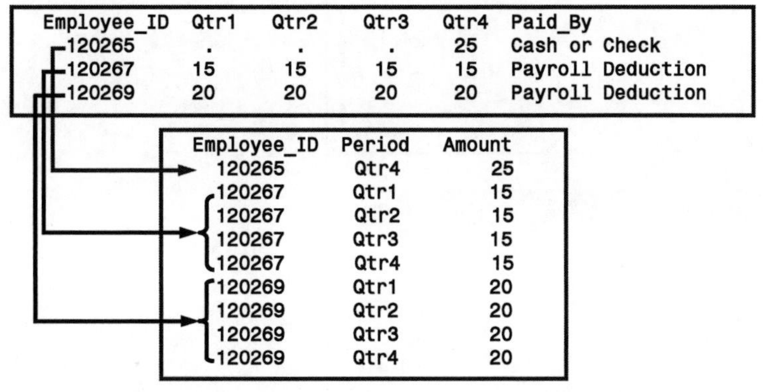

Employee_ID	Qtr1	Qtr2	Qtr3	Qtr4	Paid_By
120265	.	.	.	25	Cash or Check
120267	15	15	15	15	Payroll Deduction
120269	20	20	20	20	Payroll Deduction

Employee_ID	Period	Amount
120265	Qtr4	25
120267	Qtr1	15
120267	Qtr2	15
120267	Qtr3	15
120267	Qtr4	15
120269	Qtr1	20
120269	Qtr2	20
120269	Qtr3	20
120269	Qtr4	20

14

Rotating a SAS Data Set

The DATA step below rotates the input data set.
An output observation will be written if a contribution was made in a given quarter.

```
data rotate (keep=Employee_Id Period Amount);
   set orion.employee_donations
            (drop=recipients paid_by);
   array contrib{4} qtr1-qtr4;
   do i=1 to 4;
      if contrib{i} ne . then do;
         Period=cats("Qtr",i);
         Amount=contrib{i};
         output;
      end;
   end;
run;
```

Only include nonmissing values

15 p208d01

Compilation: Rotating a SAS Data Set

```
data rotate (keep=Employee_Id Period Amount);
   set orion.employee_donations
            (drop=recipients paid_by);
   array contrib{4} qtr1-qtr4;
   do i=1 to 4;
      if contrib{i} ne . then do;
         Period=cats("Qtr",i);
         Amount=contrib{i};
         output;
      end;
   end;
run;
```

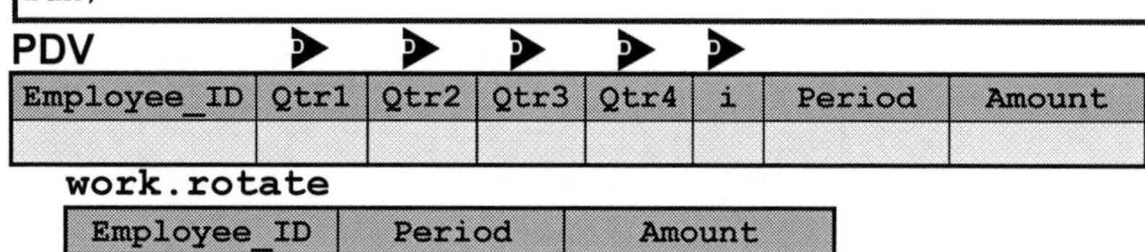

PDV

Employee_ID	Qtr1	Qtr2	Qtr3	Qtr4	i	Period	Amount

work.rotate

Employee_ID	Period	Amount

16 p208d01 ...

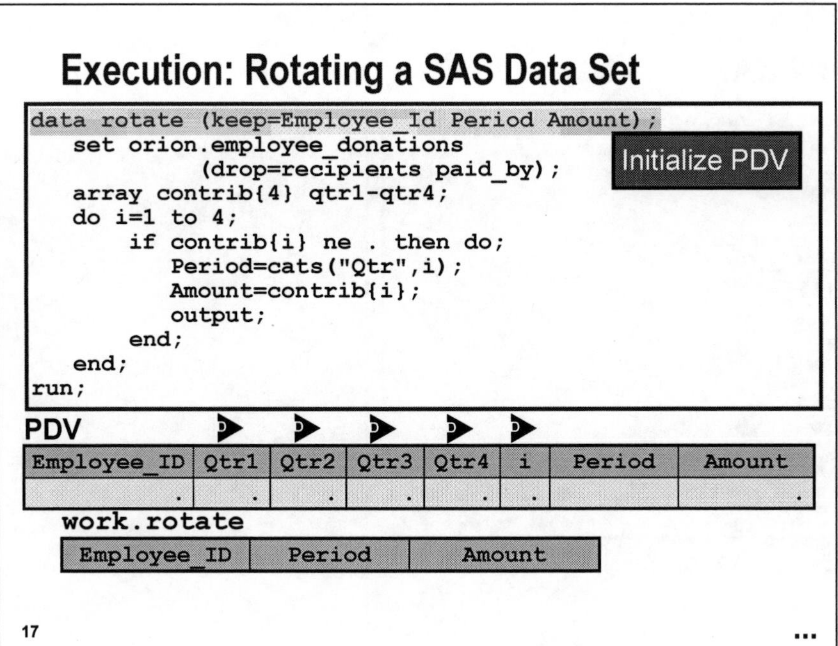
Execution: Rotating a SAS Data Set
data rotate (keep=Employee_Id Period Amount);
set orion.employee_donations
(drop=recipients paid_by);
array contrib{4} qtr1-qtr4;
do i=1 to 4;
if contrib{i} ne . then do;
Period=cats("Qtr",i);
Amount=contrib{i};
output;
end;
end;
run;
Initialize PDV
PDV
Employee_ID Qtr1 Qtr2 Qtr3 Qtr4 i Period Amount
. . . .
work.rotate
Employee_ID Period Amount
17
...

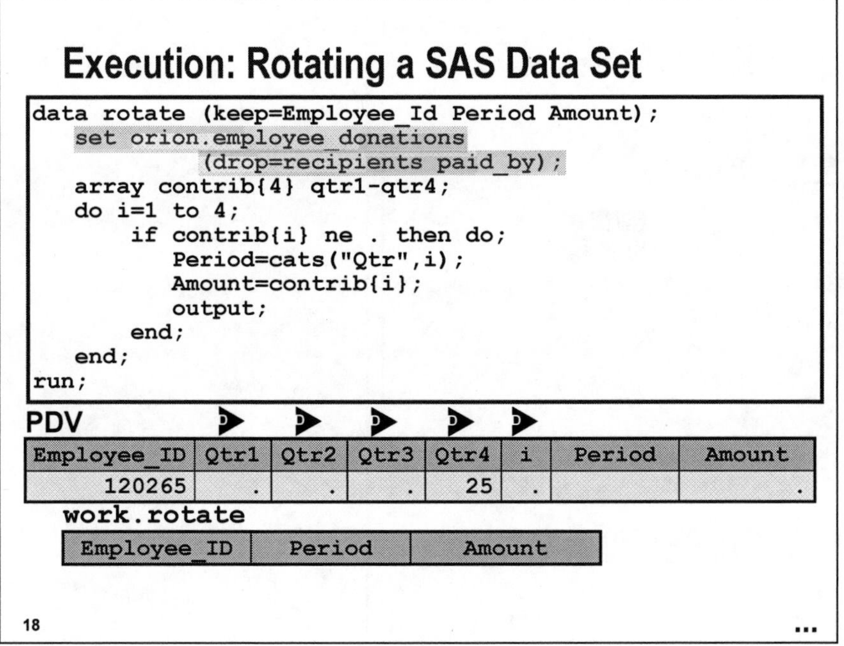
Execution: Rotating a SAS Data Set
data rotate (keep=Employee_Id Period Amount);
set orion.employee_donations
(drop=recipients paid_by);
array contrib{4} qtr1-qtr4;
do i=1 to 4;
if contrib{i} ne . then do;
Period=cats("Qtr",i);
Amount=contrib{i};
output;
end;
end;
run;
PDV
Employee_ID Qtr1 Qtr2 Qtr3 Qtr4 i Period Amount
120265 . . . 25 . .
work.rotate
Employee_ID Period Amount
18
...

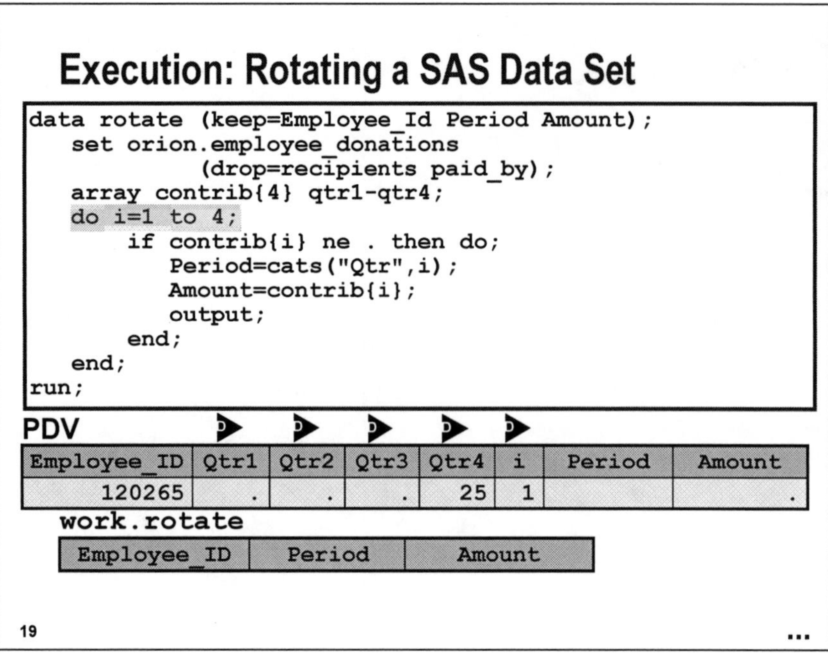
Execution: Rotating a SAS Data Set
data rotate (keep=Employee_Id Period Amount);
set orion.employee_donations
(drop=recipients paid_by);
array contrib{4} qtr1-qtr4;
do i=1 to 4;
if contrib{i} ne . then do;
Period=cats("Qtr",i);
Amount=contrib{i};
output;
end;
end;
run;
PDV
Employee_ID Qtr1 Qtr2 Qtr3 Qtr4 i Period Amount
120265 . . . 25 1 .
work.rotate
Employee_ID Period Amount
19
...

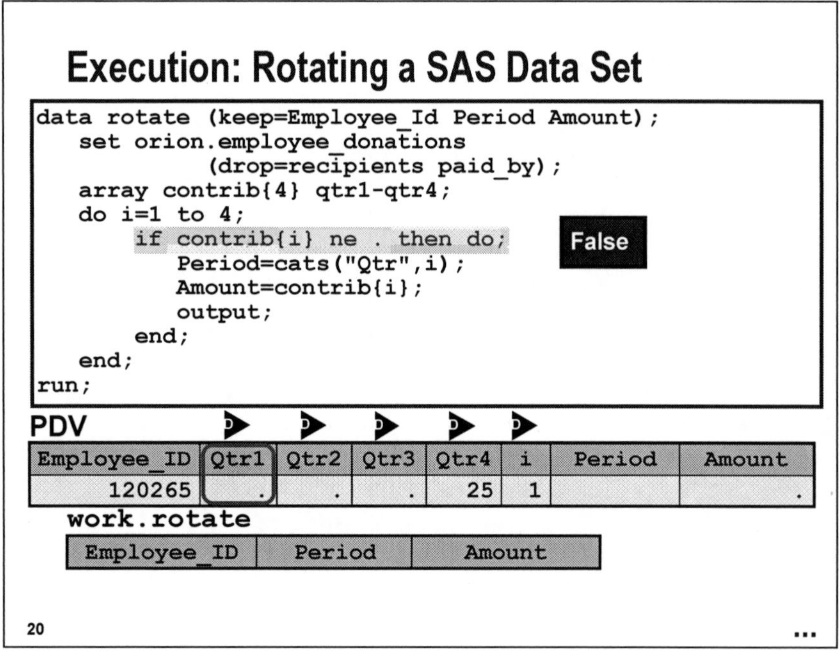
Execution: Rotating a SAS Data Set
data rotate (keep=Employee_Id Period Amount);
set orion.employee_donations
(drop=recipients paid_by);
array contrib{4} qtr1-qtr4;
do i=1 to 4;
if contrib{i} ne . then do;
Period=cats("Qtr",i);
Amount=contrib{i};
output;
end;
end;
run;
False
PDV
Employee_ID Qtr1 Qtr2 Qtr3 Qtr4 i Period Amount
120265 . . . 25 1 .
work.rotate
Employee_ID Period Amount
20
...

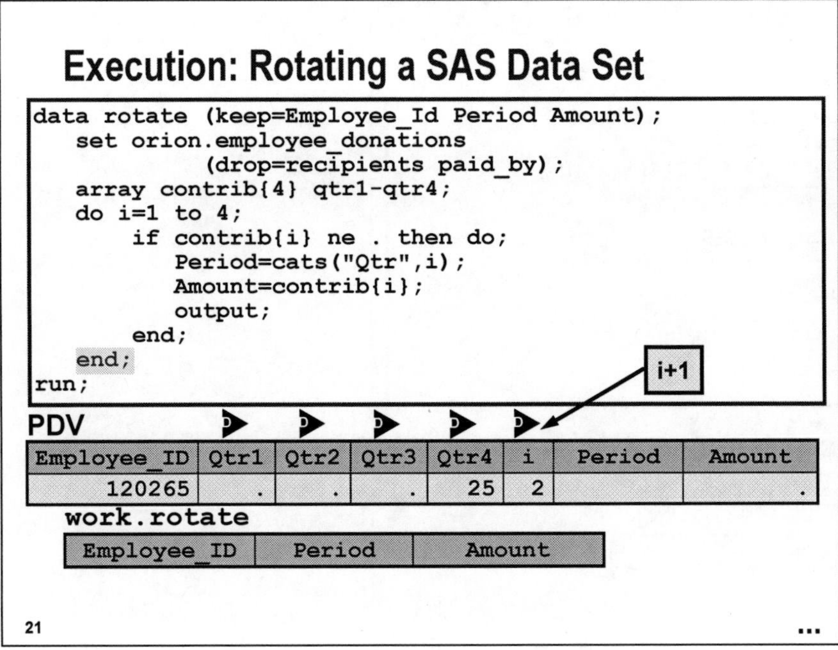
Execution: Rotating a SAS Data Set
data rotate (keep=Employee_Id Period Amount);
set orion.employee_donations
(drop=recipients paid_by);
array contrib{4} qtr1-qtr4;
do i=1 to 4;
if contrib{i} ne . then do;
Period=cats("Qtr",i);
Amount=contrib{i};
output;
end;
end;
run;
i+1
PDV
Employee_ID Qtr1 Qtr2 Qtr3 Qtr4 i Period Amount
120265 . . . 25 2 .
work.rotate
Employee_ID Period Amount
21
...

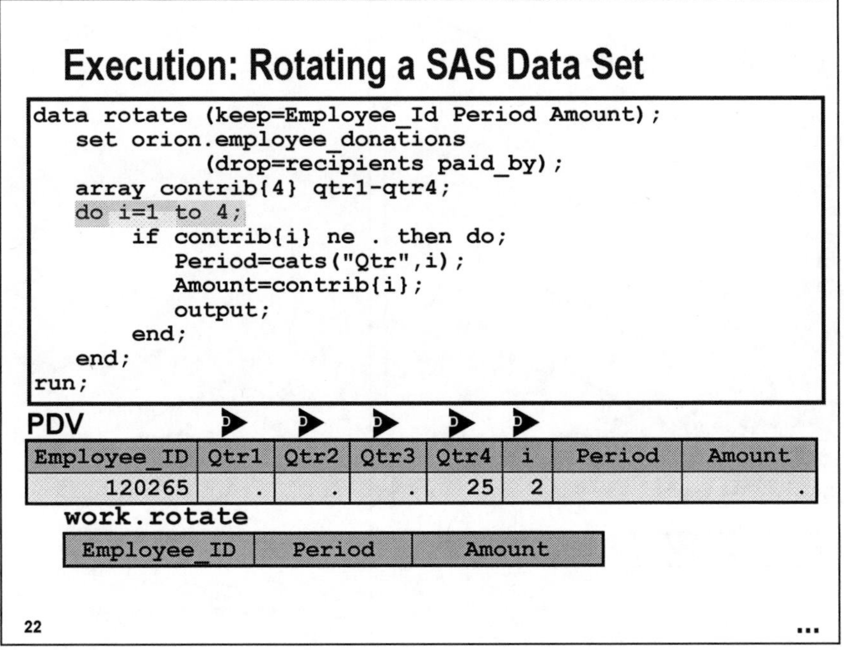
Execution: Rotating a SAS Data Set
data rotate (keep=Employee_Id Period Amount);
set orion.employee_donations
(drop=recipients paid_by);
array contrib{4} qtr1-qtr4;
do i=1 to 4;
if contrib{i} ne . then do;
Period=cats("Qtr",i);
Amount=contrib{i};
output;
end;
end;
run;
PDV
Employee_ID Qtr1 Qtr2 Qtr3 Qtr4 i Period Amount
120265 . . . 25 2 .
work.rotate
Employee_ID Period Amount
22
...

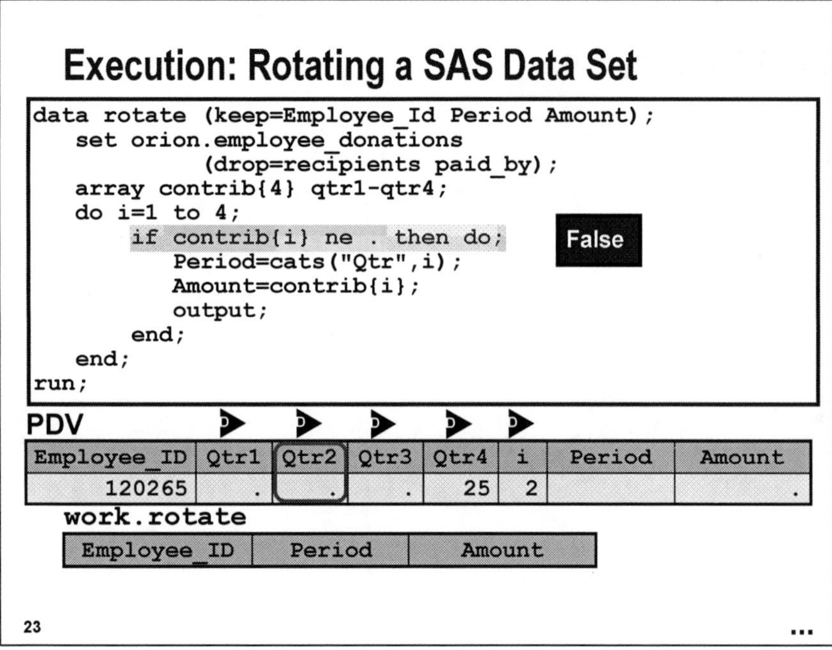
Execution: Rotating a SAS Data Set
data rotate (keep=Employee_Id Period Amount);
set orion.employee_donations
(drop=recipients paid_by);
array contrib{4} qtr1-qtr4;
do i=1 to 4;
if contrib{i} ne . then do;
Period=cats("Qtr",i);
Amount=contrib{i};
output;
end;
end;
run;
False
PDV
Employee_ID Qtr1 Qtr2 Qtr3 Qtr4 i Period Amount
120265 . . . 25 2 .
work.rotate
Employee_ID Period Amount
23
...

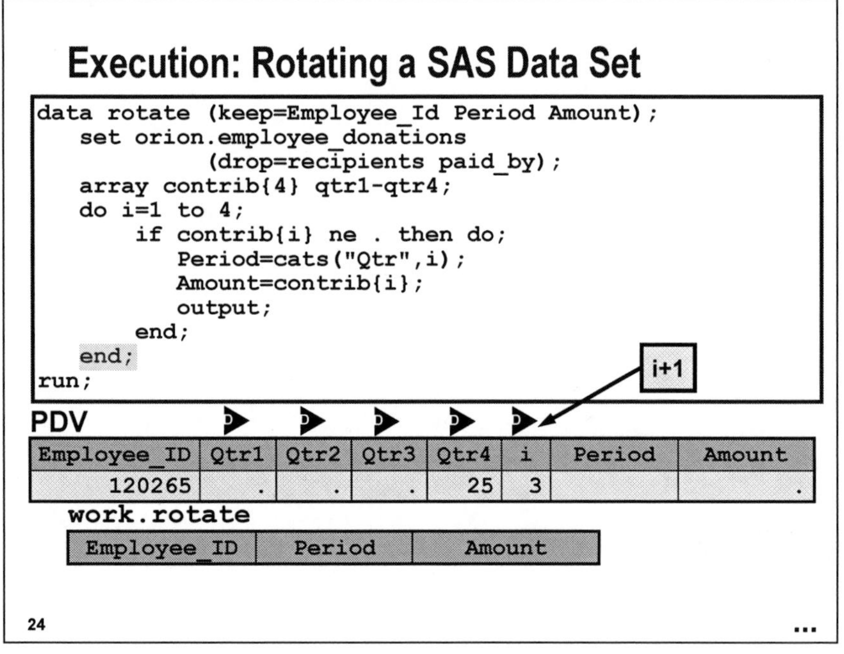
Execution: Rotating a SAS Data Set
data rotate (keep=Employee_Id Period Amount);
set orion.employee_donations
(drop=recipients paid_by);
array contrib{4} qtr1-qtr4;
do i=1 to 4;
if contrib{i} ne . then do;
Period=cats("Qtr",i);
Amount=contrib{i};
output;
end;
end;
run;
i+1
PDV
Employee_ID Qtr1 Qtr2 Qtr3 Qtr4 i Period Amount
120265 . . . 25 3 .
work.rotate
Employee_ID Period Amount
24
...

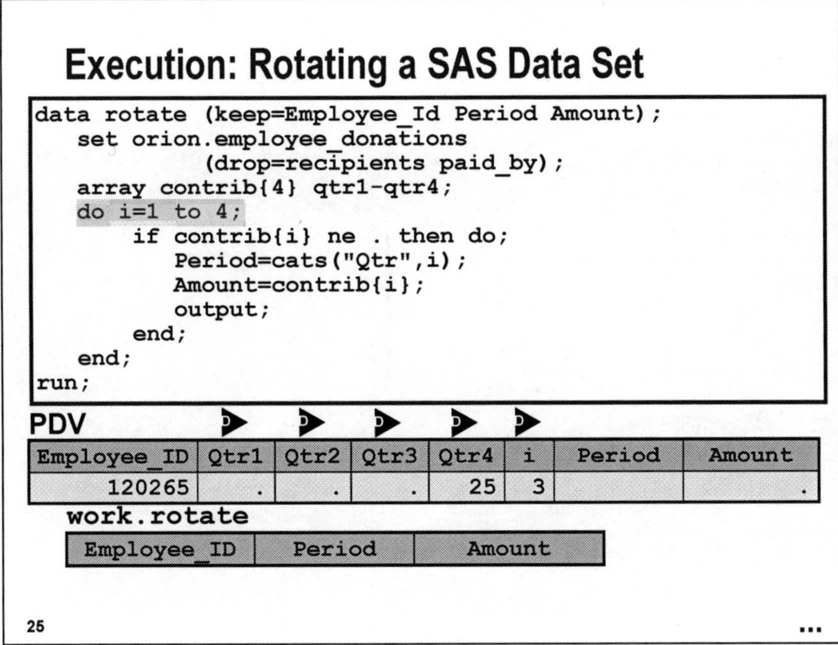
Execution: Rotating a SAS Data Set
data rotate (keep=Employee_Id Period Amount);
set orion.employee_donations
(drop=recipients paid_by);
array contrib{4} qtr1-qtr4;
do i=1 to 4;
if contrib{i} ne . then do;
Period=cats("Qtr",i);
Amount=contrib{i};
output;
end;
end;
run;
PDV
Employee_ID Qtr1 Qtr2 Qtr3 Qtr4 i Period Amount
120265 . . . 25 3 .
work.rotate
Employee_ID Period Amount
25

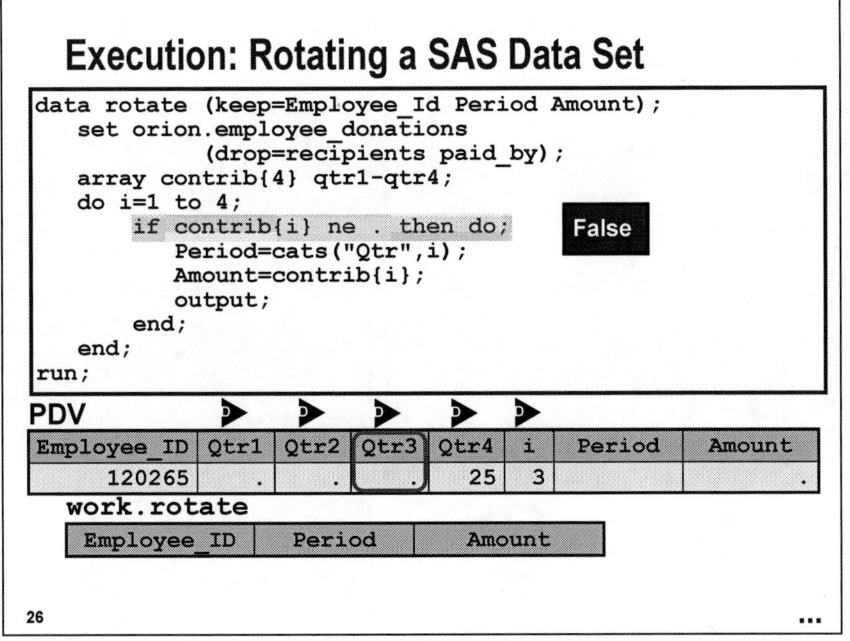
Execution: Rotating a SAS Data Set
data rotate (keep=Employee_Id Period Amount);
set orion.employee_donations
(drop=recipients paid_by);
array contrib{4} qtr1-qtr4;
do i=1 to 4;
if contrib{i} ne . then do;
False
Period=cats("Qtr",i);
Amount=contrib{i};
output;
end;
end;
run;
PDV
Employee_ID Qtr1 Qtr2 Qtr3 Qtr4 i Period Amount
120265 . . . 25 3 .
work.rotate
Employee_ID Period Amount
26

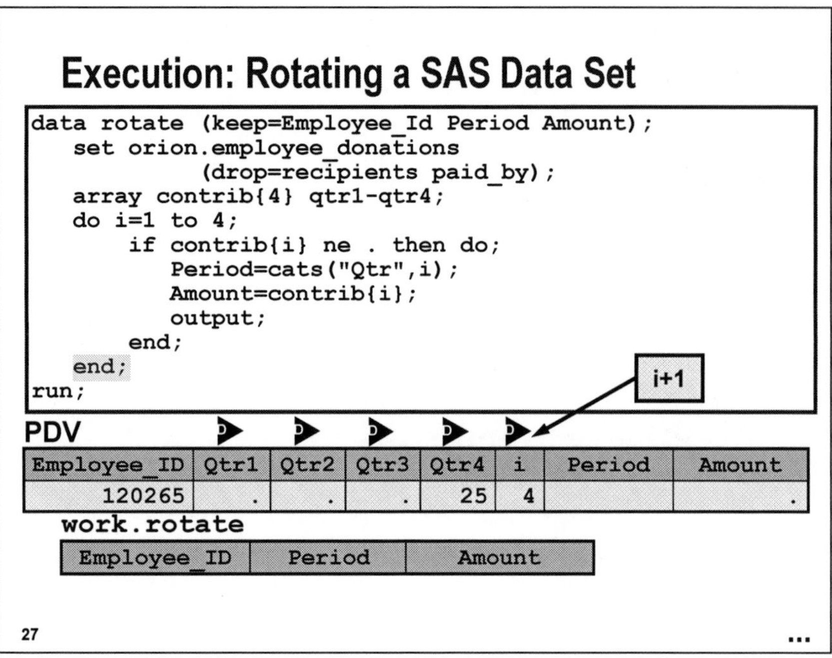
Execution: Rotating a SAS Data Set
data rotate (keep=Employee_Id Period Amount);
set orion.employee_donations
(drop=recipients paid_by);
array contrib{4} qtr1-qtr4;
do i=1 to 4;
if contrib{i} ne . then do;
Period=cats("Qtr",i);
Amount=contrib{i};
output;
end;
end;
run;
i+1
PDV
Employee_ID Qtr1 Qtr2 Qtr3 Qtr4 i Period Amount
120265 . . . 25 4 .
work.rotate
Employee_ID Period Amount
27
...

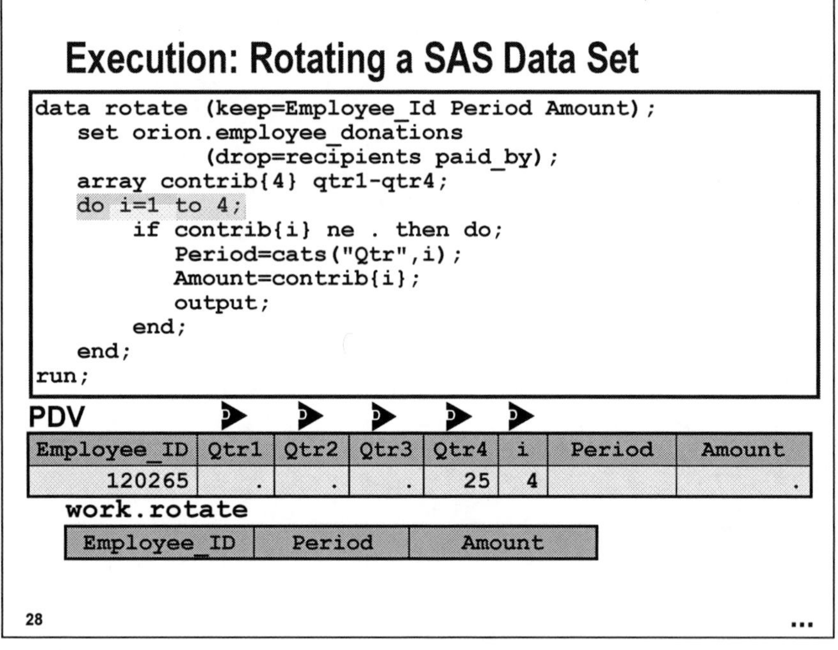
Execution: Rotating a SAS Data Set
data rotate (keep=Employee_Id Period Amount);
set orion.employee_donations
(drop=recipients paid_by);
array contrib{4} qtr1-qtr4;
do i=1 to 4;
if contrib{i} ne . then do;
Period=cats("Qtr",i);
Amount=contrib{i};
output;
end;
end;
run;
PDV
Employee_ID Qtr1 Qtr2 Qtr3 Qtr4 i Period Amount
120265 . . . 25 4 .
work.rotate
Employee_ID Period Amount
28
...

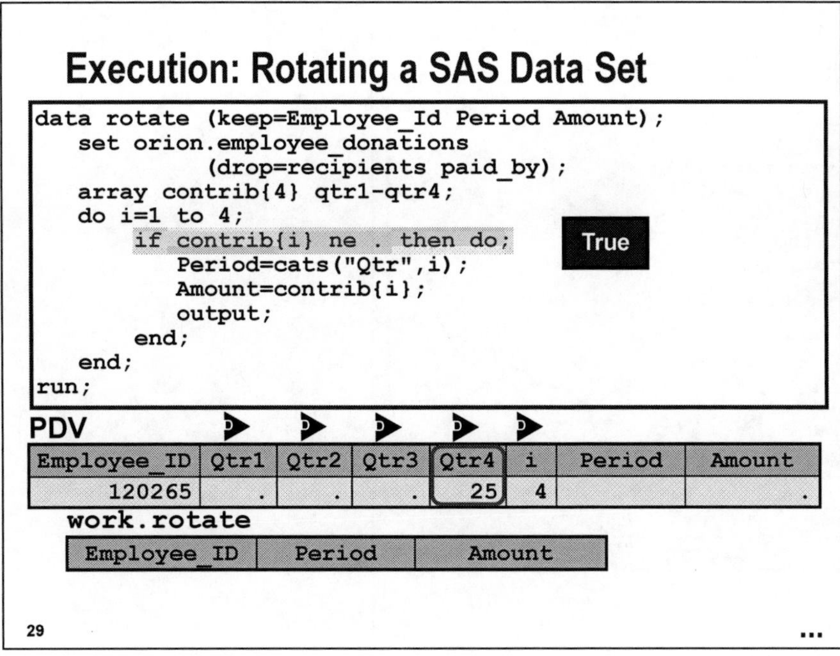

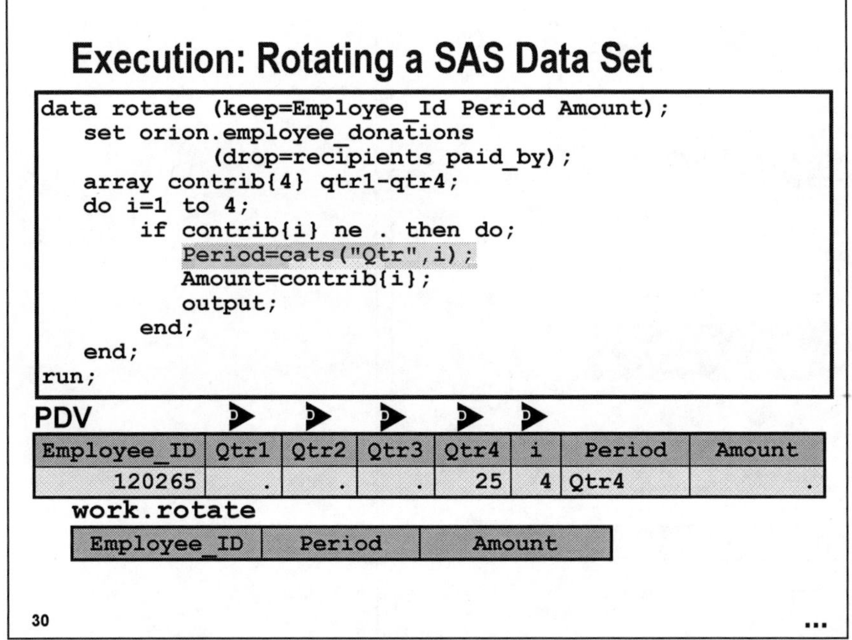

Automatic conversion occurs when you use a numeric value in character context. The functions in the CAT family remove leading and trailing blanks from numeric arguments after it formats the numeric value with the BEST12. format.

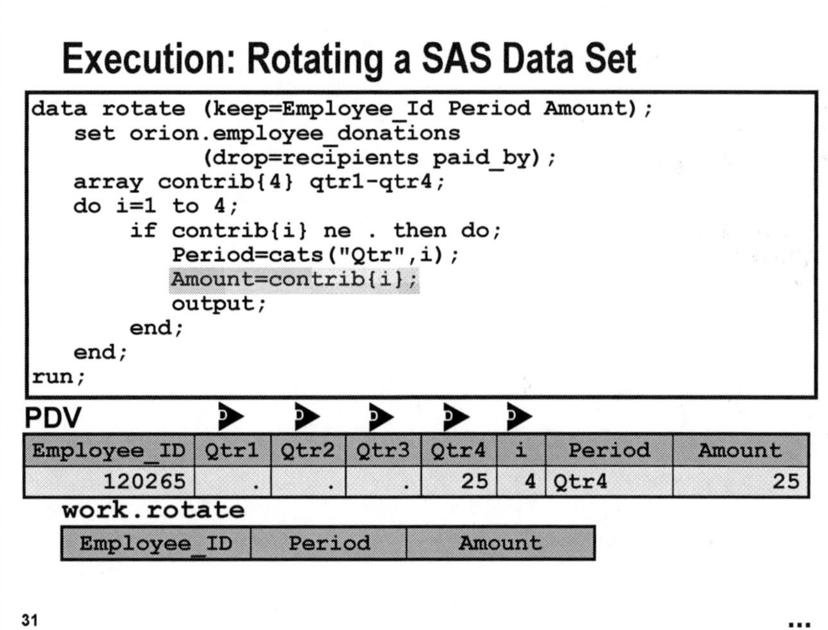
Execution: Rotating a SAS Data Set
data rotate (keep=Employee_Id Period Amount);
set orion.employee_donations
(drop=recipients paid_by);
array contrib{4} qtr1-qtr4;
do i=1 to 4;
if contrib{i} ne . then do;
Period=cats("Qtr",i);
Amount=contrib{i};
output;
end;
end;
run;
PDV
Employee_ID | Qtr1 | Qtr2 | Qtr3 | Qtr4 | i | Period | Amount
120265 | . | . | . | 25 | 4 | Qtr4 | 25
work.rotate
Employee_ID | Period | Amount
31

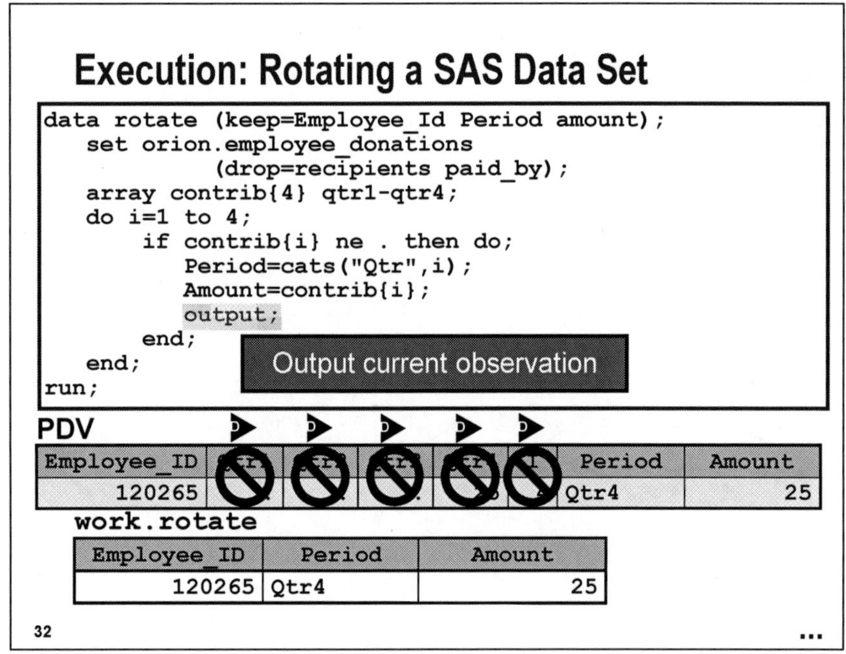
Execution: Rotating a SAS Data Set
data rotate (keep=Employee_Id Period amount);
set orion.employee_donations
(drop=recipients paid_by);
array contrib{4} qtr1-qtr4;
do i=1 to 4;
if contrib{i} ne . then do;
Period=cats("Qtr",i);
Amount=contrib{i};
output;
end;
end;
run;
Output current observation
PDV
Employee_ID | Period | Amount
120265 | Qtr4 | 25
work.rotate
Employee_ID | Period | Amount
120265 | Qtr4 | 25
32

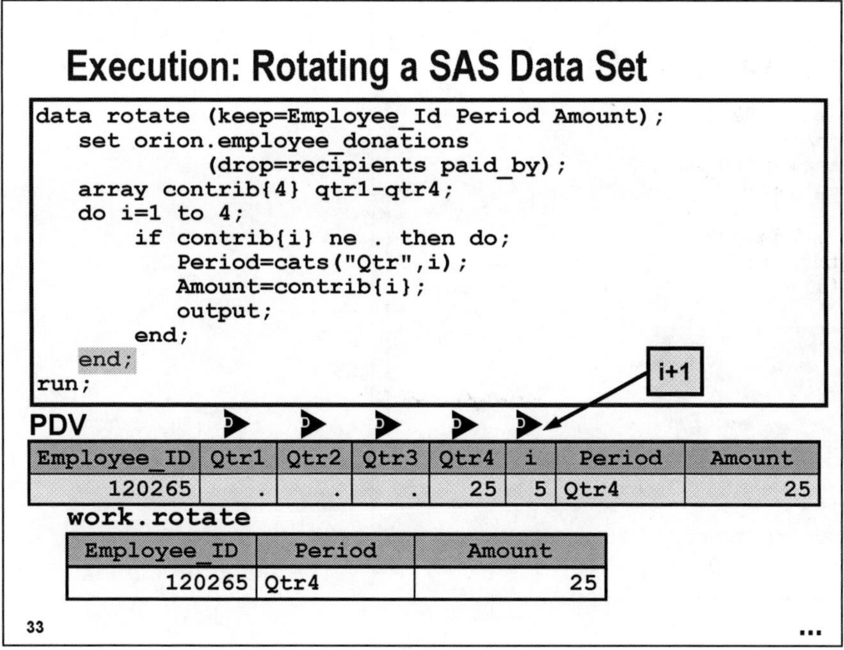
Execution: Rotating a SAS Data Set
data rotate (keep=Employee_Id Period Amount);
set orion.employee_donations
(drop=recipients paid_by);
array contrib{4} qtr1-qtr4;
do i=1 to 4;
if contrib{i} ne . then do;
Period=cats("Qtr",i);
Amount=contrib{i};
output;
end;
end;
run;
i+1
PDV
Employee_ID Qtr1 Qtr2 Qtr3 Qtr4 i Period Amount
120265 . . . 25 5 Qtr4 25
work.rotate
Employee_ID Period Amount
120265 Qtr4 25
33
...

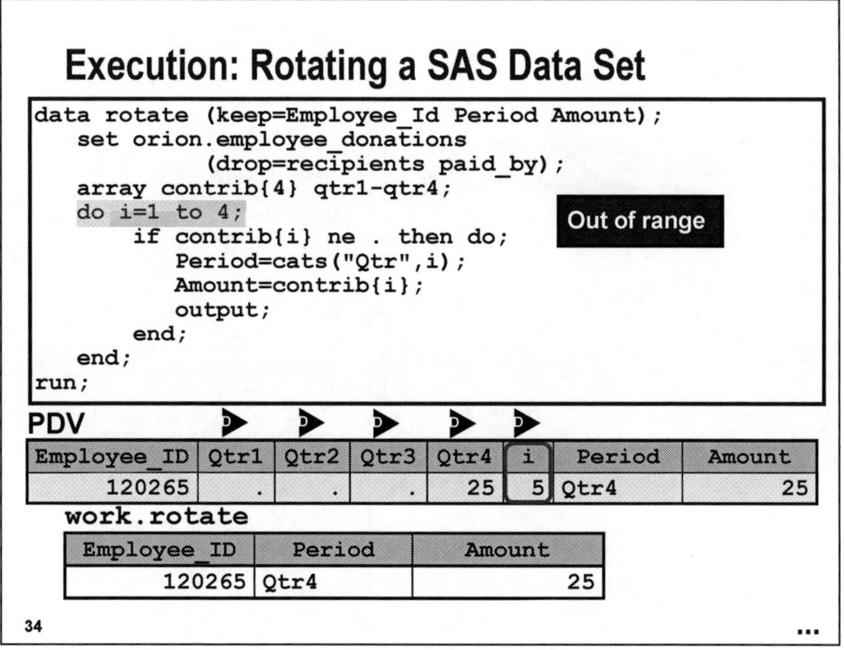
Execution: Rotating a SAS Data Set
data rotate (keep=Employee_Id Period Amount);
set orion.employee_donations
(drop=recipients paid_by);
array contrib{4} qtr1-qtr4;
do i=1 to 4;
if contrib{i} ne . then do;
Period=cats("Qtr",i);
Amount=contrib{i};
output;
end;
end;
run;
Out of range
PDV
Employee_ID Qtr1 Qtr2 Qtr3 Qtr4 i Period Amount
120265 . . . 25 5 Qtr4 25
work.rotate
Employee_ID Period Amount
120265 Qtr4 25
34
...

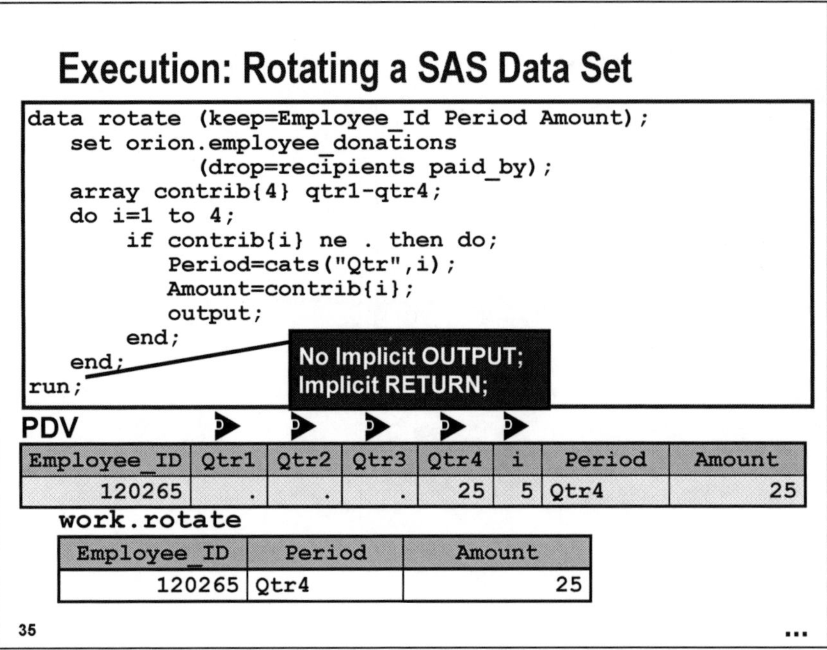
Execution: Rotating a SAS Data Set
data rotate (keep=Employee_Id Period Amount);
set orion.employee_donations
(drop=recipients paid_by);
array contrib{4} qtr1-qtr4;
do i=1 to 4;
if contrib{i} ne . then do;
Period=cats("Qtr",i);
Amount=contrib{i};
output;
end;
end;
run;
No Implicit OUTPUT;
Implicit RETURN;
PDV
Employee_ID Qtr1 Qtr2 Qtr3 Qtr4 i Period Amount
120265 . . . 25 5 Qtr4 25
work.rotate
Employee_ID Period Amount
120265 Qtr4 25
35

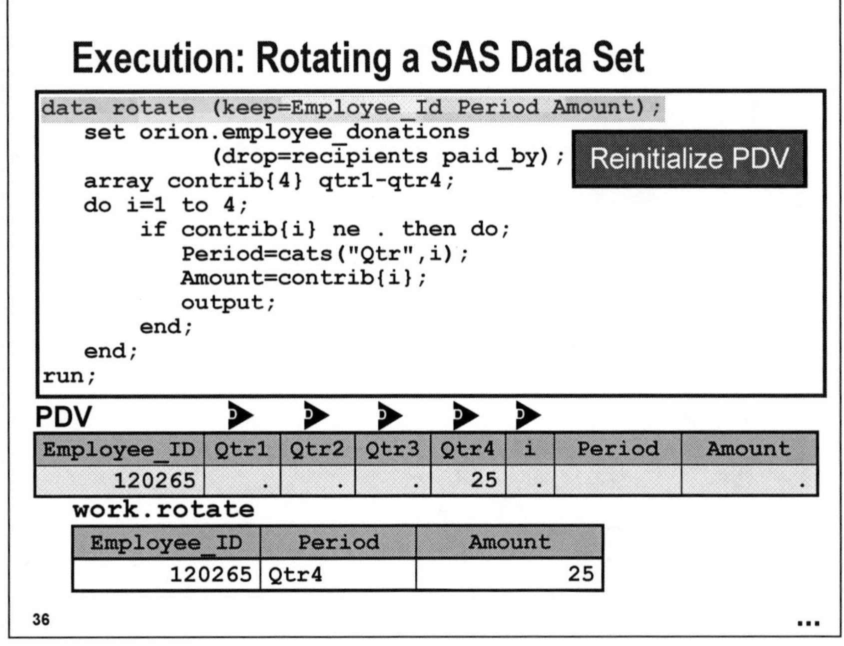
Execution: Rotating a SAS Data Set
data rotate (keep=Employee_Id Period Amount);
set orion.employee_donations
(drop=recipients paid_by);
Reinitialize PDV
array contrib{4} qtr1-qtr4;
do i=1 to 4;
if contrib{i} ne . then do;
Period=cats("Qtr",i);
Amount=contrib{i};
output;
end;
end;
run;
PDV
Employee_ID Qtr1 Qtr2 Qtr3 Qtr4 i Period Amount
120265 . . . 25 . .
work.rotate
Employee_ID Period Amount
120265 Qtr4 25
36

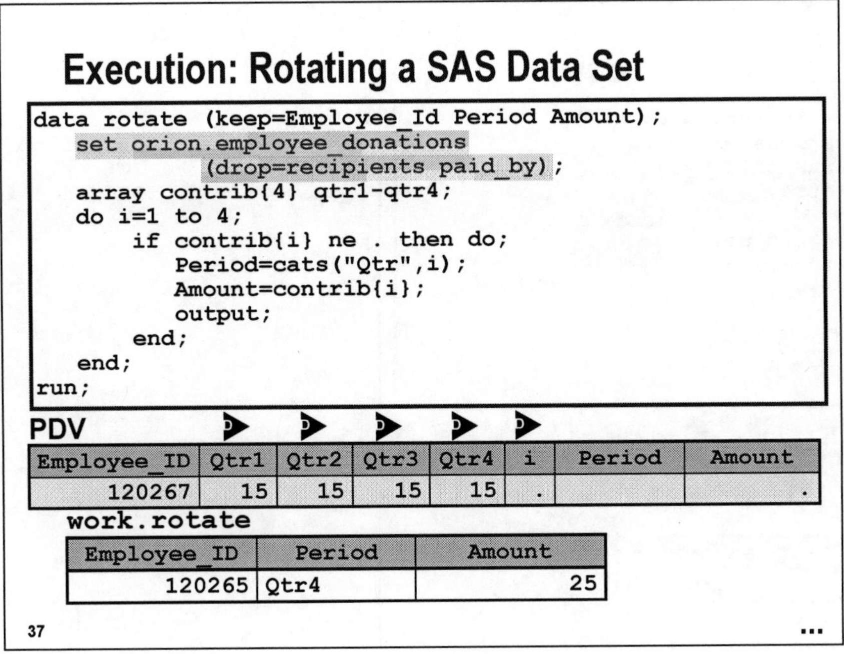
Execution: Rotating a SAS Data Set
data rotate (keep=Employee_Id Period Amount);
set orion.employee_donations
(drop=recipients paid_by);
array contrib{4} qtr1-qtr4;
do i=1 to 4;
if contrib{i} ne . then do;
Period=cats("Qtr",i);
Amount=contrib{i};
output;
end;
end;
run;
PDV
Employee_ID Qtr1 Qtr2 Qtr3 Qtr4 i Period Amount
120267 15 15 15 15 . .
work.rotate
Employee_ID Period Amount
120265 Qtr4 25
37

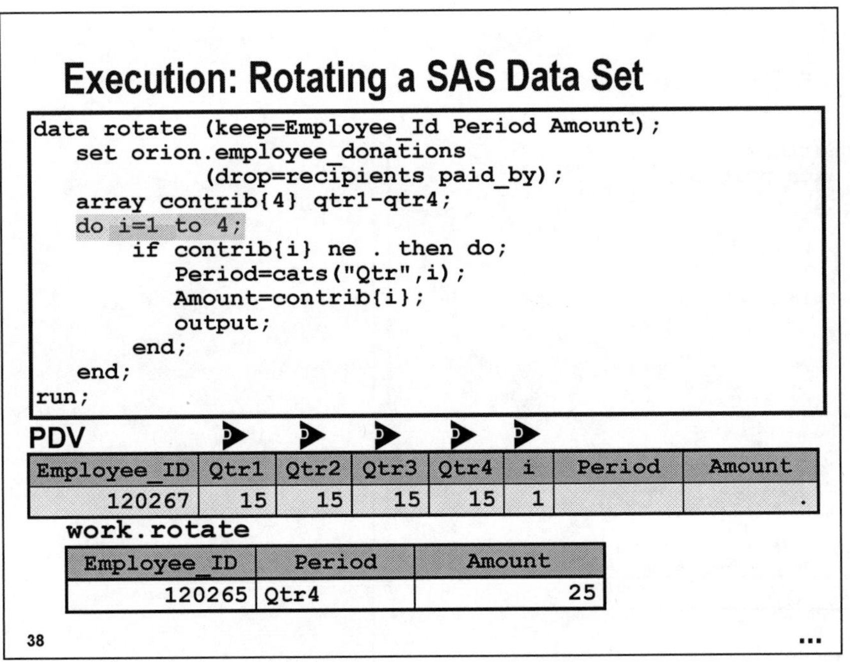
Execution: Rotating a SAS Data Set
data rotate (keep=Employee_Id Period Amount);
set orion.employee_donations
(drop=recipients paid_by);
array contrib{4} qtr1-qtr4;
do i=1 to 4;
if contrib{i} ne . then do;
Period=cats("Qtr",i);
Amount=contrib{i};
output;
end;
end;
run;
PDV
Employee_ID Qtr1 Qtr2 Qtr3 Qtr4 i Period Amount
120267 15 15 15 15 1 .
work.rotate
Employee_ID Period Amount
120265 Qtr4 25
38

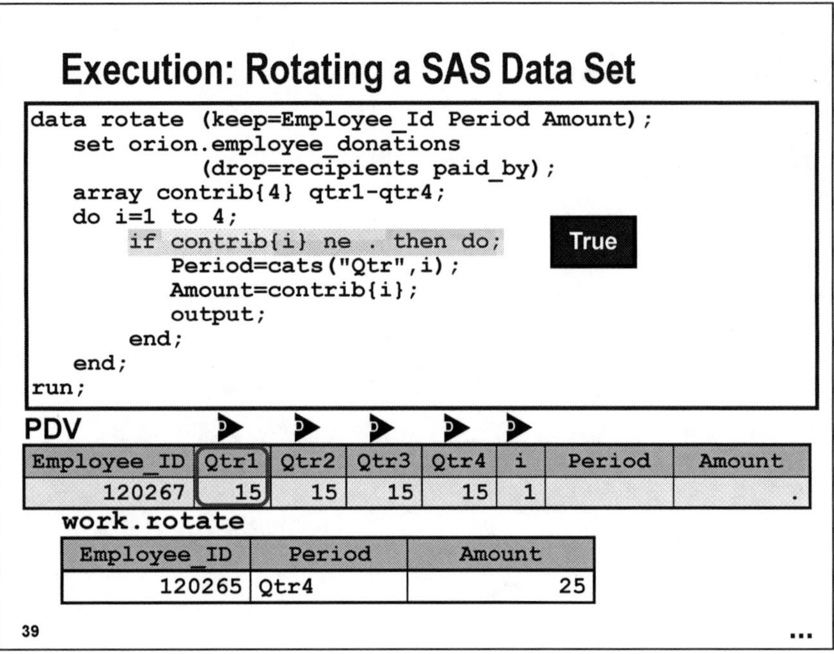
Execution: Rotating a SAS Data Set
data rotate (keep=Employee_Id Period Amount);
set orion.employee_donations
(drop=recipients paid_by);
array contrib{4} qtr1-qtr4;
do i=1 to 4;
if contrib{i} ne . then do;
Period=cats("Qtr",i);
Amount=contrib{i};
output;
end;
end;
run;
True
PDV
Employee_ID | Qtr1 | Qtr2 | Qtr3 | Qtr4 | i | Period | Amount
120267 | 15 | 15 | 15 | 15 | 1 | | .
work.rotate
Employee_ID | Period | Amount
120265 | Qtr4 | 25
39
...

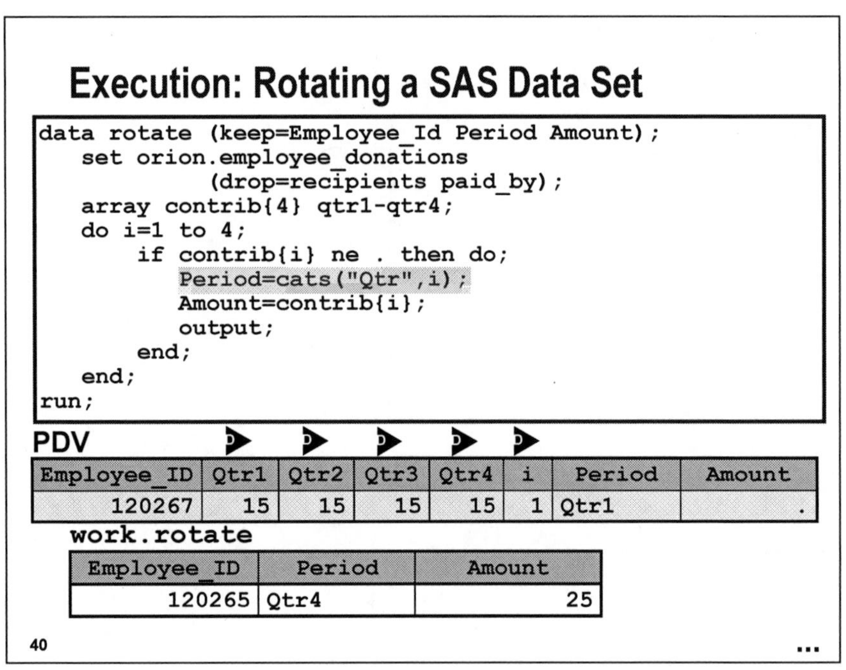
Execution: Rotating a SAS Data Set
data rotate (keep=Employee_Id Period Amount);
set orion.employee_donations
(drop=recipients paid_by);
array contrib{4} qtr1-qtr4;
do i=1 to 4;
if contrib{i} ne . then do;
Period=cats("Qtr",i);
Amount=contrib{i};
output;
end;
end;
run;
PDV
Employee_ID | Qtr1 | Qtr2 | Qtr3 | Qtr4 | i | Period | Amount
120267 | 15 | 15 | 15 | 15 | 1 | Qtr1 | .
work.rotate
Employee_ID | Period | Amount
120265 | Qtr4 | 25
40
...

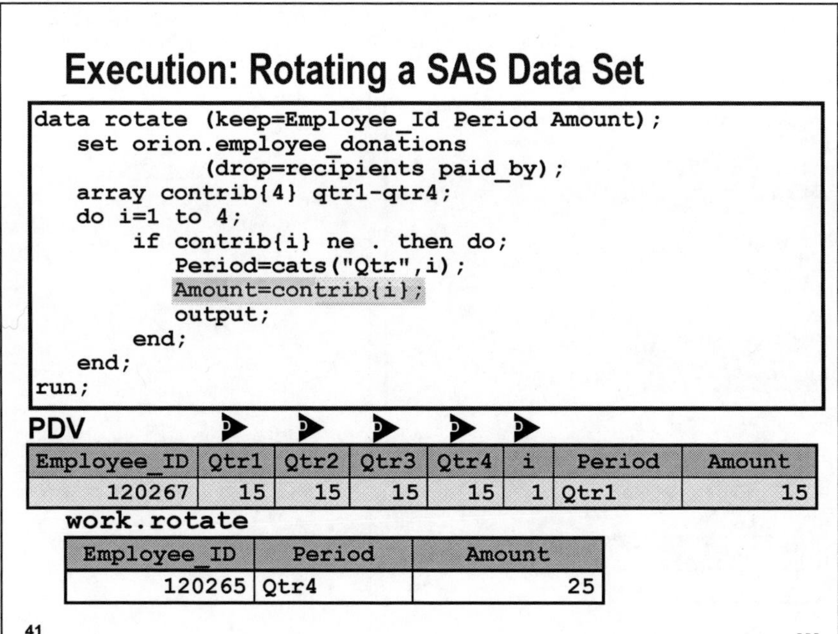
Execution: Rotating a SAS Data Set
data rotate (keep=Employee_Id Period Amount);
set orion.employee_donations
(drop=recipients paid_by);
array contrib{4} qtr1-qtr4;
do i=1 to 4;
if contrib{i} ne . then do;
Period=cats("Qtr",i);
Amount=contrib{i};
output;
end;
end;
run;
PDV
Employee_ID Qtr1 Qtr2 Qtr3 Qtr4 i Period Amount
120267 15 15 15 15 1 Qtr1 15
work.rotate
Employee_ID Period Amount
120265 Qtr4 25
41
...

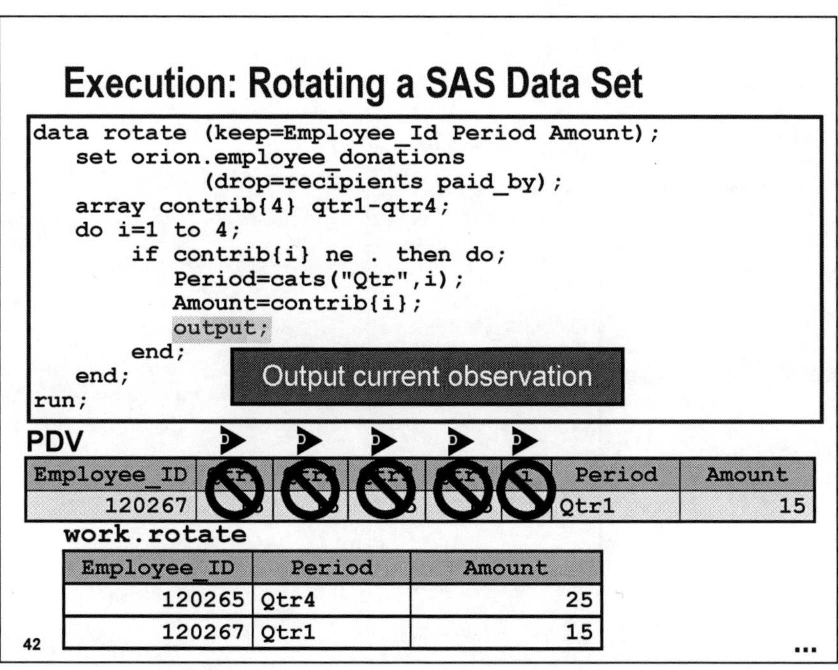
Execution: Rotating a SAS Data Set
data rotate (keep=Employee_Id Period Amount);
set orion.employee_donations
(drop=recipients paid_by);
array contrib{4} qtr1-qtr4;
do i=1 to 4;
if contrib{i} ne . then do;
Period=cats("Qtr",i);
Amount=contrib{i};
output;
end;
end;
run;
Output current observation
PDV
Employee_ID Period Amount
120267 Qtr1 15
work.rotate
Employee_ID Period Amount
120265 Qtr4 25
120267 Qtr1 15
42
...

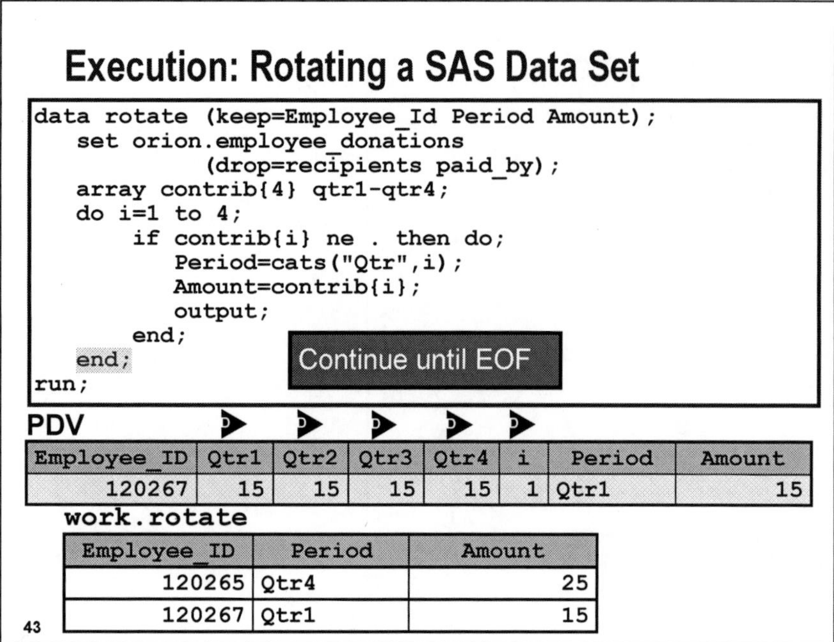

Output: The Rotate Data Set

```
proc print data=rotate;
run;
```

Partial PROC PRINT Output

Obs	Employee_ID	Period	Amount
1	120265	Qtr4	25
2	120267	Qtr1	15
3	120267	Qtr2	15
4	120267	Qtr3	15
5	120267	Qtr4	15
6	120269	Qtr1	20
7	120269	Qtr2	20
8	120269	Qtr3	20
9	120269	Qtr4	20
10	120270	Qtr1	20
11	120270	Qtr2	10
12	120270	Qtr3	5

44

p208d01

Analyzing the Rotated SAS Data Set

```
proc freq data=rotate;
   tables Period /nocum nopct;
run;
```

PROC FREQ Output

Period	Frequency
Qtr1	110
Qtr2	98
Qtr3	107
Qtr4	102

45 p208d01

Exercises

Level 1

1. Rotating a Data Set

The data set **orion.orders_midyear** contains an observation for each customer, with the total retail value of the customer's monthly orders for the first half of the year.

Partial Listing of **orion.orders_midyear** (24 Total Observations)

Obs	Customer_ID	Month1	Month2	Month3	Month4	Month5	Month6
1	5	213.10	.	478.0	525.80	394.35	191.79
2	10	188.10	414.09	2876.9	3164.59	2373.44	169.29
3	11	78.20	.	.	.	.	70.38
4	12	135.60	.	117.6	129.36	97.02	122.04
5	18	.	.	29.4	32.34	24.26	.
6	24	93.00	265.80	.	.	.	83.70
7	27	310.70	782.90	.	.	.	279.63
8	31	1484.30	293.30	.	.	.	1335.87
9	34	642.50	.	86.3	94.93	71.20	578.25
10	41	134.00	119.20	313.0	344.30	258.23	120.60

a. Rotate **orion.orders_midyear** to create an output data set, **sixmonths**, containing one observation per month for each customer.

- The data set should contain **Customer_ID**, **Month**, and **Sales**.
- Do not output an observation if the monthly total is missing.

b. Print the new data set. Verify the results.

Partial PROC PRINT Output (88 Total Observations)

Obs	Customer_ID	Month	Sales
1	5	1	213.10
2	5	3	478.00
3	5	4	525.80
4	5	5	394.35
5	5	6	191.79
6	10	1	188.10
7	10	2	414.09
8	10	3	2876.90
9	10	4	3164.59
10	10	5	2373.44
11	10	6	169.29
12	11	1	78.20
13	11	6	70.38

Level 2

2. Rotating a Data Set and Using a Lookup Table

The data set **orion.travel_expense** contains an observation for each employee business trip and includes a **Trip_ID**, the **Employee_ID**, and up to five expenses, **Exp1-Exp5**. The table below shows the type of each expense:

Exp1	Airfare
Exp2	Hotel
Exp3	Meals
Exp4	Transportation
Exp5	Miscellaneous

Listing of **orion.travel_expense**

Obs	Trip_ID	Employee_ ID	Exp1	Exp2	Exp3	Exp4	Exp5
1	1044-1	121044	345.97	568.54	235.00	320.00	.
2	0145-1	120145	256.00	675.90	343.25	125.00	67.50
3	0656-1	120656	312.26	.	236.98	325.00	45.00
4	1119-1	121119	597.80	780.99	345.87	195.00	50.75
5	0812-1	120812	345.24	865.45	534.20	430.50	76.75
6	0754-1	120754	456.00	677.40	348.90	.	67.00
7	0198-1	120198	.	175.90	173.25	167.40	65.50
8	0728-1	120728	256.00	675.00	215.25	205.00	95.50
9	0724-1	120724	.	.	343.85	125.45	61.18
10	1137-1	121137	564.90	345.87	267.50	120.00	50.00

a. Rotate **orion.travel_expense** to create an output data set named **travel** that contains one observation per nonmissing travel expense.

- The new data set should contain the variables **Trip_ID**, **Employee_ID**, **Expense_Type**, and **Amount**.
- Use two arrays in your solution: one to refer to each of the five expenses in an observation and a second array to store the expense types as a lookup table.

b. Print the new data set.

- Format **Amount** with dollar signs, commas, and two decimal places.
- Compare your results to the partial listing below.

Partial PROC PRINT Output (44 Total Observations)

Obs	Trip_ID	Employee_ ID	Expense_Type	Amount
1	1044-1	121044	Airfare	$345.97
2	1044-1	121044	Hotel	$568.54
3	1044-1	121044	Meals	$235.00
4	1044-1	121044	Transportation	$320.00
5	0145-1	120145	Airfare	$256.00
6	0145-1	120145	Hotel	$675.90
7	0145-1	120145	Meals	$343.25
8	0145-1	120145	Transportation	$125.00
9	0145-1	120145	Miscellaneous	$67.50
10	0656-1	120656	Airfare	$312.26

Level 3

3. Rotating a Data Set

The data set **orion.order_summary** contains monthly order information with multiple observations for each customer.

Partial Listing of **orion.order_summary** (101 Total Observations)

Customer_ID	Month	Sale_Amt
5	5	478.00
5	6	126.80
5	9	52.50
5	12	33.80
10	3	32.60
10	4	250.80
10	5	79.80
10	6	12.20
10	7	163.29
10	8	902.50

a. Rotate **orion.order_summary** to create an output data set named **customer_orders** that contains one observation for each customer.

- Use an array in a DATA step.
- The new data set should contain **Customer_ID**, and **Month1** through **Month12**.

b. Print the new data set. Verify the results.

Partial PROC PRINT Output (37 Total Observations)

Customer_ID	Month1	Month2	Month3	Month4	Month5	Month6	Month7 ...	Month 11	Month12
5	.	.	.	.	478.0	126.80	.	.	33.80
10	.	.	32.6	250.8	79.8	12.20	163.29	1894.60	143.30
11	.	.	.	.	.	.	.	.	.
12	.	117.6	.	.	.	48.40	.	.	.
18	.	29.4	.	.	.	.	.	.	.
24	195.6	.	46.9	.	.	.	70.20	.	.
27	174.4	.	140.7	205.0	.	91.60	403.50	.	.
31	.	.	64.2	57.3	.	609.00	.	.	760.80
34	.	.	.	.	.	642.50	.	86.30	.
41	.	36.2	.	.	19.9	.	89.80	239.30	.

8.2 Using the TRANSPOSE Procedure

Objectives

- Use the TRANSPOSE procedure to restructure a data set.

49

Business Scenario (Review)

The Orion Payroll Manager asked for a report showing the number of Orion Star employees who made charitable donations in each quarter.

Sketch of the Desired Report

Period	Frequency
Qtr1	56
Qtr2	99
Qtr3	24
Qtr4	75

50

Business Scenario – Review

The data set **orion.employee_donations** has a wide structure with one observation per employee (124 total observations).

Partial Listing of **orion.employee_donations**

Employee_ID	Qtr1	Qtr2	Qtr3	Qtr4	Paid_By
120265	.	.	.	25	Cash or Check
120267	15	15	15	15	Payroll Deduction
120269	20	20	20	20	Payroll Deduction

With a restructured, narrow data set, the FREQ procedure can be used to generate the desired output.

This example uses PROC TRANSPOSE to restructure the data.

51

Setup for the Poll

Open SAS Help and navigate to the PROC TRANSPOSE section:

SAS Products ⇨
Base SAS ⇨
Base SAS 9.2 Procedures Guide ⇨
Procedures ⇨
The Transpose Procedure ⇨
Overview: Transpose Procedure

Review the Overview section.

53

8.02 Multiple Answer Poll

Which of the following statements are true of the TRANSPOSE procedure?

a. It produces printed output.
b. It creates a new data set.
c. It often eliminates the need for a complex DATA step.
d. It transposes selected variables into observations.

54

The TRANSPOSE Procedure

General form of a PROC TRANSPOSE step:

```
PROC TRANSPOSE DATA=input-data-set
               <OUT=output-data-set>
               <NAME = variable-name>;
   <BY <DESCENDING> variable-1
     <...<DESCENDING> variable-n> <NOTSORTED>;>
   <VAR variable(s);>
   <ID variable;>
RUN;
```

NAME=	specifies a new name for the _NAME_ column. The values in this column identify the variable that supplied the values in the row.
BY	specifies the variable(s) to use to form BY groups.
VAR	specifies the variable(s) to transpose.
ID	specifies the variable whose values will become the new variables.

The BY statement requires that the data is sorted on the BY variable. The NOTSORTED option in the BY statement specifies that observations are not necessarily sorted in alphabetic or numeric order, but grouped in another way, such as chronological order. If you do not use the NOTSORTED option, then either the observations must be sorted by all the variables that you specify, or they must be indexed appropriately.

The COPY statement can be used to specify variables to be copied directly from the input data set to the output data set, without being transposed.

The TRANSPOSE Procedure

The TRANSPOSE procedure

- transposes selected variables into observations
- transposes numeric variables by default
- transposes character variables only if explicitly listed in a VAR statement.

57

Using the Transpose Procedure

Start with a simple PROC TRANSPOSE step:

```
proc transpose
     data=orion.employee_donations
     out=rotate2;
run;
```

Partial Listing of **rotate2**

NAME	_LABEL_	COL1	COL2	COL3	...	COL124
Employee_ID	Employee ID	120265	120267	120269		121147
Qtr1		.	15	20		10
Qtr2		.	15	20		10
Qtr3		.	15	20		10
Qtr4		25	15	20		10

The output is very different from the desired results. A row was created for each variable. A column was created for each of the 124 observations.

58 p208d02

Results of a Simple Transposition

Compare PROC TRANSPOSE output to the original data:

Partial Listing of **orion.employee_donations**

Employee_ID	Qtr1	Qtr2	Qtr3	Qtr4	Paid_By
120265	.	.	.	25	Cash or Check
120267	15	15	15	15	Payroll Deduction
120269	20	20	20	20	Payroll Deduction

Partial Listing of **rotate2**

NAME	_LABEL_	COL1	COL2	COL3	...	COL124
Employee_ID	Employee ID	120265	120267	120269		121147
Qtr1		.	15	20		10
Qtr2		.	15	20		10
Qtr3		.	15	20		10
Qtr4		25	15	20	.	10

All the numeric variables were transposed by default.

Paid_By, a character variable, was not transposed.

59

The **_LABEL_** column was created because permanent labels were defined in the input data set. This column is not included in the output if there are no labels in the input data set.

Results of a Simple Transposition

Partial Listing of **orion.employee_donations**

Employee_ID	Qtr1	Qtr2	Qtr3	Qtr4	Paid_By
120265	.	.	.	25	Cash or Check
120267	15	15	15	15	Payroll Deduction
120269	20	20	20	20	Payroll Deduction
120270	20	10	5	.	Cash or Check
120271	20	20	20	20	Payroll Deduction

Partial Listing of **rotate2**

NAME	_LABEL_	COL1	COL2	COL3	...	COL124
Employee_ID	Employee ID	120265	120267	120269		121147
Qtr1		.	15	20		10
Qtr2		.	15	20		10
Qtr3		.	15	20		10
Qtr4		25	15	20	.	10

Each observation (row) in the input data set becomes a variable (column) in the output data set.

60

PROC TRANSPOSE Results

The data should be grouped by **Employee_ID** with a separate observation for each transposed variable.

Partial Listing of **rotate2**

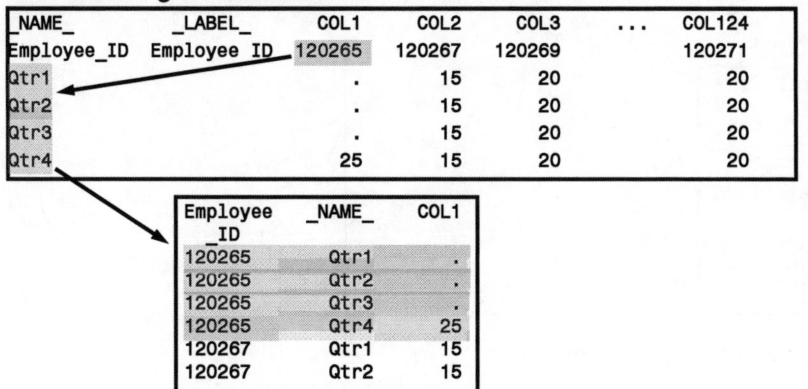

NAME	_LABEL_	COL1	COL2	COL3	...	COL124
Employee_ID	Employee ID	120265	120267	120269		120271
Qtr1		.	15	20		20
Qtr2		.	15	20		20
Qtr3		.	15	20		20
Qtr4		25	15	20		20

Employee _ID	_NAME_	COL1
120265	Qtr1	.
120265	Qtr2	.
120265	Qtr3	.
120265	Qtr4	25
120267	Qtr1	15
120267	Qtr2	15
...		

61

The BY Statement

Use a BY statement to group the output by **Employee_ID**.

```
proc transpose
     data=orion.employee_donations
     out=rotate2;
   by Employee_ID;
run;
proc print data=rotate2 noobs;
run;
```

All numeric variables other than the BY variable are transposed.

62 p208d03

Improved PROC TRANSPOSE Results

Use of the BY statement results in one observation for each transposed variable per **Employee_ID**, and includes missing values.

Partial PROC PRINT Output

```
Employee_ID    _NAME_    COL1

     120265     Qtr1        .
     120265     Qtr2        .
     120265     Qtr3        .
     120265     Qtr4       25
     120267     Qtr1       15
     120267     Qtr2       15
     120267     Qtr3       15
     120267     Qtr4       15
```

If there were additional numeric variables, an observation would be created for each.

63

The following example reads a data set, **work.donations**, with multiple observations for some employees, and an additional numeric variable, **Code**. It shows how PROC TRANSPOSE handles additional observations and variables.

Partial Listing of **work.donations**

Obs	Employee_ID	Qtr1	Qtr2	Qtr3	Qtr4	Code
1	120265	.	.	.	25	1001
2	120265	35	.	10	25	1011
3	120267	15	15	15	15	1002
4	120267	35	15	10	15	1012
5	120269	35	20	10	20	1013
6	120270	35	10	10	.	1014

```
   /* p207d03a */
proc transpose
     data=donations
     out=rotate3;
   by Employee_ID;
run;
proc print data=rotate3;
run;
```

Partial Listing of **rotate3**

Obs	Employee_ID	_NAME_	COL1	COL2
1	120265	Qtr1	.	35
2	120265	Qtr2	.	.
3	120265	Qtr3	.	10
4	120265	Qtr4	25	25
5	**120265**	**Code**	**1001**	**1011**
6	120267	Qtr1	15	35
7	120267	Qtr2	15	15
8	120267	Qtr3	15	10
9	120267	Qtr4	15	15
10	**120267**	**Code**	**1002**	**1012**
11	120269	Qtr1	35	.
12	120269	Qtr2	20	.
13	120269	Qtr3	10	.
14	120269	Qtr4	20	.
15	**120269**	**Code**	**1013**	**.**

The output contains two new variables, **COL1** and **COL2**. **COL1** has the values from the first observation for each employee; **COL2** has the values from the second observation for that employee. All numeric variables are transposed, including **Code**. The observations for **Code** are highlighted.

The VAR Statement

The VAR statement is used to specify which variables to transpose. It can include character and numeric variables.

```
proc transpose
     data=orion.employee_donations
     out=rotate2;
   by Employee_ID;
   var Qtr1-Qtr4;
run;
proc print data=rotate2 noobs;
run;
```

✎ The VAR statement has no effect in this example because **Qtr1-Qtr4** will be transposed by default.

64 p208d03b

Enhancing PROC TRANSPOSE Results

The final step is to change the default names of the new variables.

Partial PROC PRINT Output

Employee_ID	_NAME_	COL1
120265	Qtr1	.
120265	Qtr2	.
120265	Qtr3	.
120265	Qtr4	25
120267	Qtr1	15
120267	Qtr2	15
120267	Qtr3	15
120267	Qtr4	15

- Change **_NAME_** to **Period**.
- Change **COL1** to **Amount**.

65

Renaming Variables in PROC TRANSPOSE

```
proc transpose
        data=orion.employee_donations
        out=rotate2
        name=Period;
   by Employee_ID;
run;
proc print data=rotate2 noobs;
run;
```

The PROC TRANSPOSE option, NAME=, is used to rename _NAME_.

Partial Listing of **rotate2**

Employee_ID	Period	COL1
120265	Qtr1	.
120265	Qtr2	.
120265	Qtr3	.
120265	Qtr4	25
120267	Qtr1	15
120267	Qtr2	15

66

p208d04

Renaming Variables in PROC TRANSPOSE

```
proc transpose
        data=orion.employee_donations
        out=rotate2(rename=(col1=Amount))
        name=Period;
   by employee_id;
run;
proc print data=rotate2 noobs;
run;
```

The RENAME= data set option is used to change the name of COL1.

Partial Listing of **rotate2**

Employee_ID	Period	Amount
120265	Qtr1	.
120265	Qtr2	.
120265	Qtr3	.
120265	Qtr4	25
120267	Qtr1	15
120267	Qtr2	15

67

p208d04

...

 The data set option RENAME= can be used in place of the PROC TRANSPOSE NAME= option.

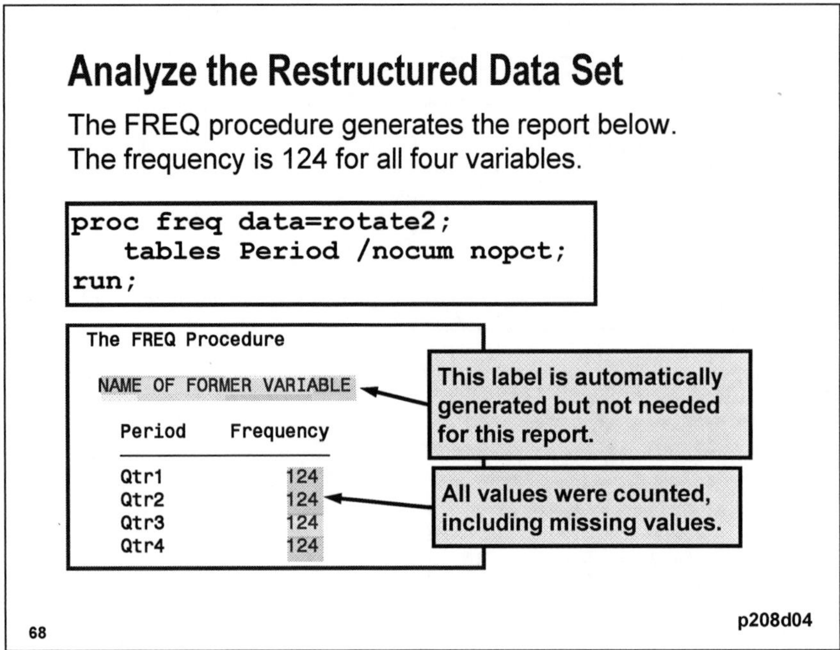

Analyze the Restructured Data Set
The FREQ procedure generates the report below.
The frequency is 124 for all four variables.
proc freq data=rotate2;
tables Period /nocum nopct;
run;
The FREQ Procedure
NAME OF FORMER VARIABLE
Period Frequency
Qtr1 124
Qtr2 124
Qtr3 124
Qtr4 124
This label is automatically generated but not needed for this report.
All values were counted, including missing values.
68
p208d04

PROC TRANSPOSE assigns the default label NAME OF FORMER VARIABLE to the **_NAME_** variable. In this example, **_NAME_** was renamed **Period**, but the label NAME OF FORMER VARIABLE still exists.

8.03 Quiz

Open **p208a01** and submit it. A LABEL statement was already added to suppress the label. Add a WHERE statement to select only observations with nonmissing **Amount** values.

```
proc freq data=rotate2;
   tables Period/nocum nopct;
   label Period=" ";
run;
```

70

p208a01

The WHERE= Data Set Option

The WHERE= data set option specifies conditions to use to subset a SAS data set.

General form of the WHERE= option:

SAS-data-set(WHERE=(*where-expression*))

The WHERE= option

- can be used on both input and output data sets
- applies only to the data set for which it is specified.

72

The WHERE statement can only be used on input data sets and applies to all input data sets. The WHERE= option can be used on a specific input or output data set.

The WHERE= Data Set Option

There is no option or statement in PROC TRANSPOSE to eliminate observations with missing values for the transposed variable. However, this can be achieved using a WHERE= data set option in the output data set.

```
proc transpose
        data=orion.employee_donations
        out=rotate2(rename=(col1=Amount)
                    where=(Amount ne .))
        name=Period;
   by employee_id;
run;
proc print data=rotate2 noobs;
run;
proc freq data=rotate2;
   tables Period/nocum nopct;
   label Period=" ";
run;
```

p208d05

73

No Missing Values

Partial PROC PRINT Output

Employee_ID	Period	Amount
120265	Qtr4	25
120267	Qtr1	15
120267	Qtr2	15
120267	Qtr3	15
120267	Qtr4	15
120269	Qtr1	20
120269	Qtr2	20
120269	Qtr3	20
120269	Qtr4	20
120270	Qtr1	20
120270	Qtr2	10
120270	Qtr3	5

PROC FREQ Output

The FREQ Procedure

Period	Frequency
Qtr1	110
Qtr2	98
Qtr3	107
Qtr4	102

The resulting data set has no missing values. Now PROC FREQ produces the desired results.

74

Business Scenario

The manager of Sales asked for a report showing monthly sales and a total for each customer.

Sketch of the Desired Report

Monthly Sales by Customer

Customer_ID	Month1	Month2	...	Month12	Total
1	1000	.		500	2000
2	.	.		200	750
3	1200	.		.	2200
4	500	150		350	1000
5	.	1000		.	2500

76

Business Scenario Considerations

The data set **orion.order_summary** contains an observation for each month in which a customer placed an order (101 total observations). The data set is sorted by **Customer_ID** and has no missing values.

Partial Listing of **orion.order_summary**

Customer_ID	Order_ Month	Sale_Amt
5	5	478.00
5	6	126.80
5	9	52.50
5	12	33.80
10	3	32.60
10	4	250.80
10	5	79.80
10	6	12.20
10	7	163.29

The number of observations per customer varies.

77

Business Scenario Considerations

The report requires rotating the columns into rows. Use PROC TRANSPOSE again to restructure the data set, and this time from narrow to wide.

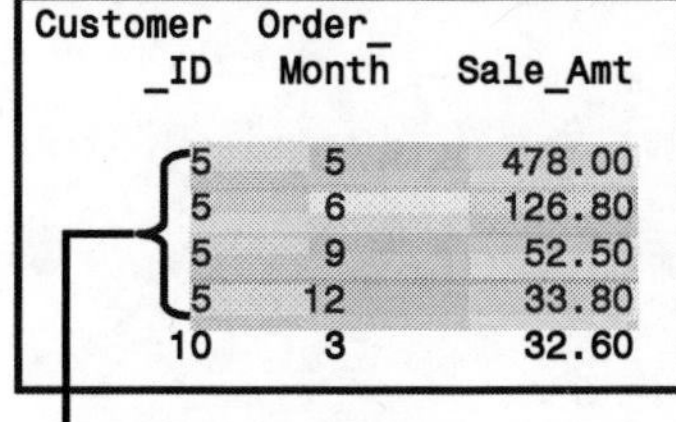

Customer _ID	Order_ Month	Sale_Amt
5	5	478.00
5	6	126.80
5	9	52.50
5	12	33.80
10	3	32.60

Desired Output

Customer_ ID	Month1	...	Month5	Month6	...	Month9	...	Month12
5	.		478.00	126.80		52.50		33.80

78

Using PROC TRANSPOSE

Start with a simple PROC TRANSPOSE.

Partial Listing of **orion.order_summary**

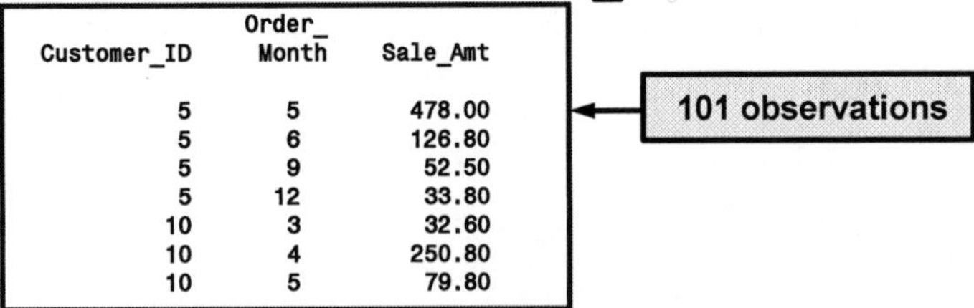

Customer_ID	Order_ Month	Sale_Amt
5	5	478.00
5	6	126.80
5	9	52.50
5	12	33.80
10	3	32.60
10	4	250.80
10	5	79.80

101 observations

```
proc transpose data=orion.order_summary
               out=annual_orders;
run;
proc print data=annual_orders noobs;
run;
```

79

p208d06

Using PROC TRANSPOSE

The resulting data set has three observations, one for each numeric variable in the input data set: **Customer_ID**, **Order_Month**, and **Sale_Amt**.

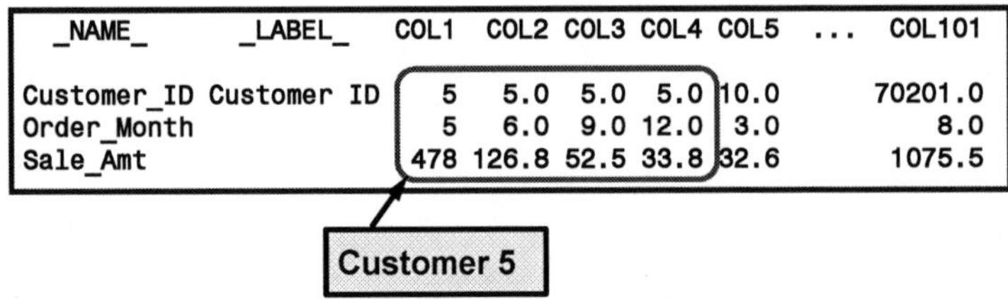

NAME	_LABEL_	COL1	COL2	COL3	COL4	COL5	...	COL101
Customer_ID	Customer ID	5	5.0	5.0	5.0	10.0		70201.0
Order_Month		5	6.0	9.0	12.0	3.0		8.0
Sale_Amt		478	126.8	52.5	33.8	32.6		1075.5

Customer 5

The variables **COL1**-**COL101** represent the 101 observations in the input data set.

Group the output by **Customer_ID**.

80

The BY Statement

The BY statement groups by **`Customer_ID`** and produces an observation for each transposed variable, **`Order_Month`** and **`Sale_Amt`**.

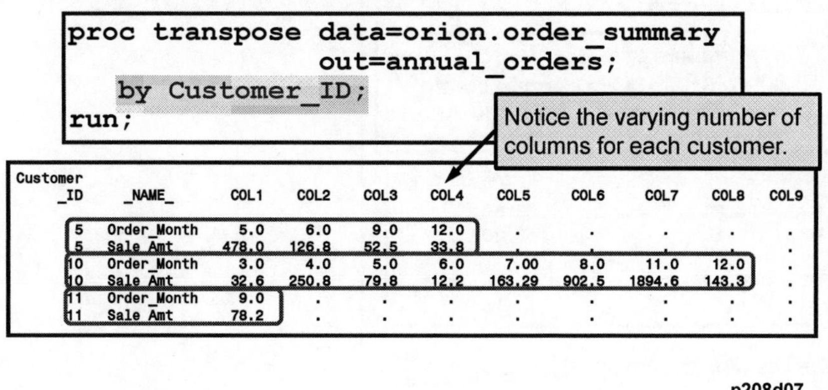

```
proc transpose data=orion.order_summary
               out=annual_orders;
   by Customer_ID;
run;
```


Customer _ID	_NAME_	COL1	COL2	COL3	COL4	COL5	COL6	COL7	COL8	COL9
5	Order_Month	5.0	6.0	9.0	12.0	.	.	.	.	.
5	Sale_Amt	478.0	126.8	52.5	33.8	.	.	.	.	.
10	Order_Month	3.0	4.0	5.0	6.0	7.00	8.0	11.0	12.0	.
10	Sale_Amt	32.6	250.8	79.8	12.2	163.29	902.5	1894.6	143.3	.
11	Order_Month	9.0	.	.	.	.	.	.	.	.
11	Sale_Amt	78.2	.	.	.	.	.	.	.	.

81

p208d07

Creating Columns Based on a Variable

Instead of transposing **`Order_Month`**, use its values to create new variables. A value of 5.0 represents orders placed in May, 6.0 represents orders placed in June, and so on.

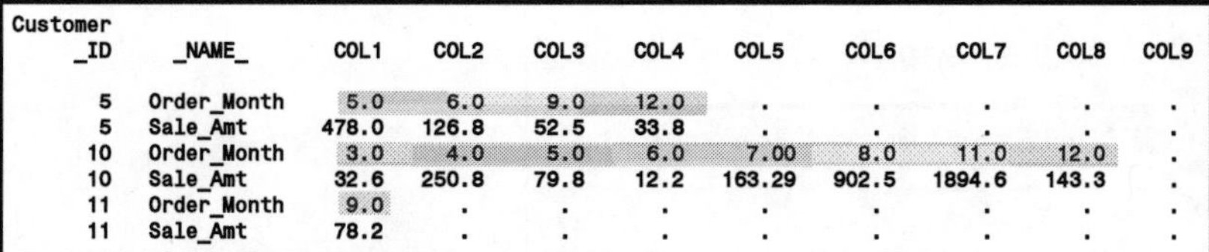

Customer _ID	_NAME_	COL1	COL2	COL3	COL4	COL5	COL6	COL7	COL8	COL9
5	Order_Month	5.0	6.0	9.0	12.0	.	.	.	.	.
5	Sale_Amt	478.0	126.8	52.5	33.8	.	.	.	.	.
10	Order_Month	3.0	4.0	5.0	6.0	7.00	8.0	11.0	12.0	.
10	Sale_Amt	32.6	250.8	79.8	12.2	163.29	902.5	1894.6	143.3	.
11	Order_Month	9.0	.	.	.	.	.	.	.	.
11	Sale_Amt	78.2	.	.	.	.	.	.	.	.

Add an ID statement.

82

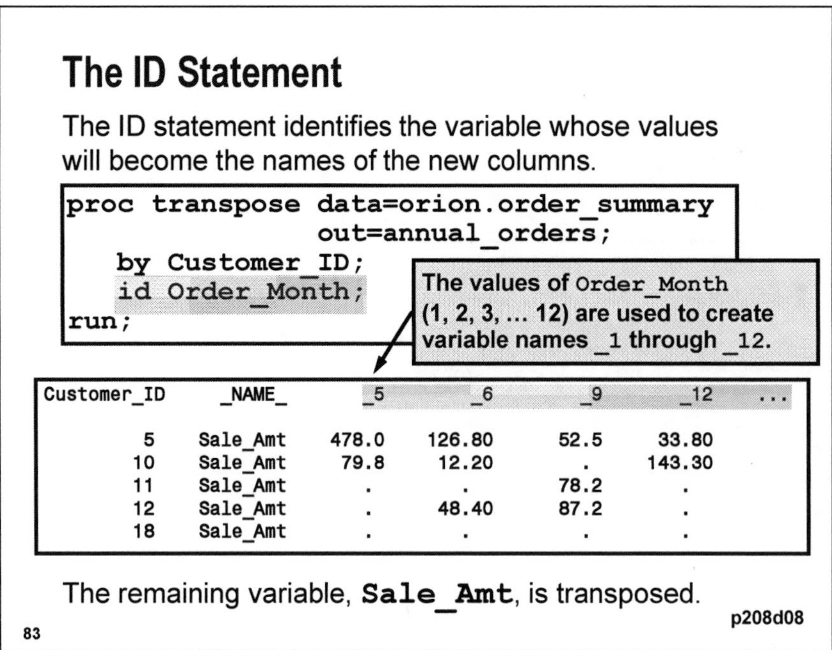

The ID Statement
The ID statement identifies the variable whose values will become the names of the new columns.
proc transpose data=orion.order_summary
out=annual_orders;
by Customer_ID;
id Order_Month;
run;
The values of Order_Month (1, 2, 3, ... 12) are used to create variable names _1 through _12.
Customer_ID _NAME_ _5 _6 _9 _12 ...
5 Sale_Amt 478.0 126.80 52.5 33.80
10 Sale_Amt 79.8 12.20 . 143.30
11 Sale_Amt . . 78.2 .
12 Sale_Amt . 48.40 87.2 .
18 Sale_Amt . . . .
The remaining variable, Sale_Amt, is transposed.
83
p208d08

The values of **Order_Month** become the names of the new variables in the output data set. Because **Order_Month** is numeric, its values are not valid SAS variable names. Each value is prefixed with an underscore to form a valid variable name. The values 1, 2, 3 become the variables **_1**, **_2**, **_3**, for example.

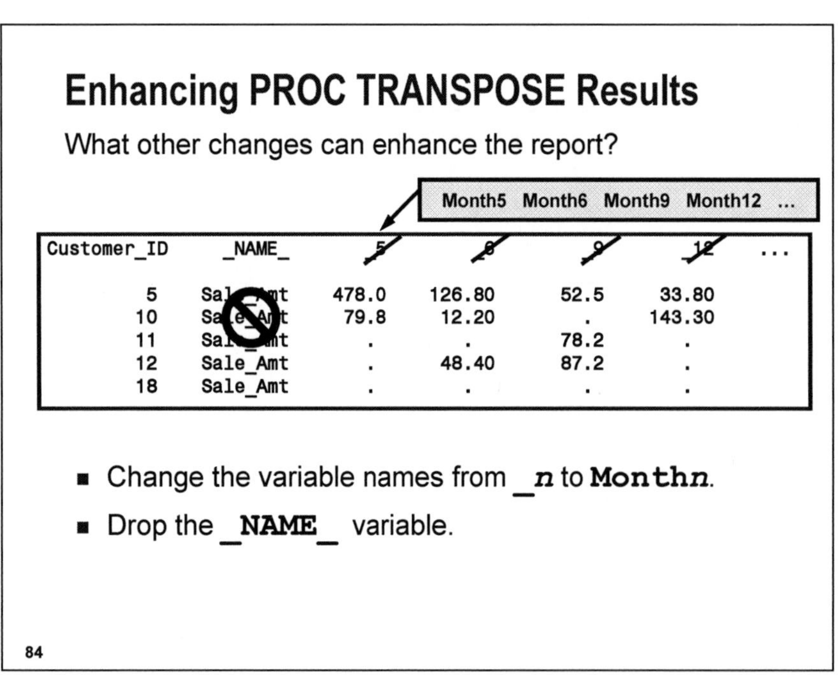

Enhancing PROC TRANSPOSE Results
What other changes can enhance the report?
Month5 Month6 Month9 Month12 ...
Customer_ID _NAME_ _5 _6 _9 _12 ...
5 Sale_Amt 478.0 126.80 52.5 33.80
10 Sale_Amt 79.8 12.20 . 143.30
11 Sale_Amt . . 78.2 .
12 Sale_Amt . 48.40 87.2 .
18 Sale_Amt . . . .
Change the variable names from _n to Monthn.
Drop the _NAME_ variable.
84

Changing the Variable Names

The PREFIX= option is used to set a prefix for each new variable name. The prefix replaces the underscore.

```
proc transpose data=orion.order_summary
               out=annual_orders
               prefix=Month;
     by Customer_ID;
     id Order_Month;
run;
```

Customer_ID	_NAME_	Month5	Month6	Month9	...
5	Sale_Amt	478.0	126.80	52.5	
10	Sale_Amt	79.8	12.20	.	
11	Sale_Amt	.	.	78.2	
12	Sale_Amt	.	48.40	87.2	
18	Sale_Amt	.	.	.	

85 p208d09

The variable _1 was changed to Month1, _2 was changed to Month2, and so on.

Dropping the _NAME_ Column

Use the DROP= data set option to drop the **_NAME_** variable.

```
proc transpose data=orion.order_summary
               out=annual_orders(drop=_name_)
               prefix=Month;
   by Customer_ID;
   id Order_Month;
run;
```

Customer_ID	Month5	Month6	Month9	Month12	Month3	...
5	478.0	126.80	52.5	33.80	.	
10	79.8	12.20	.	143.30	32.6	
11	.	.	78.2	.	.	
12	.	48.40	87.2	.	.	

86 p208d10

The PROC TRANSPOSE NAME= option or the RENAME= data set option can be used to rename **_NAME_**.

8.04 Quiz

Notice the column order in the PROC PRINT output. Why are the variables out of sequence?

Customer_ID	Month5	Month6	Month9	Month12	Month3	...
5	478.0	126.80	52.5	33.80	.	
10	79.8	12.20	.	143.30	32.6	
11	.	.	78.2	.	.	
12	.	48.40	87.2	.	.	

88

Print the Transposed Data Set

A VAR statement in the PRINT procedure specifies the desired order of the variables.

```
proc print data=annual_orders noobs;
   var Customer_ID Month1-Month12;
run;
```

Customer_ID	Month1	Month2	Month3	Month4	Month5	...
5	.	.	.	.	478.0	
10	.	.	32.6	250.8	79.8	
11	.	.	.	.	.	
12	.	117.6	.	.	.	
18	.	29.4	.	.	.	
24	195.6	.	46.9	.	.	
27	174.4	.	140.7	205.0	.	

90

p208d11

Reorder Data Set Variables (Self-Study)

The RETAIN statement can be used in a DATA step to permanently change the order of the variables in an existing data set.

```
data annual_orders;
     retain Customer_ID Month1-Month12;
     set annual_orders;
run;
```

The data set **annual_orders** is used for input and output.

⚠ It is recommended that no additional processing be performed in the DATA step

91 p208d12

The RETAIN statement is placed before the SET statement. This placement makes it the statement of first reference for the data set variables, and thus controls their positions in the PDV.

If new variables are also listed in the RETAIN statement, their values are retained from one iteration to the next. Normally new variables are reinitialized on every iteration. Retaining their values might generate undesirable results.

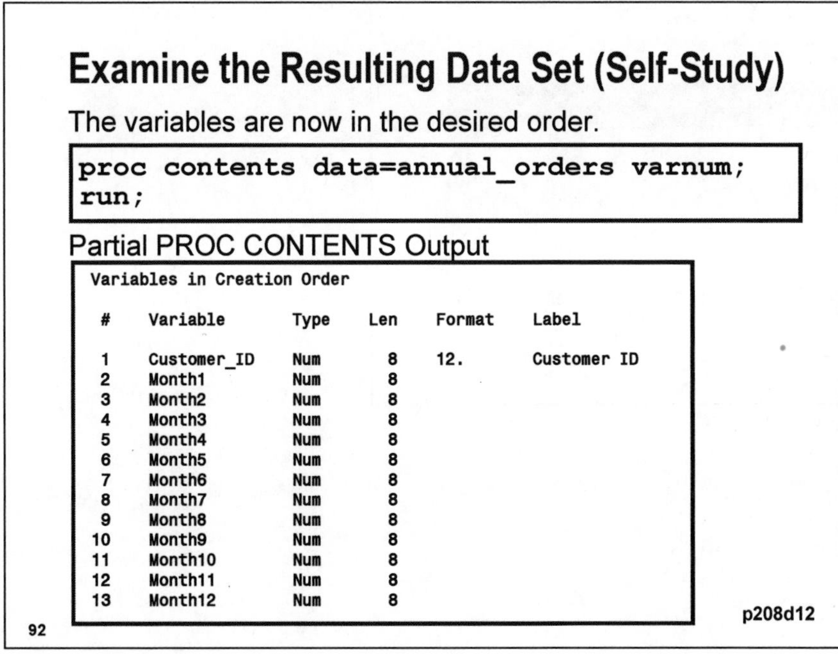

Examine the Resulting Data Set (Self-Study)

The variables are now in the desired order.

```
proc contents data=annual_orders varnum;
run;
```

Partial PROC CONTENTS Output

Variables in Creation Order

#	Variable	Type	Len	Format	Label
1	Customer_ID	Num	8	12.	Customer ID
2	Month1	Num	8		
3	Month2	Num	8		
4	Month3	Num	8		
5	Month4	Num	8		
6	Month5	Num	8		
7	Month6	Num	8		
8	Month7	Num	8		
9	Month8	Num	8		
10	Month9	Num	8		
11	Month10	Num	8		
12	Month11	Num	8		
13	Month12	Num	8		

92 p208d12

The VARNUM option lists the variables by their positions in the data set instead of listing them alphabetically.

Print the Resulting Data Set (Self-Study)

```
proc print data=annual_orders;
run;
```

Partial PROC PRINT Output

```
Customer_ID  Month1  Month2  Month3  Month4  Month5  ...

          5       .       .       .       .   478.0
         10       .       .    32.6   250.8    79.8
         11       .       .       .       .       .
         12       .   117.6       .       .       .
         18       .    29.4       .       .       .
         24   195.6       .    46.9       .       .
         27   174.4       .   140.7   205.0       .
```

93

p208d12

Advantages of Each Restructuring Method

The TRANSPOSE Procedure
Might eliminate the need for a complex DATA step
Requires very little code to restructure data

The DATA Step
Can create multiple data sets
Can direct output to data sets based on data set contributors
Enables First. and Last. processing
Enables complex data manipulation

94

Exercises

Level 1

4. Converting Observations to Variables

The data set **orion.orders_qtr1** contains an observation for each customer, with the customer's first quarter orders by month.

Partial Listing of **orion.orders_qtr1** (37 Total Observations)

Obs	Customer_ID	Month1	Month2	Month3
1	5	213.10	.	478.0
2	10	188.10	414.09	2876.9
3	11	78.20	.	.
4	12	135.60	.	117.6
5	18	.	.	29.4
6	24	93.00	265.80	.
7	27	310.70	782.90	.
8	31	1484.30	293.30	.
9	34	642.50	.	86.3
10	41	134.00	119.20	313.0
11	45	443.88	216.20	40.2
12	49	24.80	.	.

a. Use PROC TRANSPOSE to create an output data set containing multiple observations for each customer.

- Name the new data set **qtr1**.
- Name the new variables **Customer_ID**, **Month**, and **Sale_Amt** as shown below.

b. Print the new data set and verify your results.

Partial PROC PRINT Output (111 Total Observations)

Obs	Customer_ID	Month	Sale_Amt
1	5	Month1	213.10
2	5	Month2	.
3	5	Month3	478.00
4	10	Month1	188.10
5	10	Month2	414.09
6	10	Month3	2876.90
7	11	Month1	78.20
8	11	Month2	.
9	11	Month3	.
10	12	Month1	135.60
11	12	Month2	.
12	12	Month3	117.60

Level 2

5. Using PROC TRANSPOSE to Rotate Excel Data

The Excel spreadsheet Orion.xls contains an Order Summary tab, which has one row for each individual sale.

Partial Listing of Orion.xls Order Summary Tab (101 Total Observations)

Customer ID	Order Month	Sale Amt
00005	5	478.00
00005	6	126.80
00005	9	52.50
00005	12	33.80
00010	3	32.60
00010	4	250.80
00010	5	79.80
00010	6	12.20
00010	7	163.29
00010	8	902.50
00010	11	1,894.60
00010	12	143.30
00011	9	78.20

a. Use PROC TRANSPOSE to create a SAS data set, **cust_orders**, with one observation per customer.

- Submit a LIBNAME statement to access the Excel workbook.

```
libname Excel 'Orion.xls';
```

- Subset the input to read only observations with nonmissing **Customer_ID.** (Hint: Use the WHERE= data set option.)
- Include the variables **Month1**, **Month2**, and so on for each monthly order amount.

b. Print the new data set and verify your results.

1) Set the line size to **120**.

2) Display **Customer_ID** and **Month1** through **Month12**.

Partial PROC PRINT Output (37 Total Observations)

Obs	Customer_ ID	Month1	Month2	Month3	Month4	Month5	Month6	Month7	Month8	Month9
1	5	.	.	.	.	478.0	126.80	.	.	52.5
2	10	.	.	32.6	250.8	79.8	12.20	163.29	902.5	.
3	11	.	.	.	.	.	.	.	.	78.2
4	12	.	117.6	.	.	.	48.40	.	.	87.2
5	18	.	29.4	.	.	.	.	.	.	.
6	24	195.6	.	46.9	.	.	.	70.20	.	46.1
7	27	174.4	.	140.7	205.0	.	91.60	403.50	.	78.4
8	31	.	.	64.2	57.3	.	609.00	.	.	50.3
9	34	.	.	.	.	.	642.50	.	.	.
10	41	.	36.2	.	.	19.9	.	89.80	17.6	134.0
11	45	.	.	.	216.2	.	56.00	.	40.2	78.2
12	49	.	.	.	.	.	.	.	.	.

c. Restore the SAS settings.

1) Set the line size to **97**.

2) Clear the Excel libref.

Level 3

6. Transposing Multiple Variables

The data set **orion.monthly_donations** contains an observation for each employee's charitable contribution.

Use the TRANSPOSE procedure to restructure the input data set into the output data set. (Both shown below.)

- There are two variables that must be transposed: the numeric variable, **amount**, and the character variable, **acct_code**.
- Use two TRANSPOSE procedures followed by a merge.

Partial Listing of **orion.monthly_donations**

Employee_ ID	Qtr	Amount	Acct_ Code
11036	2	20	AQI2
11036	3	25	CCI2
11057	1	10	CS2
11057	2	10	CS2
11057	3	10	CS2

PROC PRINT Output

Employee_ ID	Qtr1	Qtr2	Qtr3	Qtr4	Account1	Account2	Account3	Account4
11036	.	20	25	.		AQI2	CCI2	
11057	10	10	10	.	CS2	CS2	CS2	
11608	50	.	50	.	ES2		AQ12	
11945	15	20	20	.	MI2	YYCR2	YYCR2	
12321	100	.	.	.	V22			
12325	.	.	.	125				V22
12447	35	35	35	35	ES2	ES2	ES2	ES2

8.3 Chapter Review

Chapter Review

1. Name two methods that can be used to restructure a data set.

2. What statement is used in PROC TRANSPOSE to group the data?

3. Which PROC TRANSPOSE statement names the variables to transpose?

4. Which PROC TRANSPOSE statement names the variable whose values are used to name the new columns?

97

continued...

Chapter Review

5. How can you keep PROC TRANSPOSE from writing observations with missing values?

6. Is there a PROC TRANSPOSE option to create the new columns in sequential order?

99

8.4 Solutions

Solutions to Exercises

1. Rotating a Data Set

a. Rotate **orion.orders_midyear** to create an output data set, **sixmonths**.

```
data sixmonths;
   set orion.orders_midyear;
   keep customer_id month sales;
   array months{6} month1-month6;
   do Month=1 to 6;
      if months{Month} ne . then do;
         Sales=months{Month};
         output;
      end;
   end;
run;
```

b. Print the new data set.

```
proc print data=sixmonths;
run;
```

2. Rotating a Data Set and Using a Lookup Table

a. Rotate **orion.travel_expense** to create an output data set, **travel**.

```
data travel;
   set orion.travel_expense;
   keep employee_id trip_id Expense_Type amount;
   array exp{5} exp1-exp5;
   array descr{5} $ 14 _temporary_ ('Airfare', 'Hotel', 'Meals',
                             'Transportation', 'Miscellaneous');
   do i=1 to 5;
      if exp{i} ne . then do;
         Expense_Type=descr{i};
         Amount=exp{i};
         output;
      end;
   end;
run;
```

b. Print the new data set.

```
proc print data=travel;
   format Amount dollar8.2;
run;
```

3. Rotating a Data Set

a. Rotate **orion.order_summary** to create an output data set, **customer_orders**, containing one observation for each customer.

```
data customer_orders;
     set orion.order_summary;
     retain Month1-Month12;
     array Month{12};
     by Customer_ID;
     if first.Customer_ID then call missing(of Month{*});
     Month{Order_month}=Sale_Amt;
     if last.Customer_ID;
     drop Order_Month Sale_Amt;
run;
```

b. Print the new data set. Verify the results.

```
options ls=120;
proc print data=customer_orders noobs;
run;
```

4. Converting Observations to Variables

a. Use PROC TRANSPOSE to create an output data set containing one observation per month.

```
proc transpose data=orion.orders_qtr1
               out=qtr1 (rename=(col1=Sale_Amt))
               name=Month;
   by customer_id;
run;
```

b. Print the new data set.

```
proc print data=qtr1;
run;
```

5. Using PROC TRANSPOSE to Rotate Excel Data

a. Use PROC TRANSPOSE to create a new data set that contains one observation per customer.

```
libname Excel 'Orion.xls';
options ls=120;
proc transpose data=Excel.'Order Summary$'n
                            (where=(Customer_ID is not missing))
               out=Cust_Orders (drop=_name_ _label_)
               prefix=Month;
   by Customer_Id;
     id Order_Month;
   var Sale_Amt;
run;
```

b. Print the new data set and verify your results.

```
proc print data=Cust_Orders;
   var customer_id month1-month12;
run;
```

c. Restore the SAS settings.

```
options ls=97;
libname Excel clear;
```

6. Transposing Multiple Variables

Use the TRANSPOSE procedure to restructure the **orion.monthly_donations** data set.

```
  /* Step 1 - Transpose the amount variable */

proc transpose data=orion.monthly_donations
               out=donations(drop=_name_ _label_)
               prefix=Qtr;
   var amount ;
   id qtr;
   by employee_id ;
run;
proc print data=donations;
run;
  /* Step 2 - Transpose the acct_code variable. */

proc transpose data=orion.monthly_donations
               out=accts(drop=_name_ _label_)
               prefix=account;
   var acct_code;
   by employee_id;
   id qtr;
run;
proc print data=accts;
run;

  /* Step 3 - Merge the two transposed datasets to get the final
     result */

data final;
   merge donations accts;
   by employee_id;
run;
proc print data=final;
   var Employee_id Qtr1-Qtr4 Account1-Account4;
run;
```

Solutions to Student Activities (Polls/Quizzes)

8.01 Quiz – Correct Answer

Which data set structure is more appropriate for using PROC FREQ to determine the number of charitable donations made in each of the 4 quarters (`Qtr1– Qtr4`)?

Proposed SAS program

```
proc freq data=b;
   tables Period /nocum nopct;
run;
```

(b.)

Employee_ID	Period	Amount
120265	Qtr4	25
120267	Qtr1	15
120267	Qtr2	15
120267	Qtr3	15
120267	Qtr4	15
120269	Qtr1	20
120269	Qtr2	20

PROC FREQ Output

The FREQ Procedure

Period	Frequency
Qtr1	2
Qtr2	2
Qtr3	1
Qtr4	2

11

8.02 Multiple Answer Poll – Correct Answers

Which of the following statements are true of the TRANSPOSE procedure?

a. It produces printed output.
(b.) It creates a new data set.
(c.) It often eliminates the need for a complex DATA step.
(d.) It transposes selected variables into observations.

55

8.03 Quiz – Correct Answer

Any of the following WHERE statements can be used to select observations with nonmissing **Amount** values.

```
where Amount ne .;

where Amount is not missing;

where Amount is not null;
```

```
proc freq data=rotate2;
   where Amount ne .;
   tables Period/nocum nopct;
   label Period=" ";
run;
```

PROC FREQ Output

The FREQ Procedure

Period	Frequency
Qtr1	110
Qtr2	98
Qtr3	107
Qtr4	102

71

p208a01s

8.04 Quiz – Correct Answer

Notice the column order in the PROC PRINT output. Why are the variables out of sequence?

Customer_ID	Month5	Month6	Month9	Month12	Month3	...
5	478.0	126.80	52.5	33.80	.	
10	79.8	12.20	.	143.30	32.6	
11	.	.	78.2	.	.	
12	.	48.40	87.2	.	.	

Partial Listing of **orion.order_summary**

Customer_ID	Order_ Month	Sale_Amt
5	5	478.00
5	6	126.80
5	9	52.50
5	12	33.80
10	3	32.60

The variables were created in the order that they appeared in the input data set.

89

Solutions to Chapter Review

Chapter Review Answers

1. Name two methods that can be used to restructure a data set.

   In a DATA step or using PROC TRANSPOSE

2. What statement is used in PROC TRANSPOSE to group the data?

   The BY statement

3. Which PROC TRANSPOSE statement names the variables to transpose?

   The VAR statement

4. Which PROC TRANSPOSE statement names the variable whose values are used to name the new columns?

   The ID statement

98

continued...

Chapter Review Answers

5. How can you keep PROC TRANSPOSE from writing observations with missing values?

   Use the WHERE= data set option on the output data set.

6. Is there a PROC TRANSPOSE option to create the new columns in sequential order?

   No. A DATA step can be used to re-order the columns.

100

Chapter 9 Combining SAS Data Sets

9.1 Using Data Manipulation Techniques with Match-Merging 9-3

Demonstration: Match-Merging Data Sets That Lack a Common Variable 9-14

Exercises 9-22

9.2 Chapter Review 9-27

9.3 Solutions 9-28

Solutions to Exercises 9-28

Solutions to Student Activities (Polls/Quizzes) 9-30

Solutions to Chapter Review 9-33

9.1 Using Data Manipulation Techniques with Match-Merging

Objectives

- Review match-merging of SAS data sets.
- Show examples of data manipulation techniques used with match-merging.
- Show techniques to perform a match-merge for these special cases:
  - three or more SAS data sets that lack a single common variable
  - variable names that need to be altered to obtain the correct merge results.

2

Match-Merging (Review)

Match-merging combines observations from one or more SAS data sets into a single observation in a new data set, based on the values of one or more common variables.

```
proc sort data=orion.order_fact
          out=work.order_fact;
   by Customer_ID;
   where year(Order_Date)=2007;
run;

data CustOrd;
   merge orion.customer
         work.order_fact;
   by Customer_ID;
run;
```

Customers of Orion Star

Products ordered by Orion Star customers in year 2007

p209d01

3

9.01 Multiple Choice Poll

Which statement is true concerning match-merging?

a. The MERGE statement must refer to permanent data sets.
b. The variables in the BY statement can only be in one of the data sets.
c. Only two data sets can be specified in the MERGE statement.
d. When you use the MERGE statement with the BY statement, the data must be sorted or indexed on the BY variable.

5

Match-Merging (Review)

Partial SAS Log

```
proc sort data=orion.order_fact
          out=work.order_fact;
   by Customer_ID;
   where year(Order_Date)=2007;
run;

NOTE: There were 148 observations read from the data set ORION.ORDER_FACT.
      WHERE YEAR(Order_Date)=2007;
NOTE: The data set WORK.ORDER_FACT has 148 observations and 12 variables.

data CustOrd;
   merge orion.customer
         work.order_fact;
   by Customer_ID;
run;

NOTE: There were 77 observations read from the data set ORION.CUSTOMER.
NOTE: There were 148 observations read from the data set WORK.ORDER_FACT.
NOTE: The data set WORK.CUSTORD has 188 observations and 22 variables.
```

The output data set contains both matches and nonmatches; therefore, it has more observations than either input data set.

7

Match-Merging (Review)

By default, match-merging produces matches and nonmatches.

Partial PROC PRINT Output:

Obs	Customer_Name	Gender	Quantity	Total_Retail_ Price
159	Rita Lotz	F	1	$113.20
160	Bill Cuddy	M	.	.
161	Avinoam Zweig	M	.	.
162	Avinoam Zweig	M	2	$80.40
163	Avinoam Zweig	M	2	$114.20
164	Eyal Bloch	M	.	.
165	Susan Krasowski	F	1	$121.00

The highlighted text represents the matches, which means that both data sets contributed to these observations.

How can you keep only the matches?

8

Match-Merging (Review)

The IN= data set option creates a variable that can be used to identify matches and nonmatches. The variable is initialized to zero and is set to one when the data set contributes to the current observation.

```
data CustOrd;
   merge orion.customer(in=cust)
         work.order_fact(in=order);
   by Customer_ID;
   if cust=1 and order=1;
run;
```

This program writes observations for matches only.

Partial SAS Log

```
NOTE: There were 77 observations read from the data set ORION.CUSTOMER.
NOTE: There were 148 observations read from the data set WORK.ORDER_FACT.
NOTE: The data set WORK.CUSTORD has 148 observations and 22 variables.
```

9 p209d01

9.02 Quiz

Write the appropriate IF statement to create the desired data set containing only nonmatches.

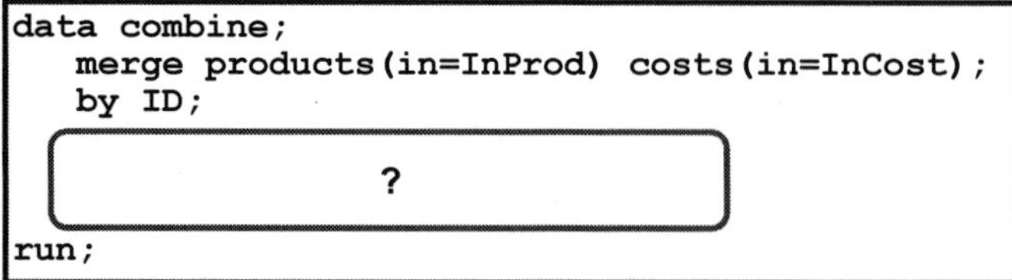

data combine;
merge products(in=InProd) costs(in=InCost);
by ID;
?
run;

Products

Product	ID
XYZ Shoe	A123
ABC Coat	B456

+

Costs

ID	Cost
B456	59.99
C789	35.75

=

Combine

Product	ID	Cost
XYZ Shoe	A123	
	C789	35.75

11

Using Data Manipulation Techniques

For this business scenario, the following techniques are needed, along with a DATA step that performs a match-merge:

- OUTPUT statement
- DROP= and KEEP= options
- First. and Last. variables
- sum statement

The techniques will be added one at a time to show how the final solution can be built and tested in small steps.

16

OUTPUT Statement

In this program, the OUTPUT statement is used to direct customers with matching orders to one data set, and customers with no orders to another data set.

```
data orders noorders;
   merge orion.customer
         work.order_fact(in=order);
   by Customer_ID;
   if order=1 then output orders;
   else output noorders;
run;
```

Partial SAS Log

```
NOTE: There were 77 observations read from the data set ORION.CUSTOMER.
NOTE: There were 148 observations read from the data set WORK.ORDER_FACT.
NOTE: The data set WORK.ORDERS has 148 observations and 22 variables.
NOTE: The data set WORK.NOORDERS has 40 observations and 22 variables.
```

17

p209d02

DROP= and KEEP= Options

The DROP= and KEEP= data set options can be used to determine which variables are written to each output data set.

```
data orders(keep=Customer_Name Quantity
              Product_ID  Total_Retail_Price)
     noorders(keep=Customer_Name Birth_Date);
   merge orion.customer
         work.order_fact(in=order);
   by Customer_ID;
   if order=1 then output orders;
   else output noorders;
run;
```

Partial SAS Log

```
NOTE: The data set WORK.ORDERS has 148 observations and 4 variables.
NOTE: The data set WORK.NOORDERS has 40 observations and 2 variables.
```

18

p209d02

9.03 Quiz

What two temporary variables are created due to the BY statement?

```
data orders(keep=Customer_Name Quantity
              Product_ID Total_Retail_Price)
     noorders(keep=Customer_Name Birth_Date);
   merge orion.customer
         work.order_fact(in=order);
   by Customer_ID;
   if order=1 then output orders;
   else output noorders;
run;
```

20

First. and Last. Variables and Sum Statement

The First. and Last. variables along with the sum statement can be used to create the values for the **summary** data set.

```
data orders(keep=Customer_Name Quantity
              Product_ID Total_Retail_Price)
     noorders(keep=Customer_Name Birth_Date)
     summary(keep=Customer_Name NumOrders);
   merge orion.customer
         work.order_fact(in=order);
   by Customer_ID;
   if order=1 then do;
      output orders;
      if first.Customer_ID then NumOrders=0;
      NumOrders+1;
      if last.Customer_ID then output summary;
   end;
   else output noorders;
run;
```

22 p209d02

Business Scenario – Final Results

noorders contains the names and birthdates of customers who did not place an order.

Partial Listing of **noorders** (40 observations total)

Customer_Name	Birth_ Date
James Kvarniq	27JUN1974
Cornelia Krahl	27FEB1974
Markus Sepke	21JUL1988
Ulrich Heyde	16JAN1939
Jimmie Evans	17AUG1954
Oliver S. Füßling	23FEB1964
Michael Dineley	17APR1959
Tulio Devereaux	02DEC1949
Candy Kinsey	08JUL1934
Rolf Robak	24FEB1939

23

Business Scenario – Final Results

orders contains orders, including customer name, ID of the product ordered, quantity, and price.

Partial Listing of **orders** (140 observations total)

Customer_Name	Product_ID	Quantity	Total_Retail_ Price
Sandrina Stephano	240100100159	1	$31.40
Sandrina Stephano	230100200029	2	$446.60
Sandrina Stephano	220200100009	2	$126.80
Sandrina Stephano	210200500016	1	$52.50
Sandrina Stephano	220101400130	2	$33.80
Karen Ballinger	220100100235	1	$32.60
Karen Ballinger	220100300037	2	$231.60
Karen Ballinger	220101400032	2	$19.20
Karen Ballinger	240700100004	3	$79.80
Karen Ballinger	230100400007	1	$12.20

24

Business Scenario – Final Results

summary contains a count of the orders placed by each customer.

Partial Listing of **summary** (37 observations total)

Customer_Name	Number Orders
Sandrina Stephano	5
Karen Ballinger	19
Elke Wallstab	1
David Black	3
Tonie Asmussen	1
Robyn Klem	4
Cynthia Mccluney	8
Cynthia Martinez	11
Alvan Goheen	3
Wendell Summersby	9

25

Special Cases

Show techniques to perform a match-merge for these special cases:

- Three or more SAS data sets that lack a common variable
- Variable names that need to be altered to get the correct merge results

27

Multiple Data Sets without a Common Variable

The following report needs to be created using data from three data sets.

Partial PROC PRINT Output

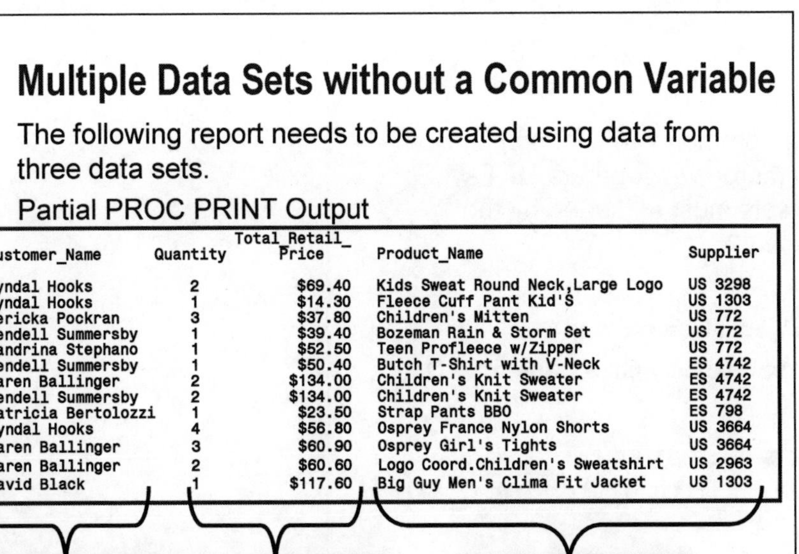

Customer_Name	Quantity	Total_Retail_ Price	Product_Name	Supplier
Kyndal Hooks	2	$69.40	Kids Sweat Round Neck,Large Logo	US 3298
Kyndal Hooks	1	$14.30	Fleece Cuff Pant Kid'S	US 1303
Dericka Pockran	3	$37.80	Children's Mitten	US 772
Wendell Summersby	1	$39.40	Bozeman Rain & Storm Set	US 772
Sandrina Stephano	1	$52.50	Teen Profleece w/Zipper	US 772
Wendell Summersby	1	$50.40	Butch T-Shirt with V-Neck	ES 4742
Karen Ballinger	2	$134.00	Children's Knit Sweater	ES 4742
Wendell Summersby	2	$134.00	Children's Knit Sweater	ES 4742
Patricia Bertolozzi	1	$23.50	Strap Pants BBO	ES 798
Kyndal Hooks	4	$56.80	Osprey France Nylon Shorts	US 3664
Karen Ballinger	3	$60.90	Osprey Girl's Tights	US 3664
Karen Ballinger	2	$60.60	Logo Coord.Children's Sweatshirt	US 2963
David Black	1	$117.60	Big Guy Men's Clima Fit Jacket	US 1303

28

9.04 Quiz

Any number of data sets can be merged in a single DATA step. However, the data sets must have a common variable and be sorted by that variable.

Do the following data sets have a common variable?

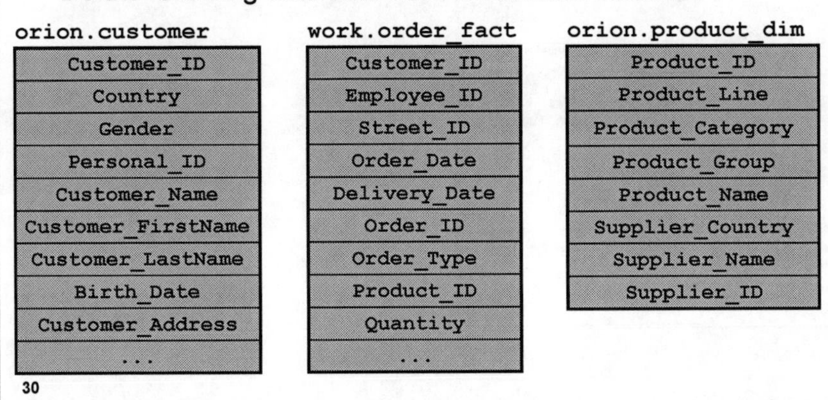

30

Match-Merge without a Common Variable

If data sets do not share a common variable, combine them by using a series of merges in separate DATA steps. As usual, the data sets must be sorted by the appropriate BY variable.

Step 1: Merge **orion.customer** and **work.order_fact** by **Customer_ID**.

Step 2: Merge the results of Step1 and **orion.product_dim** by **Product_ID**.

32

Without a Common Variable – Step 1

Merge **orion.customer** and **work.order_fact** by **Customer_ID**.

```
proc sort data=orion.order_fact
          out=work.order_fact;
   by Customer_ID;
   where year(Order_Date)=2007;
run;

data CustOrd;
   merge orion.customer(in=cust)
         work.order_fact(in=order);
   by Customer_ID;
   if cust=1 and order=1;
   keep Customer_ID Customer_Name Quantity
        Total_Retail_Price Product_ID;
run;
```

orion.customer is in order by Customer_ID

33 p209d03

Without a Common Variable – Step 2

Merge the results of Step 1, **CustOrd**, with **orion.product_dim** by **Product_ID**.

```
proc sort data=CustOrd;
   by Product_ID;
run;

data CustOrdProd;
   merge CustOrd(in=ord)
         orion.product_dim(in=prod);
   by Product_ID;
   if ord=1 and prod=1;
   Supplier=catx(' ',Supplier_Country,Supplier_ID);
   keep Customer_Name Quantity
        Total_Retail_Price Product_Name Supplier;
run;
```

Product_dim is in order by Product_ID

34

p209d03

Match-Merging Data Sets That Lack a Common Variable

p209d03

1. Perform a match-merge on three data sets: **orion.customer**, **orion.order_fact**, and **orion.product_dim**.. The first two data sets have **Customer_ID** as a common variable. The last two data sets have **Product_ID** as a common variable. Data is needed from all three data sets, and multiple merges are required.

2. Submit Step 1. It sorts **orion.order_fact** by **Customer_ID**, creating **work.order_fact**. The DATA step match-merges the output from the sort, **work.order_fact**, with **orion.customer** by **Customer_ID**. The variable **Product_ID** is kept in the new data set so that it can be match-merged with **orion.product_dim** in the next step.

```
*** Step 1 **************************************************;
proc sort data=orion.order_fact
          out=work.order_fact;
   by Customer_ID;
   where year(Order_Date)=2007;
run;

data CustOrd;
   merge orion.customer(in=cust)
         work.order_fact(in=order);
   by Customer_ID;
   if cust=1 and order=1;
   keep Customer_ID Customer_Name Quantity
        Total_Retail_Price Product_ID;
run;
```

3. Examine the output data set, **work.CustOrd**. Notice that it contains only matches, with a total of 148 observations.

4. Submit Step 2. It sorts **work.CustOrd** by **Product_ID**. The DATA step match-merges **work.custord** with **orion.product_dim** by **Product_ID** to get additional product information.

```
*** Step 2 **************************************************;
proc sort data=CustOrd;
   by Product_ID;
run;

data CustOrdProd;
   merge CustOrd(in=ord)
         orion.product_dim(in=prod);
   by Product_ID;
   if ord=1 and prod=1;
   Supplier=catx(' ',Supplier_Country,Supplier_ID);
   keep Customer_Name Quantity
        Total_Retail_Price Product_Name Supplier;
run;
```

5. Examine the output data set, **work.CustOrdProd**. It is in order by **Product_ID**.

6. Submit the PRINT procedure to display the first 15 observations in the newly merged data set, **work.custordprod**.

```
proc print data=CustOrdProd(obs=15) noobs;
   var Customer_Name Quantity Total_Retail_Price
       Product_Name Supplier;
run;
```

Altering Variable Names

With match-merging, two situations might require altering variable names:

- The BY variables have different names in the input data sets being merged.
- The data sets being merged have identically named variables that must both be kept in the merged output.

In both cases, the RENAME= data set option can be used to alter the variable names to get the desired results.

37

Business Scenario – Create Gift List

The Excel workbook **`BonusGift.xls`** contains a list of suppliers that want to send gifts to customers who purchased more than a specified minimum quantity of a product.

Use **`work.CustOrdProd`** and **`BonusGift.xls`** to determine the customers that will be sent gifts.

`work.CustOrdProd`

Customer_Name
Quantity
Total_Retail_Price
Product_Name
Supplier

`BonusGift.xls`

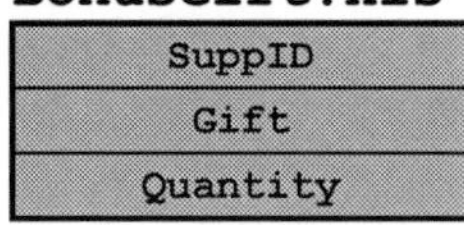

SuppID
Gift
Quantity

38

9.05 Quiz

Which statements correctly access the **`Supplier`** worksheet in the Excel workbook?

a.

```
libname bonus 'BonusGift.xls';

proc print data=bonus.Supplier;
run;
```

b.

```
libname bonus 'BonusGift.xls';

proc print data=bonus.'Supplier$'n;
run;
```

BonusGift.xls [Compatibilit...

	A	B	C
1	SuppID	Gift	Quantity
2	BE 5922	Tote Bag	1
3	CA 16814	Gift Card	1
4	DK 755	Coupon	1
5	ES 4742	Travel Mug	2
6	NL 16542	Mini-Light	1
7	NL 2995	Belt Pouch	2
8	PT 1684	Umbrella	1
9	SE 109	Gift Set	1
10	US 10225	Coupon	1
11	US 1303	Gift Card	2
12	US 15218	Tote Bag	1
13	US 1747	Travel Set	1
14	US 2963	Backpack	1
15	US 3298	Travel Bag	1
16	US 3808	Coupon	1
17	US 3815	Mini-Light	1
18	US 4646	Gift Card	1
19	US 772	Travel Mug	1
20			
21			

Supplier

40

Business Scenario – Details

The data sets **`work.CustOrdProd`** and **`BonusGift.xls`** must be merged on values that are in two differently named variables.

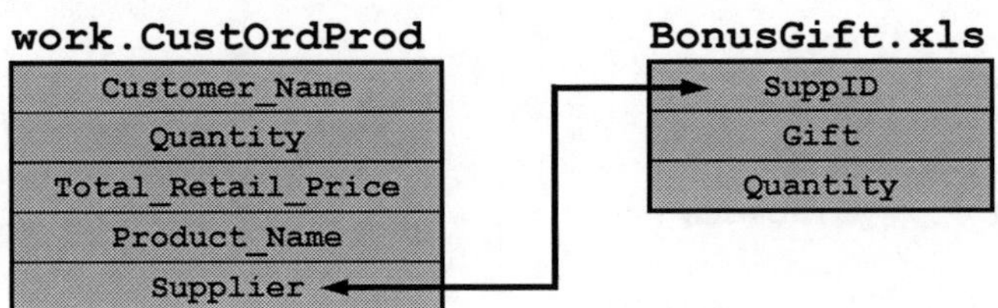

The variables must have the same name for the match-merge to work correctly.

42

Business Scenario – Details

You want to keep merged observations where the value of **Quantity** in **work.CustOrdProd** is more than the value of **Quantity** in **BonusGift.xls**.

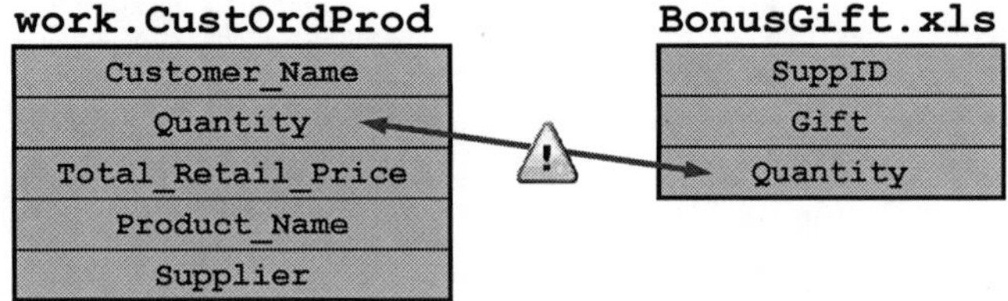

The variables must have different names so that you can use a subsetting IF statement to compare them.

43

Create Gift List – Solution

Access the Excel workbook, specify the worksheet to use, and release the workbook after the DATA step.

```
libname bonus 'BonusGift.xls';

data CustOrdProdGift;
   merge CustOrdProd(in=c)
         bonus.'Supplier$'n(in=s
            rename=(SuppID=Supplier
                    Quantity=Minimum));
   by Supplier;
   if c=1 and s=1 and Quantity > Minimum;
run;

libname bonus clear;
```

44 p209d04

Create Gift List – Solution

Use the RENAME= data set option to ensure that the BY variable has the same name to use for merging.

```
libname bonus 'BonusGift.xls';

data CustOrdProdGift;
   merge CustOrdProd(in=c)
         bonus.'Supplier$'n(in=s
            rename=(SuppID=Supplier
                    Quantity=Minimum));
   by Supplier;
   if c=1 and s=1 and Quantity > Minimum;
run;

libname bonus clear;
```

45 p209d04

Create Gift List – Solution

Change the name of the **Quantity** variable from the Excel worksheet so that it can be use in a subsetting IF.

```
libname bonus 'BonusGift.xls';

data CustOrdProdGift;
   merge CustOrdProd(in=c)
         bonus.'Supplier$'n(in=s
            rename=(SuppID=Supplier
                    Quantity=Minimum));
   by Supplier;
   if c=1 and s=1 and Quantity > Minimum;
run;

libna
```

Quantity value from the CustOrdProd data set

Renamed Quantity value from the 'Supplier$'n data set

46 p209d04

Create Gift List – Solution

Use the IN= option and a condition in the subsetting IF statement to keep only the matches.

```
libname bonus 'BonusGift.xls';

data CustOrdProdGift;
   merge CustOrdProd(in=c)
         bonus.'Supplier$'n(in=s
            rename=(SuppID=Supplier
                    Quantity=Minimum));
   by Supplier;
   if c=1 and s=1 and Quantity > Minimum;
run;

libname bonus clear;
```

47 p209d04

Create Gift List – Solution

Fifty-two customers qualified for gifts.

Partial SAS log

```
207  libname bonus 'BonusGift.xls';
NOTE: Libref BONUS was successfully assigned as follows:
      Engine:        EXCEL
      Physical Name: BonusGift.xls
208
209  data CustOrdProdGift;
210     merge CustOrdProd(in=c)
211           bonus.'Supplier$'n(in=s
212              rename=(SuppID=Supplier
213                      Quantity=Minimum));
214     by Supplier;
215     if c=1 and s=1 and Quantity > Minimum;
216  run;

NOTE: There were 148 observations read from the data set WORK.CUSTORDPROD.
NOTE: There were 18 observations read from the data set BONUS.'Supplier$'n.
NOTE: The data set WORK.CUSTORDPRODGIFT has 52 observations and 7 variables.
NOTE: DATA statement used (Total process time):
      real time           0.04 seconds
      cpu time            0.03 seconds
```

48

Create Gift List – Output

Sort the data set by customer name prior to printing the list of customers and the gifts that they should receive.

```
proc sort data=CustOrdProdGift;
   by Customer_Name;
run;

proc print data=CustOrdProdGift;
   var Customer_Name Gift;
run;
```

49

p209d04

Create Gift List – Output

The output below shows the list of customers and gifts.

Partial PROC PRINT output

```
Customer_Name           Gift

Alvan Goheen            Travel Mug
Angel Borwick           Belt Pouch
Cynthia Martinez        Travel Set
Cynthia Martinez        Gift Card
Cynthia Martinez        Travel Mug
Cynthia Mccluney        Tote Bag
Cynthia Mccluney        Tote Bag
Cynthia Mccluney        Gift Card
David Black             Backpack
Dericka Pockran         Coupon
Dericka Pockran         Travel Mug
Dericka Pockran         Travel Mug
```

50

p209d04

Exercises

Level 1

1. Match-Merging Two Data Sets

The data set **orion.web_products** contains an observation for every product available for sale on Orion Star's wholesale Web site.

Partial Listing of **orion.web_products**

Product_ID	Price	Product_Name
120400304333	114.36	Smasher Super Rq Ti 350 Tennis Racket
120400305288	53.26	Knife
120400305846	107.74	Big Guy Men's Air Deschutz Viii Shoes
120400308766	40.96	Big Guy Men's Packable Hiking Shorts
120400308849	12.23	Wood Box for 6 Balls
120400310496	128.99	Comfort Shelter
120400311211	69.16	Tipee Summer Sleeping Bag
120400311220	160.49	Perfect Fit Men's Stunt Skates
120400315870	156.49	Grandslam Ultra Power Tennisketcher

The data set **orion.web_orders** contains a list of orders made in a single day from the Web site. Each observation contains the product ID, the quantity ordered, and the customer's name.

Partial Listing of **orion.web_orders**

Product_ID	Quantity	Customer
120400305288	16	Carglar Aydemir
120400305288	19	Sanelisiwe Collier
120400305846	13	Candy Kinsey
120400305846	13	Cynthia Martinez
120400305846	10	Rolf Robak
120400308766	13	Ahmet Canko
120400310496	15	Oliver S. Füßling
120400311220	13	Ramesh Trentholme
120400311220	9	Avni Argac
120400311465	13	Thomas Leitmann
120400312556	7	Robyn Klem

 The two data sets are sorted by **Product_ID**.

a. Create **three** data sets:

- A data set named **revenue** contains the product code (**Product_ID**), the price (**Price**), the quantity sold (**Quantity**), the product name (**Product_Name**), the customer name (**Customer**), and the revenue generated from each sale (**Revenue**). **Revenue** is a new variable that is equal to **Price*Quantity**.
- A data set named **notsold** contains the product code (**Product_ID**), price (**Price**), and product name (**Product_Name**) for each product that was not sold.
- A data set named **invalidcode** contains the product code (**Product_ID**), quantity (**Quantity**), and customer name (**Customer**) for each observation in the **web_orders** data set that does not have a corresponding product code in the **web_products** data set.

b. Print the three data sets with appropriate titles. The data sets should contain 39, 7, and 4 observations, respectively.

Partial Listing of **revenue** (39 Observations)

```
                                       Revenue from Orders

  Product_ID    Price Product_Name                           Quantity Customer                Revenue

120400305288    53.26 Knife                                     16    Carglar Aydemir          852.16
120400305288    53.26 Knife                                     19    Sanelisiwe Collier      1011.94
120400305846   107.74 Big Guy Men's Air Deschutz Viii Shoes     13    Candy Kinsey            1400.62
120400305846   107.74 Big Guy Men's Air Deschutz Viii Shoes     13    Cynthia Martinez        1400.62
120400305846   107.74 Big Guy Men's Air Deschutz Viii Shoes     10    Rolf Robak              1077.40
120400308766    40.96 Big Guy Men's Packable Hiking Shorts      13    Ahmet Canko              532.48
120400310496   128.99 Comfort Shelter                           15    Oliver S. Füßling       1934.85
```

Listing of **notsold** (7 Observations)

```
                    Products Not Ordered

  Product_ID        Price     Product_Name

120400304333       114.36     Smasher Super Rq Ti 350 Tennis Racket
120400308849        12.23     Wood Box for 6 Balls
120400311211        69.16     Tipee Summer Sleeping Bag
120400317183       164.82     Smasher Rd Ti 70 Tennis Racket
120400329978       114.47     Tipee Twin Blue/Orange
120400330339        31.74     Small Belt Bag, Black
120400330967        38.73     Duwall Pants
```

Listing of **invalidcode** (4 Observations)

```
                Invalid Orders

  Product_ID       Quantity    Customer

120400311465          13       Thomas Leitmann
120400312556           7       Robyn Klem
120400315078          23       Tonie Asmussen
120400326278          10       Theunis Brazier
```

Level 2

2. Handling Same-Named Variables and Different Data Types for BY Variables

The data set **orion.web_products2** contains an observation for every product available for sale on Orion Star's wholesale Web site.

Partial Listing of **orion.web_products2**

```
    Product_ID        Price     Name

   120400304333      114.36     Smasher Super Rq Ti 350 Tennis Racket
   120400305288       53.26     Knife
   120400305846      107.74     Big Guy Men's Air Deschutz Viii Shoes
   120400308766       40.96     Big Guy Men's Packable Hiking Shorts
   120400308849       12.23     Wood Box for 6 Balls
   120400310496      128.99     Comfort Shelter
   120400311211       69.16     Tipee Summer Sleeping Bag
   120400311220      160.49     Perfect Fit Men's Stunt Skates
   120400315870      156.49     Grandslam Ultra Power Tennisketcher
```

The data set **orion.web_orders2** contains a list of orders made in a single day from the Web site. Each observation contains the product ID, the quantity ordered, and the customer's name.

Partial Listing of **orion.web_orders2**

```
    Product_ID       Quantity     Name

   120400305288          16       Carglar Aydemir
   120400305288          19       Sanelisiwe Collier
   120400305846          13       Candy Kinsey
   120400305846          13       Cynthia Martinez
   120400305846          10       Rolf Robak
   120400308766          13       Ahmet Canko
   120400310496          15       Oliver S. Füßling
   120400311220          13       Ramesh Trentholme
   120400311220           9       Avni Argac
   120400311465          13       Thomas Leitmann
   120400312556           7       Robyn Klem
```

> The two data sets are sorted by **Product_ID**. **Product_ID** is numeric in **orion.web_products2** and character with a length of 12 in **orion.web_orders2**.

a. Create a new data set, **web_converted**, from the **orion.web_products2** data set. Change the type of **Product_ID** to character. (Use **web_converted** to merge with **orion.web_orders2** in the next step.)

Hint: Use the RENAME= data set option to change **Product_ID** to some other name, such as **nProduct_ID**, the LENGTH statement to declare a new character variable named **Product_ID**, and an assignment statement with a PUT function to explicitly convert the numeric value in **nProduct_ID** into a character value in **Product_ID**.

b. Create **three** new data sets:

- A data set named **revenue** contains the product code, the price, the quantity sold, the product name, the customer name and the revenue generated from each sale. **Revenue** is calculated as **Price*Quantity**.

  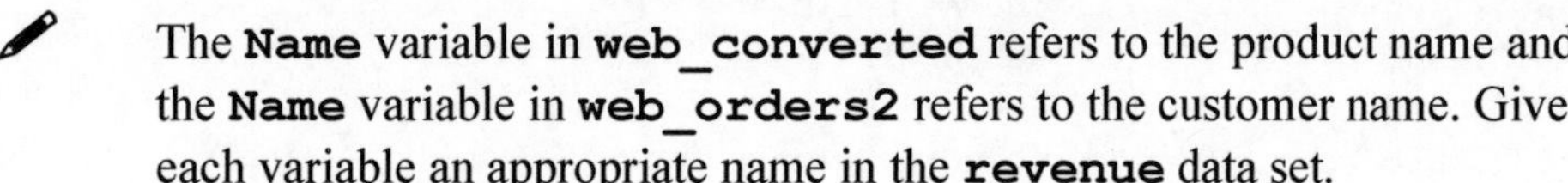

  The **Name** variable in **web_converted** refers to the product name and the **Name** variable in **web_orders2** refers to the customer name. Give each variable an appropriate name in the **revenue** data set.

- A data set named **notsold** contains the product code, price, and product name for each product that was not sold.
- A data set named **invalidcode** contains the product code, quantity, and customer name for each observation in the **web_orders2** data set that does not have a corresponding product code in the **web_products2** data set.

c. Print the three data sets with appropriate titles. The data sets should contain 39, 7, and 4 observations, respectively. (The data sets you create might have different variable names than the ones shown here.)

Partial Listing of **revenue** (39 Observations)

Revenue from Orders

Product_ID	Price	Product_Name	Quantity	Customer	Revenue
120400305288	53.26	Knife	16	Carglar Aydemir	852.16
120400305288	53.26	Knife	19	Sanelisiwe Collier	1011.94
120400305846	107.74	Big Guy Men's Air Deschutz Viii Shoes	13	Candy Kinsey	1400.62
120400305846	107.74	Big Guy Men's Air Deschutz Viii Shoes	13	Cynthia Martinez	1400.62
120400305846	107.74	Big Guy Men's Air Deschutz Viii Shoes	10	Rolf Robak	1077.40
120400308766	40.96	Big Guy Men's Packable Hiking Shorts	13	Ahmet Canko	532.48
120400310496	128.99	Comfort Shelter	15	Oliver S. Füßling	1934.85

Listing of **notsold** (7 Observations)

Products Not Ordered

Product_ID	Price	Name
120400304333	114.36	Smasher Super Rq Ti 350 Tennis Racket
120400308849	12.23	Wood Box for 6 Balls
120400311211	69.16	Tipee Summer Sleeping Bag
120400317183	164.82	Smasher Rd Ti 70 Tennis Racket
120400329978	114.47	Tipee Twin Blue/Orange
120400330339	31.74	Small Belt Bag, Black
120400330967	38.73	Duwall Pants

Listing of **invalidcode** (4 Observations)

```
                 Invalid Orders

  Product_ID     Quantity    Name

 120400311465       13       Thomas Leitmann
 120400312556        7       Robyn Klem
 120400315078       23       Tonie Asmussen
 120400326278       10       Theunis Brazier
```

9.2 Chapter Review

Chapter Review

1. By default, match-merging places matches and nonmatches in the output data set. True or False?

2. Two SAS data sets need to be merged, but the BY variables have different names. What can be done to enable the data sets to be merged?

3. What conditions must be met before three or more SAS data sets can be merged in a single DATA step?

53

9.3 Solutions

Solutions to Exercises

1. **Match-Merging Two Data Sets**

   a. Create **three** data sets.

```
data revenue
   NotSold(keep=Price Product_ID Product_Name)
   InValidCode(Keep=Product_ID Quantity Customer);
   merge orion.web_products(in=InProduct)
         orion.web_orders(in=InOrders);
   by Product_ID;
   if InProduct and InOrders then do;
      Revenue = Quantity * Price;
      output revenue;
   end;
   else if InProduct and not InOrders then output notsold;
   else if not InProduct and InOrders then output invalidcode;
run;
```

   b. Print the three data sets with appropriate titles.

```
title 'Revenue from Orders';
proc print data=revenue noobs;
run;

title 'Products Not Ordered';
proc print data=notsold noobs;
run;

title 'Invalid Orders';
proc print data=invalidcode noobs;
run;
title;
```

2. **Handling Same-Named Variables and Different Data Types for BY Variables**

   a. Create a new data set, **`web_converted`**, from the **`orion.web_products2`** data set. Change the type of **`Product_ID`** to character.

```
data web_converted(drop=nProduct_ID);
   length Product_ID $ 12;
   set orion.web_products2(rename=(Product_ID=nProduct_ID));
   Product_ID=put(nProduct_ID,12.);
run;
```

b. Create **three** data sets.

```
data revenue
   NotSold(keep=Price Product_ID Product_Name)
   InValidCode(Keep=Product_ID Quantity Customer);
   merge web_converted(in=InConv rename=(Name=Product_Name))
         orion.web_orders2(in=InOrders rename=(Name=Customer));
   by Product_ID;
   if InConv and InOrders then do;
      Revenue = Quantity * Price;
      output revenue;
   end;
   else if InConv and not InOrders then output notsold;
   else if not InConv and InOrders then output invalidcode;
run;
```

c. Print the three data sets with appropriate titles.

```
title 'Revenue from Orders';
proc print data=revenue noobs;
run;

title 'Products Not Ordered';
proc print data=notsold noobs;
run;

title 'Invalid Orders';
proc print data=invalidcode noobs;
run;
title;
```

Solutions to Student Activities (Polls/Quizzes)

9.01 Multiple Choice Poll – Correct Answer

Which statement is true concerning match-merging?

a. The MERGE statement must refer to permanent data sets.

b. The variables in the BY statement can only be in one of the data sets.

c. Only two data sets can be specified in the MERGE statement.

(d.) When you use the MERGE statement with the BY statement, the data must be sorted or indexed on the BY variable.

6

9.02 Quiz – Correct Answer

Write the appropriate IF statement to create the desired data set containing only nonmatches.

```
data combine;
   merge products(in=InProd) costs(in=InCost);
   by ID;
   if InProd=0 or InCost=0;
run;
```

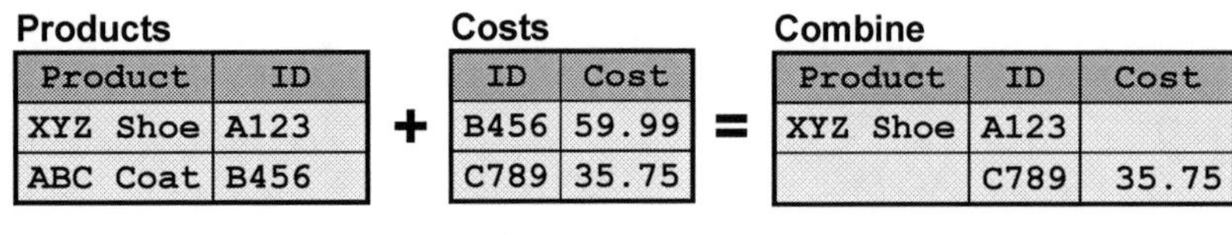

Products

Product	ID
XYZ Shoe	A123
ABC Coat	B456

\+ **Costs**

ID	Cost
B456	59.99
C789	35.75

= **Combine**

Product	ID	Cost
XYZ Shoe	A123	
	C789	35.75

12

9.03 Quiz – Correct Answer

What two temporary variables are created due to the BY statement?

```
data orders(keep=Customer_Name Quantity
              Product_ID Total_Retail_Price)
     noorders(keep=Customer_Name Birth_Date);
   merge orion.customer
         work.order_fact(in=order);
   by Customer_ID;
   if order=1 then output orders;
   else output noorders;
run;
```

`First.Customer_ID` and `Last.Customer_ID`

21

9.04 Quiz – Correct Answer

Do the following data sets have a common variable?

No, these data sets do not share one common variable. Therefore, they cannot be combined in a single DATA step.

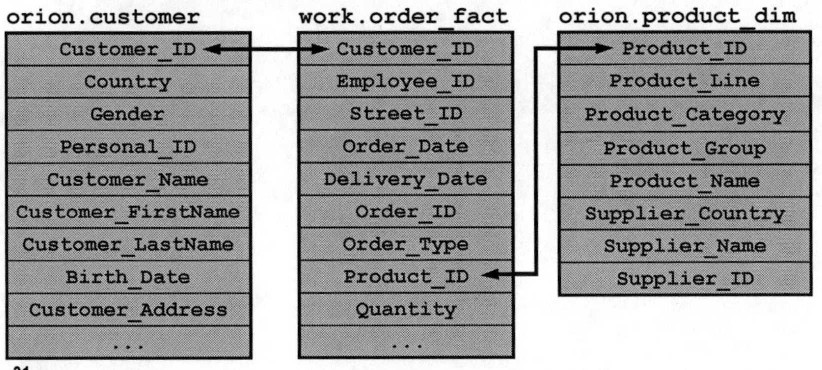

31

9.05 Quiz – Correct Answer

Which statements correctly access the **Supplier** worksheet in the Excel workbook?

a.

```
libname bonus 'BonusGift.xls';

proc print data=bonus.Supplier;
run;
```

(b.)

```
libname bonus 'BonusGift.xls';

proc print data=bonus.'Supplier$'n;
run;
```

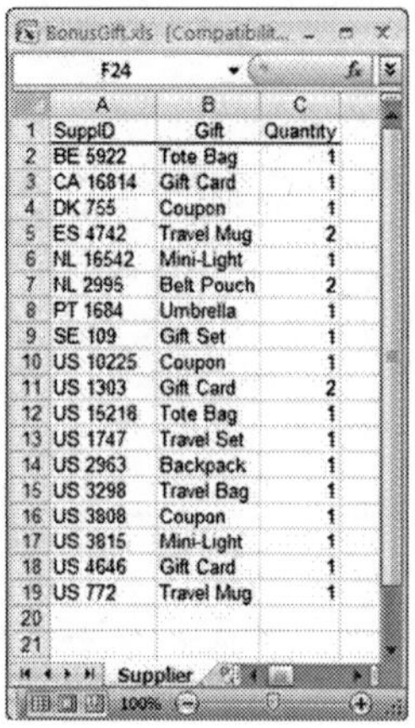

BonusGift.xls [Compatibilit...

F24

	A	B	C
1	SuppID	Gift	Quantity
2	BE 5922	Tote Bag	1
3	CA 16814	Gift Card	1
4	DK 755	Coupon	1
5	ES 4742	Travel Mug	2
6	NL 16542	Mini-Light	1
7	NL 2995	Belt Pouch	2
8	PT 1684	Umbrella	1
9	SE 109	Gift Set	1
10	US 10225	Coupon	1
11	US 1303	Gift Card	2
12	US 15218	Tote Bag	1
13	US 1747	Travel Set	1
14	US 2963	Backpack	1
15	US 3298	Travel Bag	1
16	US 3808	Coupon	1
17	US 3815	Mini-Light	1
18	US 4646	Gift Card	1
19	US 772	Travel Mug	1
20			
21			

Supplier

100%

41

Solutions to Chapter Review

Chapter Review Answers

1. By default, match-merging places matches and nonmatches in the output data set. True or False?

   True. By default both matches and nonmatches are placed into the output data set.

2. Two SAS data sets need to be merged, but the BY variables have different names. What can be done to enable the data sets to be merged?

   The RENAME= data set option can be used to ensure that the BY variables have the same name.

54

continued...

Chapter Review Answers

3. What conditions must be met before three or more SAS data sets can be merged in a single DATA step?

   All the data sets must have a common variable and must be sorted by that variable.

55

Chapter 10 Other SAS Languages

10.1 An Overview of Other Languages....................10-3

10.2 Using the SQL Procedure....................10-5

Exercises....................10-21

10.3 The SAS Macro Language....................10-25

Exercises....................10-37

10.4 Chapter Review....................10-40

10.5 Solutions....................10-41

Solutions to Exercises....................10-41

Solutions to Student Activities (Polls/Quizzes)....................10-44

Solutions to Chapter Review....................10-47

10.1 An Overview of Other Languages

Objectives

- Describe other languages available in SAS.

3

Other SAS Languages

The languages that are available in SAS include the following:

- the SAS language
- SQL
- macro
- SCL
- SAS/C

Until now the focus was on the SAS language.
This chapter introduces SQL and the macro language.

4

Why Learn SQL?

SQL (Structured Query Language) is a standardized language used by many software products.

The SQL procedure in SAS

- can be used to retrieve, join, and update data in tables
- can perform more efficient join operations than DATA step merges in some cases
- can replace the need for multiple DATA and PROC steps with one query.

5

Why Learn Macro?

The SAS macro language permits code substitution as well as automatic code generation and execution.

Macro programming makes more efficient use of a SAS developer's time by

- simplifying program maintenance
- generating flexible, customizable code
- executing code iteratively.

6

10.2 Using the SQL Procedure

Objectives

- Explain the purpose and syntax of the SQL procedure.
- Use the SQL procedure to query a SAS data set.
- Use the SQL procedure to create a SAS data set.
- Use the SQL procedure to join SAS data sets.

8

10.01 Multiple Choice Poll

Which of the following best describes your experience level with the SQL procedure?

a. Over one year
b. Six months to one year
c. Less than six months
d. I have seen SQL code but not written any.
e. No experience with SQL

10

The SQL Procedure

The SQL procedure enables you to write ANSI standard SQL queries in a SAS program.

With PROC SQL you can access the following:

- SAS data sets
- other database data, with the appropriate SAS/ACCESS engine

This section focuses on accessing SAS data sets.

11

The SQL Procedure

The following table shows SAS terms and the equivalent SQL terminology:

SAS Term	SQL Term
Data Set	Table
Observation	Row
Variable	Column

When using SQL to access a table, remember that you are accessing a SAS data set.

12

The SQL Procedure: Syntax Overview

The PROC SQL statement signals the start of an SQL procedure.

The QUIT statement ends an SQL procedure.

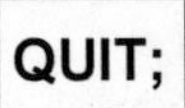

13

If the QUIT statement is omitted, the SQL procedure remains in memory to process subsequent queries. A QUIT statement or the start of another step terminates the SQL procedure and removes it from memory.

The SQL Procedure: Syntax Overview

An SQL SELECT statement (also called a *query*) is submitted to query SAS tables. A query contains smaller building blocks named *clauses*.

The following clauses are discussed in this section:

- SELECT
- FROM
- WHERE

14

The SELECT Clause

The SELECT clause identifies columns to include in the query result.

```
SELECT var-1, var-2 ...
```

Columns listed in the SELECT clause are separated by commas. There is no comma following the last column in the list.

```
SELECT *
```

To select all columns, use an asterisk in place of the column names.

15

The FROM Clause

The FROM clause identifies the SAS table(s) from which to read.

```
FROM SAS-table ...
```

16

The WHERE Clause

The WHERE clause identifies a condition that must be satisfied for a row to be included in the PROC SQL output. A WHERE clause can contain any of the columns in a table, including unselected columns.

```
WHERE where-expression
```

✎ The *where-expression* can be a compound expression using logical operators.

17

Using PROC SQL to Query a Table

A query identifies the columns to include in the result, the table to be queried, and a WHERE clause, if desired.

General form of a PROC SQL query:

```
LIBNAME libref 'SAS-data-library';
PROC SQL;
     SELECT var-1, var-2...
          FROM SAS-table-1...
          <WHERE where-expression>
     ;
QUIT;
```

A RUN statement is not needed because the query is executed when the semicolon is reached.

18

The SELECT statement syntax shows the clauses allowed and the order in which they must be written.

```
SELECT column-1<, column-2>...
       FROM table-1<, table-2>...
       <WHERE expression>
       <GROUP BY column-1<, column-2>...>
       <HAVING expression>
       <ORDER BY column-1<, column->...<DESC>>;
```

Business Scenario

The director of sales wants a report listing employee IDs, titles, and salaries for his direct reports. Use a query to examine the **orion.sales_mgmt** table.

```
options ls=80;
proc sql;
     select *
     from orion.sales_mgmt;
quit;
```

19

p210d01

Query Results

The output includes all rows and all columns from **orion.sales_mgmt**.

```
Employee     Start_
  _ID         Date      End_Date     Job_Title              Salary

121143     01JUL2001    31DEC9999    Senior Sales Manager   $95,090
121144     01NOV1995    31DEC9999    Sales Manager          $83,505
121145     01APR1980    31DEC9999    Sales Manager          $84,260
121147     01SEP1991    31DEC9999    Secretary II           $29,145

             Birth_     Emp_Hire_    Emp_Term_
Gender        Date        Date         Date          Manager_ID

  M        26NOV1973    01JUL2001        .             121142
  F        28JUN1968    01NOV1995        .             121142
  M        22NOV1953    01APR1980        .             121142
  F        28MAY1973    01SEP1991        .             121142
```

20

10.02 Quiz

Open and submit **p210a01**. The query displays all variables in the **orion.sales_mgmt** table. Modify the SELECT clause to display only **Employee_ID**, **Job_Title**, and **Salary**.

```
proc sql;
   select *
   from orion.sales_mgmt;
quit;
```

22

p210a01

Output: A Simple SQL Query

By default a query generates a report. It does not create a table.

PROC SQL Output

Employee ID	Employee Job Title	Employee Annual Salary
121143	Senior Sales Manager	$95,090
121144	Sales Manager	$83,505
121145	Sales Manager	$84,260
121147	Secretary II	$29,145

What if you want to use the results to create a data set?

24

The CREATE TABLE Statement

Use the CREATE TABLE statement to create a table with the results of an SQL query.

General form to create a table from a query:

```
LIBNAME libref 'SAS-data-library';
PROC SQL;
    CREATE TABLE table-name AS
    SELECT var-1, var-2...
        FROM SAS-table-1...
        <WHERE where-expression>
    ;
QUIT;
```

25

Create a Table

The CREATE TABLE statement creates an output data set or SAS table. The results are not displayed in the Output window.

```
proc sql;
   create table direct_reports as
      select employee_id, job_title, salary
      from orion.sales_mgmt;
quit;
```

Partial SAS Log

```
38   proc sql;
39      create table direct_reports as
40         select employee_id, job_title, salary
41         from orion.sales_mgmt;
NOTE: Table WORK.DIRECT_REPORTS created, with 4 rows and 3 columns.
42   quit;
```

26

p210d02

Display the SAS Table Using an SQL Query

Use an SQL query to display the table. The NUMBER option includes a column of row numbers similar to the Obs column generated by the PRINT procedure.

```
proc sql number;
   select *
      from direct_reports;
quit;
```

PROC SQL Output

Row	Employee ID	Employee Job Title	Employee Annual Salary
1	121143	Senior Sales Manager	$95,090
2	121144	Sales Manager	$83,505
3	121145	Sales Manager	$84,260
4	121147	Secretary II	$29,145

27

Display the SAS Table Using PROC PRINT

You can use the PRINT procedure to display the new table, because it is a SAS data set.

```
proc print data=direct_reports;
run;
```

PROC PRINT Output

Obs	Employee_ID	Job_Title	Salary
1	121143	Senior Sales Manager	$95,090
2	121144	Sales Manager	$83,505
3	121145	Sales Manager	$84,260
4	121147	Secretary II	$29,145

28

p210d02

Business Scenario

The director wants employee names added to the previous report. The names are not in the **orion.sales_mgmt** table, but they are in **orion.employee_addresses**. Both tables must be used to get the required data.

Partial Contents of **orion.employee_addresses**

```
Alphabetic List of Variables and Attributes
     #    Variable         Type    Len
     6    City             Char     30
     9    Country          Char      2
     1    Employee_ID      Num       8
     2    Employee_Name    Char     40
     8    Postal_Code      Char     10
     7    State            Char      2
     3    Street_ID        Num       8
     5    Street_Name      Char     40
     4    Street_Number    Num       8
```

30

Using PROC SQL to Join Tables

To join two or more SAS tables, list them in the FROM clause separated by commas.

General form of an SQL inner join:

```
LIBNAME libref 'SAS-data-library';
PROC SQL;
     SELECT var-1, var-2...
          FROM SAS-table-1, SAS-table-2...
          <WHERE where-expression>
     ;
QUIT;
```

31

Using PROC SQL to Join Tables

The **Employee_ID** column appears in both tables, so it must be qualified to identify which variable is selected. To qualify the column, use the table name as a prefix when the column is referenced.

```
proc sql number;
   select sales_mgmt.employee_id,
          employee_name,
          job_title,
          salary
   from orion.sales_mgmt,
        orion.employee_addresses;
quit;
```

32

p210d03

10.03 Quiz

Open **p210a02,** submit the program, and view the output. It joins **orion.sales_mgmt** (4 rows total) and **orion.employee_addresses** (424 rows) to obtain the names of the director's four direct reports.

```
proc sql number;
     select sales_mgmt.employee_id,
          employee_name,
          job_title,
          salary
     from orion.sales_mgmt,
        orion.employee_addresses;
quit;
```

Does the output show the names of the four direct reports as desired?

34

p210a02

A Cartesian Product

Each row in **orion.sales_mgmt** was combined with every row in **orion.employee_addresses**.

sales_mgmt

```
121143  Senior Sales Manager $95,090
121144  Sales Manager        $83,505
121145  Sales Manager        $84,260
```

employee_addresses

```
121044  Abbott, Ray
120145  Aisbitt, Sandy
120761  Akinfolarin, Tameaka
120656  Amos, Salley
```

Partial PROC SQL Output

```
1  121143  Abbott, Ray          Senior Sales Manager    $95,090
2  121143  Aisbitt, Sandy       Senior Sales Manager    $95,090
3  121143  Akinfolarin, Tameaka Senior Sales Manager    $95,090
4  121143  Amos, Salley         Senior Sales Manager    $95,090
```

You need to specify the join criteria for matching rows. Select only the rows with matching **employee_id** values.

36

Conceptually, when two tables are specified in a join, each row of the first table is matched with every row of the second table to produce a *Cartesian product*, which is stored in an internal or intermediate table. The number of rows in the intermediate table is equal to the product of the number of rows in each of the source tables. The intermediate table becomes the input to the rest of the query, although some of its rows might be eliminated by the WHERE clause.

The WHERE Clause

A WHERE clause is used to specify the join criteria and possibly other subsetting criteria.

WHERE *join-condition(s)*
    <**AND** *other subsetting conditions*>

join-condition can be any valid SAS condition.

When the conditions are met, the rows are displayed in the output.

37

Joining on a Common Variable

This task requires matching the values of **employee_id** in both tables. This is referred to as an *inner join*.

employee_id from **orion.sales_mgmt** =
employee_id from **orion.employee_addresses**

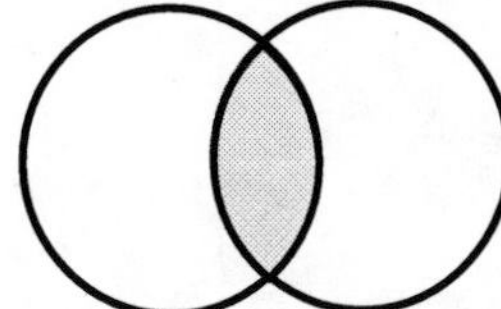

38

Joining on a Common Variable

```
proc sql;
   select sales_mgmt.employee_id,
          employee_name,
          job_title,
          salary
   from orion.sales_mgmt,
        orion.employee_addresses
   where sales_mgmt.employee_id =
         employee_addresses.employee_id;
quit;
```

The WHERE clause specifies the join condition, that the value of **employee_id** is the same in both tables.

p210d04

39

A WHERE clause can use logical operators to include join conditions as well as other subsetting conditions.

```
where sales_mgmt.employee_id = employee_addresses.employee_id
      and Salary > 900000;
```

Output: Joining on a Common Variable

PROC SQL Output

Employee ID	Employee_Name	Employee Job Title	Employee Annual Salary
121144	Capachietti, Renee	Sales Manager	$83,505
121143	Favaron, Louis	Senior Sales Manager	$95,090
121145	Lansberry, Dennis	Sales Manager	$84,260
121147	Sneed, Christine	Secretary II	$29,145

40

An inner join is equivalent to a DATA step merge in which both data sets contribute to the merge. The following program is an equivalent process using the SORT procedure and a DATA step.

```
proc sort data=orion.staff out=staff;
   by employee_id;
run;
proc sort data=orion.employee_addresses out=addresses;
   by employee_id;
run;

data sqlEquiv (keep=employee_id job_title salary employee_name);
      merge staff (in=inStaff) addresses (in=inAddr);
   by employee_id;
   if instaff and inaddr;
run;

proc print data=sqlEquiv;
run;
```

10.04 Quiz

The **orion.customer** and **orion.country** tables both have a column named **Country** containing a country abbreviation. Open **p210a03** and add a WHERE clause to join the tables based on matching values of **Country**.

```
proc sql;
   select customer_id, customer_name,
          customer.country, country_name
   from orion.customer,
        orion.country
   where [                          ]
     ;
quit;
```

42 p210a03

Assigning an Alias for a SAS Table

You can specify an alias for a SAS table. The alias can replace the table name in a query.

> **FROM** *SAS-table-1* <AS> *alias-1*,
> *SAS-table-2* <AS> *alias-2* ...

An alias can be any valid SAS name.

44

Assigning an Alias for a SAS Table

```
proc sql;
   select s.employee_id,employee_name,
          job_title,salary
   from orion.sales_mgmt as s,
        orion.employee_addresses as a
   where s.employee_id = a.employee_id;
quit;
```

PROC SQL Output

Employee ID	Employee_Name	Employee Job Title	Employee Annual Salary
121144	Capachietti, Renee	Sales Manager	$83,505
121143	Favaron, Louis	Senior Sales Manager	$95,090
121145	Lansberry, Dennis	Sales Manager	$84,260
121147	Sneed, Christine	Secretary II	$29,145

45 p210d05

Advantages of PROC SQL and the DATA Step

With the SQL procedure you can
join tables and produce a report in one step without creating a SAS data set
join tables without presorting the data
use complex matching criteria.

With the DATA step you can
create multiple data sets
direct output to data sets based on data set contributors
use First. and Last. processing
use DO loops and arrays
perform complex data manipulation.

46

Exercises

Level 1

1. Modifying an Inner Join

An existing PROC SQL inner join combines information from the **orion.discount** and **orion.product_dim** tables on the matching product IDs.

- The table **orion.discount** contains discount information.
- The table **orion.product_dim** contains product descriptions.
- Both tables have a column named **Product_ID**.

a. Open and submit the program **p210e01**. Examine the output.

Partial PROC SQL Output

```
                                                 Supplier       Start
Product Name                                     Country         Date
-----------------------------------------------------------------------
Osprey Girl's Tights                             US         01DEC2007
Big Guy Men's Woven Warm Up                      US         01JUL2007
Woman's Foxhole Jacket                           US         01JUL2007
Armadillo Road Dmx Men's Running Shoes           CA         01JUN2007
Armadillo Road Dmx Women's Running Shoes         CA         01JUL2007
```

b. Modify this program as follows:

- Display the columns **Product_ID**, **Product_Name**, **Start_Date**, **End_Date**, and **Discount** as shown below.
- Modify the WHERE clause so that only rows with **Discount** greater than or equal to 60% are returned.

Hint: Add an AND to the WHERE clause to put in the condition for **Discount**. Also, remember to qualify any columns that appear in both tables.

Partial PROC SQL Output

```
                                                                                  Discount
                                                                                        as
                                                                                   Percent
                                                                                        of
                                                                                    Normal
                                                                                    Retail
                                                                   Start             Sales
   Product ID  Product Name                                         Date   End Date  Price
------------------------------------------------------------------------------------------
 220100100309  Big Guy Men's Woven Warm Up                     01JUL2007  31JUL2007    60%
 220100100536  Woman's Foxhole Jacket                          01JUL2007  31JUL2007    60%
 220100700023  Armadillo Road Dmx Men's Running Shoes          01JUN2007  30JUN2007    70%
 220100700024  Armadillo Road Dmx Women's Running Shoes        01JUL2007  31JUL2007    60%
 220100800001  Bra Top Wom.Fitn.Cl                             01AUG2007  31AUG2007    70%
```

Level 2

2. Coding a PROC SQL Inner Join

- The table **orion.order_fact** contains a group of orders.
- The table **orion.product_dim** contains descriptions of products.
- Both tables have a column named **Product_ID**.

Partial Listing of **orion.order_fact** (617 Total Rows, 12 Total Columns)

```
     Product_ID         Order_ID    Quantity

   220101300017       1230058123        1
   230100500026       1230080101        1
   240600100080       1230106883        1
   240600100010       1230147441        2
   240200200039       1230315085        3
```

Partial Listing of **orion.product_dim** (481 Total Rows, 8 Total Columns)

```
     Product_ID     Product_Name

   210200100009     Kids Sweat Round Neck,Large Logo
   210200100017     Sweatshirt Children's O-Neck
   210200200022     Sunfit Slow Swimming Trunks
   210200200023     Sunfit Stockton Swimming Trunks Jr.
   210200300006     Fleece Cuff Pant Kid'S
```

Write a PROC SQL inner join to combine information from these tables.

- Use the column **Product_ID** to match rows.
- Display columns **Order_ID**, **Product_ID**, **Product_Name**, and **Quantity** in the results.
- Add an appropriate title.

Partial PROC SQL Output

```
                    Detail Information for Ordered Products and Quantities

                                                                               Quantity
        Order ID    Product ID  Product Name                                    Ordered
      ---------------------------------------------------------------------------------
      1243960910  210200100009  Kids Sweat Round Neck,Large Logo                      2
      1234198497  210200100017  Sweatshirt Children's O-Neck                          1
      1235926178  210200200022  Sunfit Slow Swimming Trunks                           2
      1240886449  210200200023  Sunfit Stockton Swimming Trunks Jr.                   1
      1242149082  210200300006  Fleece Cuff Pant Kid'S                                1
      1237789102  210200300007  Hsc Dutch Player Shirt Junior                         1
      1236701935  210200300052  Tony's Cut & Sew T-Shirt                              2
      1233920786  210200400020  Kids Baby Edge Max Shoes                              1
      1233920786  210200400070  Tony's Children's Deschutz (Bg) Shoes                 1
      1241086052  210200500002  Children's Mitten                                     3
```

Level 3

3. Comparing PROC SQL Inner Joins and Outer Joins

- The table **orion.order_fact** contains a group of orders.
- The table **orion.employee_addresses** contains personal information for employees.
- Both tables have a column named **Employee_ID**.

a. Write a PROC SQL inner join in order to combine information from these tables.

- Join the tables based on the column **Employee_ID**.
- Use the alternative syntax featuring the ON clause to code this inner join.
- Display the columns **Employee_Name**, **City**, and **Order_Date** in the results.
- Order the results based on **Order_Date**.
- Create a table named **work.matches** from the query results.
- Display the new table with an appropriate title.

Consult SAS Help for information on using the ORDER BY clause.

Partial PROC PRINT output (324 Total Rows)

```
                    Matches from the Order and Address Tables

                                                          Order_
            Obs      Employee_Name        City              Date

              1    Washington, Donald    Miami-Dade     11JAN2003
              2    Simms, Doungkamol     Melbourne      28JAN2003
              3    Shannan, Sian         Sydney         27FEB2003
              4    Carhide, Jacqulin     San Diego      15MAR2003
              5    Chantharasy, Judy     Melbourne      22MAR2003
              6    Shannan, Sian         Sydney         25MAR2003
```

b. Change the inner join that you wrote in part **a** so that you include all rows from **`orion.order_fact`** and matching rows from **`orion.employee_addresses`**.

- Create a table named **`work.allorders`** from the query results.
- Display the new table with an appropriate title.

✎ Consult SAS Help for information on using a LEFT JOIN.

Partial PROC PRINT output (617 total rows)

```
                  Order Dates, with Employee Information when Available

                                                               Order_
                  Obs      Employee_Name        City              Date

                    1    Washington, Donald    Miami-Dade     11JAN2003
                    2                                         15JAN2003
                    3                                         20JAN2003
                    4    Simms, Doungkamol     Melbourne      28JAN2003
                    5    Shannan, Sian         Sydney         27FEB2003
                    6                                         02MAR2003
                    7                                         03MAR2003
                    8                                         03MAR2003
```

10.3 The SAS Macro Language

Objectives

- State the purpose of the macro facility.
- Describe the two types of macro variables.
- Create and use macro variables.
- Display the values of macro variables in the SAS log.

50

Purpose of the Macro Facility

The *macro facility* is a text-processing facility that supports symbolic substitution within SAS code.

The macro facility enables you to

- create and resolve macro variables anywhere within a SAS program
- write and call macro programs (macros) that generate custom SAS code.

This section focuses on macro variables.

51

Types of Macro Variables

There are two types of macro variables:

- *Automatic* macro variables store system-supplied information such as date, time, or operating system name.
- *User-defined* macro variables store user-supplied information in symbolic names.

52

System-Defined Automatic Macro Variables

Automatic macro variables are set at SAS invocation and are always available. These include the following:

Name	Description
SYSDATE	Date of SAS invocation (DATE7.)
SYSDATE9	Date of SAS invocation (DATE9.)
SYSDAY	Day of the week of SAS invocation
SYSTIME	Time of SAS invocation
SYSSCP	Abbreviation for the operating system: OS, WIN, HP 64, and so on
SYSVER	Release of SAS software being used.

To refer to a macro variable, use *¯o-variable-name*.

53

Using Automatic Macro Variables

Automatic macro variables can be used to avoid hardcoding values. In the program below macro variables are referenced to display system information within footnotes.

```
proc print data=orion.customer_type noobs;
title "Listing of Customer_Type Data Set";
footnote1 "Created &systime &sysday, &sysdate9";
footnote2 "on the &sysscp System Using Release &sysver";
run;
```

Macro variable references are replaced with the values of the corresponding macro variables.

54 p210d06

Using Automatic Macro Variables

The automatic macro variable references are resolved **prior to compilation**.

```
proc print data=orion.customer_type noobs;
title "Listing of Customer_Type Data Set";
footnote1 "Created 10:24 Wednesday, 25JAN2008";
footnote2 "on the WIN System Using Release 9.2";
run;
```

55

Output: Using Automatic Macro Variables

Partial PROC PRINT Output

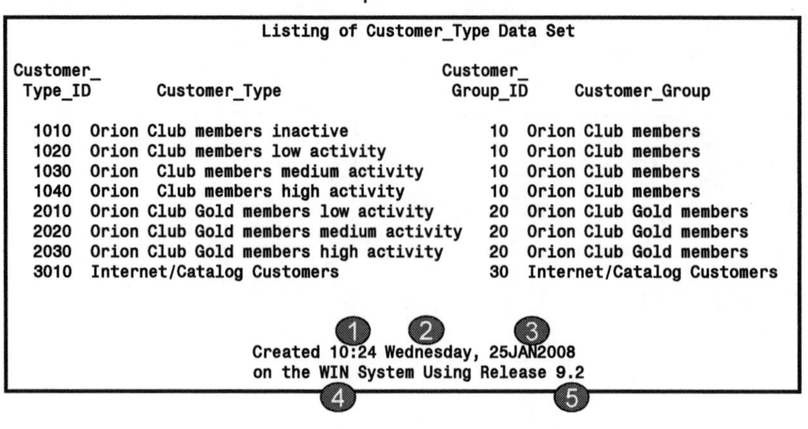

```
                          Listing of Customer_Type Data Set

Customer_                                      Customer_
 Type_ID        Customer_Type                   Group_ID     Customer_Group

   1010   Orion Club members inactive              10   Orion Club members
   1020   Orion Club members low activity          10   Orion Club members
   1030   Orion  Club members medium activity      10   Orion Club members
   1040   Orion  Club members high activity        10   Orion Club members
   2010   Orion Club Gold members low activity     20   Orion Club Gold members
   2020   Orion Club Gold members medium activity  20   Orion Club Gold members
   2030   Orion Club Gold members high activity    20   Orion Club Gold members
   3010   Internet/Catalog Customers               30   Internet/Catalog Customers

                       Created 10:24 Wednesday, 25JAN2008
                       on the WIN System Using Release 9.2
```


56

Use %PUT to Display Macro Variables

The %PUT statement displays the names and values of all automatic macro variables.

```
%put _automatic_;
```

Partial SAS Log

```
1    %put _automatic_;
AUTOMATIC AFDSID 0
AUTOMATIC AFDSNAME
AUTOMATIC AFLIB
AUTOMATIC AFSTR1
AUTOMATIC AFSTR2
AUTOMATIC FSPBDV
AUTOMATIC SYSBUFFR
AUTOMATIC SYSCC 0
AUTOMATIC SYSCHARWIDTH 1
AUTOMATIC SYSCMD
AUTOMATIC SYSDATE 25JAN08
AUTOMATIC SYSDATE9 25JAN2008
```

57

10.05 Quiz

Submit a %PUT statement to display the values of all automatic macro variables.

What are the values of the SYSVER and SYSSCP macro variables?

59

Business Scenario

A developer manually changes the year values each time that the following program is submitted. Use user-defined macro variables to simplify program maintenance.

```
proc print data=orion.order_fact;
   where year(order_date)=2006;
   title "Orders for 2006";
run;
proc means data=orion.order_fact mean;
   where year(order_date)=2006;
   class order_type;
   var total_retail_price;
   title "Average Retail Prices for 2006";
   title2 "by Order_Type";
run;
```

62 p210d07

Creating a Macro Variable

User-defined macro variables can make SAS programs more flexible and easier to modify. Use the %LET macro statement to create a macro variable and assign it a value.

General form of the %LET statement:

%LET *variable=value*;

- *variable* follows SAS naming conventions.
- *variable* is created and assigned *value*.
- If *variable* already exists, its *value* is overwritten.

63

The %LET Statement

value can be any string.

- The length is between 0 (*null value*) and 65,534 (64K) characters.
- A numeric value is stored as a character string.
- Mathematical expressions are **not** evaluated.
- The case of *value* is preserved.
- Quotation marks bounding literals are stored as part of *value*.
- Leading and trailing blanks are **removed** from *value* before the assignment is made.

%LET *variable=value*;

64

Examples of the %LET Statement

```
%let year=2006;

%let city=Dallas, TX;
```

Name	Value
year	2006
city	Dallas, TX

65

10.06 Quiz

Complete the rest of the table.

```
%let year=2006;

%let city=Dallas, TX;

%let fname=     Marie   ;

%let name=" Marie Hudson ";

%let total=10+2;
```

Name	Value
year	2006
city	Dallas, TX

67

Create and Use a Macro Variable

Use a %LET statement to create a user-defined macro variable, **year**, and a macro variable reference, **&year**, to obtain the value of the macro variable.

```
%let year=2006;
proc print data=orion.order_fact;
   where year(order_date)= &year;
   title "Orders for &year";
run;
proc means data=orion.order_fact mean;
   where year(order_date)= &year;
   class order_type;
   var total_retail_price;
   title "Average Retail Prices for &year";
   title2 "by Order_Type";
run;
```

69

p210d08

...

Resulting Code: After Symbolic Substitution

The macro variable references are resolved prior to compilation. The references are replaced with the corresponding text value. The resulting code is sent to the compiler.

```
proc print data=orion.order_fact;
   where year(order_date)= 2006;
   title "Orders for 2006";
run;
proc means data=orion.order_fact mean;
   where year(order_date)= 2006;
   class order_type;
   var total_retail_price;
   title "Average Retail Prices for 2006";
   title2 "by Order_Type";
run;
```

70

10.07 Quiz

Examine the program below. What change(s) must be made to generate reports for 2007?

```
%let year=2006;
proc print data=orion.order_fact;
   where year(order_date)= &year;
   title "Orders for &year";
run;
proc means data=orion.order_fact mean;
   where year(order_date)= &year;
   class order_type;
   var total_retail_price;
   title "Average Retail Prices for &year";
   title2 "by Order_Type";
run;
```

72

p210a04

Displaying Macro Variable Values in the Log

Enable the SYMBOLGEN system option to write a message to the SAS log each time that a macro variable is resolved.

General form of the SYMBOLGEN system option:

```
OPTIONS SYMBOLGEN;

OPTIONS NOSYMBOLGEN;
```

✎ The default option is NOSYMBOLGEN.

74

Displaying Macro Variable Values

Use the SYMBOLGEN option to see the result of macro variable resolution in the SAS log.

```
options symbolgen;
%let year=2006;
proc means data=orion.order_fact mean;
   where year(order_date)=&year;
   class order_type;
   var total_retail_price;
   title "Average Retail Prices for &year";
   title2 "by Order_Type";
run;
```

75

p210d09

Displaying Macro Variable Values

A message is written to the SAS log each time that a macro variable is resolved.

```
options symbolgen;
%let year=2006;
proc means data=orion.order_fact mean;
   where year(order_date)=&year;
SYMBOLGEN:  Macro variable YEAR resolves to 2006
   class order_type;
   var total_retail_price;
SYMBOLGEN:  Macro variable YEAR resolves to 2006
   title "Average Retail Prices for &year Orders";
   title2 "by Order_Type";
run;
```

76

Using Macro Variables within a SAS Literal

The resulting code might require quotation marks. If so, the macro variable reference should be enclosed in double quotation marks.

```
%let site=Melbourne;
proc print data=orion.employee_addresses;
   where City="&site";
   var Employee_ID Employee_Name;
   title 'Employees from &site';
run;
```

Notice that the macro variable reference, **`&site`**, is enclosed in double quotation marks in the first reference above and single quotation marks in the second reference.

p210d10

77

Substitution within a SAS Literal

Double quotation marks allow macro variable resolution and single quotation marks prevent macro variable resolution.

```
%let site=Melbourne;
proc print data=orion.employee_addresses;
   where City="&site";
   var Employee_ID Employee_Name;
   title 'Employees from &site';
run;
NOTE: There were 41 observations read from the data set
ORION.EMPLOYEE_ADDRESSES.
      WHERE City='Melbourne';
```

`Site` resolved in double quotation marks.

Partial PROC PRINT Output

```
       Employees from &site

          Employee_
  Obs        ID         Employee_Name

    2      120145       Aisbitt, Sandy
   24      120168       Barcoe, Selina
```

`Site` did not resolve in single quotation marks.

78

Substitution within a SAS Literal

There is no SYMBOLGEN message for the second reference to **site** because it is not resolved.

```
options symbolgen;
%let site=Melbourne;
proc print data=orion.employee_addresses;
   where City="&site";
SYMBOLGEN:  Macro variable SITE resolves to Melbourne
   var Employee_ID Employee_Name;
   title 'Employees from &site';
run;

NOTE: There were 41 observations read from the data set
ORION.EMPLOYEE_ADDRESSES.
      WHERE City='Melbourne';
```

79 p210d11

Use %PUT to Display Macro Variables

To display the names and values of all user-defined macro variables, use this form of the %PUT statement:

```
%put _user_;
```

Partial SAS Log

```
%put _user_;
GLOBAL SITE Melbourne
GLOBAL YEAR 2007
```

To display both user-defined and automatic macro variables, use this form of the %PUT statement:

```
%put _all_;
```

80

Exercises

Level 1

4. Replacing a Hardcoded Value with a Macro Variable

a. Modify the program **p210e04** to display only customers in Germany.

- Open the file **p210e04**.
- Submit the program.
- Modify the program by creating a macro variable named **`location`** and use it in place of the hardcoded value, `DE`. (DE is the country code for Germany.)
- Submit the program and verify your results.

PROC PRINT Output

```
                    Customers in DE

 Obs     Customer_ID    Customer_Name          Gender

   3               9    Cornelia Krahl           F
   5              11    Elke Wallstab            F
   7              13    Markus Sepke             M
   8              16    Ulrich Heyde             M
  11              19    Oliver S. Füßling        M
  18              33    Rolf Robak               M
  23              42    Thomas Leitmann          M
  26              50    Gert-Gunter Mendler      M
  31              61    Carsten Maestrini        M
  33              65    Ines Deisser             F
```

b. Change the value of **`location`** to `ZA` to display customers in South Africa and resubmit the program. (ZA is the country code for South Africa.) Verify your results.

PROC PRINT Output

```
                    Customers in ZA

 Obs     Customer_ID    Customer_Name          Gender

  53            2550    Sanelisiwe Collier       F
  54            2618    Theunis Brazier          M
  56            2806    Raedene Van Den Berg     F
  57            3959    Rita Lotz                F
```

Level 2

5. Creating and Using a Macro Variable

a. Generate a report showing a list of all employees earning at least a designated minimum salary.

- Write a program to create a macro variable, **minSal**, and set its value to represent a minimum salary of $60,000.
- Use the **orion.employee_payroll** data set and the PRINT procedure to generate the report below.
  - Format **birth_date**, **employee_hire_date**, and **employee_term_date** with the DATE9. format.
  - Add an appropriate title and verify your results.

Partial PROC PRINT Output (34 Total Observations)

Employees Earning at Least $60000

Obs	Employee_ID	Employee_ Gender	Salary	Birth_ Date	Employee_ Hire_Date	Employee_ Term_Date	Marital_ Status	Dependents
1	120101	M	163040	18AUG1976	01JUL2003	.	S	0
2	120102	M	108255	11AUG1969	01JUN1989	.	O	2
3	120103	M	87975	22JAN1949	01JAN1974	.	M	1
99	120259	M	433800	25JAN1964	01SEP1989	.	M	1
100	120260	F	207885	02DEC1964	01NOV1984	.	M	2
101	120261	M	243190	21FEB1969	01AUG1987	.	O	1
102	120262	M	268455	21OCT1969	01SEP1988	.	M	2
108	120268	M	76105	01SEP1974	01MAY1997	.	S	0
124	120659	M	161290	16JUL1949	01JAN1974	.	M	3
125	120660	M	61125	06JUN1978	01MAR2005	.	S	0

b. Modify the previous solution to display employees who earn at least $100,000. Verify your results.

PROC PRINT Output

Employees Earning at Least $100000

Obs	Employee_ID	Employee_ Gender	Salary	Birth_ Date	Employee_ Hire_Date	Employee_ Term_Date	Marital_ Status	Dependents
1	120101	M	163040	18AUG1976	01JUL2003	.	S	0
2	120102	M	108255	11AUG1969	01JUN1989	.	O	2
99	120259	M	433800	25JAN1964	01SEP1989	.	M	1
100	120260	F	207885	02DEC1964	01NOV1984	.	M	2
101	120261	M	243190	21FEB1969	01AUG1987	.	O	1
102	120262	M	268455	21OCT1969	01SEP1988	.	M	2
124	120659	M	161290	16JUL1949	01JAN1974	.	M	3
417	121141	M	194885	19JUN1944	01JAN1974	.	S	0
418	121142	M	156065	14FEB1969	01MAY1993	.	M	2

Level 3

6. Using Macro Variable Delimiters

Debug and correct the program **p210e06**.

- Open the program and submit it.
- View the error in the SAS log.
- Set the appropriate system option to debug the program.
- Resubmit the program and identify the error.
- Use the SAS documentation to determine how to delimit a macro variable reference.
- Correct the code and resubmit it. Verify your results.

Hint: In SAS documentation, select **SAS Products** ⇨ **Base SAS** ⇨ **SAS Macro Reference** ⇨ **Macro Variables** ⇨ **Using Macro Variables**.

PROC PRINT Output

```
Obs    Country    Country_Name       Population

 1       AU       Australia          20,000,000
 2       CA       Canada                      .
 3       DE       Germany            80,000,000
 4       IL       Israel              5,000,000
 5       TR       Turkey             70,000,000
 6       US       United States     280,000,000
 7       ZA       South Africa       43,000,000
```

10.4 Chapter Review

Chapter Review

1. Which clause is used in an SQL query to identify the desired columns?
2. Which clause identifies the input tables?
3. What statement is used to create a data set using the output of a query?
4. Is it necessary to use a table name to qualify every column name in an inner join?

83

continued...

Chapter Review

5. What type of macro variables are &sysver and &sysdate9?
6. What statement is used to create a user-defined macro variable?
7. What is a macro variable reference?
8. How can you display all macro variables?
9. What system option writes the value of a macro variable to the log when it is referenced in a program?

85

10.5 Solutions

Solutions to Exercises

1. **Modifying an Inner Join**

   a. Open **p210e01**, submit it, and examine the output.

   b. Modify the program to display different variables and add a WHERE clause.

```
proc sql;
   select d.Product_ID, Product_Name, Start_Date, End_Date, Discount
      from orion.discount as d, orion.product_dim as p
      where d.Product_ID=p.Product_ID and Discount >= .6;
quit;
```

2. **Coding a PROC SQL Inner Join**

   Write a PROC SQL inner join.

```
title 'Detail Information for Ordered Products and Quantities';
proc sql;
   select Order_ID, o.Product_ID, Product_Name, Quantity
      from orion.order_fact as o, orion.product_dim as p
      where o.Product_ID=p.Product_ID;
quit;
title;
```

Alternate Solution:

```
title 'Detail Information for Ordered Products and Quantities';
proc sql;
   select Order_ID, o.Product_ID, Product_Name, Quantity
      from orion.order_fact as o
         INNER JOIN
      orion.product_dim as p
      on o.Product_ID=p.Product_ID;
quit;
title;
```

3. Comparing PROC SQL Inner Joins and Outer Joins

a. Write a PROC SQL inner join based on **Employee_ID**.

```
proc sql;
   create table work.matches as
   select Employee_Name, City, Order_Date
      from orion.Order_fact as o
         INNER JOIN
      orion.Employee_addresses as a
         on a.Employee_ID=o.Employee_ID
      order by Order_Date;
quit;

title 'Matches from the Order and Address Tables';
proc print data=work.matches;
run;
title;
```

b. Change the inner join that you wrote in part **a** to include all rows from **orion.order_fact** and matching rows from **orion.employee_addresses**.

```
proc sql;
   create table work.allorders as
   select Employee_Name, City, Order_Date
      from orion.Order_fact as o
         LEFT JOIN
      orion.Employee_addresses as a
        on a.Employee_ID=o.Employee_ID
      order by Order_Date;
quit;

title 'Order Dates, with Employee Information when Available';
proc print data=work.allorders;
run;
title;
```

4. Replacing a Hardcoded Value with a Macro Variable

a. Modify the program **p210e04** to display only customers in Germany.

```
%let location=DE;
title "Customers in &location";
proc print data=orion.customer;
   var customer_id customer_name gender;
   where country="&location";
run;
```

b. Change the location to `ZA` to display the customers in South Africa.

```
%let location=ZA;
title "Customers in &location";
proc print data=orion.customer;
   var customer_id customer_name gender;
   where country="&location";
run;
```

5. Creating and Using a Macro Variable

a. Generate a report showing a list of all employees earning at least $60,000.

```
%let minSal=60000;
title "Employees Earning at Least $&minSal";
proc print data=orion.employee_payroll;
   where salary >= &minSal;
run;
```

b. Modify the previous solution to display employees who earn at least $100,000.

```
%let minSal=100000;
title "Employees Earning at Least $&minSal";
proc print data=orion.employee_payroll;
   where salary >= &minSal;
run;
```

6. Using Macro Variable Delimiters

Debug and correct **p210e06**.

```
%let lib=orion;
%let ds=country;
proc print data=&lib..&ds;
   var country country_name population;
run;
```

Solutions to Student Activities (Polls/Quizzes)

10.02 Quiz – Correct Answer

Modify the SELECT clause to display **Employee_ID**, **Job_Title**, and **Salary**. **List the columns in the desired order in the SELECT clause.**

```
libname orion 'SAS-data-library';
proc sql;
   select employee_id, job_title, salary
   from orion.sales_mgmt;
quit;
```

Employee ID	Employee Job Title	Employee Annual Salary
121143	Senior Sales Manager	$95,090
121144	Sales Manager	$83,505
121145	Sales Manager	$84,260
121147	Secretary II	$29,145

23

p210a01s

10.03 Quiz – Correct Answer

No, the output contains many more rows than expected.

```
/* SQL query to join two SAS tables */
proc sql number;
    select sales_mgmt.employee_id,
           employee_name,
           job_title,
           salary
    from orion.sales_mgmt,
         orion.employee_addresses;
NOTE: The execution of this query involves performing one or more
      Cartesian product joins that can not be optimized.
quit;
```

There is no WHERE clause to specify a join condition, so a Cartesian product was created. The result contains 1696 rows (4 * 424).

35

10.04 Quiz – Correct Answer

The **orion.customer** and **orion.country** tables both have a column named **Country** containing a country abbreviation. Open **p210a03** and add a WHERE clause to join the tables based on matching values of **Country**.

```
proc sql;
   select customer_id, customer_name,
          customer.country, country_name
   from orion.customer,
        orion.country
   where customer.country=country.country
     ;
quit;
```

43

p210a03s

10.05 Quiz – Correct Answer

Submit a %PUT statement to display the values of all automatic macro variables.

```
%put _automatic_;
```

What are the values of the SYSVER and SYSSCP macro variables?

Answers will vary, but for many installations the value of SYSVER is 9.2 and the value of SYSSCP is WIN.

60

10.06 Quiz – Correct Answer

Complete the rest of the table.

```
%let year=2006;

%let city=Dallas, TX;

%let fname=      Marie    ;

%let name=" Marie Hudson ";

%let total=10+2;
```

Name	Value
year	2006
city	Dallas, TX
fname	**Marie**
name	**" Marie Hudson "**
total	**10+2**

68

10.07 Quiz – Correct Answer

Examine the program below. What change(s) must be made to generate reports for 2007? **Change the value assigned in the %LET statement.**

```
%let year=2007;
proc print data=orion.order_fact;
   where year(order_date)= &year;
   title "Orders for &year";
run;
proc means data=orion.order_fact mean;
   where year(order_date)= &year;
   class order_type;
   var total_retail_price;
   title "Average Retail Prices for &year";
   title2 "by Order_Type";
run;
```

73

p210a04s

Solutions to Chapter Review

Chapter Review Answers

1. Which clause is used in an SQL query to identify the desired columns?

   The SELECT clause

2. Which clause identifies the input tables?

   The FROM clause

3. What statement is used to create a data set using the output of a query?

   CREATE TABLE *table-name* AS

4. Is it necessary to use a table name to qualify every column name in an inner join?

   No. A column name must be qualified only if it exists in more than one table.

84

continued...

Chapter Review Answers

5. What type of macro variables are &sysver and &sysdate9?

   Automatic macro variables

6. What statement is used to create a user-defined macro variable?

   The %LET statement

7. What is a macro variable reference?

   An & followed by a macro variable name

8. How can you display all macro variables?

   ```
   %put _all_;
   ```

9. What system option writes the value of a macro variable to the log when it is referenced in a program?

   The SYMBOLGEN option

86

Chapter 11 Learning More

11.1 SAS Resources 11-3

11.2 Beyond This Course 11-6

11.1 SAS Resources

Objectives

- Identify areas of support that SAS offers.

3

Education

Comprehensive training to deliver greater value to your organization

- More than 200 course offerings
- World-class instructors
- Multiple delivery methods: instructor-led and self-paced
- Training centers around the world

http://support.sas.com/training/

4

SAS Publishing

SAS offers a complete selection of publications to help customers use SAS software to its fullest potential:

- Multiple delivery methods: e-books, CD-ROM, and hardcopy books
- Wide spectrum of topics
- Partnerships with outside authors, other publishers, and distributors

http://support.sas.com/publishing/

5

SAS Global Certification Program

SAS offers several globally recognized certifications.

- Computer-based certification exams – typically 60-70 questions and 2-3 hours in length
- Preparation materials and practice exams available
- Worldwide directory of SAS Certified Professionals

http://support.sas.com/certify/

6

Support

SAS provides a variety of self-help and assisted-help resources.

- SAS Knowledge Base
- Downloads and hot fixes
- License assistance
- SAS discussion forums
- SAS Technical Support

http://support.sas.com/techsup/

7

User Groups

SAS supports many local, regional, international, and special-interest SAS user groups.

- SAS Global Forum

- Online SAS Community: www.sasCommunity.org

http://support.sas.com/usergroups/

8

11.2 Beyond This Course

Objectives

- Identify the next set of courses that follow this course.

10

Next Steps

To learn more about this:	Enroll in the following:
How to use SQL to manipulate and merge data files	SAS® SQL 1: Essentials — 2-day course (or 4 half-day Live Web sessions)
How to write SAS programs that are reusable, dynamic, and easily maintained	SAS® Macro Language 1: Essentials — 2-day course (or 4 half-day Live Web sessions)
DATA step programming techniques and comparing the efficiencies of various techniques	SAS® Programming 3: Advanced Techniques and Efficiencies — 3-day course (or 6 half-day Live Web sessions)
Creating reports	SAS® Report Writing 1: Using Procedures and ODS — 3-day course (or 5 half-day Live Web sessions)
Preparing for the SAS Certification Exam	SAS® Certification Review: Base Programming for SAS®9 — 2-day course (or 4 half-day Live Web sessions)

11

Next Steps

In addition, there are prerecorded short technical discussions and demonstrations called e-lectures.

http://support.sas.com/training/

12

Appendix A Index

%

%LET statement, 10-30–10-31
%PUT statement, 10-28

A

accumulating variable
  creating, 3-3–3-16
array processing, 7-34–7-46
ARRAY statement, 7-39
arrays
  defining, 7-41–7-42
  processing with a DO loop, 7-43–7-46
  using, 7-52–7-68

B

BY-group processing, 3-24–3-25

C

Cartesian product, 10-16
CAT functions
  numeric conversions, 5-95
CATX function, 5-37–5-39
CEIL function, 5-61
character values
  manipulating, 5-10–5-24, 5-29–5-52
CMISS function, 5-65
COMPRESS function, 5-50–5-51
concatenating operator, 5-40
conditional execution
  SELECT group, 2-26–2-30
converting variable type, 5-73–5-100
course overview, 1-15–1-22
CREATE TABLE statement
  SQL procedure, 10-12

D

data
  accumulating totals for groups, 3-21–3-41
  manipulating using functions, 5-3–5-5
  nonstandard, 4-7
  sorting by variables, 3-34–3-35
  standard, 4-7
  summarizing by groups, 3-29–3-32
data conversion, 5-75–5-79
  character to numeric, 5-82–5-83
  numeric, 5-95
  numeric to character, 5-89–5-91
data file
  reading raw with formatted input, 4-3–4-19
data manipulation techniques, 9-3–9-21
data set
  restructuring, 8-3–8-23, 8-28–8-48
  rotating, 8-8–8-23
  structure, 8-4
data sets
  combining, 9-3–9-21
  creating multiple, 2-21–2-22
DATA step
  advantages, 10-20
data types
  converting values between, 5-73–5-100
DEBUG option, 6-17–6-20
debugging techniques, 6-17–6-20
  using the DEBUG option, 6-17–6-20
  using the PUTLOG statement, 6-3–6-11
DO UNTIL statement, 7-22
DO WHILE statement, 7-21
double trailing @, 4-65–4-72
DROP statement, 2-37
DROP= data set option, 2-38–2-42, 9-7
DSD option
  INFILE statement, 4-61–4-62

E

END= option
  SET statement, 6-10
errors
  logic, 6-4
explicit OUTPUT statement, 2-5

F

FIND function, 5-43–5-46
First. values, 3-25–3-28, 3-36–3-39
First. variables, 9-10
FIRSTOBS= data set option, 2-46–2-47
FLOOR function, 5-61
FROM clause

SQL statement, 10-8
functions, 5-3–5-5
descriptive statistic, 5-65–5-67
manipulating character values, 5-10–5-24, 5-29–5-52
truncating numeric values, 5-58–5-69

G

groups of data
summarizing, 3-29–3-32

I

IF statement, 3-31
placement of subsetting, 4-48
IN= data set option, 9-5
INFILE statement
DSD option, 4-61–4-62
informats, 4-10–4-11
INPUT function, 5-80–5-81
INPUT statement, 4-12
multiple, 4-25–4-28
INT function, 5-62

K

KEEP= data set option, 2-40–2-41, 9-7

L

Last. values, 3-25–3-28, 3-36–3-39
Last. variables, 9-10
LENGTH function, 5-16
line pointer controls, 4-29–4-32
list input, 4-52–4-74
logic errors
identifying using the DEBUG option, 6-17–6-20

M

macro facility, 10-25–10-36
macro variables
automatic, 10-26–10-27
creating with %LET statement, 10-30
displaying using %PUT statement, 10-28, 10-36
displaying values, 10-32–10-34
user-defined, 10-26
within a SAS literal, 10-35–10-36
match-merging, 9-3–9-21
with Excel data, 9-15–9-21
MISSOVER option, 4-58

N

numeric values
truncating, 5-58–5-69

O

OBS= data set option, 2-45–2-47
observations
selecting, 2-35–2-50
OTHERWISE statement
SELECT group, 2-27
output
multiple observations, 2-3–2-15
OUTPUT statement, 9-7
explicit, 2-5

P

PROPCASE function, 5-21–5-22
PUT function, 5-92–5-94

R

raw data
reading, 4-5
raw data files
reading, 4-52–4-74
reading and subsetting, 4-24–4-48
reading with formatted input, 4-3–4-19
repetitive calculations
performing with arrays, 7-34–7-46
RETAIN statement, 3-5–3-6
ROUND function, 5-59–5-60

S

SAS arrays
using, 7-52–7-68
SAS data sets
writing to multiple, 2-20–2-30
SAS functions, 5-3–5-5
SAS Help facility, 1-6–1-14
SAS informats, 4-10–4-11
SAS macro language, 10-25–10-36
SAS System
languages, 10-3–10-4
SCAN function, 5-32–5-34
SELECT clause
SQL statement, 10-8
SELECT group
conditional execution, 2-26–2-30
OTHERWISE statement, 2-27
SET statement

END= option, 6-10
single trailing @, 4-41
SORT procedure, 3-24
SQL. See Structured Query Language
SQL procedure, 10-5–10-20
advantages, 10-20
CREATE TABLE statement, 10-12
joining tables, 10-14
query, 10-9
syntax, 10-7
WHERE clause, 10-9
SQL statement
FROM clause, 10-8
SELECT clause, 10-8
Structured Query Language, 10-4
SUBSTR function, 5-13–5-14, 5-46
SUM function, 3-14
sum statement, 3-15–3-16

T

tables
assigning an alias, 10-19–10-20
joining on a common variable, 10-17–10-18
joining with the SQL procedure, 10-14
TRANSPOSE procedure, 8-28–8-48
TRANWRD function, 5-48

V

variable lists, 5-6–5-8
variables
converting to antoher data type, 5-84–5-88
creating an accumulating total, 3-3–3-16
creating with arrays, 7-54–7-60
selecting, 2-35–2-50

W

WHEN expression
multiple values, 2-28
WHERE statement, 2-50
WHERE= data set option, 8-39